THE LIFE & WORK
OF
AN ENGLISH LANDSCAPE ARCHITECT

Rembrandt Gravure   Painted by Sir Hubert Herkomer, R.A.

Thomas H. Mawson, F.L.S., P.P.T.P.I.

From a portrait by Sir Hubert Herkomer, R.A.

THE LIFE & WORK OF AN ENGLISH LANDSCAPE ARCHITECT

'I LOOK BACKWARD THAT I MAY
THE BETTER PRESS FORWARD.'

An Autobiography by
Thomas H Mawson F.L.S

Corresponding Member of the Royal
Fine Arts Commission ; — Past
President of the Town Planning Inst;
Late Lecturer on Landscape Design
Liverpool University; Corresponding
Member of the American Society of
Landscape Architects ; Etc, Etc.

The Grimsay Press

The Grimsay Press
an imprint of
Zeticula
57 St Vincent Crescent
Glasgow
G3 8NQ
Scotland

http://www.thegrimsaypress.co.uk
admin@thegrimsaypress.co.uk

Viridarium Library of Garden Classics
Series Editor: Douglas Coltart
http://www.viridarium.co.uk

First published in 1927 by Chapman & Hall
This edition Copyright © Douglas Coltart 2012

First published in this edition 2012
ISBN-13 978-1-84530-070-8

DEDICATED TO

MY WIFE

To Whose Discernment and Encouragement
I Owe Any Success I May Have
Achieved

LIST OF CHAPTERS.

Church of the Twelve Apostles
Salonica
G. Bankart Munson /21

LIST OF ILLUSTRATIONS.

List of Illustrations.

List of Illustrations.

" *Landscape architecture is primarily a fine art,
and as such its most important function is to create
beauty in the surroundings of human habitations, and
in the broader natural scenery of the country ; but
it is also concerned with promoting the comfort, convenience, and health of urban populations, which have
scanty access to natural scenery, and urgently need
to have their hurrying work-a-day lives refreshed
and calmed by the beautiful and reposeful sights
and sounds which Nature, aided by the landscape
art, can abundantly provide.''*

CHARLES W. ELIOT.

Bust of Author by Joyce Reddrop, exhibited at the Royal Academy, 1917.

PREFACE

FOR the past three years it has been necessary that I should "go slow," the most difficult thing in the world for one whose whole working life has been spent in a profession of such absorbing interest as that of the Landscape Architect, a profession the followers of which are borne into every corner of the globe and brought into contact with many interesting personages.

The situation must, however, be faced, for with declining bodily powers I am no longer able to pursue the life of constant travel and physical and mental exertion which, thank God, I have not only lived for nearly fifty years, but have enjoyed as, I think, few men would have enjoyed it.

It is thus fortunate that at this juncture my doctor, anxious to find an outlet for mental powers deprived of their usual field of activity, and many friends who at one time or another had shown a kindly interest in stories of happenings in many lands culled from experiences incidental to my life-work, conspired to urge upon me the writing of either an autobiography or an extensive collection of reminiscences. Such an agreeable task, I was assured, would give me the opportunity to live my life again without physical or mental stress, and at the same time provide a contribution to the history of Landscape Architecture during the half-century of my connection with this fascinating but so sadly neglected and travestied branch of creative art.

The task has proved a most congenial one, and the result has far outstripped its original purpose. My intention had been to write an account of my life-work which might prove interesting and inspiring to members of my family, and particularly to those on whom has fallen the task of carrying on the work so dear to my heart. Since, however, the following pages have been written, several of my oldest and most trusted friends to whom they have

been submitted for opinion and criticism, as well as for the verifica-
tion of details, have strongly advised me to allow their publication,
urging the consideration, which carried great weight with me,
that an account of my early efforts and struggles would be inspiring
to young men facing great odds, and who may not possess sufficient
vision to convince them of their ability to win through.

The decision to agree to this request brings with it the obligation to explain certain matters without which the personal *ego* in
the text might appear too insistent even for an autobiography, and
certain modest achievements, originally related only for the ears
of kind and indulgent friends, to be a little over-emphasised. If
I may reasonably claim to have advanced in my profession, and
in turn to have contributed to its advancement as a creative art,
there are certain factors which have materially assisted me.

First of all, there is the strong influence exerted by my early
circumstances, which compelled me to devote my energies to the
practical side of garden-making, so that my artistic inclinations
and love of the beautiful have always been under the control of,
and severely restricted by, practical considerations, thus preventing
any possibility of my falling a prey to that dilettantism which has
militated against the success of so many men with greater opportunity and of greater genius than I possessed.

Then, again, I consider that I was most fortunate in entering
the profession of Landscape Architecture at a time of special
opportunity. With the general wane in every field of art which
marked the mid-Victorian period, the profession was fast losing
its status as a means of serious art-expression, and was falling
entirely into the hands of ill-informed amateurs obsessed with
those crude conceptions of the " picturesque " which at that
period produced such disastrous results—results from which we
are not yet totally emancipated, and which even to-day produce
wriggling paths, impossible contours, white spar rockeries, and a
distressing confusion of little aims.

If we exclude the work of three or four men who were growing
old, and whose creations still retained something of the traditions
of the craft, it became evident that Landscape Architecture had
outrun its claim to serious consideration, and so the moment was
opportune for any young man with a passion for the arts and some
practical knowledge of architecture, horticulture, and forestry, to
attempt a revival of intelligent and scholary garden design. Such
a revival, during the period of my life-work, has been general and

widespread, and many enthusiastic men and women, with whom I have had pleasant relationships, and with most of whom I have collaborated at one time or another, have been contributors equally with myself to this renaissance.

A third factor, and one which has perhaps helped me more than any other, is my great good fortune in having appreciative clients, to whose generous encouragement I owe a debt I can never repay, and who, in many instances, realising the uncertainties and disappointments that must always attend work in which one of the greatest factors is the sport of a variable and uncertain climate, have allowed me to correct inevitable mistakes, often at considerable expense to themselves.

Again, I have been equally fortunate in my assistants, both those in my office and those engaged upon directing the actual spadework on the ground. Among the former I naturally retain a special regard for those who, coming to me as articled pupils, and in some instances quite early in my career, have remained with me as assistants in various capacities, and thus have permanently identified their fortunes and careers with those of my firm. Among the latter, also, there are a number of men who, beginning as boys attendant on the foreman in charge of some piece of park or garden construction, have developed a special aptitude and love for the work, and have, through sheer grit and determination, educated themselves to the position of " landscape foreman " (as the post is termed, for lack of a better name), capable of appreciating and translating into actuality the best traditions of my practice. To both classes, in a profession such as mine, in which the personal element and its interpretation are so important, it is obvious that I must owe, and should gratefully acknowledge, a debt of loyal service.

Lastly, but by no means least in the factors which have made for success, I would mention the way in which my work has naturally and inevitably brought me into direct personal contact with many notable personalities—leaders in government, art, letters, and industry,—from whom I have learned much that has been helpful to me in my career.

And, as this book, in common with most autobiographies, must partake somewhat of the nature of a " swan song," I may perhaps add a word to those on whom, coming after me, will fall the task of carrying forward, upholding, and developing the prestige of the profession to which I belong. I would say, shortly and categorically, that art and practice must run together. Whatever advances have been made in Landscape Architecture, they are as nothing compared with those which are possible. All the good and generous clients are not yet dead, and, in spite of many irritating hindrances and restrictions, the work of those who follow may proceed happily under the inspiration which the cult of the beautiful will always provide.

I believe that the usefulness of the Landscape Architect to the general public is sure to meet with increasing recognition, side by side with a growth in public taste, and that his work will provide him with abundant opportunities and inspiration for the provision of those amenities on which the happiness and well-being of the community so largely depend. To assist him in this is one of the chief aims I have had before me in the writing of this book.

Finally, many of the men and women referred to in this volume are no longer living. I trust that what I have said about them may help to keep their memories green. If, in referring to the living, I should inadvertently have transgressed, I apologise.

THOMAS HAYTON MAWSON.

High Street House,
   Lancaster,
     August, 1927.

END OF GLADE, LEWISTON MANOR, DORSET.
From " The Art and Craft of Garden Making."

CHAPTER I.

ABOUT one hundred and eighty years ago Joseph Mawson was architect and clerk of works on the Lowther Castle Estate, and from that time onward some one or other of his descendants has carried forward the traditions so established in at least one department of constructive art, while even amongst those not so actively engaged there have been many who have taken a keen interest in the skilled handicrafts of the country, and still others, as in the case of my father, who have inherited the faculty for art criticism which has given them a somewhat unusual status in the country communities in which they have lived. Such an appreciation of design in its many manifestations seems to be born in some people, and I believe my family are among them. Anyway, the following almost unbelievable stories tend to show that I possessed at the earliest age those powers of observation so necessary to creative art.

As boy and youth I retained a vision of a tall, comely nurse in whose arms I nestled during my introduction into the world, and she always wore dress and apron of a very quaint pattern. On one occasion I gave my mother a somewhat minute description of the nurse and her apron, and she replied, " Well, that is a very good description of Nurse Standing."

This may seem incredible, and it may be that my early imagination pictured the whole, and by chance the dream corresponded to the real. But such an explanation would not apply to a second incident of the same kind. In August of 1914 my wife and I were the guests of Lady and Sir William Hesketh Lever (as he then was) at Roynton Cottage, Rivington Pike, and on Bank Holiday our hosts took us for a motor run through the Trough of Bowland, returning by Wyreside, Scorton, Garstang, and Preston. About a quarter of a mile beyond Scorton we came to a bridge of simple

The Life and Work of An English Landscape Architect.

and somewhat peculiar design. " Stop ! " I called ; " I have found the bridge for which I have been searching for fifty years." The explanation is that I was born in the village, and although my parents left before I was six years of age, the bridge, the quaintness of which had impressed itself irradicably upon my memory, corresponded exactly to my impression of it. I merely mention these two incidents to show that from my earliest infancy the observation of quaint and beautiful objects and scenes has been quite natural to me. This faculty never left me, but rather developed into a passion so pronounced that by the time I had reached my twelfth year I knew intimately every old door-head, date-stone, sundial, quaint gateway, oriel or mullioned window, for miles round my home. True, I often played truant when the passion was most impelling, but I was fortunate in having the sympathy of an understanding schoolmaster, who wisely discerned that nature and art were my best lesson books.

I was born in 1861 in Scorton, a picturesque village lying midway between Preston and Lancaster, of parents who during the cotton famine had passed with great courage and fortitude through a period which proved the ruin of so many Lancashire families. My father had somehow gained a very sound English education, notwithstanding the fact that he started work as a young boy. Part of the explanation is that Dr. Mackereth, a distant relative, was rector of Halton, my father's birthplace, and it was he who taught my father his Latin and algebra, and gave him a love for good literature.

Somehow this kindly rector's influence seemed to remain with my father through life, as he was not only an industrious but also a very discerning and methodical reader, who recognised that an artisan, with a home and family to provide for, could not waste time upon spasmodic and unproductive study. It has been my privilege through life to meet many men in humble circumstances who possess the same instinct for good reading, and the men are invariably interesting characters. My father's sympathies and interests were, however, widespread, and included religion and politics.

Although brought up as an Anglican, with sincere regard for his rector, my father early came under the influence of noncon-formity, to which he brought a fine lovable character, a mind unusually well stored, a charm of address, and an appealing musical voice and unquestioned sincerity. He would have made an ideal pastor, but misfortune drove him into business, for which he had not the least aptitude. In politics he was an ardent Gladstonian, and an earnest exponent of the fiscal policy of the Manchester School; but although such an uncompromising Liberal, he enjoyed the close friendship of many men of opposing views.

My mother was of a very different temperament—practical, proud, alert, and very ambitious for the success of her children. These qualities were associated with a delicate constitution. Even when given up by the doctors, she would not relinquish her five young children, and her indomitable will and faith in the Great Healer pulled her through. She lived to the age of seventy-six. My mother, who had a keen sense of humour and a very sane if material outlook on life, was, like my father, a nonconformist, and in her youth had a reputation as a public speaker. Nevertheless, she did not share with my father to the same extent his regard for the village conventicle which we attended, nor his zeal for politics. Her small contribution to these activities may have been to some extent dictated by prudence and a regard for the needs of her family. I remember a rather amusing incident arising out of these differences of opinion. On one occasion an evangelist was engaged to conduct a week's mission in our village. The whole place was worked up to a white heat of religious fervour, and the gratitude of the fathers of the community was great. They decided to show their appreciation by presenting the evangelist with a sum of money on his departure. My father proposed a contribution of fifteen shillings, but my mother thought our reasonable obligations would be met by a donation of five shillings, and, as usual, her view carried the day. The next day I was sent with ten shillings in a purse to pay for the last load of coal—and lost it! My father piously considered this a visitation of the Almighty, but my mother thought it a case for a sound thrashing, and I got it!

As a family we adored father and feared mother, but with the lapse of time, and with all the facts of our home life in the right perspective, we not only revised our estimates, but came to regard my mother as a wonderful personality.

When I was about six years of age my parents removed to Lancaster, where my father's brothers were in business as builders. In that quaint old county town my father purchased two plots of land on the Freehold Park Estate, and on part of it erected a pair of semi-detached houses, one of which we occupied. It was here, at the age of seven, that I got my first taste for gardening.

The Life and Work of An English Landscape Architect.

Up to this time I had been a very delicate child, and the cure for my ailments was open-air work. My father purchased for me a small spade, and I was taught to dig a straight line. The soil was fairly light and easy to work, but even so, as I take account of boys of seven of to-day, I am almost driven to doubt if I really did dig over these two plots of ground, and yet such is the fact. Turning over the soil gave me an appetite and a zest for life such as I had never experienced before. From digging I got to planting and sowing, my father and mother directing or taking part in the work. With what fascination I dug out the trenches to a straight line, and then, after laying in manure, planted the potatoes a foot apart by my measure stick! Then came the sowing of onions, carrots, turnips, marrowfat peas, and broad beans, and the planting of cabbage and cauliflower plants. Then with my own pennies I bought packets of candytuft, mignonette, virginian and ten-weeks stocks and clarkias, but I remember that I wanted more than anything a double white primrose and a Rex Theodore double polyanthus, but my pennies were spent, and before I could save up enough the plants were " off the market."

Watching the peas, beans, and potatoes push through the ground, and taking part in sticking the peas and hoeing the potatoes, thinning out the onions, carrots, and turnips to their right distances, was the beginning of my technical training as a horticulturist, and gave me a keen interest in all Nature's handiwork. I thus gained vigour of mind and body so quickly that I was soon well enough to attend a dame's school, where I met other children of my own age.

To my great sorrow, my parents had to give up their home, and the garden for which I had such a great affection, to reside at Ingleton, in the West Riding of Yorkshire, where my father had secured a position. For some time we lived in a quaint white-washed cottage with mullioned windows, with one of those carved door-heads peculiar to this locality. The house included a walled-in garden or garth, but it was overgrown with bindweed, and the fruit trees were all neglected. The soil was on a heavy clay, and therefore quite unsuited to my strength, and for some time my interest waned; while my father, with his strong independent character, chafed at being under a landlord, and soon purchased ground on which to build a cottage. The site was very well chosen, because, although it stood at the end of a row of old cottages, it had a southern exposure, overlooking a valley through which ran

Family History and Early Influences.

the river Greta, with wooded slopes and panoramic distances. The old cottages, on the other hand, faced east and the public road, so we were very private, with no possibility of interrupted views, as the adjoining land was formed of a series of bluffs which were too precipitous for building purposes. The view down the valley of the river Greta was one of the finest prospects I have ever seen, and thus early I was taught the value of fine panorama.

My parents were much too poor to allow of my being sent away to school, so, very much to their grief, I had to attend the Church school in the village. Fortunately the young schoolmaster was a man of character and good address, who took a great liking to me, and spent endless time, and exercised great patience, in instructing me. Samuel Coburn has always remained one of my ideal gentlemen. He was a man to look up to, very severe at times, but possessing great insight into a boy's character.

My father took a keen interest in our studies, which he supplemented by talks on natural history, of which he was a keen student, and I remember how interested we were in his descriptions of birds and animals, and the coloured illustrations in many treasured volumes.

Of course I had to go to Sunday school, which had as its superintendent Joseph Carr, a country gentleman of small means. I wonder if any other Sunday school in the country was ever presided over by such a genius for the work? An entire absence of monkish, religious sentimentality, and recognition that what was needed was not so much theology as an expansion of our powers of observation, were his dominant characteristics. He could not sing a note, and we had convulsions when he tried; but when he addressed us in the simplest language on the great Creator's work he was entrancing. He was also inspiring, creating for the boys great visions of what they might be and do in the world. Altogether, I think this Sunday school did much to fire my imagination and prepare me for my life-work.

I attended the Church school between the ages of nine and twelve, and during this time generally managed to rise two forms or standards in the year. By that time, however, one of my uncles living in Lancaster needed an office boy, whose duties would be to make tracings of contract drawings and keep a check on materials sent to buildings in course of construction. Although I was so young, my uncle engaged me, and took me into his home and allowed me certain liberties and off time for the study of drawing.

The Life and Work of An English Landscape Architect.

At the age of twelve I commenced and pursued, in spite of vicissitudes, serious study in drawing at the Lancaster Mechanics' Institute under Mr. Gilbert, uncle to Sir Alfred Gilbert, the sculptor. Mr. Gilbert was an able instructor, deeply interested in the success of his students.

While in my uncle's office I learnt much of the preparation of working drawings and the use and quality of building materials. In fact, the work constituted the best technical training I could have had.

At the age of fourteen, having made some progress in my studies, it was practically decided that I should enter the designing department of the old Lancaster firm of Gillows, but about this time my father purchased a small property known as Langber End, midway between Ingleton and Bentham, with the object of turning it into a nursery and fruit farm. The project was never a sound one, as most of the land lay high and was heavy to work, being a stiff clay soil. It was far away from the markets, and in a poor residential neighbourhood. The only economic advantage which it possessed was that it was near cheap coal for heating the tomato houses and vineries which my father proposed to erect. However, he was keen on the project, and asked me to return to work on the property.

Knowing little of the business aspect of the enterprise, but having a great affection for my father, and a great love of open-air life, I was delighted at the prospect. This making of a new homestead and the cultivation of a nursery and fruit farm seemed to have an air of romance about it. It appealed to my imagination, and I was all enthusiasm for the work. My brother Robert, about eighteen months younger than I, was taken from the village school, and together we began to turn the pasture land into cropping ground by double-trenching it in the most approved manner.

First we marked out a trench eighteen inches wide, cut off the turf three inches thick, and dug out a deep spit of about eight or ten inches, spading the loose part and the loosened subsoil. Then we lifted the turf from the next line of trench and laid it grass downward in the bottom ; we then dug the soil to a full spit's depth and laid it on the turf, and finished by spreading on the top of this the loose soil from the bottom of the trench, which was then picked or loosened as before, and the process repeated. We two boys of twelve and a half and fourteen did our sixty square yards day by day, and did not think we had done a fair day's work if we fell short of this quantity.

While the preparation of the ground was going forward, the builders were busy erecting a new house on the highest part of the ground—a comfortable, fine square house of eight rooms, with a vinery at one end. There was no water supply, so we had to dig huge cisterns, not only for the domestic supply of the house, but also for nursery purposes.

I enjoyed the work, and spent my evenings and free time in studying garden books and botany. How I became possessed of so many books I do not recollect, but I do remember someone giving me Henfry's Botany and Mrs. Beeton's Gardening Book, and three volumes of "The Gardener's Assistant," and I bought out of my own money a copy of " How to Earn £600 per Year from an Acre of Ground," a book that was very unconvincing.

My principal sources of instruction were " The Gardener's Chronicle " and " The Journal of Horticulture," every line of which I read week by week. In this way I became acquainted with the successes of noted exhibitors. Amongst these exhibitors was the Rev. Frederick Horner, the grandson of the famous Dr. Horner, of Hull, the noted collector of tulips during the period which is known to horticulturists as the tulip-mania period. Mr. Horner the younger still carried on the family tradition for tulip growing and hybridising with such success that he swept all before him on exhibition tables, but he was better known as a grower and exhibitor of auriculas, a hardy plant of which I was passionately fond.

About a year before the time of which I speak, Mr. Horner had rented a property in the adjoining village, and here he established his prize collections of auriculas and tulips. With that reverence for great men which I have always felt, for a long time I was diffident in approaching Mr. Horner. At last one day in March I walked over to Burton and ventured to lift his brass knocker, and within a few minutes introduced myself to the reverend gentleman, who gave me a kind welcome, though he was evidently amused to find a boy of fourteen who had walked miles for the express purpose of seeing his auriculas and tulips. In a few minutes we were walking across an untidy garden in the direction of what I thought was a peach-house, built against a wall with a southern aspect, a structure very dilapidated and unpainted. This was about sixty feet in length and perhaps eight

The Life and Work of An English Landscape Architect.

feet in width, divided into three compartments, the whole being heated from one end with a common brick flue. We entered by the far and cooler end. The house was filled with auriculas, including the latest successful exhibits, which were just on the wane. After Mr. Horner had explained the points between a good and a bad auricula, such as form and size of flower, the placing of the corona and its pistil, we passed the second house, out of which the stage had been cleared to admit of tulips being planted on the ground level. For size and colour I have never seen anything approaching these tulips. Of course very few of them were in commerce. I was told they were shy producers.

Here again I listened to an eloquent talk on the history and development of the tulip, and the different classes into which it is divided. It was, however, in the last compartment that I received my most complete surprise and enchantment, for the house contained nothing but orchids, mostly in flower and all in perfect condition. The nepenthes and odontoglossums, along with some of the smaller varieties of dendrobiums, were hanging from the roof, whilst on the stage were extremely fine plants of dendrobiums Wardianum, cattlyias of sorts, also masdevallias and cypripediums. Yet the whole range of glass was not worth more than £20, and the house and plants, notwithstanding their luxuriance, looked as if they received little attention. The only explanation one can give in such circumstances is that plants and flowers grow for those who love them. However, this was a new experience in my study of horticulture, the influence of which I never forgot. I have ever since wished to possess a collection of orchids, but this is a hobby for those with leisure or money.

I ought here to add that whilst living with my uncle in Lancaster I had managed to learn a good deal of horticulture, because my uncle was a keen amateur gardener and a grower of choice British ferns, and I remember with what delight I used to memorise the Latin names of his rarer specimens. I still remember dozens of his rarest and most perfect plants—Scolopendrum crispum crestata, Lastrea dilatata grandiceps, Athyrium felix fœmina, Multifida, and Polypodium cambrica crispum. Thus my reading, combined with my love of the work and my previous experience with my uncle, combined with the actual contact with new trees, shrubs, and plants of various kinds, was quickly giving me a grasp of the theory and practice of horticulture.

Close to us lived an old lady, the widow of a gardener, whose

Family History and Early Influences.

books she affectionately retained. Here I spent many of my evenings devouring books on horticulture, which to me seemed very precious possessions. Amongst these was a Parkinson's Herbal, Loudon's Encyclopedia of Gardening, a quaint Journal of Husbandry, and copies of Loudon's Landscape Gardening and Repton's Fragments. These books, together with my studies in drawing and the elements of architecture, fired my boyish imagination and set the direction of my hopes for a career, and accidentally turned my thoughts and studies towards Landscape Gardening.

About this time I came into possession of " Uvedale Price on the Picturesque," and Gilpin's " Forest Scenery." The former I read in conjunction with Repton's Fragments. I never read a novel with more absorbing interest than the keen controversies between Repton and Sir Uvedale Price, and I remember that my sympathies were all with Repton.

In the fruit farm and nursery it soon became evident that my father had undertaken a greater venture than his capital or physical strength warranted. With his usual optimism he had made a careful estimate of capital outlay in so far as this was ascertainable, but he had entirely omitted maintenance charges to cover the period until the fruit trees and nursery crop could bring an adequate return. Like hosts of pioneer cultivators of the soil, he had assumed that catch crops would meet working expenses. This began to worry him so much that he lost heart and strength, and developed a chronic illness from which he died within two years.

To me my father's death was the greatest sorrow of my life, for not only did I regard him with sincerest filial affection, but I had the most profound belief in everything he undertook.

Imagine the position of my mother, left with an undeveloped enterprise and burdened with the accumulated debts of my father's illness, with four children—three boys, of whom I was the eldest, and my sister, a little over eighteen. Wonderful did my mother become in those dark days. She inspired us with energy and purpose, and we responsively worked like trojans, determined to make good and realise my father's ambition if that were attainable. For a year and a half we struggled on, only to find that success in our present position was impossible. Then it was that my mother, with courage and foresight, determined to remove to London, to which she was an entire stranger, but where she felt it would

The Life and Work of An English Landscape Architect.

be possible to find openings where her boys could get a sound training in some of the metropolitan market gardens. No sooner was the decision arrived at than I was despatched there to explore the land, with twenty shillings in addition to my train fare, the intention being that I should obtain a situation and hold on as best I could until I could fix up an opening for my two younger brothers.

By good fortune I first called to see the late Mr. John Wills (now Wills and Segar), of Onslow Crescent, of whom I had often heard as a great floral decorator and landscape gardener. He evidently took a liking to me, and engaged me at a salary of eighteen shillings a week, telling me to report the next morning at six o'clock. I thought this a stroke of good fortune, and felt certain I could soon increase my salary to a pound a week. Within three months I had found openings for my two brothers with Mr. William Iceton, of Roehampton, a grower for Covent Garden Market. The arrangement was that if my brothers came up to my description he would pay them twelve and fourteen shillings a week respectively. I was so delighted that I wrote to my mother to come at once, as we were now assured of two pounds four shillings per week, which I was quite sure would soon increase. In a month she had a sale by public auction of furniture and stock, retaining only a few household treasures and linen, and about twenty-five pounds, the rest of the proceeds of the sale being devoted to reducing our indebtedness, any accounts left unpaid being accepted as a family liability; and, let me add, my mother insisted on every penny being paid, and as we all felt that it devolved upon us to clear my father's memory of any charge of insolvency, we carried out my mother's wish.

Thus I had arrived at the age of eighteen, and the end of one period of my life and the entrance to another plane of existence and effort. For this sphere I had had few educational advantages and a comparatively hard struggle, and whatever may be said for or against such conditions, I am convinced that they formed the finest training possible for a boy of my temperament. I am assured that easier circumstances would not have resulted in the same fruition and energy. To a boy so placed there is a sense of romance in exploration and conquest : this feeling creates a wholesome attitude of mind ever leading him to wider horizons ; he knows instinctively that head and heart must always be at school if his ideals are to be achieved. When I look back and try to estimate the value of the influences controlling my budding youth, I am

Family History and Early Influences.

profoundly impressed with the good fortune which these influences had bestowed upon me. Fond parents ambitious for their children's future were combined with a home in which sane, frugal living was a sound preparation for high service and wholesome thinking, and where good fiction, good music, and good literature were daily discussed.

I was also most fortunate in my drawing-master, and later in meeting with friends who provided me with entrancing works on landscape gardening and natural scenery, which appealed to my innate pleasure in nature and carried on the work begun by my early introduction to the delights of gardening.

In London came my actual introduction to practical commercial horticulture, and in my first experiences of collective business methods and the growing knowledge of men which these gave me, I found exactly what was needed. By nature inclined to abstract meditation rather than to purposeful action, I was, by the circumstances in which I now found myself, compelled to conquer this inclination, and this was so thoroughly accomplished that I became really fond of hard work, a characteristic which, with diminishing powers, I still retain. Naturally, my studies did not follow any definite plan, and to this extent I was at a disadvantage, as I had not acquired the orderly habits which regulated study inculcate.

It was my good fortune to serve a master and work with men who possessed the fixed habit of steady application, and who worked with the hum and momentum of a spinning-top.

As to recreation, beyond the rough-and-tumble games at school and with my brothers, I had none. Life to me from my very early years was one of set purpose. My cherished dream was Landscape Architecture. The boyish delight with which I devoured the books lent me by the gardener's widow remains as a beacon light now to be looked back upon: then, it beckoned onwards. Mixing with men of set purpose and steady application in London was just what was needed. I observed, and formed similar habits.

Although I was a most impressionable youth, the sudden transition from the quiet country to the whirl of the metropolis did not divert me from my purpose. It was wisely ordered that I should have no money for the ordinary city amusements indulged in by my workmates, as all my earnings were needed at home, the hive whence my brother and I sallied forth to gather our daily store, and whither we returned each evening to pour into the sympathetic ear of our mother an account of our experiences,

The Life and Work of An English Landscape Architect.

our successes and defeats, and to receive from her good cheer and sage advice.

During my period of residence in Lancaster a good part of my leisure had been spent in sketching, in my own way, the ancient historic castle and fine Georgian buildings, and especially the old doorways, for which the town is famous. Later on, when at Ingleton, famed for its waterfalls and romantic river scenery, I used to note and store my memory with the pictures of the entrancing views in which the district abounds. Nor did this personal bent fail to find outlet during my residence in London, where in my scanty spare time I made excursions, necessarily as cheaply as possible, to special spots noted for their rural beauty, which I again tried to analyse and sketch. Ah ! if I had only had some capable person to direct those early tentative efforts.

As the reader will discover, it has been one of the dreams of my life to establish a national school for instruction in the art of landscape design ; and, bearing in mind what I have just said as to my own early studies, so diffusive in their aims and partial in their results, just for the lack of a little sympathetic and expert guidance, the motive which has inspired the wish will be obvious.

THE BROTHERS ISAAC, ROBERT R., AND THOMAS H. MAWSON.

CHAPTER II.

EARLY DAYS IN LONDON.

ABOUT the time of our removal to London my only sister contracted what proved to be a very happy marriage, and so it was a still further diminished household, consisting of my mother and two brothers, that settled down in a cottage near Barnes Common, about half a mile from Mr. Iceton's nurseries, which were situate in Putney Park Lane. The rent was thirty pounds a year, and we let the upper part to a young couple, because we could not afford to furnish more than half the house ; but somehow our part, under the controlling genius of my mother, soon assumed the character of a comfortable flat. We lived frugally on our small united income, and consequently kept in good health. It was a great change from our comfortable home in Yorkshire, where, when things came to the worst, there was at least a home-fed chicken or there were a few eggs to make a meal for hungry lads. Looking back, I am amazed at my mother's thrift during those difficult days, at the perfect control which she exercised over us boys, and the tact with which she inspired us to reach our utmost possibilities.

John Wills, for whom I was working, was a remarkable man. Starting life as an apprentice in a Lancashire garden, he had attained no small fame as a floral decorator and by his garden design—though garden " arrangement " would be a better description of his work.

As a garden designer Wills laid out the grounds at Lacken, near Brussels, for King Leopold of Belgium, who bestowed upon him a Belgian decoration in recognition of his work. He was also made a Chevalier of the Legion of Honour for his scheme of decoration at the Paris Exhibition of 1875. At the time I entered his service he had built up an enormous business, which he had converted into a public company, with head offices and

The Life and Work of An English Landscape Architect.

conservatories at Onslow Crescent, Warwick House, in Regent Street, and nurseries at South Kensington and Annerley. He had succeeded beyond his most sanguine dreams as a floral decorator, being much in request by royalties and great personages, and it is probably safe to say that some of his creations in this department have never been excelled. I have never seen any of his work as a landscape gardener which manifested any grasp as a planner, but his skill in arranging plants for decorative effects was of service to him in working out his schemes for planting in the open.

Notwithstanding his phenomenal success, John Wills was not satisfied. There were yet other fields to be won ! He had, so it is said, an ambition to outrival Veitch's as a distributor and grower of rare plants, including orchids, and to become equally famous as a seedsman. But he had long passed middle age, and his driving force was not equal to his programme. He was, however, a man of wide powers and great imagination, and had a clear grasp of the essential factors of his business.

At the time I began work at Onslow Crescent the firm had a great reputation for its floral decorations, which resulted in schemes for one or two balls and receptions every day of the week. My first work was to select the plants and palms from the conservatories and despatch them to their respective destinations. Very soon I was sent out to arrange some of the less-important commissions, filling in my time at the office. Gradually I was trusted, during periods of great pressure, with small but quite important work, and allowed to follow my own ideas.

These were not always successful, and occasionally led to trouble. One afternoon, for instance, I was asked to undertake a table decoration for Mrs. Jacob Bright, who had a house in Onslow Square. It was an important occasion, because Gladstone, John Bright, Lord Granville, and other famous Liberal politicians, were to be there.

The occasion and the opportunity delighted me, and I determined to win my laurels. My plan was a simple one. I obtained a circular tray in the centre of which I placed a block of ice about thirty inches high, then around the edge I arranged a fringe of *Isolepus gracilis* which had previously been carefully washed. This grass overhung on to the white tablecloth. I think I filled the tray to within half an inch of the rim with water, in which floated white and blue water lilies (*nymphea alba* and *nymphea stellata*). The family were delighted, and I went home that night feeling that I had placed my foot on the first rung of the ladder of fame.

Next morning I learnt, to my great distress, that the scheme had ended in disaster, and that John Wills had been sent for. Mr. Wills said that Mr. Bright complimented him on his very imaginative young man, but suggested that his assistant should be given a little practical training. Then he explained that the decoration was very much admired until the ice began to melt; then the *Isolepus* acted as syphons, and simply flooded the entire table, with the result that the guests had to retire to the drawing-room until the table could be cleared and re-set. Of course so long as the windows were closed the ice block remained intact, but directly the windows were opened it melted !

For two years I stayed with John Wills, living the whole time at Putney, catching the train every morning at Putney Bridge Station at 5-45 a.m. so as to be at work shortly after 6 a.m. I used to bring my food with me, and was given half an hour for breakfast and an hour and a quarter for lunch. The latter meal occupied no more than a quarter of an hour, leaving me with a full hour in which to run into that treasure house, the South Kensington Museum. The unique collection of works of art and treasures of craftsmanship, covering a wide field, was a perfect revelation to me, and for a long time so fascinated me by its intrinsic beauty that I did not find time for study along the special lines adapted to my specific needs. This phase, however, passed, and I began to study the treasures around me from their constructive and decorative standpoints as examples of design and craftsmanship. Unfortunately, I had neither previous knowledge nor anyone to guide me, otherwise this period might have counted for much more in formulating my ideas in design and proportion than it did. Nevertheless, personal observation and discernment being there, and being eagerly employed, I am sure that I owe much to the use I made of my luncheon hour at the South Kensington Museum.

During my stay with John Wills I met many famous people who called on business. The two I remember most distinctly were Lady Dorothy Neville and Holman Hunt, both of whom I met years later under very different circumstances.

The only plans or drawings I saw while at Onslow Crescent were of a very elementary character, and I believe Wills, like many another professing landscape gardener of that period, depended in a large measure upon verbal instructions given on the site.

The Life and Work of An English Landscape Architect.

Although I saw little of practical landscape work during this period, I heard much discussion of a critical character of the work of other professors of the art, including that of Robert Marnock, Edward Milner, Edward Kemp, and others, and studied with great interest any illustrations of their work which came my way, and, when opportunity occurred, I visited parks and gardens laid out by them and others. At the end of two years of useful and instructive work, disaster fell on the Wills business, which went into liquidation, and I, along with many others, had to leave and find employment elsewhere.

Looking up the files of "The Gardener's Chronicle," I saw that Messrs. Kelway and Son, of Langport, Somerset, a firm which was rapidly coming into prominence, wanted an assistant. As the positions and salaries of my two brothers had greatly improved, my mother urged me to apply for the post. I did so, and was selected to fill the vacancy. The work was not congenial, and seemed to open up no avenue such as I sought. I also found that I was inexperienced in the work of invoicing plants, the majority of which were quite new to me, so to save the firm the necessity of discharging me, I gave in my notice and left after six weeks' service. During this period, however, I took a keen interest in the stock and the means of propagation, and determined to make, under freer conditions, a study of hardy herbaceous and alpine plants, a knowledge of which I felt was absolutely essential if I was to succeed as a designer of gardens.

I was now close upon twenty-one years of age, and for the second time had to search the files of the horticultural journals for a post. I found a vacancy advertised by Thomas S. Ware, of the Hale Farm Nurseries, Tottenham, a firm noted for its vast collection of hardy plants. I applied for the position, and was successful in getting it. The salary was only twenty-two shillings a week, but that did not matter, such was my enthusiastic determination to gain a thorough knowledge of hardy plants, and here was my chance.

Thomas S. Ware was a tall, stately old gentleman, who for the greater part of his life had been a draper, until he married the daughter of the former owner of the Hale Farm Nurseries. Upon the death of his father-in-law he took over what had become a flourishing retail business. He scarcely knew one plant from another, but he had the good sense to recognise his deficiency, and devoted his energies to business organisation, leaving the

Early Days in London.

cultural and technical part of the business to his out-door manager, Mr. Amos Perry. The latter was one of the best known experts in hardy flowering plants in the country, and an authority who was regularly consulted by the editors of horticultural papers when asked to name and prescribe the culture of the many rare and curious plants sent to them for identification.

When I first joined the staff, Mr. Ware was beginning to take less part in the business organisation, which gradually fell into the hands of Francis Fell, a very capable and ambitious man, and a tremendous worker, who was dominated by a desire to do big things in a big way. To him was due the foundation of the firm's extensive wholesale business, which soon outran in volume of trade the retail department.

Francis Fell and I soon became close friends, a friendship additionally cemented by the fact that our fathers, then both dead, had been boys together.

The Hale Farm Nurseries were very extensive—about one hundred and twenty acres, I believe, divided into eight large departments, each under a trained expert, and all grouped under Amos Perry, their head ; and it is safe to say that at this time no nursery in the country possessed a stock so varied and of so high a quality.

During the spring and summer months I used to turn out with my note-book at six o'clock in the morning, and again in the evening after the day's work was done, studying, comparing, and tabulating descriptions of various plants, and allocating each to its genus or family. This brought me into friendly relations with all the managers of departments and foremen, who were never tired of answering my questions and adding to my stock of knowledge. They even consulted me on various matters, and asked my opinion upon the comparative merits of the plants under their charge. One of these men was James Smith, the foreman in charge of the aquatic and sub-aquatic plants, British ferns, and miscellaneous plants suitable for wild gardens.

I was very soon promoted to the charge of the firm's extensive correspondence, and thus got into touch with many interesting people. There was Miss Jekyll writing about daffodils ; Dr. Hogg about the correct naming of ivies ; Dr. Masters wanting to know something about a rare iris ; Reynolds Hole writing about carnations ; Dr. Ellacombe interested in peonies ; Mr. Cyril Flower (later Lord Battersea) writing about delphiniums :

The Life and Work of An English Landscape Architect.

Robert Marnock wanted Alpine plants ; the Rev. George Rawson sent specimens of his beautiful long-spurred aquilegias ; Mr. Davies, of Newry, sent berries of his new hybrid pernettyas ; Mr. William Robinson wrote from time to time about nympheas and other aquatic plants. To me this meeting, even at second hand, with so many people famous in horticulture, was most inspiring. Many of these correspondents I later met personally, and with some I struck up a lasting acquaintance.

In the winter months I attended the local Technical School evening classes for the study of botany and the principles of agriculture. I regret that I have forgotten our lecturer's name. He was a character, possessing the power of illuminating the driest subject and investing it with an importance which was irresistible. Young and lanky, with a shock of red hair, he wore a paper collar and a paper front, which continually flipped out of his waistcoat. But no matter, when he was lecturing we were all earnest scholars sitting at the feet of a Gamaliel. I am sure he has gone far since those days.

In the middle of my second year it was suggested that I should come into closer contact with the firm's wholesale customers within fifty miles of London. It was properly urged that this personal contact with some of the firm's best customers would give me some advantage when dealing with their correspondence. The consequent journeys were of the greatest educational value. They enlightened me as to the various floral and horticultural require-ments of the metropolis and of the country in general, and opened my eyes as to what constituted fine collections of rhododendrons, azaleas, and roses, and as to the best manner of displaying them. Amongst the nurseries which I visited were those of Messrs. Paul's, of Waltham Cross and Cheshunt, Anthony and John Waterer's extensive Rhododendron Nurseries at Woking and Bagshot, and many others, including those of George Jackman, of Woking, which contained most interesting and representative collections of hollies and conifers. In addition to the above, the nurseries at Wimbledon owned by Mr. Thompson must not be omitted. They contained what was probably the finest selection of street and avenue trees in the country, and many interesting shrubs of exceptional interest to me. In Kingston Vale I had many oppor-tunities of seeing the extensive nurseries owned by Messrs. Veitch and Sons, with their wonderful avenue of *Picea Nobilis Glauca.* At Tunbridge Wells I saw the nurseries owned by Mr. Crisp, the propagator of clematis and Japanese maples, which he grew in enormous quantities. I also visited Messrs. Turners' nurseries at Slough, and saw their fine collection of roses and shrubs.

The best fruit-tree nurseries in those days were Osborn's, of Fulham ; Bunyard's, of Maidstone ; Lane's, of Berkhamstead ; and Rivers', of Sawbridgeworth, all of which came within my range.

While never consciously forgetful of my employer's interests, and really in pursuit of them, I made the acquaintance of the heads and managers of all these establishments. Whether or not it was my youthful enthusiasm which helped me, I cannot say, but in every case I received the greatest kindness and help, my attention always being drawn to anything rare and beautiful.

Although not naturally gifted with a good memory, I gradually acquired the happy knack of assimilating botanical names, so that I was able somewhat rapidly to gain a wide knowledge of the material by the aid of which I was later able to express some of my ideas in garden design. Only recently I saw a fine plant of *Desfontania spinosa* in flower, and immediately the name flashed to my mind, and memory sprang back to the early days when I first saw the shrub, over forty years ago.

During these trips I became acquainted with a well-known firm of nurserymen on the Surrey side of the river, which carried on business as contractors for landscape garden work as a separate department. They had a compact, high-class, profitable business, which at this time was run by father and son, the father being the landscape gardener. He was a nice old man, and a good example of the contracting landscape gardener. The son had no genius for this work, nor indeed any other except the financial part, and in this way ran his father as a monetary asset. Realising that his father was getting old, he approached me, and with a view to my taking up his father's work offered me a partnership on advantageous terms. I was now twenty-three, and the offer attracted me very much, not only because I was promised a free hand in reorganisation and development of the landscape department, but also for reasons which I will now state.

These reasons were, first, that the offered partnership would give me the opportunity for the practical application of my ideas on garden design ; and, secondly, further the idea of settling down in a home of my own, which just then began to appeal to me.

At Tottenham I had rooms with one of our departmental foremen, and every afternoon on my way from work I made a

The Life and Work of An English Landscape Architect.

detour *via* High Street, to purchase some little delicacy for my evening meal. Returning, I passed the hospital, and the emergency hospital for scarlet fever, run by the general hospital, the two being about three hundred yards apart. Every day, about the same time, the night nurse walked from the general to the emergency hospital, and she and I could not help meeting, but we were much too proper to notice one another—indeed, as in so many versions of the old, old story, so ever new, we would not see each other ! Then, as we both became conscious that we were acting rather foolishly, and, still in silence, passed with a heads-erect, nose-in-the-air sort of pose, we felt that someone really ought to introduce us ! (I know this was the true state of two agitated minds, for later we compared notes.) One day she failed to appear at the usual place, but as I passed the fever hospital I saw her at the open window rearranging a vase of half-dead flowers for the children's ward.

This was too much for the young horticulturist, who stammered out : " Nurse, you cannot make anything decent out of those flowers ; let me bring you some fresh ones." And for the love of her patients she agreed. From that day onwards the children's ward was supplied with fresh flowers. The rest was inevitable, and in one month's time I was introduced by Anna Prentice, daughter of the late Dr. Edward Prentice, of North Walsham, Norfolk, to her guardian and the trustee of her small property, permission being given me to pay my addresses to her openly. So began a love story which ever afterwards had a pronounced bearing on my progress and after-career.

This naturally decided the question of the acceptance of the offer of the partnership which had been made to me, and it was arranged that at the end of six months, subject to the permission of her guardian, we should marry.

When I handed in my notice to leave at Ware's, every inducement and argument, including an offer of a junior partnership, was offered me to stay with the firm. My time with them had been very pleasant and very instructive ; and I explained that had they had a landscape department I should gladly have stayed, but that I must follow the line of development which I had marked out for myself, even though it were not so profitable as the acceptance of a partnership in their business would have proved. With many regrets, therefore, but with high hopes and great determination, I left ; but so long as the original firm remained in existence I

Early Days in London.

kept up a correspondence with them, and sometimes revisited the nurseries.

I started my new work, and had the satisfaction of seeing the business developing, and as I considered everything was progressing satisfactorily, I thought I was justified in marrying. Anna Prentice and I were therefore married at Trunch Church, Norfolk, on August 1st, 1884, and departed to the Lake District on our honeymoon. Then came a bolt from the blue, which seemed for a time to point to a disastrous ending to all my hopes and plans. During our honeymoon I received a letter from the son of the Surrey nurseryman with whom I had conducted the partnership negotiations, informing me that his father objected to the ratification of the partnership arrangement. If agreeable to me, I was told, I could work for a salary—a salary which, by the way, was quite inadequate to meet my new responsibilities.

After the first shock of our disappointment my wife and I decided that we should make a plunge and start a family business, which should also provide for my brothers, and, being on the spot, we explored the possibilities of the English Lake District for our purpose. The more we saw of the district, the more we liked the prospect which opened out before us, so we looked out for a site for what we called our " home nursery," to become eventually the business centre for what we were quite sure would become a considerable organisation. Before leaving the district we gave instructions to a local estate agent to find a site for us. This was in August, 1884.

In January of the following year we heard from the agent that a suitable site, rather less than an acre in extent, with a cottage and a shop, could be rented on a long lease, on terms apparently reasonable. We telegraphed, instructing him to close. In another five weeks the Mawson Brothers, along with my wife and my mother, established themselves in Windermere.

Most of our new neighbours were very sorry for us : other people had tried the same thing and failed. Our neighbours argued that when any important work was to be done, the local gentlemen sent to Manchester, Chester, or London, and so it always would be, and so on. Nothing daunted, we set to work to make a survey of our nursery site, and to plan the new offices, propagating houses, and frame yards.

Our programme was to establish a nursery and contracting landscape business for my brothers, I to obtain, as a member of

The Life and Work of An English Landscape Architect.

the firm, all the landscape gardening I could get hold of, but to separate the professional practice from the business directly the latter was sufficiently firmly established. This programme was adhered to, the separation taking place in 1889. Such is the early history of the Lakeland Nurseries.

The second year saw us moving very slowly, and our finances were very strained. No wonder that sometimes we bore anxious looks. Every day we met at my mother's for afternoon tea, and discussed the problems which were uppermost; but if anyone hinted throwing up the sponge, he was at once decisively squashed by my mother. So we went back with fresh determination and worked as long as light permitted.

When matters had become really serious, I received a letter from Mrs. Arthur Severn (John Ruskin's niece), of Brantwood, Coniston, to say she had recommended me to Mr. Bridson, a gentleman who moved in the best county circles and exercised a great influence locally. He was just completing Bryerswood, a new house at Sawrey, on the western side of Windermere, and wanted advice on the laying out of his garden. I lost no time in seeing Mr. Bridson and submitting my designs. Within a few days I had made my survey, taking all necessary levels, and prepared a preliminary plan of the prospective gardens. The plan was carefully discussed by Mr. and Mrs. Bridson, especially in relation to the commanding view obtainable across Windermere, embracing the landscape on the other shore and the lake. Finally, the scheme was adopted, with slight modifications, an estimate of cost was prepared, and the work placed in our hands, all within a fortnight. I secured a splendid old fellow as foreman, one of the old-fashioned school, thoroughly versed in constructional garden work, hard working, and loyal. Old Kidd stayed with us as long as he could work, and we never lost money on any contract carried out under his superintendence.

At this stage there happened one of those incidents which bind men together and make even sceptics believe in the principles of altruism. We started work on Monday, and on the Wednesday following Mr. Bridson asked me to go to his private business room for a chat. When I got there he said : " Well, Mr. Mawson, I am a business man, and I, like every other business man, have experienced times when I was glad to see a cheque. As you are just starting business, it has occurred to me that you would not mind if I gave you a cheque for £200 on the work. When you

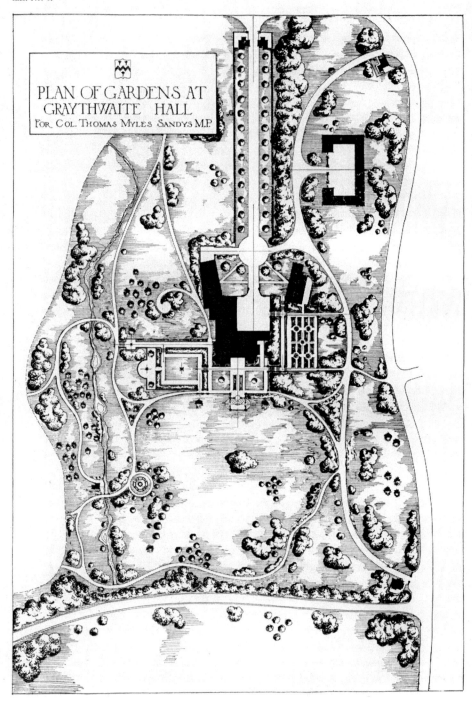

PLAN OF GARDENS AT
GRAYTHWAITE HALL
For Col. Thomas Myles Sandys M.P.

want more, let me know ! " That cheque was a godsend, and its moral value was far greater than its exchange value. It showed that I had won the confidence of my first client. That confidence I retained to the end of this gentleman's life.

Mr. and Mrs. Bridson entertained on a liberal scale, and amongst the guests I met Lady Bective, who was keenly interested in garden design, and particularly in the development of the grounds at Bryerswood. It was here also that I first met Captain Bagot, who had just inherited Levens Hall, and many were the talks we used to have about the Captain's quaint world-famous gardens, their history and points of interest. It was at Bryerswood that I first met Colonel Sandys, whose large estate at Graythwaite Hall adjoined the Bridsons' property. I also met here Mr. Knill Freeman, the well-known Bolton architect, who designed both Bryerswood and the new additions to Graythwaite Hall, as well as many other people interested in garden design. This work led almost immediately to our firm being employed by others in the Lake District, including some work for Sir Henry Moore, K.C.B., of Crook, a great Eastern scholar. In addition to his valued services and oft-sought advice as a General, Sir Henry was the most lovable old gentleman I have ever met, and as picturesque as he was lovable. At ninety the old man would walk to Windermere and back, a distance of four miles each way, with a spring and a swing which put to shame many a man half his age.

He had just built additions to his family home, and my work was to extend the lawns and walks round the new additions, and to lay out a few rose beds and do a little planting along the boundaries to emphasise the vistas, the foregrounds being somewhat uninteresting. My client was an able amateur water-colour artist, and followed all my recommendations with a critical and an understanding interest. He was also interested in the way the work was carried out, and made many sage and quaint observations. For instance, when I remarked that the cost of the work was more than I had anticipated, he replied, " You are a young man : take the advice of an old one. Whenever you have to choose between a big expenditure coupled with a good job, and a small expenditure with a bad one, choose the first—the pain of paying the account is momentary ; the satisfaction with the work is permanent. A bad job is quickly paid for, but the dissatisfaction with the work is lasting, and you will find that your client will forget how little of his money you spent, but curse you eternally

The Life and Work of An English Landscape Architect.

as a bad workman." Many a craftsman and architect has experienced the truth of these remarks, which have special force in executing garden schemes, where so much can be scamped, the results not being apparent at once.

Several other Lake District commissions fell to us, but our signal success at this period was gained when, on the introduction of Mr. Bridson, I was commissioned to prepare a comprehensive scheme for the improvement of the gardens and park at Graythwaite Hall for Colonel Sandys, M.P. I really felt the great responsibility of this work on account of its extent, the status of my client, and the unique opportunities which the site and the dominating residence presented. To this work I brought all my energies and the accumulated stores of my previous experience and study. The plan which I evolved so truly represents the extent of my attainments and my conception of what constituted garden design, that I reproduce it herewith (Illus. No. 6). As will be evident, I devoted much thought to the successful linking of the gardens with the house on the one hand, and the house and garden with the landscape on the other.

The plan is interesting as showing the progress I had so far made in the art of Landscape Architecture—the " mistress art," as an American has called it. It shows the conception I had of the combination of the formal and the informal, technically known as the composite style. It was carried out almost exactly as planned, together with later and further proposals for reinstating the carriage court to the north side of the house in the position which it originally occupied.

This work was of a very difficult and expensive nature, owing to the fact that everywhere a thin veneer of soil overlay the tough native rock, which was difficult to quarry. The property was, however, beautifully wooded with noble trees, including some characteristic old yews growing near the house and within the pleasure grounds.

At the time my services were requisitioned, my client had been in possession of the property for seventeen years, spending the entire rent roll and more on the estate, which extended from two miles north of Lake Side Station to and comprising most of the village of Hawkshead, a distance of at least six miles. The entire area of Esthwaite Lake and a part of each of the two villages of Sawrey Infra and Sawrey Ultra were also included.

Colonel Sandys was member of Parliament for Bootle, and

boasted that one of his forebears sat in the Parliament of King John. The Colonel had the reputation of being the only Tory in the House ; stern and autocratic, with a reserve that was very difficult to penetrate. He accepted most conscientiously the responsibilities of his position, and exercised over his estate a beneficent paternalism. He was a staunch Protestant, and one of the founders of the Protestant League. Gladstone was to him the arch-fiend, and many were the stories he told me of the great statesman's alleged intrigues, all of which I am sure he firmly believed ; and yet the dear old Colonel was in many respects an advanced Liberal. He believed that work, and work alone, gave a man his right to live. He was in advance of the Liberal policy of better housing, to which he gave effect on his own estate, and he believed in every workman being paid a living wage, with regular employment.

He anticipated the provisions of the old-age pensions, with its medical clauses. He paid fees to a doctor so that medical attendance might be provided for the entire estate. He also provided a nurse when required. If measles or scarlet fever broke out on his domain, the Colonel worried until all fear of infection had disappeared.

Towards the end of my work, one day I remarked to my client, " You have spent a vast sum of money on this property during the last twenty years or more ? " " Yes," he replied, " I have spent one hundred and twenty thousand pounds." " Do you never regret it ? " I asked. " Never ! " was the reply, as he turned round to me ; then he continued : " A brother officer of mine, who left the Army at the same time as I did, has also spent one hundred and twenty thousand pounds—but on horse-racing. I pride myself that I have made the better choice, and that others will feel for generations to come some of the advantages of what some might call my extravagance, but which I regard as economy."

I visited the work at Graythwaite three days a week, driving in all weathers, summer and winter, in a small open trap. Whilst at Graythwaite I often met Mr. Knill Freeman and his resident architect, Mr. Dan Gibson, and also George Gregory, a well-known Parliamentary solicitor and legal adviser to Colonel Sandys.

Mr. Gregory was at the time building Riverside, near Staines, the late Mr. T. E. Colcutt being his architect, and he asked me to lay out his gardens. This was my first commission at any

The Life and Work of An English Landscape Architect.

distance from home, and it opened up visions of expanding possibilities which within a very few years were to be realised.

It was now five years since we took up our permanent residence at Windermere. During this period the volume of business had grown by leaps and bounds, and my landscape practice was on its feet. In these five years the firm had carried out a number of improvements or extensions to gardens, but my personal work consisted increasingly in consultations and the preparation of designs, and in the occasional superintendence of work carried out under the direction of the client's head gardener, or under that of one of our landscape foremen, who employed local labour, paid directly by my clients. My direct contribution to the volume of trade, and every penny I made beyond a bare living wage, went into the Nursery to swell its working capital. Still, financial worries seemed to increase, for whilst our balance-sheet showed splendid progress, most of the concrete value of the business was in stock. At the same time the liquid capital was unequal to the weekly wages, bills, and other liabilities. In short, our capital was unequal to the volume of business we were doing. We almost reached a second crisis in our enterprise when, fortunately, my wife received a small but unexpected legacy, every penny of which went into the business, raising it from what looked like inevitable disaster, and allowing us to take more land and to stock it with trees and shrubs, for which there was a regular demand both for our planting schemes and for sale in the district.

To equip myself for still larger enterprise I studied hard, my principal text-books being "Loudon's Landscape Gardening," "The Works of Repton" (which, it will be remembered, I had studied as a boy), and particularly "How to Lay Out a Garden," by Edward Kemp, whom I still regard as the best exponent of the landscape style—or, as Kemp called it, "the gardenesque style." I also commenced to study the works of Ruskin, of whom I became an admiring disciple, and have so remained.

Naturally, I visited every park and garden within reach which had been laid out by men of repute in my profession, including Sefton Park, Liverpool, and Birkenhead Park, and the Miller and Avenham Parks at Preston, respectively the work of the Frenchman Andre, Sir Joseph Paxton and Kemp, and Ernest Milner. I also made a careful study of the landscape garden effects arranged as a setting to the Furness railway stations, and private gardens such as Levens, Holker, Sir James Ramsden's place at Furness Abbey,

Keswick, and many other smaller places of interest. No effort was too great if only it led to my increased efficiency as a designer of gardens.

During the later part of this period I endeavoured to improve my draughtsmanship by studying with artists resident in the district, and by sketching from nature, generally in company with my now old friend and secretary, John Dyer, who has a very critical mind in art matters, and a caustic and expressive style of criticism, which I encouraged him to exercise liberally in our mutual problems incidental to my work.

In my early years, and in my struggles for advancement, I had associated mainly with workmen who possessed ideas in abundance in the nugget. These ideas, however, needed a good deal of refining before they could be submitted to criticism from people of culture and refinement. I now perceived that it was with such people that I should be brought into contact if I were to succeed in my profession. I therefore began to think of schooling and educating myself in appropriate ideas, and, what is equally important, clothing these ideas in suitable language so that even " he who runs may read." It is fitting and proper that superior ideas be presented in courtly dress. Many a first-rate idea or scheme is lost because it is clumsily presented, and many a second or third rate idea is preferred to the more excellent one because pleasingly set forth. Anyone versed in architectural or similar competitions knows how, even when adjudged by competent assessors, a tricky perspective view wins first place for a comparatively poor plan and elevation, while the scheme of distinctive merit is rejected owing to its author having sent in drawings in a cruder, if more honest, style of draughtsmanship.

In my desire to overcome my conscious defects, I was led, as a first step, to join the village Debating Society—that forum which has produced so many orators. In these rugged training grounds many distinguished parliamentarians have discovered that they possessed the gift of swaying and convincing men by native eloquence. Such, however, was not my purpose. Among the society's workers and supporters were several men of culture and leisure, who always maintained a high level of debate on subjects of real importance, and who mildly and reprovingly insisted upon a high tone of language and expression, which was just the discipline I needed. Into these debates I threw myself with energy, preparing myself for each weekly meeting by reading and study. I soon

The Life and Work of An English Landscape Architect.

found my level, and by steady improvement, after three years, I was elected president of the society.

These were the distinctively formative years of my career, during which many forces contributed to my evolution. By no means the least important was the influence of the two pastors of the Carver Memorial Church, Windermere, where I sat for twelve years under two learned divines, Doctors Taylor and Adamson. Usually little credit is given to the influence of the clergy of our churches, and their contributions to the formation of character is seldom recognised. Is it surprising, then, that to me my church was, in addition to being a source of spiritual refreshment at a very strenuous and trying time, a " secondary school," presided over by men of great ability, fully abreast with modern thought, and not afraid of expressing liberal views in matters of theology. Dr. Taylor, the first pastor, was Professor of Analytical Theology in Glasgow, and it was said of him that he made Fairbairn of Oxford. He attracted Americans to his church when paying visits to Lakeland, and I remember once listening to a keen argument between him and Dr. Henry Ward Beecher, the famous American preacher. I forget the point at issue, but I thought that our pastor got the best of the argument. Dr. Taylor was not only a very eloquent preacher, but the arrangement of his matter followed so lucidly in clarified logical sequence, that I could remember the whole of his discourse—and, as a matter of fact, I often gave a rehearsal of the sermon to my mother when she was unable to attend. These perfect compositions were so simplified in utterance that all padding and unessential word passages were eliminated, and the pastor's principle began to have an effect upon my work. I began to reach after the same qualities ; mere attempts at following or copying nature began to have less and less attractions for me, whilst art compositions based on reason attracted me more and more.

Dr. Taylor was popular with the young folks of the church, but he was sometimes a trial to aged orthodoxy, as may be gathered from his remarks to his congregation after a visit to Rome. He told us one Sunday morning of one of his experiences in St. Peter's.

He said : " My daughters and I visited St. Peter's Cathedral in Rome. After admiring Cellini's splendid colonnade, with the great dome rising behind it silhouetted against a deep blue sky, we mounted the great stairway and entered the Cathedral, the interior of which I found created in me a deep sense of devotion. Just then my attention was drawn to a girl of about ten and a boy about eight years of age, passing deftly, almost on tip-toe, towards the statue of St. Peter, crossing themselves as they passed along. When they got up to the statue they stood with clasped hands and bowed heads for a moment, then the little girl got her brother by the middle, and by great energy lifted him until he kissed the toe of St. Peter. Then the little fellow endeavoured to lift up his sister, but try as he would he could not do it, and I could see the little girl's tears were beginning to flow; so I approached quietly and lifted the little girl so that she could perform her act of devotion, at which my eldest daughter exclaimed, ' Oh, father, whatever will the people of the Carver Memorial Church say ? ' To which I replied, ' I don't care what they say. It has done the little girl good, and it's done me good too, and that's justification enough.' "

Dr. Adamson was less scholastic—or, shall I say, less academic? But he had the finest presence of any minister I have ever seen or known, and was as fine and lovable as he looked, always anxious to help with advice and encouragement ; just the sort of man one would choose as a father confessor, if needed. As it was, he was a staunch friend and adviser, exercising an influence in the home which was even greater than that which he exercised in the pulpit. Dr. Adamson was more devoted to art and the poets, especially Wordsworth, than Dr. Taylor. He had also a fine sense of the value of form and order in public worship, and I can imagine that had he been in a position to introduce such an innovation, his church, which was well adapted for the purpose, would have seen a high development in beautiful music and liturgy. Unlike his predecessor, who feared no one, he unfortunately feared certain members of his flock who were unworthy to tie his shoe-strings. Taylor would say, " The ignorant have no right to an opinion, nor the half-ignorant the right to rule any community by the rushlight of their half-formed ideas." Adamson would say, " My brother, what do you think about the matter, and what would be your advice under existing conditions ? "—knowing all the time that the advice given would be unworthy of adoption. I loved and admired both men, but the greatest lesson which I learnt was that democratic institutions work best when there is a strong and fearless autocrat as leader.

My last recollection of Pastor Adamson was as he, with outstretched hands, pronounced the benediction in the tiny but beautiful Congregational Church at Hest Bank, of which the reader will hear later, with its evening shadows dimly pierced by

The Life and Work of An English Landscape Architect.

the lights from the candelabras. The benign figure, and the massive leonine head with its rich halo of curling grey locks, silhouetted against the green panelled background, were poem and picture combined. I would gladly give a good deal to possess his portrait posed in that last great act of worship.

I have done but scanty justice to these two grand old men and the influence they exercised over me, but I feel that more cannot properly be said here. I can only repeat that both were to me great schoolmasters.

THE REV. WILLIAM ADAMSON, D.D.

CHAPTER III.

GREAT AMBITIONS AND GREATER NECESSITIES.

I HAD now arrived at a point at which I had fully established myself in my work as a designer of private gardens. Not that I was satisfied. That failing I never allowed myself to encourage. On the contrary, I have always instinctively cultivated a critical outlook, an attitude which once led one of my best clients to remark : " I have never known you to express satisfaction with anything you ever did " ; to which I replied : " I hope you never will, for then I should know that I had reached the full scope of my limitations." It was not so much my plans which I doubted, as my ability, on many occasions, to prevent my clients introducing all sorts of inconsistencies and anachronisms, such as rock and rustic work near the house, where work of an architectural or formal character was needed; or, on the other hand, the introduction of formal and architectural details amidst natural rural scenery.

These inconsistencies have always arisen from the inability on the part of the gardening public to understand the definite principles underlying the art of garden design. The consequent repeated disappointments in my work led me to decide on the compilation of a book dealing with the art and craft of garden making, for which I began about this time to collect material. My idea was to lay down some sort of standard which might, I thought, influence my clients and encourage them to insist on the best of what I was capable. My growing confidence in myself fostered my ambition to undertake work of greater importance, not only for the private clients for whom I had so far mostly worked, but also for public authorities, which I felt would lead to more profitable employment, a consideration which was becoming pressing owing to the increased cost of living which always accompanies an increasing and growing family. I also

31

The Life and Work of An English Landscape Architect.

felt that the time was rapidly approaching when I must definitely withdraw from the nursery business, which was now well established and under the able direction of my two brothers, for whom I had done everything which affection and family interest dictated, a point of view with which they were in entire agreement.

At this juncture I saw in my morning paper an account of a big scheme for a public park at Hanley in Staffordshire, and I decided to do what only a few years before I would have regarded as a very unprofessional act. I decided to " get after " the work, and at once I got together a number of my plans, along with certain articles I had contributed to the horticultural papers, wired to a member of Parliament whom I knew very well (and who knew my work) asking for an introduction to Mr. Woodall, the member for the Hanley Division, and then made my way to Hanley. Receiving next morning a letter of introduction to Mr. Woodall, who was staying in the district, I repaired thither, and was welcomed by him, and after inquiries as to the work I had done, and an examination of the drawings I brought with me, he gave me a letter of introduction to Mr. Joseph Lobley, the engineer for the borough. This I duly presented at half-past two in the afternoon.

I apologised for taking a course of action which was unusual amongst professional men, to which he laughingly replied that two men of considerable reputation had already been in communication with him. He then looked at my plans, which evidently impressed him, for he told me that the Parks Committee would be sitting at three o'clock, and that he would do his best to induce them to see me, but that I must not be surprised if he failed, because it was quite an unusual course to take.

At three o'clock Mr. Lobley left me in his private room whilst he attended the Committee, and at a quarter past I was asked to walk into the Committee room, where I was introduced to the Mayor, Aldermen, and Councillors. I was very nervous, but I did my best to brace myself up for an ordeal, and soon found I was dealing with a committee of gentlemen who were wondrous kind, one of them endeavouring to put me at my ease by saying they " had all been young and enterprising once," and that they appreciated the same quality in others. " And now to business," said the Mayor. " On what terms," he asked, " are you prepared to do the work ? " " Five per cent. on the cost of the work, and expenses," I replied. " This places us in a rather difficult position,"

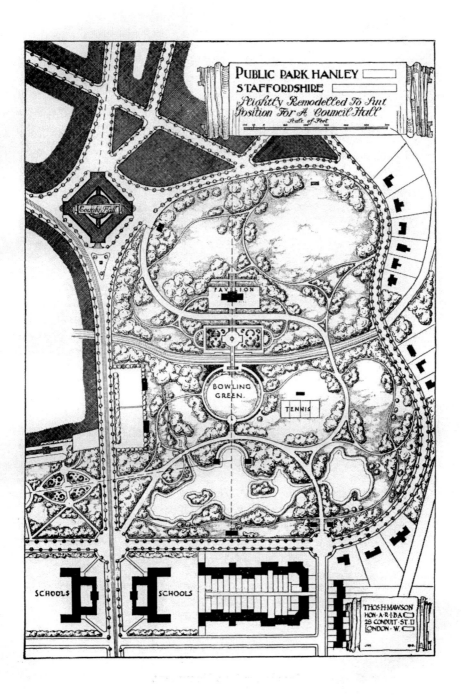

PUBLIC PARK HANLEY
STAFFORDSHIRE
Slightly Remodelled To Suit
Position For A Council Hall
Scale of Feet

VIEWS OF THE LAKE, HANLEY PARK.

Great Ambitions and Greater Necessities.

he said, " because [handling a letter] I have here a letter from a landscape gardener of repute offering to do the work for three per cent., and of course we have to safeguard the ratepayers' interests." " Mr. Mayor and gentlemen," I replied, " I am sorry I cannot accept less for my services than the recognised fee. All I can promise is to earn it. Only one thing more I can say, and it is this : If you appoint me, Hanley Park will be my first great public work, and I cannot afford to do less than my utmost to give you satisfaction." I was then asked to retire, but in ten minutes was back again to be told that the Committee had passed a resolution recommending my appointment as expert to the Council, and I knew that instead of my youth being regarded as a detriment it won the hearts of these seasoned old Aldermen and Councillors.

In about ten days I had a letter from Mr. Challinor, the Town Clerk, informing me that the Council had accepted the Parks Committee's recommendation, and appointed me as their Landscape Architect, and asking me to attend the next meeting of the Parks Committee. Mr. Lobley wrote asking me to be prepared with certain tentative proposals for dealing with the park area, not for the purpose of adoption, but rather to focus discussion, and thus draw out some idea of the requirements. To do this I had to spend a week on the site, which contained a number of old pit-shafts and enormous spoil-banks, whilst the remainder of the land was used as a tip for pottery refuse. The site extended to one hundred and five acres, twenty-five of which Mr. Lobley had decided should be developed for building purposes, whilst eighty acres were to be devoted to the park and recreation grounds.

I have often remarked since that I must have been a very young man when I agreed to convert this waste of pits, mounds, and rubbish-tips, under which was buried all the good soil there ever was on the land, into a pleasant public park. Never, excepting at Burslem and on the East Park, Wolverhampton, has it been my lot to transform such an unpromising site into quiet lawns and tree-planted spaces. It was a risky undertaking, which might have ended in disaster.

Try to imagine the site with which I had to deal. Any soil that remained was very thin, overlying a stiff, tenacious clay, and in many places this was badly water-logged. Here and there were a few stunted and shrivelled thorns and ash trees that had once been part of a hedge. The only redeeming feature of the site was its southern slope, but this was largely nullified by the fact that

The Life and Work of An English Landscape Architect.

across the middle of the property was an exceptionally utilitarian canal at an awkward level, which carried an enormous amount of traffic for the local potteries and ironworks.

In addition to this, along the eastern boundary were a number of potteries with numerous bottle-shaped kilns belching forth fumes and smoke, poisoning the air and making vegetation very difficult to establish, while on the south side the outlook was over Stoke-on-Trent, generally lying in a pottery mist. On the west we overlooked the irrigation works, beyond which was more or less open country, and on the north lay the town of Hanley, with some small works in the foreground. Such were the conditions with which I had to deal, and which I was determined to coax or bully into a beautiful pleasance.

The plan Illus. No. 8 shows the general principle upon which I proceeded, and its main proposals were laid in rough sketch form before the next meeting of the Parks Committee. The general conception of the lay-out, which was dictated by the contours, was irregular but harmonious, with free groupings of trees and shrubs, following the natural contours, and a lake for boating on the lowest part of the site. The two views Illus. Nos. 9 and 10 show the lake as matured from different points of view. This sheet of water serves two practical purposes : first, it clarifies the air of the chemical fumes and favours the growth of the surrounding foliage and supplies a source of revenue to the park.

Into this free landscape treatment was introduced a certain proportion of formality and architectural adornment, which culminated in a formal terrace, which with its pavilion, fountains, and gardens provided a social centre for the district. This treatment of my subject greatly appealed to the Mayor and his committee, who urged me to go ahead with my plans with all possible speed.

At the first meeting after my appointment, the Mayor said : " Mr. Mawson, we don't know whether we ought to tell you or not, but after seeing your rough ideas, we are so pleased with our choice of a landscape architect that we feel we may tell you that one of the three men who were in the running with you, writes to say he ' is surprised that we have appointed an entirely unknown man for such an important piece of work.' We are giving you a chance to make that sort of letter impossible in the future. In the meantime, we have replied that if you are not already famous, we believe you are going to be."

Great Ambitions and Greater Necessities.

From this it will be seen that I was peculiarly fortunate in having as my first committee of a public authority men of great human understanding and kindliness.

The next business was to get out my working drawings for the entire park. These were approved, along with my estimate for £25,000, an estimate which was subsequently considerably increased owing to additional works undertaken on my recommendation, and the great expense of obtaining secure foundations for the various structures on undermined land. Arrangements were made for the ceremony of cutting the first sod, which was a great event. The town of Hanley rose to the occasion, and provided me with my first experience of a public function.

One thing which impressed me was the tremendous enthusiasm of the general public and ratepayers. The idea of it all seemed to raise them socially and materially above the level of other Pottery towns. The concourse of people at the ceremony was simply amazing, and the civic enthusiasm was unbounded. The Mayor, Aldermen, and Councillors, along with the élite of the town and distinguished guests from adjoining towns, started their day with a Mayor's luncheon. I was given a seat at the high table, and had to listen with pleasurable embarrassment to complimentary speeches eulogising my plans.

Alderman Hammersley, the orator of the Council, complimented the perspicuity of vision of the Parks Committee, who in their endeavour to produce a park which should be a classic example for all other towns, had made the most exhaustive inquiries and had discovered a budding genius, and of course all the members of the Council applauded, whilst I bowed my acknowledgments.

The master of ceremonies announced to the Mayor, Aldermen, and Gentlemen that " carriages are at the door." The day was fine, with a blue sky overhead—specially blue, I may remark, for a Pottery town. We then took our places and drove between crowds of cheering ratepayers to the site of the park, where a military band played Handel's " Largo " as we proceeded to the gaily decorated platform from which the speeches were to be made before and after the sod-cutting, and I was called upon to describe the designs. I have not the least recollection of what I said or how I said it, but I remember clearly the great goodwill which was shown to me, which at once endeared the pottery folk to me.

With the assistance and advice of Mr. Lobley, the borough

The Life and Work of An English Landscape Architect.

engineer, I soon had the work in progress, many hundreds of men being employed on half-time, during a period of industrial distress.

So much has been said about the unemployed, who are too often regarded as unemployable, that I would like to say one word on their behalf. Park construction is not like working a cultivated garden ; it is for the most part heavy navvy work with pick and spade, requiring hardened hands and hard muscles for its successful pursuit. These men were used for the most part to light indoor occupations. Many of them and their families were suffering from want, and were only too anxious for the work. Poor fellows, they scarcely knew one end of a spade from the other ; but they persevered, only to blister their hands until they were cracked and raw. The men were taken on in relays on the basis of three days' work and three days' play. In each of the play periods the hands got tender again, and the work became in many cases a period of pain and discomfort. Certain of the men dropped out from sheer inability to go on, and then the rest were taken on full time, and did good, conscientious work, gradually getting into condition, which gave them a zest for open-air occupations.

This work led to others, and when I had been engaged on this park about six months I was asked to advise the Burslem Town Council upon their new park. The site was not so large as the Hanley one, but it was well situated in relation to the centres of population. From a cultural standpoint it was even worse than Hanley, for the whole centre of the site was a series of enormous pit-mounds and spoil-banks. However, I went to work with my designs on the assumption that somehow the soil to cover them could be found.

My uphill experiences with the Hanley site now stood for an asset of some value, and I knew that if a covering of soil could be obtained, success would follow. Fortunately for both me and the park, as luck would have it, we were able to obtain several thousands of loads of suitable surface soil from a developing building estate not far distant. Thus another almost insuperable difficulty was providentially surmounted, and another chapter of my history, the design and construction of public works, was promisingly begun.

ROCKY CASCADE IN BELLEVUE PARK, NEWPORT, MON.

CHAPTER IV.

I ENTER OPEN COMPETITIONS FOR THE DESIGN OF PARKS.

ABOUT the time that I was engaged upon the work of laying out parks for Hanley and Burslem, the Local Government Board sent out to municipalities a recommendation that they should alleviate the prevalent distress arising from unemployment by promoting works of public utility, the Board promising special facilities for the speedy passing of plans and the raising of loans. This led to a number of authorities acquiring lands for park purposes, followed by calls for competitive designs for their development.

I have come to regard competition as an unsatisfactory method of obtaining plans, because what generally happens is that about twenty firms spend each fifty to a hundred pounds in preparing a design which, if lucky, may win the premium of one hundred guineas. Instructions may follow to superintend the carrying out of the work, but in the greater majority of cases the whole matter ends with the winning of the premium. Competitions, however, appeal peculiarly to ambitious young men, and at the time of which I speak I was distinctly of this class. I therefore threw myself into this new sphere of work with all the enthusiasm of which I was capable.

By this time I had got my own office and the nucleus of an organisation and a small staff who were just as keen as myself to win laurels for the office. We worked early and late, working at one competition after another for over a year. We sent in our first design, and waited the result with confidence, till one morning a letter bearing the seal of the town clerk to the municipality that had advertised the competition, arrived, advising me that my drawings had won third place. In a month's time we were waiting the result of the second competition, in which we were not placed at all. Then the result of the third competition was advertised,

The Life and Work of An English Landscape Architect.

and we were placed second. And so it went on with depressing persistence, until I had exhausted all my capital. Then came the thirteenth advertisement, this time by the Newport, Monmouthshire, Town Council, who had been presented by Lord Tredegar with a twenty-seven-acre site. The premiums offered were £100, £50, and £25, and I felt, with the gambler's optimism, that if only I could afford another try I would win. My friends and my two brothers were very anxious that I should not risk the expense of another competition. The latter in particular pointed out that I really had made a good fight for it, but it was clear that I was not a winner; that in any case my practice called for the whole of my time and energies.

It was at this juncture that my wife decided the question, urging that as I had been in for twelve competitions and lost, this would mean ruin to my reputation unless I proved that I was capable of winning. Perhaps thirteen would prove my lucky number. I felt that this line of argument was absolutely sound, and that I simply had at all risks to go on until I did win.

Next day I was on my way to Newport, where I stayed the night, calling upon Mr. Conyers Kirkby, the borough engineer, next morning at 10 o'clock. Mr. Kirkby, who was a genial character, received me kindly, explaining that he had heard of my work in the Potteries, and that he would have preferred his Council to have consulted me, and thus have saved him a lot of work preparing surveys and plans for the competition. He then gave me two additional copies of the survey, and directed me to the site. "Jump on to a tram," he said, "and go to the terminus, then take the road to your right, and it is the first field you come to on your right again."

I followed my directions, and on arriving at the field unfolded my survey plan and began my observations. The field was approximately the size and shape of the site indicated on the plan, and the fall of the land approximately that shown by the contours, but in every other respect there was little correspondence between them. For hours I tried to harmonise the site with the survey, and at last returned to explain my dilemma to Mr. Kirkby and get his explanation. To my amazement he was very apologetic about the survey, which, he explained, had been done by a young pupil who had never been known to do anything correctly. "He was, however, the only man I could spare for the work!" "What, then, am I to do about it?" I asked. "All you can do is to go

Design of Parks and Gardens.

home and spread your tracing paper over the survey, and make your design on the assumption that it is correct." I decided to act on his advice; indeed, how otherwise could I compete?

My plans and report were ready and despatched in time for the Parks Committee and Selection Committee. Late in the afternoon of the date of the meeting I had a telegram from Mr. Kirkby, which read as follows :—

Mawson, Landscape Architect, Windermere.

Parks Committee have selected your design recommendation to the Council for first premium. Accept my heartiest congratulations.   Kirkby.

A week later I had a letter from the Town Clerk informing me that his Council had adopted the recommendation of the Parks Committee and awarded me the first premium, for which he enclosed me the Council's cheque for £105. The letter also stated that the General Purposes Committee would meet that day fortnight, and requested my attendance.

By the same post came a local newspaper which gave a long description of the winning plan, and a report of the Council meeting, which included explanatory remarks by Mr. Kirkby, who said : " I am pleased that Mr. Mawson has won the first premium, because he has given greater care to the study of the site than any other competitor."

My delight and that of my staff were unbounded, for we all felt that we had wiped out a reproach. My wife took the matter as an expected and assured result. Her " I-told-you-so " attitude was quite pardonable !

In a fortnight I presented myself again at the Town Hall, where Mr. Kirkby introduced me to the Town Clerk, who in turn introduced me to the Mayor, Aldermen, and Councillors in the council chambers, where I had to listen to congratulatory addresses from the Mayor and several Aldermen. I thanked them heartily, for I felt very proud and grateful for the honour they had paid me. This was to me the third rung of the ladder of fame of which I had always dreamed. The Mayor then informed me that they wished me to accompany them to the site of the park, as they would like me to explain the features of my design on the ground. At the door there were waiting for us about six carriages, each with a pair of horses, and when we had taken our places we moved forward down Commercial Street, turning to the right at the bottom ; but imagine my utter dismay and consternation when we passed the field I had studied, and drove

The Life and Work of An English Landscape Architect.

on to the next one! My surprise can be imagined as I realised I had never seen the site I had planned; but I pulled myself together to meet the impact with stoical come-what-may sort of courage, or perhaps it was the courage of desperation.

Having entered the field, I directed my clients to the advantages of the site, the picturesque old elms, the charm of certain views, and the necessity for screening certain disturbing details of the middle distance. They became so absorbed in these major factors, which were entirely new to them (and, let me add, to me), that they did not press me to explain my plans further, but wandered off in groups to discover other vistas. One old Alderman, however, was evidently deeply interested in what I proposed to do about a group of splendid old elms which in their setting formed a very delightful glade, with a small stream meandering down the vista which they made.

" Where does your lake go, Mr. Mawson? "

" Just where those trees are."

" What will happen to them? "

" They will disappear."

" I am awfully sorry for that."

" So am I."

" Then why remove them? "

" Simply because you have asked for a lake, and I have shown it in the only position in which it could possibly go; but I am bound to tell you that you ought never to have asked for it, for a park like this does not require a lake. In any case a rocky stream with cascades would have been far more suitable and retained for us those splendid elms."

" Would you mind, Mr. Mawson, telling the Committee what you have just told me? "

To this I readily agreed, discerning that this was my opportunity to save my front.

The Alderman called upon the Mayor to collect his Councillors together to hear my explanations. I told them that I had so far adhered in my designs to the conditions of the competition, but that the Alderman had extracted from me the confession that in my opinion the plans did not do full justice to the site; that, in particular, I thought the lake which they had called for ought not to appear, and instead we ought to have a rocky glade and cascade in its place.

" What," asked the Mayor, " do you propose? "

Design of Parks and Gardens.

" That you should give me five weeks to redraft my plans," a suggestion which raised quite a cheer. My proposal was put to the meeting and passed unanimously. I was then thanked for my courage in criticising my own plans. It was with feelings of profound relief that I emerged from behind this smoke-screen. Illus. No. 11 shows the rocky cascade which took the place of the proposed lake, and which is a perennial source of delight to lovers of the park.

In some three months we were ready for the first tree-planting, a ceremony performed by the donor, Lord Tredegar, who made a charming short speech, which I think still further increased the affection which the people of Newport entertained for him. One incident pleased him very much. I was not satisfied with the way in which the hole for the tree was prepared by the contractor, so without the least thought or hesitation I handed to him my silk hat, took the spade and completed the hole as I thought it should be. Lord Tredegar watched me with approving interest, and said : " Well done, Mawson ; you know the practical side of your job."

Having turned the corner from failure to success, fortune seemed to smile on me. Another competition for a public park was advertised within a few months, and I again entered and won. This time it was for the East Park, Wolverhampton, an area of fifty acres, consisting entirely of cinder-heaps, excepting for a flooded depression which gave an opportunity for a lake large enough for boating. Like the Hanley Park, there was an outer fringe of land to be laid out as a building estate. Thus, in both cases the park and surroundings provided material for miniature town-planning schemes. Lord Tredegar, by the way, was one of the few survivors of the charge of the Light Brigade in the Crimean War.

About this time the late Mr. Dan Gibson, with whom I had worked at Graythwaite Hall, where he acted as resident architect, joined me as a junior partner. Leaving Graythwaite, he had gone up to London, working as a valued assistant in the office of Messrs. Ernest George and Peto, returning to Lakeland to recuperate after a severe illness. At the time I was much overworked myself, and I offered him a share in my practice. Gibson, who was one of the handsomest, most courtly, and able men I have ever known, exercised a great influence on the work of the office, and set up as high an ideal for the architectural section of our work as I had

The Life and Work of An English Landscape Architect.

striven for in landscape expression. His skill as an architect is shown in the entrances and lodges at East Park and the conservatory in the West Park, Wolverhampton, and in a lesser degree in the large pavilion in Hanley Park.

About the same time a competition of a quite different order was advertised. It was for the planning of a part of Lord Forrest's estate, near Wellington, Shropshire, as a model residential area. I had already prepared the plans for the lay-out of the building estate at Storrs, Bowness-on-Windermere, and the Heathwaite building estate, Windermere, and the work appealed to me ; so I again entered the arena, but with considerable doubt as to my ability when pitted against adepts in this branch of my adopted profession. The problems involved were particularly difficult, and the scheme as a whole was much larger than anything I had so far attempted. I decided, however, to make the attempt, and went to Wellington for a few days so that I might study the possibilities of the site, and at the same time form some idea by local inquiries as to the size of plots most needed. In this lay-out I anticipated the restrictions of Mr. John Burns' Town Planning Act, and the recommendation of the National Housing and Town Planning Council. The plans were developed on the basis of a self-contained suburb, with its own shopping centre, schools, churches, club, and recreation ground, with wide tree-planted boulevards for the main arteries and avenues of trees in the residential quarters. Finished plans were carefully drawn from my roughly developed ideas on the site, and beautifully coloured by my staff, who were becoming expert in pictorial rendering of competitive drawings. The plans were presented in due course, and to my surprise were awarded the first premium.

This success encouraged me to enter town-planning competitions, and within a few months of my first success I submitted a scheme for the lay-out of the Endcliffe Hall Estate, Sheffield. In my designs I took the fine old hall and its gardens as the main focus of my scheme, reserving them as a park and social centre. The promoting syndicate paid me the compliment of asking me to name the assessors, and I proposed Mr. Aston Webb (now Sir Aston) and Mr. Ernest Milner, neither of whom was at the time known to me excepting by his work. The plans were despatched, and the awards shortly after advertised, but, to my keen disappointment, I was not even awarded a place. By the next post, however, I received a personal letter from Mr. Milner informing me that though my scheme was by far the best submitted, they had no option but to disqualify me, because I had violated the conditions. My plans had been sent in under my own name instead of under a *nom de plume*, as directed by the advertisement. The printed conditions made no mention of this, and I, concluding that they gave the full instructions, had omitted to study the original advertisement, so I lost the £100 premium.

After several other small competitions in which I had a good proportion of successes, and having won from first to last over five hundred pounds in premiums, I decided that I would retire from the field and take part only in those competitions where I was specially invited.

When I first took part in competitions my reasonable desire was to measure my ability against that of other men. After a long period of whirling excitement, however—one set of competitive plans treading fast upon the heels of, if not actually overlapping, another—I realised that my original motives were no longer the controlling passion, but that, on the contrary, I was pitting my luck, rather than my skill, against that of other men. In short, it was my way of having a flutter. I was becoming a gambler. To make my introspection all the more accusing, I realised that I had discovered and was using certain catchy tricks which are well known to those who enter professional competitions, and which, even where the plans are judged by a capable assessor, have much to do with the result. The use of these tricks implies a moral declension from the high motives that inspire all good art. I was winning by giving the Councillors what they wanted, instead of seeking to raise their ideals of what was right and proper. It was my pastor, the old doctor, who made me see the matter in its proper setting. I can still recall his words : " You have a saying that you know what you like, but does it ever occur to you that God Almighty intended you to know what you ought to like ? If you come to think of it, you will discover that this knowing what you ought to like is the measure of the difference between yourself and your dog." Only grey-haired old men of authority can afford to speak like that.

Another reason which carried great weight with me was the absurdity of allowing the men on local committees, who, however well meaning and however practical and level-headed, could make no pretension to art culture, to adjudicate upon schemes submitted to them by men who had devoted a life's study to their subject.

The Life and Work of An English Landscape Architect.

In no other profession would the expert submit his decisions to the judgment of the amateur, and I did not see why landscape architecture should be an exception to this rule. I still think this was a right and proper view to take in the interests of the profession, and I have steadily endeavoured ever since to induce public authorities to employ a professional assessor, and have even gone the length of offering my services in this capacity without fee. In every case the reply has been that the Council "know what they want"!

Having told the story of my first success in a public-park competition, let me narrate my last, which followed my decision to desist from such pursuits. The circumstances I thought justified the violation. Receiving a flattering letter from a borough engineer to say that his Council had expressed a special wish that I should compete, because the conditions prevailing were similar to those which I had successfully solved in the Pottery towns, I determined to submit a scheme. I was conscious that my plans were equal to those of any of my previous winning schemes, and better than most of them. They were carefully detailed with special designs for the entrances, lodges, bandstands, and every other important feature. It was therefore with some surprise that I learnt that I was entirely out of the running. I was so puzzled that I made a special journey to see the plans which were on exhibition. Judge of my chagrin and disappointment when, instead of discovering a new star, I saw that the award had been given to the veriest amateur, whose architectural details were simply pages from an ironmonger's catalogue pasted on to sheets of Whatman's paper! The explanation is simple. The members of the Town Council understood ironmongers' catalogues, but they did not possess the least glimmering of the art of landscape architecture.

SIR W. CUNLIFFE-BROOKS AND GUESTS AT GLEN TANA.

MIDDLEMASS BEY, THOMAS H. MAWSON, HON. MARGARET CROSS, LADY CROSS, LORD CROSS, SIR GEO. BADEN-POWELL, BART.,
MIGNONETTE MIDDLEMASS, LADY BADEN-POWELL, SIR WM CUNLIFFE-BROOKS.

CHAPTER V.

THE arrangement with my friend Dan Gibson lasted just two years, and, strange as it may appear, it was our success that finally led to its dissolution. My idea in seeking the partnership was to secure by our joint efforts a higher degree of architectural expression in the gardens which I planned. I had at this time no thought of proceeding beyond the legitimate limits of landscape architecture, but such were Gibson's genius and skill in every department of applied design, that no sooner had he made the round of my clients, than he was busy with every conceivable kind of speciality undertaken by any architect. Ecclesiastical, domestic, and garden designs, along with designs for furniture, decorations, bookbinding, and jewellery, jostled one another, and, as I feared, sometimes under pressure of work relegating garden design to a secondary place. In addition, he collected for my clients, china, furniture, silver, pewter, tapestries, prints, and miniatures, and every other imaginable artistic antique. His knowledge of these matters was wide and extensive, he having spent what veritably amounted to years of his life at the South Kensington, the Wallace, and other collections ; and, in addition, he seemed to have an instinct for discovering the genuine example. I was a keenly interested amateur, and would have been delighted to develop this side of our practice, but I saw that the motto was, " Keep within your compass." Gardens were my asset, and antiques and horticulture were not homely companions.

To an extent unrealised at the time, however, there was a keen bond of sympathy between us, and we both gained much by our collaboration—I by gaining a much wider appreciation of architectural detail, and Gibson by a widened grasp of he fundamentals of composition ; so that within a week of our dissolution I was pouring work into Gibson's office, the most

45

The Life and Work of An English Landscape Architect.

important being a new, or almost new, house at Wood, South Tawton, Devonshire (of which more hereafter), where together we planned the house, garden, park, the home farm buildings, the decorative furniture, he even going to the extent of selecting the silver, china, and linen.

My principal contribution to Gibson's work was the preparation of the first ground plan of the house and its relation to the terraces and garden scheme. Gibson's contribution to my own work (the garden scheme) was the alteration to the lodge, to which I added the gate piers, wrought-iron gates, and wing walls at a later period.

At the time that Gibson and I joined forces I had, in addition to my public-park work, the work which I was still carrying out at Graythwaite Hall for Colonel Sandys, and much other interesting work, such as that for Sir William Cunliffe-Brooks at Glen Tana, Aboyne; the Marquis of Bute at Mount-Stuart, Isle of Bute; Major Macrae-Gilstrap at Ballimore, Argyllshire; Colonel Campbell at Ormidale; Mr. Walter Whitehead at Colwyn Bay, and many others.

Sir William Cunliffe-Brooks was in many ways the most generous and yet the most tyrannical client for whom I have ever worked. Nothing could exceed his interest in one's work and its development, and nothing was too much for him to do to get me the right sort of introduction to his friends. To him I owed my clients, Sir Alan Mackenzie; Lord Erroll, of Slains Castle, Aberdeenshire; and Mrs. Pickering, of Kincardine-O'Neil. My introduction to Sir William came through a fine old Shropshire squire, Mr. Frank Stanier of Peplow Hall, who warned me that Sir William would prove a difficult client, at the same time expressing confidence that I had the qualities to win his goodwill. This I think I succeeded in doing completely, but doubtless I was largely indebted to Sir William's friends, who, whilst loving the old man, had a just estimate of his temperament. " Now, Mr. Mawson," said one of these warning friends, " whenever Sir William takes morning prayers, look out for a squall and go very slow." True enough this warning was understood by everyone, who for another reason regretted his ministrations, as it was a real joy to listen to Lady Brooks reading morning prayers: she had the perfect voice and intonation for a set form of liturgy.

My new client had an absolute passion for building and road-making, and kept a regular staff of two hundred and fifty workmen. Before he died he had rebuilt Glen Tana House, and

Bridge and Tower of Ess, Glen Tana, Aboyne.

Two Years' Collaboration.

every farm-house and cottage on the estate. He also in a large measure rebuilt, or added to, the village of Aboyne, and carried out extensive improvements to Aboyne Castle, where his son-in-law, the Marquis of Huntly, resided. He was a tremendous worker, and methodical withal. Every morning at six in summer and seven in winter he was downstairs with his secretary dictating replies to the vast correspondence which he conducted.

One morning Lord Swansea, passing through the verandah, remarked as he saw his host immersed in work, " I tell you what, Brooks ; I wouldn't have your job for ten thousand a year." " Neither would I," grunted Sir William, a reply which, I imagine, was well within the mark !

I have said that my client was methodical in his work, and his professional advisers, whoever they might be, had to conform to his plans.

Promptly at seven o'clock in the morning the piper's wail began, first indistinctly as he left his cottage, and then by degrees gathering power as he approached. At five minutes past he was going the round of the house, piping as if to waken the dead. At ten minutes past a footman came with a cup of tea, informing you that your bath was ready ; then breakfast at 7-45 ; prayers at 8-20 ; next the carriage and pair with the piper (who was general factotum) at 8-30, and away to the minute. Every day there was a big programme of work. First the widening of the bridge of Ess, then planning out on the ground the lines for new roads and carriage-ways, then on a mile to where an important fence wall was being erected. This I believe to be the finest dry walling in Great Britain, a fact on which my client greatly prided himself. From this point we would drive to where a pipe track was being laid to supply the village of Aboyne with water, and at each place he went into the most minute discussion of every detail of plan and construction, making any alteration which suggested itself to his fertile brain. This was one of the difficulties experienced by every adviser, whether architect or engineer. There was no finality. A poor man cannot afford to change a contract ; a rich one can do so as often as fancy suggests.

By this time we were ready for a lunch of sandwiches, followed by a cup of tea, always carried in a stone bottle, packed in a carefully lined and upholstered basket, for in those days thermos flasks were not invented.

In half an hour we would be on our way again to a farm-house

The Life and Work of An English Landscape Architect.

and outbuildings in the process of reconstruction. Here there would be many details to settle with the masons, carpenters, plumbers, and others, plans to be gone into and corrections to be made. From here we would go to Ladywood, near Aboyne, where my client was laying out an estate for feuing, which is a system of perpetual leasehold, the purchaser of the land paying a ground rent annually. This estate, by the way, was a gem for the purpose. It was advantageously situated close by the lovely river Dee, and was beautifully inset with the surrounding hills, and plentifully interspersed with the native Scots fir.

Leaving the feuing estate we would go perhaps to Aboyne Castle, the ancient seat of the Huntlys, where my client would unfold his big plans for additions and improvements. Then we would fall to discussing the arrangement of the gardens and home policies and new avenues.

From the Castle we would drive in the direction of Dinnett and inspect all Sir William's farms *en route*, discuss also sites for new schools, look at one or two fishing lodges, and so to Dinnett. A halt by the roadside for another cup of tea would mark off this portion of the day's work, for it was now about four o'clock. Then on again, calling on the way home to see some more men engaged on widening roads, and in the same neighbourhood the foresters fencing-in rough land to be planted in the autumn. If we were lucky we would reach Glen Tana by 6-45.

For such a wild spot Sir William seemed to have a wonderful system of letter delivery. At some prearranged place in the morning's drive a gillie would meet him with the morning's budget ; in the afternoon at another place with the afternoon's letters. These were opened by the piper, and as we went along handed in turn to Sir William, who read them page at a time, marked them with a blue or a red pencil, and placed them, according to his classification, in one of his four capacious letter pockets, to be dealt with next morning whilst the rest of the household, excepting his secretary, were asleep.

Every day our journeyings were varied somewhat, and throughout my stay at Glen Tana it was my business to spend each day with my client, and to be consulted about every conceivable matter. My principal task, however, was to advise on the lay-out of the roads meeting at the Bridge of Ess, the wing walls extending beyond the bridge, and the new entrance to the Park.

For hours sometimes we would discuss and then peg out

our lines, reviewing the operation over and over again until my client was satisfied. Then Sir William would turn to his foreman mason and say, " Well, Donald, if only I were younger and richer, I would do all that Mr. Mawson advises me to do " ; to which Donald would reply, " Weel, Sir Wullyum, ye'd better get on wi' the work, for ye'll ne'er be younger ; and perhaps if you were richer, someone would be aye the poorer " ; or some other bit of distinctively Gaelic pleasantry would be exchanged.

On the estate there was a unique little church contrived out of the ruins of an old manor-house kitchen, on which Sir William and Mr. Truffitt, his architect, had expended much ingenuity. It was divided into nave and choir ; the floor was laid to a pattern in granite and red porphyry, the roof timbers were of locally grown peeled pine, overlaid with home-grown pine boards, and covered with rough slate flags. A strange but Gothic effect was produced by rows of stags' skulls, their antlers making a perfect forest overhead, many of them " royals." Inscribed upon each skull was the name or initials of the sportsman who had brought the stag down. The seats were constructed in semi-rustic fashion, out of home-grown timbers, and upholstered with home-grown wool and covered with deerskins. In one of the window slits was a beautiful stained-glass window depicting the Saint of the Forest. The effect upon the mind was that you were in a baronial hall, or in the comfortable private chapel of an old baron. In the church an Anglican service was held every week, on one Sunday in the morning and on the next in the afternoon, alternating morning and afternoon with the adjoining parish of Kincardine-O'Neil, thus enabling one priest, the Rev. Mr. Nash, to act as incumbent of the two parishes.

At dinner on the first Sunday after my arrival Lady Brooks asked me what I thought of their little church, to which I replied that it was both quaint and beautiful. This answer did not seem quite to satisfy my hostess, so I continued : " Do you wish me to be critical ? If you do, I would venture to add that although I think it so beautiful, it seems strange to me that you should apply the trophies of sport to the decoration of your church." To which my hostess replied : " We consider these stags' heads the most beautiful thing the forest produces, and that is why we use them to beautify our church."

Much to my surprise, one Good Friday morning the carriage and pair came to the door as usual. " I hope," said Sir William,

The Life and Work of An English Landscape Architect.

" you do not mind going to the Bridge of Ess to peg out the position of the new entrance to the Park." " Certainly not," I replied. " My church imposes no special restrictions." " That's all right," said my client. " We will drive on to church later." So away we went, and began laying down and discussing our lines.

When we were at our busiest, with several men driving in pegs, Mr. Nash drove past, scarcely nodding, but looking very much annoyed. " Sir William," I said, " Mr. Nash does not approve."

Sir William : " What matter ? "

" How if he refers to us in his sermon this morning ? "

" He daren't do it."

" Well, I wouldn't like to bet on that."

" I say he dare not do it. I pay his stipend."

" I think Mr. Nash is a courageous man, and he will speak that which he believes it his duty to say, regardless of his stipend."

Sir William was a fearful man when upset, and it was quite clear I had upset him, and so he never uttered another word on the way to church, and we arrived late.

True to his principles, Nash chastised us publicly about the neglect of Holy Day. " It matters not whether you are servants, professional men, or masters, it is your bounden duty to obey the commands of your Holy Church. I say it matters not what or who you are ; and yet it does matter, for those who are exalted have the greater responsibility."

I shall never forget the row between vicar and squire in the churchyard after the service. I enjoyed it. Nash maintained his ground. Never did an A Becket reprove his king with greater courage and candour. Nothing that Sir William said had the slightest effect upon the clergyman. He spoke from his conscience, believing that there was no appeal. I do not say that his words reached Sir William's conscience, nor do I maintain that conscience in such matters is unerringly right ; but the vicar administered a castigation, and it was sensibly felt by my client.

Sir William was difficult to manage for days after that, and so I made an excuse to return home ; but I paid many subsequent visits, and so did also my partner, Gibson.

At Glen Tana I met many interesting people, including Tommy Gibson Bowles, who was a terrible tease when in the humour, and Sir George Baden Powell, a charming man and a keen politician, who, though a Conservative, was a strong Free Trader, and not afraid to attack an opponent. He had the knack of doing this quite drastically and completely, without hurting the other's feelings. This is a wonderful gift possessed by very few politicians.

Sir William was one of the best *raconteurs* I have ever known, and he himself had many interesting experiences. I remember, for instance, telling him a story about Gladstone, related to me by my client, Colonel Sandys, describing how the veteran statesman, with his personal charm, won the Midlothian election. " I believe every word of that story," said Sir William, " for I have experienced the fascination of his evil eye. One night," he continued, " when a very important discussion was on, Gladstone fixed me with his eye and literally dragged me into the Government lobby ; but just then he transfixed another victim, and the spell being broken, I bolted ! "

Life at Glan Tana was in many respects most interesting. Each evening the gillies deposited in the dining-room the kill of the day, whether of rod or gun, and then the company rose ceremoniously, inspected the kill, paid compliments, and heard comparisons from Bailey, the head gillie. One evening something went wrong, and Bailey was in disgrace. " Do you know you are a fool, Bailey ? " said Sir William. " Yes, Sir William," replied Bailey, touching his hat, or rather his hatless head.

The next evening it was the butler's turn, and this time for something for which he was not in the least responsible. But our host was so impatient that poor Parker could not get in a word of explanation. Later, someone quietly explained what had happened, and Sir William decided to make ample reparation. At the end of dinner Sir William called to the butler. " Parker, stand here, for I wish to explain as publicly as I made my charge against you, that I was wrong. I wish to say that you are not as great a fool as I thought you were. Does that satisfy you ? " " Yes, Sir William," was the docile answer.

These were merely his foibles. The apparently irascible old martinet had many lovable qualities which endeared him to a large circle of friends. His benefactions were on the grand scale. He was a most considerate employer, a generous landlord, but the quality one most loves to dwell upon is his fondness for children, with whom he was on intimate terms, and children's hospitals must have gained much from this attribute. Two hours of almost every night during his later life was spent in making albums for the hospitals. He must have spent pounds weekly

The Life and Work of An English Landscape Architect.

on pictorial magazines for cutting up, and on linen, mounted paper, and books wherein to paste the pictures.

To Gibson and me he was a generous client. His capacity for rapidly mastering the contents and incidence of our plans, which he always thoroughly and completely understood, was phenomenal. It was not too much for him if he received plans by every post. These he would return with his blue-pencil notes, and ask for amended drawings, for which he did not mind in the least paying ; but although most of the plans were carried out, the work as executed was always a travesty of our designs—so much so that the only pieces I remember with any satisfaction were the lay-out of the roads and entrance at the Bridge of Ess and the sub-division lay-out for the Ladywood feuing plan at Aboyne. The most ambitious scheme we prepared for our client was for new avenues and entrances, extensive lawns and gardens, and a new carriage court at Aboyne Castle. This work was never even commenced. It was his intention to carry it out, but his death supervened before he could get sufficient of his large staff of workmen disengaged from the then schemes in hand.

As already stated, it was at Glen Tana that I met Sir Alan Mackenzie, Sir William's neighbour at Glen Muick, near Ballater, for whom my partner and I practically rebuilt the family mansion of Brackley, the dower-house, to which we added terraces and gardens and a new avenue. In later years we carried out still further works at Brackley for Sir Victor, the son and successor of Sir Alan.

Sir Alan was a very charming and lovable man, intensely fond of his home, and, as he once told me, never miserable except when in London. Like many Scotch landlords, he was a very keen forester, and formed many new and extensive plantations on his estate. He once told me that he took a personal interest in every farmer and cottager on his estate, adding that he did not believe in the absent landlord. In contrast with our Glen Tana work, that for Sir Alan went through almost without alteration.

Sir Alan introduced me to Lord Erroll, who had just retired from the command of the " Blues," and who, after the South African war, was in residence at the family seat, Slains Castle, Cruden Bay, near Peterhead. By request, one day I broke my journey at Aberdeen, where I stayed the night, and proceeded next morning to Ellon, where a conveyance awaited me, as the railway to Cruden Bay was not laid at that time. The morning was fine

Two Years' Collaboration.

but cloudy, and the drive very enjoyable. There had been a good deal of rain, and more was in prospect. At Cruden Bay there was a fairly large fisherman's village, and at the end of the main street stood the entrance to Slains Castle, approached by a winding driveway. The Castle is most romantically situated on the cliffs overlooking the Kyles of Buchan. It is not old, and architecturally is not massive enough in appearance to suit the huge surrounding rocks or the cliffs. It has none of the impressive stability or grandeur of the ruined coast castles of Scotland, nor is it characteristic of the architecture of Aberdeenshire, though the ground it occupies is spacious. The most satisfactory part of the Castle is its entrance, which stands at the top of a flight of fourteen wide steps, and I imagine from its south-west exposure that these steps must be almost inaccessible during strong winds. As I drove up to this entrance, Lord Erroll, a soldierly looking man, apparently in his prime, was waiting to welcome me. A moment before I had noticed a hospital nurse at one of the windows, and my client immediately explained that Lady Erroll could not see me until dinner, as she was suffering from acute neuralgia, but that he would show me round the place and explain some of the improvements which they hoped I might find practicable.

After an hour's study of these problems I noticed a lady dressed in a sou'-wester, mackintosh, and wader boots, with a fishing-rod over her shoulder, whilst a man, evidently one of the footmen, was marching behind carrying a pannier. Apparently the two were out on a fishing expedition, and I mentally wished them good luck and went on with my work.

About 1-30 we went in to lunch, and met a well-known litterateur and his wife, to whom I was introduced. In the afternoon I asked for a couple of labourers, and at once began my survey, as there were no plans available to a larger scale than the ordnance maps, which were too small for my purpose.

At dinner I met Lady Erroll, who regretted she had not been able to meet me on arrival, and we at once plunged into conversation concerning the possibilities of growing shrubs for gardens and plantations, about which she was extraordinarily optimistic; but somehow the dinner did not go with that splendid swing which the hungriest spot on the East Coast seemed to demand. Meantime, his lordship made a remark which I did not catch, but presently the Countess replied, " Well, my dear, it really was excusable ";

The Life and Work of An English Landscape Architect.

then holding her two hands as a lady will do (proving her inability to measure when explaining the length of anything), she began to describe the length of something, but changing the length at each moment. She went on, " Without exaggeration, it was." " A concertina trout, my lord," interjected Mr. Sturgis. Then I learnt that the lady I had seen bent upon fishing was Lady Erroll, who had hooked and lost a big sea-trout, with which she was in difficulties, when the footman, in his excitement, jumped into the river and spoilt a new suit of livery. Possessing a practical mind, my host did not think that any trout, however long and heavy it might be, was worth such a sacrifice !

My partner and I carried out considerable work at Slains Castle, including an architectural carriage court, tennis lawns, and croquet lawns, and in this way we contrived a little shelter for some of the hardier maritime pines, sea buckthorn, rosemary, and a few other trees and shrubs which may generally be grown on the sea coast. Our plantations round the Castle were, however, rather disappointing, though lower down, in the direction of Cruden, the new plantations of sea buckthorn, gorse, broom, and pines succeeded fairly well. On the whole, I have come to the conclusion that there are certain places on the East Coast which scarcely justify the employment of a landscape architect unless he can also plan the house and arrange for a walled-in and protected garden, with the house itself as a wind-screen.

My visits to Slains were, however, very pleasant, and the results not perhaps considered by my clients to be so unsatisfactory as I myself thought, as I was asked at a much later date to plan for them another garden in Surrey.

One of the most interesting recollections of my visits to Slains Castle was of the family history, in which Lord Erroll was apparently being carefully coached by his old nurse, then a pensioner, and whose forebears had been in the family service for over two hundred years. She could recount every stirring incident and every bit of romance and tragedy in the military, political, religious, and social history of the Erroll family, and her pride in it was only equalled by that of the family she and her forebears had served, whom she regarded as having many times saved Scotland and the Empire. Needless to say, old Margaret was a person of some importance.

Another notable client who came to me for advice was Lord Bute, whose name I have already mentioned, and who wished to

SHRUBLANDS, WINDERMERE.

consult me respecting the improvement of his grounds at Mount Stuart, and the construction of a *Via Dolorosa*, or Way of the Cross, of an unusual kind. Mount Stuart House had just been rebuilt, along with a beautiful private chapel, at a cost, it is said, little short of a million pounds, to the design of Sir Rowan Anderson, the famous Edinburgh architect.

Like many who have adopted Roman Catholicism, Lord Bute was more Romish than the Romans. He was an authority on mediæval history and many matters relating to the ancient guilds and crafts, on which he had written learned treatises. Naturally a " book-worm," with his mental strength impaired by physical weakness, my client had become a recluse, seldom walking in the open air. Lady Bute explained this at our first interview, and at the same time threw out the hint that my chief claim to her goodwill would be my ability to tempt Lord Bute out of doors. If only I succeeded in doing this, she would be amply repaid even if I did not succeed in persuading him to carry out a fractional part of my proposals. There seemed to be no difficulty in getting the Marquis out, whatever the weather, and I found him a delightful man, full of his special subjects, and quite ready to talk about them. Somewhat to my surprise, he was also well versed in horticultural lore, with a special preference for conifers. In his time he had been an experimenter, and he often spoke to me about his vineyards in South Wales and the liquors he made from his vintage.

The first year's work I undertook at Mount Stuart was the transformation of a rather uninteresting stream which flowed down the wooded hills north of the house, between artificial walled banks. We varied its monotonous, even slope, gathering up the flow into pools at places and then projecting it over rugged cascades formed with the boulders plentifully sprinkled about in the adjoining woods. The principal waterfalls were arranged as foreground to the view from a much-used bridge. For this work I had as foreman a capable Scotsman named Calder, who had a genius for realising one's ideas from rough sketches. The result when complete was most beautiful, and much more like generous, wayward nature than the stream as we found it. Along the banks we made meandering woodland walks and laid out wild gardens, which, like the rocky stream, greatly pleased my client.

On one of my visits the Marquis gave me a rough plan of the Way of the Cross in Jerusalem, which had been prepared for him by the Bishop of Clifton, and asked me to study the possibilities

The Life and Work of An English Landscape Architect.

of creating a corresponding " Way " and its " Stations " on the wooded slopes behind Mount Stuart House, which are known to all who travel from Glasgow to the Isle of Bute. Indeed, they are the most prominent feature of the island, and give a luxuriant aspect to this part of it. This work was something quite new to me, but I seized upon the idea, and, truth to tell, my ultra-Protestant upbringing did not impose any barrier, as I was quite able to enter sympathetically into the ideals underlying my work, and realised that for my client the walk to Calvary meant much.

Never was there a more ideal setting for a memorial and sacrificial way—the solemn majesty of the mature beech trees, with their almost classical beauty, the clean silver-grey of the tree trunks, the soft velvety moss covering the ground, and overhead the tender green of the opening leaves silhouetted against a blue sky, bespoke the sentiment perfectly, whilst the gentle lapping on the pebbly shore had a voice which was distinctly sedative. This was indeed a spot for meditation.

The roads between each station and the next ascended all the time, until at last the highest plateau was reached, from which the storms had partly cleared the trees. Here we fixed the spot for Calvary, whilst in a dell one hundred and fifty feet away was the perfect spot for the Church of the Sepulchre.

When we had together fixed the routes, we discussed details, with the result that my friend Gibson was asked to prepare sketches for the oratories at each station, the Cross of Calvary, and for the Church of the Sepulchre, work exactly suited to his wonderful genius for the interpretation of mediævalism. I have never seen a more beautiful set of drawings, and I regret exceedingly that all our office records of this work were destroyed. I remember somewhat accurately, however, the design for the great crucifix, thirty feet high, which as seen from the Kyles of Bute would have been silhouetted against the sky. I remember also something of the design for the bronze doors and grille to the tiny Church of the Sepulchre.

Most of the road-making for this interesting work was laid down, but meanwhile the strength of the Marquis was diminishing, and the architectural adjuncts were never executed.

I may perhaps add one little incident of interest before closing this account of our work at Mount Stuart. On one occasion I was watching the head gardener planting a hedge of Turner's Crimson Rambler Rose, at that time in great favour, when

Two Years' Collaboration.

Mr. James Dickson, a famous Irish rose-grower, called on his annual round. " Mr. Mawson," he said, " the sight of that rose always makes me ill, for it always reminds me of the loss of a fortune. For thirty years it was growing in our nurseries amongst a batch of rose species imported from China, and we never saw a penny in it. Then Charles Turner, of Slough, also imported a set of roses from the same district, which flowered the next season, and amongst them was this scarlet rambler, in which they saw a commercial asset of great possibilities. Immediately they began to propagate by every method known to the expert rose-grower, filling one propagating house after another. Next year they exhibited the plants in flower at the Royal Horticultural Society's Show, where it created a sensation and an unprecedented demand. Of course we hurried up when we saw what was wanted, but Turner came in at 10s. 6d. to 21s. ; we were ready when the price had gone down to 2s. 6d. Only think of it, Mr. Mawson—we had that rose growing and blooming for thirty years."

The agent for the Bute estate was his lordship's cousin, Colonel John Stuart, with whom I sometimes stayed at Foley House, Rothesay. He introduced me to Major Macrae Giltrap, who had just purchased Ballimore, an extensive property on Loch Fyne in Argyllshire. The house, designed by Hamilton of Glasgow at a time when Scotch domestic architecture was at a low ebb, was being remodelled and extended by William Leiper, R.S.A., of Glasgow, an able exponent of the Scotch Baronial style, and a man whom I came to know intimately as a friend greatly admired, and with whom I had the pleasure of working on many subsequent occasions.

The journey to Ballimore is by boat from Rothesay to Tighnabruaich, and I remember that on my first visit I saw Clianthus Damperi (the Australian Elephant Flower), which I had always regarded as a greenhouse climber, in full flower growing on the wall of the Royal Hotel. In these days there were no motor-cars : the roads were very bad, and the drive of eleven miles to Ballimore was sometimes a painful experience.

The gardens were originally unimportant and commonplace, but the house occupied an imposing site overlooking an expansive lawn to the south, a ravine and wooded background on the west, and Loch Fyne on the north. My new client was anxious to possess a garden which should be a suitable setting to the house, and a source of pleasure and profit to his family and friends.

I prepared a general plan showing the lay-out of the entire garden, and my partner prepared the details for the terrace garden, house, and bridge. The greater part of this work was carried out successfully, but the isolation of Ballimore, and thus the difficulty of obtaining suitable labour, were very great, and we had to fall back on the most costly of all labour, that of the fishermen, who generally work very spasmodically and inefficiently when employed on ground work. The great opportunity we had was the cascading of the stream at the bottom of the dell, which flowed in a northerly direction and was confined between meandering walls. For this work we had splendid moss-covered granite, admirably suited to the work, lying within easy reach of the stream. It was successfully carried through for me by Mr. Pulham, of rock-building fame, but the stone bridge which was to grip the main terraces with the opposite bank and the rose garden which we proposed to form on the level of the terrace, were never carried through, and I think that the scheme as a whole greatly suffered from this omission.

From Ballimore I was introduced to Colonel Campbell of Ormidale, for whom I made certain plans for the improvement of his gardens, but how much or how little of my proposals were ever realised I do not know.

During our two years of collaboration (1898 and 1899) Gibson not only carried out much work in Scotland, but also in England, the most important of which was for Walter Whitehead, at that time senior surgeon of the Manchester Infirmary, and a man of considerable wealth, who had just purchased the Flagstaff, Colwyn Bay, a famous view-point which visitors and residents alike had made their own.

When the purchase of the property was announced there was the keenest disappointment and much railing against the Urban District Council for their failure to acquire the property for the public. For this site we were instructed to design a large country house, with stables, gate-houses, terraces, gardens, and new drives.

Our client met the opposition to the sequestration of the Flagstaff by promising to allow the public free access to the property when he had adapted it, only retaining for his own private use a small and really unimportant part—viz., the immediate surroundings of the new residence. Under the impression that they had to deal with a liberal resident, those responsible actually

Two Years' Collaboration.

conveyed to the new owner a cattle pound without which the lower lodge entrance could not have been made.

In view of the promise given, I prepared my plans on the principle of a semi-public pleasance, but had to alter them to the needs of the owner of a private place, and this was the last I ever heard of the Flagstaff being restored to the use of the public.

In the meantime, the old pound has been incorporated in the grounds. The work, so far as it progressed, was very interesting; indeed, I became so enthusiastic that I asked, and was granted, permission to alter some of my own work, of which more in a later chapter. To-day the Flagstaff is complete in almost every particular, excepting for the residence which was to crown the site. This was never erected, but the gardens and plantations show what can be done on a very difficult and exposed site, and its educational value was to me considerable.

Another garden of a totally different character was designed for the Misses Ashton, of Little Onn Hall, Gnosall, Staffordshire, a comfortable, commodious, and even beautiful Tudor house occupying the site of an old monastery. The plans for this work are interesting as showing the progress I had made in the direction of a more ordered lay-out ; most of my designs being at once carried out by my very appreciative and generous clients, who were fully in sympathy with them. These plans are illustrated in "The Art and Craft of Garden Making."

I mention this fact because there is no doubt that my leanings towards that which my clients called the "formal" manner disturbed some of my friends and repelled others. This fact is well shown by the fate of our work for Mr. Naylor, of Cuerdon Hall, near Warrington. Mr. Naylor, who posed as an art collector and man of taste, asked me to prepare a design for his gardens, which certainly needed remodelling. In it were awful examples of oyster-shell garden houses, white spar rockeries, and rustic absurdities, which appealed to him as not quite the thing. The site was a very difficult one, with the house on the lowest ground ; but there were opportunities, and these we endeavoured to interpret. I made a careful survey with levels, and on the data secured composed my plans, bringing in Gibson to assist with the architectural details. Together we produced one of the best designs so far turned out of the office, and I remember with what pride I showed them to Mr. Naylor, and the cold douche which I experienced when he remarked with great severity : "This

THE CORBELS, WINDERMERE.

isn't art. If I wanted straight lines I could have done them myself."

I merely relate this incident for the purpose of showing the deplorable state into which landscape architecture had fallen. Mr. Naylor represented a wide class of garden-owners who had no conception of garden design beyond that debased form illustrated in current literature and characteristic of the efforts of the nursery gardener.

Another client of a somewhat similar outlook and temperament was at one time a Nonconformist minister, but becoming a London financier, had done well in the City. With his great wealth he had purchased a beautiful property in Sussex, on which he had built what he was pleased to call a Tudor house, in the most flambuoyant red terracotta. The site demanded building materials of soft silver-greys and dun-brown and russety reds, with here and there a splash of faded purple. What, then, was one to do with a house like this dominating such a site? The first impulse was to surround it with green cloistered courts enclosed by pleached lines of limes and rose-covered pergolas. This was my fatal mistake. For I was afterwards told, what I already suspected, that my client had designed the house himself, after scouring all England for Tudor details. Every conceit of this period was somehow woven into the house, together with a few strange inventions of his own to give a touch of modernity to the whole. And, of course, my pleached alleys and pergolas would hide it all. Precisely! Here again I failed to impress my generous client, and had to lament the loss of further work which might have been ever so profitable. However, I took it all stoically, though regretfully, and we parted friends. Nevertheless, I should have liked to have seen that garden materialise!

One of the last schemes on which Gibson and I collaborated was a formal garden at Ashton-on-Ribble for W. W. Galloway, Esq., a partner in the famous firm of Horrockses, Crewdson and Co., of Preston, who gave us practically a free hand, though studying with care each detail as it came along. About the same time we planned the house and gardens at Brockhole, Windermere, for W. Gaddum, Esq., a Manchester man with a passion for Lakeland, and the fortunate possessor of a beautiful site on the shores of the lake between Troutbeck Bridge and the Low Wood Hotel. Both house and gardens are so well known to visitors to Windermere and the district as to need little description. Gibson was

The Life and Work of An English Landscape Architect.

entirely responsible for the design of the house, while I arranged the terraces, gardens, entrance drives, and plantations.

Much other work of a purely architectural character for churches, chapels, cottages, small houses (including thirteen cottages of varying accommodation for members of my own family) was flowing into the office, and there is no doubt that prospects for the future were very bright. Moreover, while Gibson was responsible for most of the architectural side of the practice, he always consulted me in respect to planning, especially when considering the ground plan of the house in relation to the garden. In the same way, I had the greatest assistance and sanest criticism from Gibson whenever he felt he could help. Both, therefore, regretted the dissolution of our partnership, but we realised that our interests were too varied, and interfered, on my part, with the steady pursuit of landscape architecture ; moreover, it created difficulties for me when I was asked to collaborate with other architects. Our break did not affect our personal relationship. My second son became a pupil in Gibson's office the week following the dissolution of our partnership, and during the week that it was dissolved I introduced him to the best client he ever had, William Lethbridge, of Wood, South Tawton, Devonshire.

Wych Cross Place, Forest Row, the Residence of Douglas Freshfield, Esq.

Wych Cross Place.—The Gardens Below the Main Terrace.

CHAPTER VI.

I BECOME AN AUTHOR.

I HAVE already hinted at some of the reasons which prompted me to become the author of a book on garden design. Following out this idea, I had for years been collecting data, eventually deciding upon the title, " The Art and Craft of Garden Making." The idea for the plan, arrangement, and scope finally adopted, first occurred to me after reading the concluding paragraph of the third edition of Edward Kemp's excellent book, " How to Lay Out a Garden," which runs as follows :—

It is much to be regretted that architects and landscape gardeners do not more usually work together, in complete unison, from the very commencement of any undertaking in which they are jointly consulted ; and he who would produce a work in which the relation of the two arts to each other, and the elements of garden architecture and of architectural gardening, should be skilfully handled and tastefully illustrated, would deserve the thanks of the entire community.

The compilation of such a book was an audacious enterprise, for which at the time I was not fully equipped, but the fact that a long time had elapsed since I first began to collect material proved a great advantage, because I had travelled far from the old and more insular position to a greater appreciation of architecture in relation to gardens. The many gardens constructed to my designs showed this evolutionary process, and the collaboration with my friend Dan Gibson certainly accelerated my progress in the direction of a logical blending of the architectural with the horticultural. Formerly Nature with me had been conductor, and Art first fiddle ; now the order was reversed, with Art wielding the conductor's baton. I seldom lost my sense of the value which comes by contrast, and my love of plants and flowers doubtless saved me from the vagaries and banalities of the extreme cult of architectural gardening. My conception of architecture was not yet very highly developed, and leaned towards simplicity, quaintness, and the

63

The Life and Work of An English Landscape Architect.

picturesque. This is clearly indicated by Illus. Nos. 15 and 16, the latter showing a small house I designed and built for myself, and the other one planned a year later for my brother Robert, both at Windermere. In these I adhered to the architectural traditions of the Westmorland dales. Similarly, I would at the time have slavishly followed the traditions of any locality wherein I was working, a state of mind which was doubtless, to some extent, the natural result of my passion for the works and views of Professor Ruskin.

Notwithstanding, by the time I was ready to collect and arrange the material, my training, experience, and outlook on garden design justified, I thought, my desire to fulfil Kemp's wish, and to write a book defining the relationship between art and nature as applied to gardens. For a book of this character there was an undoubted need, and I was assured that if a satisfactory work were produced, written from a new standpoint, it would win the approval of the garden-loving public.

A description of my methods of working on my books may be of interest, especially to others who are trying to make time, in a very busy life, for literary composition. My practice had so vastly increased and was spread over so much greater territory that I was often several nights in the train in a week, my travels totalling at least twenty thousand miles a year. My days were occupied in consulting clients, sometimes making a survey, meeting contractors, and discussing the progress of the work in detail with the landscape foreman in charge; and the evenings, if staying the night with my client or at an hotel, in working out details for further elaboration by the office staff at Windermere. It will thus be seen that, except when in the train, my leisure moments were few, and thus, like Kemp, I was compelled to do my writing there or in odd moments when waiting for a connection. The drawback to writing under these conditions is the lack of continuity, both in style and in sequence, and I soon found it almost impossible to proceed without first working out a plan of the chapters, and then of the correlation of all the points to be covered by each chapter. Once I had settled this arrangement to my satisfaction, the problem of connected writing was much simplified. My method of overcoming the difficulties mentioned has proved so satisfactory that, to a greater or lesser extent, I have followed it ever since. Still, the conditions under which I worked were not such as to promote logical sequence in my writing.

I Become an Author.

Fortunately my *fidus Achates*, John Dyer, has a great capacity for editorial work, and to him I handed my rough MS. a chapter at a time. This was then typewritten, put into its proper order, and corrected. I then took the " copy " away with me on my journeys, re-editing it and arranging the numbers and order of the necessary illustrations.

A point of real difficulty in the preparation of my first book arose from the necessity for selecting actual examples of garden design to illustrate and apply the theories and principles of design and methods of construction discussed. Obviously, I could appreciate more vividly the problems presented by my own work, its difficulties, its failures, and, to a large extent, its successes, than I could those of the work of others, and, at every point in my writing, examples to illustrate the matter immediately under discussion flashed to my mind, sometimes because the struggle with difficult problems had produced exceptionally happy results, at other times from the point of view that it is from our failures that we learn. On the other hand, I fully appreciated the difficulty of so doing without placing undue emphasis on the personal *ego*. In an autobiography one may, and indeed must, live again one's own little failures, triumphs, and experiences ; but in what is, after all, a text-book, one has always the feeling that the personal element should as far as possible be kept in the background.

Thinking the matter over carefully, however, I came to the conclusion that the loss to my book would be so real unless I drew freely on the results of my own experiences, used my own garden plans, and described, both by photographs and by letterpress, the details of my own work and the motives underlying it, that any criticism which resulted from my action in so doing must be faced. Criticism, generally, though by no means always, couched in terms intended to be constructive and helpful, has undoubtedly resulted, but I have the further excuse for the course I have taken in this matter, if excuse were necessary, that all the great writers on garden design whose names I have so often mentioned, adopted the same methods in their books, and obviously from the same motive.

Of the illustrations, all those representing plans and working drawings were prepared by my staff from those actually used on the ground ; but in the design of the cover and the chapter headings, and of the perspective views, I had the invaluable help of my old friend the late C. E. Mallows, and my colleague Dan Gibson.

The Life and Work of An English Landscape Architect.

Finally, the whole of my manuscript was read over for me by the Reverend Eric Robertson, at this time Vicar of St. John's, Windermere. Readers of Mr. Robertson's well-known work, " Wordsworthshire," will appreciate the value of his criticism and suggestions.

The writing of the preface, I was warned, was a matter of supreme importance, for, said my friends, the reviewer is a busy man who judges from this portion of the book whether or not the remainder is worthy of an extended study. Apart from this aspect of the matter, it appeared to me that the preface should define the art I was seeking to promote.

The following extracts show fairly conclusively my own position in relation to it :—

Garden-making, it has been said, is the only art in which, owing to accidental development and unlooked-for groupings, the realisation surpasses the original conception. A caustic critic, seizing upon this statement, has referred to landscape gardening as an art which relies upon accident for its effects. Whilst not fully admitting the justice of this criticism, it must be allowed that the writings and practice of many who have undertaken to lay out gardens have given cause for it. The responsibility of this does not, however, rest entirely with the landscape gardener, for no such desirable object as garden-making has suffered so much from the inattention of those who were most capable of guiding and advising. This is the more remarkable when we consider the immense interest which has been taken in horticulture during the last fifty years.

In the course of an extensive practice, having had considerable opportunities for studying gardens, more especially garden design in relation to the house and its architectural character, I have realised the fact that one must always be a complement of the other. I therefore, on the one hand, sympathise with those architects who claim the right to design the setting to their houses, and, on the other, with those landscape gardeners who have felt, more especially in the later years of practice, that to ensure a successful garden it is necessary to have some part in the arrangement and disposal of the house on the site, and in the selection of the site itself. In either case the range of subjects to be mastered before this ideal can be reached is so great as to make many men shrink from undertaking it. By giving in a handy form experience gained in the special department of garden design, I venture to hope that some of the difficulties which now face architects who essay to design the gardens, will be considerably lessened. If I fail in this, I still hope to show that garden designers are much more in sympathy with architectural ideals than recent writers would have us suppose.

Throughout this work I have endeavoured to make it clear that while I consider a formal treatment the one most likely to give satisfactory results, I do not think the " Art and Craft of Garden Making " is advanced by a slavish adherence to style or tradition. In my own practice, I am bound to confess, I have often executed work which could not be justified by prescribed rules or canons of art, and yet to me the effect has been harmonious.

Finally, the book was by permission gratefully dedicated to my old friend and client, Colonel Sandys of Graythwaite Hall.

With the whole of the MS. and illustrations complete, I went up to London to find a publisher, but received everywhere the most depressing reception and advice. Any new work which I have ever published has received the same treatment, so that I have now come to regard publishers as incorrigible pessimists. Perhaps this attitude is the right one to adopt with young authors, though I sometimes doubt it.

At the well-known publishing house of Batsford one of the partners complimented me on my energy and ambition, and even went so far as to admire some of the plans and drawings. " It is a pity, however," he said, " that there is no sale for a book of that sort. Why," he added, " you could not sell two hundred and fifty copies. If, however, you go to the manager of the Publishing Department at the ' Country Life ' office, he might help you."

So, rather dejected, I called, as suggested, on the manager at the " Country Life " office, only to be told there was little sale for a book on garden design, but if I could persuade Messrs. Batsford to agree, they would allow their name to appear with Batsford's as selling agents. " But, mind you," he added, " we can take no financial responsibility."

I then returned to Mr. James Batsford, who added, " Of course, Mr. Mawson, if you can afford to pay for the printing, we will do our utmost to sell the book."

I accepted the position, made a contract with a firm of printers, and delivered to Batsford and " Country Life " an edition of one thousand copies, costing £660, and waited the results of the reviews with some little anxiety. It was, however, a thrilling experience, and one which I suppose is felt by every budding author awaiting the fiat of Fleet Street.

The first review appeared in about a fortnight after publication. It was from " The Times," and to my huge delight was favourable, even complimentary :—

" Those who have gardens to make and who want to know how they can make them to advantage will find much to assist and guide their taste in ' The Art and Craft of Garden Making,' by T. H. Mawson. . . . The author has plenty of ideas and a very pretty taste."

Other excellent reviews quickly followed in " Country Life," the " Manchester Guardian," the " Spectator," and in the

The Life and Work of An English Landscape Architect.

" Daily Chronicle," and finally I received a notice in almost every well-known provincial paper in the country.

As a result of these notices the first edition was disposed of in three months at 21s. per copy, which, however, after deducting copies for the press and publishers' charges, still left me with a small loss, which I was sure future editions would wipe out.

I need only add that at the time of writing I am engaged upon the preparation of the fifth edition of this work, the fourth and enlarged edition, published at 50s., having been out of print for some considerable time.

I know of no satisfaction which surpasses that of winning the support of the press on a first literary venture, and I must say that the reviewers were more than kind to me ; even the reviews which were frankly critical were helpful and gave many useful suggestions, which I endeavoured to incorporate in the later editions. Many other improvements, mainly suggested by private correspondents, were adopted, so that quite a number of people contributed to the ultimate success of my first book. Frankly, my opinion is, now that the glamour of a garden is so potent, that far too many of the reviewers over-emphasised the value of my contribution to garden literature. This view will be endorsed if comparison be made between the first and the fourth editions.

As a result of this book and its reception in the press, I was inundated with requests from editors for interviews and articles, and from secretaries of literary and lecture societies to lecture on various cognate subjects, whilst foreign publishers asked for the rights of publication in their own countries ; but very few of these requests could be met. I gave a lecture on the " Unity of House and Garden " before the Royal Institute of British Architects, and three lectures on " Garden Design " before the Royal Horticultural Society, all of which were published in their respective journals.

I enjoyed this work almost as much as writing my book, notwithstanding that I found the task of preparing a lecture very exacting, and the collection and arranging of the slides to illustrate it even more so. The strenuous life which I was living would not allow of this additional strain, already heightened by the enthusiasm which I felt for my work. The result was a breakdown which laid me aside for many weeks during one of the most critical periods of my career. Success was bringing its penalties as well as its rewards.

In some respects the publication of my book brought

unexpected results, and the flowing current of my professional career was having its impetus broken by cross-currents. For this I was entirely responsible, and if only I had stopped to think I would have realised that I was taking too much for granted. It was quite right and proper, thought some of my clients, for an architect to propose formality. That is what they expected him to do, but they came to me because they thought I could do good landscape gardening and copy nature, and I had disappointed them. I was regarded as a heretic.

Undoubtedly I was losing caste as a landscape gardener, and I had not yet " arrived " as a landscape architect, but I felt I was on the way, since it was the way I was determined to go ; indeed, it was the only route I could conscientiously follow, and my resolution was strengthened by my collaboration with Gibson.

It was unfortunate, however, that this time of crisis in my professional career coincided with a period of domestic financial outlay on an increased scale. When one is confronted with this responsibility, however one may be upheld by the certainty that the course one is pursuing is altruistically correct, the financial rewards of one's services cannot be entirely ignored.

At the time of which I am writing I had just built " The Corbels," Windermere (see Illus. No. 16), with all the attendant expense of going into a new and larger house. We had a family of six children, with two sons and one daughter at school. It was rather difficult going, and my wife and I had to practise rigid economy, more especially as we had built a holiday bungalow for our young folk at Hest Bank, which also required a certain expenditure for maintenance.

As an offset to the loss of practice I have just described, the first clients which came to me as a result of my new attitude to my profession as laid down in my book more than compensated both practically and professionally. They were Douglas W. Freshfield, of Wych Cross Place, Forest Row, in Sussex, and the late William Lethbridge, of Wood, South Tawton, Devonshire, whom I have already mentioned. Both brought work to me of exceptional extent and importance. They accepted whole-heartedly the principles advanced in my book, and as they were both interested in art, and particularly in architecture, whilst possessing also a great love of nature, my lines were indeed fallen in pleasant places, so that in every respect I was most fortunate and worked hard to acquit myself creditably. Their respective gardens were illustrated

The Life and Work of An English Landscape Architect.

in the later editions of my first book, and are otherwise well known to the garden-loving public. (See Illus. Nos. 17, 18, 19, and 20.)

I had long known Mr. Freshfield by reputation as a member of the Council of the Royal Geographical Society. As the famous president of the Alpine Club, he was an intrepid traveller beyond the beaten tracks in Japan, the Himalayas, Uganda and the mountains adjoining, Syria, the Caucasus, the Apennines, and the greater part of the Alpine regions. I had read some of his fascinating books on travel, and several of the articles he had contributed to the geographical journals. It was with some trepidation that I set out to meet a man of such august presence and imperious dignity, as I imagined him to be, but my preconceived notions and fears proved to be quite ill-founded. I was met by a genial gentleman who at once set me at ease, and with whom I could arrive readily at a perfect understanding with regard to tastes and projects. Then I was introduced to Mrs. Freshfield, whose charming graciousness was so natural and spontaneous. She immediately won my admiration and homage.

Kidbrooke Park was such a desirable residence, and its parklands so well matured, that I wondered at their decision to build a large residence on a new site. But both Mr. and Mrs. Freshfield explained that sunsets and fine prospects were a necessity of life, and that in wandering through Ashdown Forest they had found a site where these two advantages could be enjoyed to the full, but they were a little doubtful as to the possibility of carving a garden, which was also a necessity, out of primeval forest.

After lunch, by which time Mr. Fisher, their prospective architect and son-in-law, arrived, we drove to the site, entering Ashdown Forest at Wych Cross, about three miles east of Forest Row on the main high road to Uckfield. Within the forest we drove down a rough track for about half a mile in a western direction until we came to a natural clearing. There was no need to ask if this was the chosen spot. It was perfectly ideal for the purpose, with a slope to the south extending down to a deep valley with a clear limpid stream wandering through it. Down to this point, east and west of the central glade, the ground is thickly studded with fine alternating masses of Scotch fir, silver birch, and patrician beech, of noble dignity and proportions. Beyond the hollow were extensive green pastures, crowned here and there with a mass of Scotch firs, which bravely broke the sky line. Extending farther were rolling Sussex downs, with those open views of enormous extent extending right to the coast, for which this county is so justly famous.

The higher ground behind the site chosen for the house was occupied by massed beech trees, giving a sheltered background, and beyond the beech trees was purple-heathered Ashdown Common.

We there and then fixed the exact spot on which the house was to be built, and arranged for scaffoldings to be erected to the various floor heights to make sure of the views. These settled, we fixed the levels of the several terraces, and studied with minute care the positions of terrace walks and the heights of the balustrades and parapet walls to ensure the garden setting of the house being a fitting and effective foreground to the forest and the landscape beyond. Thus closed my first day's collaboration with both architect and clients ; it provided a delightful beginning, and the results have fully justified my urgent advice to many clients before and since, that the architect for the house and the architect for the garden should collaborate from the very first.

Having settled the site and the main supporting terrace, I was asked to present a plan for a complete lay-out to cover a considerable area in addition to the long drive and carriage court, also for tennis and croquet courts, alpine and wild gardens, herbaceous borders, woodland glades, walled-in fruit and vegetable gardens and orchard, covering in all about twenty acres. The scheme also included a large range of plant houses, vineries, and peach houses, and positions were arranged for bothies, gardeners' cottages, garage and stables, the whole making a very complete and well-appointed residential estate, all of which was carved out of virgin forest in such a manner as not to destroy its dominating natural character.

This commission raised a problem the solution of which has been debated by garden designers from the earliest beginning of the profession. One school argues that under the conditions which existed at Wych Cross, any new work should imitate nature, the other school believing that art in contrast with nature will provide the best results. In my solution I adhered to formality within the limits of the spacious terraces built of the local sandstone, merging these gradually, by intermediate stages, into the wild landscape. This course was the basis of the recommendations which I placed before my clients. The consequent plan, which I prepared, was carried out in its entirety. That the result

The Life and Work of An English Landscape Architect.

justified the methods employed will be evident from the two photographs given in Illus. Nos. 17 and 18, and taken within two years of the completion of the work, showing how quickly the new work acquired an appearance of maturity, and how harmoniously it merged into that which was already " fixed and abiding."

Throughout the execution of this very important commission, extending over two and a half years, I must at times have almost exhausted the patience of my clients, for it taxed all belief that we could ever evolve anything out of the sea of mud which, during the progress of the work, seemed to flow over the forest like molten lava; but they never doubted my ability to evolve order out of chaos, and indeed they often encouraged me when I seemed to be losing confidence in myself. Mr. Edmund Fisher, the able architect (who, by the way, was brother to the popular and learned Minister of Education, Dr. H. A. L. Fisher), also proved the most charming of colleagues, always anxious to have my opinion on his schemes, and at the same time always pleased to give helpful criticism whenever his aid was sought. His death during the war robbed the architectural profession of a very able exponent.

To give to the gardens an aspect of matured age, we transplanted a number of ancient yews from distant parts of the forest. These were removed with great balls of earth, each yew weighing from four to five tons. That trees some of which may have been from 600 to 900 years old could be successfully transplanted in this manner may seem impossible; nevertheless, so successful was this work that we lost only one tree.

The virgin soil of Ashdown Forest varied in character, some parts being a stiff loam, other parts light and gravelly. On the lower parts there were lots of boggy peat, admirably suited to the growth of rhododendrons, azaleas, kalmias, andromedas, and other peat-loving plants, while on the higher ground there was a thin crest of dry peat which suited ericacious plants to perfection. In other parts of the garden roses did equally well, as bushes, standards, or pillars. Only when we came to the fruit trees did we meet with disappointment, many varieties of apples, pears, and plums recommended by experienced fruit growers refusing to respond to the generous treatment given to them. My clients, were, however, fortunate in their first head gardener, Mr. John Drew, who, by experimenting during several years, finally succeeded in obtaining satisfactory crops. Though simple and straightforward, Mr. Drew looked learned. He gave judgments with reasoned

Illus. No. 19.

PLAN·OF·HOUSE·AND GARDEN·IN·A·COPPICE PLANTATION

STABLE BLOCK

KITCHEN GARDEN

TENNIS LAWN

CARRIAGE COURT

BOWLING GREEN

SCALE of FEET

The Life and Work of An English Landscape Architect.

deliberation, knew the Kew hand lists from A to Z, and possessed the genius for planting shown by so many Kewites, and yet he retained a generous love of nature and enthusiasm for all country craft. Our chosen name for Drew from the first was " the Professor," which title proved prophetic, for a few years later he was appointed Professor of Horticulture at Reading University College. Here he organised a strong department which has rendered notable service to the profession of horticulture. This department, since his death, continues to attract a large number of students.

The problem set before me by Mr. Lethbridge was a very different one, and has in part been dealt with in the description of my collaboration with Dan Gibson. The site was immensely more difficult to handle than that in Ashdown Forest, as the contours ran diagonally across it, necessitating a deep cutting for the carriage court on the west side, and a filling of at least twelve feet on the east, before we could obtain a level space on which the house could be made to appear to rest comfortably. The plan and sections in " The Art and Craft of Garden Making " show how the problems were dealt with, whilst the photographic view of the south front (Illus. No. 20) shows how happily house and garden blend.

The gardens extend southwards, the character of the lay-out changing by imperceptible degrees until it ends in a large placid pool or lake and a cascaded stream.

Upon the completion of this garden some years later, the owner, who was a most appreciative client, presented me with a beautiful copy of " The Praise of Gardens," by A. F. Sievking, handsomely bound in a cover designed by Dan Gibson. On the fly-leaf he wrote—

To the Author and Begetter
of the Gardens at Wood.
In grateful appreciation.
From the Owner.
19.9.05.

At his death, which occurred at Davos Platz, Switzerland, I felt that I had lost a dear and understanding friend. William Lethbridge was one of the finest types of English gentlemen I have ever met, and a scholar withal.

SOUTH FRONT, WOOD, DEVON.

CHAPTER VII.

MISFORTUNES AND COMPENSATIONS.

A T this critical and difficult juncture in my career I received
several hard knocks. I have already referred to our work
for Walter Whitehead at Colwyn Bay, upon which Gibson
and I were engaged. This work was given to me on the understanding that I should be responsible for the business part of
both the architectural work and the gardens and management, to
which I foolishly agreed.

My client was a man of very considerable private means
in addition to his professional emoluments. He was senior surgeon
to the Manchester Infirmary, and possessed a lucrative private
practice as well. He liked to surround himself with a circle of
convivial friends of a class as mixed as it was large. One of his
friends was the contractor for the building. This gentleman was, I
daresay, a worthy man, but whatever his abilities, I feared that for
the proprietor to make such an exceptional friend of one with whom
strict business relationships would normally exist could not but
prejudice my position, and especially make it difficult for me to
insist upon the standard and quality of the work which, as a client,
he had a right to demand. Before the works were far advanced I
had to protest that the friendship was undermining my authority,
and that I was not satisfied with either the progress of the work
or its quality.

In the gardens matters progressed much better, but certain
of the work did not come up to my ideals of what was possible or
desirable. This I frankly explained to my client. " By all means
have the work done as you would like it," said he ; but, nevertheless,
I felt we were not getting on well together as client and adviser.
The upshot of it all was that we agreed to part, and I was asked to
submit my account, which amounted to something over five
hundred pounds, every penny of which had been well earned.

The Life and Work of An English Landscape Architect.

To my astonishment, Mr. Whitehead sent in a counter-claim for over one thousand pounds for alleged defective work, the very work which I myself had complained about. As he put it, he had my own condemnation of this work, and gave me to understand that if I pressed my claim for the payment of my professional charges, he would press his counter-claim, whatever the cost might be. I knew my man, and had some idea of the length of his purse. I also knew that I could not afford to jeopardise my professional reputation even though I might win my case. I have lost greater sums since then, but the loss of this money, and the unreasonable methods pursued in such an impossible set of circumstances, formed one of the bitterest experiences of my life.

A much heavier blow was awaiting me, the impact of which nearly overwhelmed me.

Although my professional practice had been quite distinct from my brothers' business for many years, there was a rare bond of comradeship and affection between us, which was strengthened by the fact that all three of us had married into the same family. My brother Robert and I had married sisters, who were the daughters of the late Dr. Prentice, of North Walsham, and who upon the death of their father had become the wards of their uncle, Mr. Thomas Bidwell, of Trunch of Norfolk, who himself had an only daughter. My younger brother married the latter (Miss Bidwell), and thus the three girls who had been brought up together as of one family became part of our family. It was indeed a peculiarly happy family, and as we all three built ourselves houses within a short distance of each other, we had daily reunions when at home. My elder brother Robert and I were both full of admiration for my youngest brother, who was in many ways a remarkable young fellow, full of generous impulses, and a sage counsellor, and in this respect quite beyond his years. He was a man of exceptional business capacity, a popular employer of labour, an earnest social worker and a keen sportsman, and withal possessing a unique sense of humour. For several days during the month of March in the austere spring of 1901 he had had a hard cough, but with his usual untiring devotion to business went on with his work, maintaining that he was suffering only from a cold, until, matters becoming worse, he was obliged to consult his doctor, who at once put him to bed, the doctor showing his anxiety by making a second visit the same night. It was declared to be a case of pneumonia.

Misfortunes and Compensations.

Although the patient made a great fight for life, at the end of the seventh day he passed away.

Not until he had gone did I realise the extent to which I had looked to him for encouragement, and sometimes, in disasters of the Whitehead kind, for material support, which he ungrudgingly extended to me.

This incident marked an epoch in my career. I discovered, as I have said, that in business matters and in my small investments I had relied almost entirely on my brother. Now I had to combine business with art, and had for some time to work hard to gain a little capacity in this direction, and this fact in part led to the reorganisation of my practice and the opening of a London office.

In regard to my own special work as a designer, it must be remembered that at this period I was only at a transitional stage, though always moving forward. In this connection I remember Sir Edwin Lutyens saying to me that " he had noticed that architects taking up gardens often gravitated towards a very natural style, while landscape gardeners often gravitated towards extreme formality, and that the point at which the two crossed probably marked the most desirable standpoint." Two examples may be given in support of this view. Kent, who was really a great architect, was responsible for the landscape eccentricities of Stowe Park, whilst Sir Joseph Paxton, who started life as a gardener, planned the Crystal Palace and its gardens, the architectural formality of which can only be guessed at by those who visit Sydenham nowadays.

During this year I was engaged upon many new works, mostly gardens, some of which were satisfactory, while others were the reverse. Amongst the first was a terraced rose garden at Capenwray Hall, near Carnforth, the seat of Colonel Marton, for many years member of Parliament for the Lancaster division. The Colonel was a cordial man, brimming over with humour and high spirits, and abounding with quaint expressions, and, as usual with men of buoyant temperament, had a large circle of friends. The gardens and park at Capenwray had been laid out between the years 1850 and 1855 by Edward Kemp, and were typical of this expert's ripe manner. It was a pleasure to me to have the opportunity of adding a feature which I am assured would have been in accord with his wishes.

Whilst at Capenwray I was able quite unexpectedly to render Colonel Marton good service, which won me his esteem for the

The Life and Work of An English Landscape Architect.

remainder of his life. One day he was describing his property south of Heysham Docks, then let at a low agricultural rental. "Colonel," I said, "why not plan out the whole of this property in prospect of a new seaport town." "'Pon my word, Mawson," he replied, "that's a capital idea. When can you let me have your plan?"

In three months' time I presented my scheme, and in less than a year the Midland Railway scheduled the foreshore rights, which they eventually acquired and paid for, not at agricultural-land values, but on the basis of its prospective building-land value.

In the same year I met Mr. C. F. A. Voysey, an architect who had rapidly risen to fame as one of the leaders of the Arts and Crafts movement, and as the exponent of a quaint simplicity in domestic architecture which had caught the public taste. He possessed a charming character, which one could well understand after listening to a sermon by his father, the Rev. Charles Voysey, who had been deprived of his living in Cumberland because of his heterodoxy.

The son told me that when his father and the family came to London, so great was the sensation caused by his father's supposed apostasy that their landlady turned them out of their lodgings. Fortunately, Mr. Voysey was a man to be respected, and in London he quickly gathered together many rich and powerful supporters, who established him at Swallow Street Theistic Church, Piccadilly, where he attracted a large and very intellectual congregation.

C. F. A. Voysey had been commissioned to build two houses on the Storrs Estate, Windermere, one for Mr. Currer-Briggs and one for Mr. Buckley, and in the latter case I was commissioned to do the gardens, so that I came in frequent contact with the architect.

On one of his visits to Windermere, Voysey was taken ill, and he sent for me to recommend a doctor. I advised my own physician, Doctor Mason, but Doctor Brooksbank, Mason's partner, arrived, and was introduced by name to the patient. "What did you say your name was?" asked Voysey. "I thought I sent for Mason!" "My name is Brooksbank, and I am come because Doctor Mason, my partner, is away from home." "Brooksbank! Brooksbank! did you say?" "Yes; that is my name." "Is your father the Rev. Walter Brooksbank?" "Yes; he is my father." "Then

Misfortunes and Compensations.

do you know your father turned my father out of his living, and now you come to doctor me. *I won't have you!*"

Notwithstanding this untoward beginning, the two men came to have a great regard for each other, and both agreed, I think, that their fathers had acted a little precipitately.

Another story of Voysey is, I think, worth relating. Once when I was at the Arts Club as the guest of Andrew Prentice, who was the illustrator and author of a splendid volume on the Spanish Renaissance, Voysey and his father on passing to their table spoke to me. Much to my surprise, Prentice did not recognise them. "Why," I asked, "did you not greet Voysey?" "Is that Voysey?" said Prentice. "Can't you give me an introduction after dinner?" "With the greatest pleasure," I replied, seizing my opportunity when Voysey came into the smoking-room.

Both men seemed pleased to meet, but in a few minutes, Prentice, coming to the end of his salutations, and wishing to strike some congenial topic, said: "I wonder, Mr. Voysey, if you have ever designed anything after the manner of the Spanish Renaissance?" "Mr. Prentice," said Voysey, "I have only one book in my office, and it is a Bradshaw's Railway Guide, which, I am sorry to say, I have to use much oftener than I like." Prentice was not pleased, but I explained that Voysey's reply was simply meant as an expression of his attitude towards all book learning relating to architecture. Voysey, in fact, said, or intended to infer, that that alone is art which has its spontaneous birth in the inner consciousness, and that books in general kill imagination. How far this was a pose of his, and how far the fruit of genuine conviction, I will not pretend to say.

An interesting client of this date was Henry Martin, a Halifax manufacturer who purchased Cringlemere, a beautiful property on the high road between Troutbeck and Ambleside. Mr. Martin, like many another Yorkshire manufacturer, was a collector of pictures, Chippendale furniture, and Wedgwood china; but though a charming and generous client, he was a collector at heart and loved variety, and I soon found that what he really wanted in his gardens was not a pleasance, but an arboricultural museum. I know he felt my restraining influence irksome.

My brother Robert carried out the work for me, and he and Mr. Martin thoroughly enjoyed themselves during my long absences. "Come along, Robert," Martin would say; "your brother is away to-day, so we can do exactly what we like." And

The Life and Work of An English Landscape Architect.

in would go another hundred conifers, whilst another twenty
men would be set to work on an extension to the rock garden.
To-day Cringlemere is interesting principally from its collection
of specimen conifers and choice shrubs, which succeed admirably
on this elevated site. Howbeit, his successor has been obliged
drastically to thin them out.

Early in the following year my old friend W. Leiper, R.S.A.,
introduced to me two clients at Stirling for whom he was
at this time erecting new houses. One was Charles A. Buchanan
of Deroran, and the other William Renwick of Mar Gate, both of
Stirling. They were comparatively small places, but I enjoyed
the work immensely, as these clients were very appreciative and
really fond of their gardens. From Deroran I was introduced to
the Pullars of Perth, and designed or superintended the construction
of gardens for three members of this well-known family.

During this year I also designed several unimportant town-
planning schemes, including the little seaside resort of Hest Bank,
on Morecambe Bay, and certain building estate developments in
Yorkshire and Westmorland.

In the autumn I was asked by Mr. G. Macalpine (afterwards
Sir George) to lay out the grounds round a new house which he
was erecting to the designs of Mr. Thompson, who was a relative
and a well-known Glasgow architect. This work gave me new
experience of the needs of suburban gardens near Lancashire
manufacturing towns, where the soil was on a stiff clay, and the
atmosphere more or less laden with smoke. Mr. Macalpine was
an interesting man, with a great understanding of the difficulties
attendant upon the construction of a beautiful garden in close
proximity to Accrington. The extent of the grounds was about
three acres, and proportionate to the needs of the family and the
scale of the house. It was, of course, rather distressing to be so
strictly limited in regard to the trees and shrubs which could be
relied upon to flourish, but what we lost in this respect was made
up for by terraces and other architectural features which relieved
the monotony of the shrubberies, and we also succeeded admirably
with our herbaceous borders and rose gardens. In the end, in
spite of many very trying limitations, we created a garden which
gave lasting pleasure to my client and his family.

FÉTE AT FOOTS CRAY PLACE, THE RESIDENCE OF LORD WARING.

CHAPTER VIII.

LIGHTS AND SHADOWS ON THE PATHWAY.

WITHIN a year of the publication of my work, "The Art and Craft of Garden Making," there was a great accession of new clients who, having read the book, realised what my aims on garden design really were. This made my practice easier, and secured for me a greater freedom than I had hitherto possessed. The work helped me in many other ways, for my clients now knew my artistic standpoint before consulting me, with the result that from the very first we worked together in full sympathy.

The resulting advantages were great, and in most cases my work as landscape architect progressed much more smoothly and with greater satisfaction both to myself and to my clients, while the reorganisation of my practice as the fruit of more extended experience led to more careful control of work in progress.

On looking through my old ledgers I find that during this year I was engaged on no fewer than thirty garden and town planning schemes, some twenty of which represented work for new clients, many of whom became my fast friends. Amongst these was Mr. Samuel Waring (now Lord Waring) of Foots Cray Place, Kent, for whom I prepared an extensive scheme which involved a great terrace to accord with the Palladian style of the mansion, and the complete reorganisation of the extensive gardens and grounds. Mr. Waring, as the head of the firm of Waring and Gillow, was himself engaged in a crusade against the ugliness of the furniture in the homes of that day, recognising the fact that good taste was not necessarily expensive, but rather the result of knowledge based upon simplicity, proportion, and practical utility, and that the best periods of English decorative art and furniture, modified and adapted to suit the conditions of the times, could be applied to the houses of almost all classes of society. He made it his mission to endeavour to educate the British public

The Life and Work of An English Landscape Architect.

into a better appreciation of the beautiful by applying these principles, thus making their homes more attractive. Mr. Waring pursued these ideals with unremitting energy, and, having regard to the enormous improvements which have taken place during the past half-century in decorative art and furniture, he has effected a work of great national value, and contributed to the general recognition and adoption of the New English Renaissance which is now so widespread. It is not surprising, then, that, filled with enthusiasm for this ideal in his own particular sphere, he proved an exacting though appreciative client whose judgment I speedily came to recognise as sound, and often original. Possessed of great discrimination and a tremendous driving force, together with keen business instincts, he was ever ready to recognise like qualities in others.

Mr. Waring was an early riser, working on an average sixteen hours a day (and often for seven days in the week), and yet finding time to discuss with minutest care every drawing prepared for the improvement of his grounds. Like other men who have won success, he is a methodical worker, and always knew exactly what he wanted to discuss with me before we met. It is quite probable that he has, somewhere in his house, a card index with notes of every interview I had with him. It is interesting to see that he is still working, year by year, at the evolution of my original plan, which in its main features has undergone but minor alterations. Lord Waring has been one of my best friends, and has introduced me, as time and occasion warranted, to many new clients, including Queen Alexandra and Mr. Gordon Selfridge.

Another client who came to me about this time was Sir Robert Affleck, Bart., of Dalham Hall, Newmarket. The Hall was a typical Georgian country mansion, without projecting wings or end pavilions, or possibly, as I first saw it, the central block from which the usual wings and pavilions had disappeared. In any case, the Hall, occupying an exceptional site, was an interesting example of domestic architecture, which was probably at one time surrounded by beautiful gardens and terraces, all of which had very likely disappeared at the same time as the wings.

It was the wish of Sir Robert and Lady Affleck to restore these gardens, and my task was to work out what I regarded as an interpretation of what the garden for such a house should be. I must have succeeded fairly well, because my clients afterwards found an old plan of the original garden which very closely

Lights and Shadows on the Pathway.

resembled my own plans. Unfortunately, shortly afterwards Sir Robert lost a great part of his fortune, which compelled him to part with the property soon after I submitted the plans, the purchaser being Mr. Cecil Rhodes.

My friend C. E. Mallows assisted me with the designs for the terraces and other architectural details, and when Sir Robert parted with his estate he thoughtfully handed on our plans with his strong recommendations to the purchaser. The result was that we were shortly sent for, I to interview Colonel Frank Rhodes at Dalham about the gardens, whilst Mallows was asked to meet Cecil Rhodes at his hotel in town regarding the house. My interview with Colonel Rhodes and his sister was a very pleasant one. Both were deeply interested in my plans. Mallows' interview with the great man was not encouraging. It was probably his first experience of a great South African magnate.

" Well, Mr. Mallows," said Cecil Rhodes, " I have sent for you to take down my instructions for additions to Dalham Hall, which I have just purchased. Here are the plans, and on this side I wish you to arrange a business room for myself, with a secretary's room and strong room adjoining, and then a waiting-room and a separate entrance, and somewhere you must arrange for a bath and cloak-room. Over these rooms I wish you to have a complete suite of apartments for my secretary, for whom you must provide a separate staircase."

Mallows, with generous enthusiasm, remarked : " Mr. Rhodes, that is splendid ; but you have said nothing about the corresponding wing to the south."

" There will be no corresponding wing on the south side."

" But, Mr. Rhodes, you will destroy the balance of parts which Dalham calls for."

" I don't care a fig about balance of parts ; all I care for at the moment is to find an architect willing to carry out my instructions. I hope, Mr. Mallows, that you understand this."

How Mallows tried to satisfy his client and his artistic conscience at the same time was shown by the drawing of Dalham Hall exhibited at the Royal Academy in 1901. He never regarded it as one of his masterpieces, and his work for Cecil Rhodes gave him little pleasure. Unfortunately, he could not afford to treat his client as a famous sculptor is said to have treated Mr. Rhodes some time before. Mr. Rhodes's autocratic treatment of my friend Mallows was probably accounted for by the fact that the South

The Life and Work of An English Landscape Architect.

African financier was already in the grip of that fatal illness from which he died before any of our plans had reached the contract stage. If we were disappointed by the work not going forward, we had the satisfaction of being well treated by the executors, who paid our fees on a generous scale.

As I was, about this time, often collaborating with Mallows, the latter decided, for the sake of convenience, to take rooms in the same building as myself at 28, Conduit Street. He secured two adjoining my own, connected by a joint consulting room, an arrangement which worked very well.

My London office was from the first placed in charge of James Crossland, my first pupil, who is still with the firm, and who during this period became as well known to my clients as I was myself. Crossland is a hard worker, and, like all my assistants, most loyal to the interests of the firm.

Our offices at Windermere were partly rebuilt and adapted for us by my old partner, Dan Gibson, and they still rank as the most effective bit of architecture in the village. They consisted of two larger rooms, my own and the drawing-office, together with a third queer, irregular box-like place, which was used by my book-keeper and private secretary. All the rooms were taxed to their fullest capacity. I have a lingering affection for this little office, so soon to be outgrown by my ever-expanding practice, and this is where I did much of my best work, which included many small but quite interesting gardens in the Lake District, amongst which I remember especially a garden at The Yews, Storrs, for Mr. (afterwards Sir James) Scott; gardens at Blackwell for Mr. Edward Holt (now Sir Edward); a range of orchid houses at Hole Hird, Windermere, for Mr. Groves, and many others.

This year I also gained in the same week two clients, both German Jews. As will later be seen, I do not use this appellation in any derogatory sense, for I have known several such men who possessed many fine qualities. One of them was a friend and partner of Mr. Cecil Rhodes, and a man of good repute in South African mining and land companies. The other was a power in the City, where he carried on a large business as a stockbroker. The former had purchased a marine villa with many acres of land on the south-east coast, and the other a similar property on the south coast. These two men knew each other, and somehow each knew that I was engaged by the other, and each gave me the same advice in almost identical words. Said

Lights and Shadows on the Pathway.

Jacobs, the South African : " I am sorry to learn, Mr. Mawson, that you have arranged to design a garden for Mr. Abrahams. Let me warn you to be extremely cautious in all your business arrangements, and never on any account undertake any liability for payment for any part of the work ! " Said Abrahams : " I learn you are undertaking considerable work for Mr. Jacobs. I am sorry it is too late to advise you, but be very careful in your business arrangements, and on no account undertake any liability."

Jacobs spent about £8,000, and although he fell on bad times, he met every penny of his liability, both to the contractors and to his architects. It was with great pleasure that we heard that after two years' hard work he had regained his financial stability. Abrahams was reputed to be one of the luckiest men on 'Change, but I found he had already quarrelled with four architects, that each had had his fees disputed, and that every tradesman and contractor who had worked for him had met with precisely the same treatment.

Of course, directly I learnt what my client's methods were I ought to have cleared out, but I was confident that with caution and diligence I might steer through where others had failed. Before the completion of my work, however, which as a garden was one of the best bits of work I had ever done, I found my client finding fault with every item. The stone was bad and the bricks were too soft, and the workmanship was faulty. The shrubs were of poor quality, and of the wrong kind. The yews for the hedges were not luxuriant and bushy enough ; weeds came up on the lawns, and therefore I had permitted bad seeds to be used, and so on. This was my client's way of avoiding payment of my accounts, and when pressed he refused point-blank to settle, and I lost heavily.

So are the rough and uphill experiences of life mingled and contrasted with appeal to one's sense of humour and interest in human nature.

Jacobs is now a highly respected member of New York society and a man of influence. Of the other I do not know anything, except that he met his match when arguing the legal fare with a taxi-driver.

Whilst the work was in progress my services were requested by Mr. A. C. de Lafontaine, at that time the owner of the famous and beautiful Athelhampton Hall, near Dorchester. As he had already spent large sums upon the restoration of the old house and a formal garden on its south side, all excellently designed and

The Life and Work of An English Landscape Architect.

executed, I could not help wondering why I had been consulted. My work was to replan the entrance and main drive, and the gardens north of this house and drive, and to find a site and plan for a new stable and garage. Some of this, I understand, was carried out, but my work was merely to supply plans.

Whilst staying at Athelhampton one of my fellow-guests was Lady Dorothy Neville, whom I had frequently met when I was with John Wills, of South Kensington, but under very different circumstances. Lady Dorothy smoked and talked incessantly, and her talk was a revelation of the Walpole genius for brilliant satire, which, however, was always cast in the vein of generous wit and humour. Her stories of Beaconsfield, Gladstone, Sir William Harcourt, and Joseph Chamberlain were priceless. For Harcourt she seemed to have a very high regard, but not for Chamberlain.

The Boer War was in progress when I last met her, and not going very well for us. One evening, on going through her letters, she said she had just heard from Lady Mary (who Lady Mary was I don't remember), who was simply heart-broken because her husband had been taken prisoner by De Wet. " And to think," said Lady Dorothy, " he expected such a good time. Indeed, he had his tennis racquet with him, because he is a crack player, and the last time I stayed with Mary she was sending him such lovely comforts." " Well," asked my client, " what could she send out to South Africa ? " " I don't quite remember," said Lady Dorothy, " excepting that there was a lot of scented soap." Of course this was not intended as a statement of fact, but as a subtle stab at a certain type of young officer now extinct.

Lady Dorothy ought to have been the owner of Athelhampton, for I have never seen a lady fit her surroundings so perfectly : she was part of the place.

Athelhampton is in the centre of the Hardy country, and I remember hearing on one of my first visits to the mansion a strange story of prudish exclusiveness which at this time seems truly amazing. A new-comer to the district who knew Thomas Hardy well, proposed to give a garden party at which the novelist was to be the honoured and lionised guest of the day. The invitations read " to meet Thomas Hardy." So incensed, however, were the local squirearchy over the publication of " Tess " that no one accepted. Lady Dorothy Neville was present when this story was related, and she told us that Gladstone had a similar reception in Midlothian, but the Grand Old Man was far-seeing enough to

Lights and Shadows on the Pathway.

turn the rebuff to political account, and it is said that the men who had refused to meet him socially ended by taking seats on his political platform.

Towards the end of the year Viscount Downe asked me to advise him upon the gardens at Wykeham Abbey, one of his country seats between York and Scarborough. Wykeham is a noble old Georgian house, with central block and wing loggias terminating in pavilions, one side of which contained the estate offices, and the corresponding block the stables. Probably it was designed by Carr, of York, or some other able architect of the period.

At the time of my visit the gardens were in ruins, and looked for all the world as if the terraces and other formal garden accompaniments suitable to such a mansion had been ruthlessly torn down by some mad landscape gardener, but in the ruins and pedestals lying about the place there was ample evidence of its former glory. In my plans I endeavoured, as at Dalham Hall, to restore some of the place's former scale and detail. This, however, was one of those numerous commissions which are confined to the preparation of plans which may be carried out as opportunity permits by the estate architect and the head gardener. I never learnt just how much or how little of my design was executed. Speaking generally, work, or rather commissions, of this character do not prove satisfactory, especially in the less formal gardens, which are often completely spoiled by ignorant or unsympathetic interpretation, though in the present instance, with Lord and Lady Downe in charge, there was, of course, nothing of the sort to fear.

In this year I also had as a client Sir Richard Cooper, of Shenstone Court, Staffordshire, a well-known agriculturist and the owner of the famous sheep-dip works at Berkhamsted. Sir Richard was one of the most liberal and energetic members of the Royal Agricultural Society. He was by nature an experimenter given to coddling everything within his sphere of influence. Shenstone was a large, uninspiring house of the early Victorian type, formal and harmless, occupying a favourable site slightly elevated above the surrounding park.

What struck me particularly on my first visit was the starved, unhappy-looking trees in the park and gardens, and it took me some time to discover the cause. On closer examination I found that a trench had been cut round each tree and filled up with new soil

The Life and Work of An English Landscape Architect.

and manure. Of course, in doing this the trees had been severed from the feeding roots which sustained them, and the park became practically denuded of timber. My work, however, was to advise upon the gardens, and not to criticise Sir Richard's experimental forestry.

The best position for a garden worthy of the name lay along the west front, where the ground sloped gently down for about two hundred feet to a brook, then rose again gently on the opposite bank, which was planted with larch, spruce, and poplars, producing a ragged see-saw line against the sky.

I walked round the gardens and expressed my views as to what was possible and desirable, to all of which my client agreed ; thereupon I made a survey and rough sketches, and left, promising to prepare plans for the first stage of the work. The plans, when I adapted them to the spot levels, worked out extraordinarily well. The ground allowed of broad, spacious terraces giving ideal proportions, and the tranquil stream was expanded right opposite the drawing-room window to a circular pool, which again suggested a water pavilion and pergola, with stepped bridges, the whole forming quite a charming garden picture. These plans were ready in three weeks, so I wrote to fix an appointment, when, to my surprise, I was told that my proposals were already carried out, and that there was no need for plans, but would I come and give further advice. I went and saw what my client understood to be a proper interpretation of my recommendations. The result was appalling. But I gave further advice, and went through the same process of preparing plans, to be told for a second time that the work had already been carried out—again, as I later saw, with the same amazing results. I relate this experience because in the course of a long professional career I have met numerous clients who seemed to think that after they had got an idea for which they would pay handsomely, they, as amateurs, were quite capable of doing the rest. Never have I known a case in which the result was ever approximately satisfactory. In Sir Richard's case, however, I am convinced that it was not a question of amateurish over-confidence, but rather the result of that impatient energy which had stood him in such good stead as a business man, and that sense of power and the ability to do things which often accompany great wealth. I have in dozens of cases known of beautiful houses spoilt by this restless energy, which trusts the building of a new wing to the local builder rather than give time

Lights and Shadows on the Pathway.

and thought to the preparation of architects' plans involving the patient solution of all the incidental problems, both æsthetic and practical.

From what has already been said it will be clear that for a man who was ever a student of his art my opportunities of acquiring experience, both as a designer of gardens and in the practical execution of my work, were almost unique. It must be remembered that whereas in domestic architecture a house designed for, say, the English Lake District may be almost as much in keeping with the moors of Devonshire, the success of a garden depends in a large measure upon its interpretation of the possibilities of the locality, site, soil, and atmospheric conditions. This is one reason why garden-making is always so difficult and yet so entrancing. No design can ever be repeated, and every new site reveals a distinct set of conditions which have to be dealt with before success can be achieved.

Here I must acknowledge the great practical assistance I received from my brother, the late Robert Mawson, who was responsible for the carrying out of more than half the gardens which I designed. For family and professional reasons I could not, of course, permit him to carry out any of my work by contract, but we devised a method of payment on the basis of actual cost plus a fixed profit which was much appreciated by my clients, and which was not open to the objections which might be raised where the architect was presumably interested on personal grounds in the fortunes of his contractor. By this means the practical side of my work was placed in the hands of a man of great technical experience on whom I could absolutely rely, and with a remarkable gift for visualising plans and their adaptation to the actual conditions of the site. My brother had also the faculty of utilising his men to the greatest advantage, and possessed a genius for winning the respect of his employees, while demanding honest service.

Under this arrangement I visited my work, on the average, once a month, and from the fact that my commissions extended from the North of Scotland to the South of England it will be seen that this entailed much night travelling and irregular meals. In addition to my regular work I had in hand the preparation of the second and considerably enlarged edition of my book.

Looking back on these strenuous days, I am amazed at the amount of work I was able to accomplish, because, although ably supported by my assistants, I made myself responsible for all the

The Life and Work of An English Landscape Architect.

basic sketch plans and designs, and in addition I made many of the original surveys of the sites of future work.

Notwithstanding the difficult clients referred to, this strenuous year was crowned with satisfactory progress. Even the awkward clients were helpful, for they taught me many lessons of professional diplomacy which were of profit in succeeding years, for I was not naturally possessed of that form of shrewdness which involves a distrust of one's fellow-men.

In addition to the demands of my practice, I visited some of my earlier works to compare actual matured results with the ideal aimed at, and many shocks on the one hand and pleasant experiences on the other awaited me. In this way I learnt many valuable lessons from both success and failure, and accumulated much experience. This study of ideals and their realisation is still my principal method of advancement, and it is by constant contact with realities that I gradually, but with painful slowness, learn to combine the two.

CHAPTER IX.

THREE YEARS OF HARD WORK AND INTERESTING EXPERIENCES.

THE following three years marked another stretch in the eager road of achievement reaching forth into unknown possibilities, and full of those strange new beginnings which give to life its spice and zest. Blessed with good health throughout this period, though never exactly robust, I advanced steadily and happily, and my imagination ever went ahead with greater freedom still, though there were occasions when I failed through frailty or fear. It was a period of strenuous work, rewarded by the making of many new friends and full of that immense satisfaction which comes from a sense of achievement.

In the first place, I began to realise that I was building up a permanent practice with a clientèle of which any man might be proud. As one of my clients said, " There's nothing like a love of gardens for cementing friendships," and the opportunity for forming friendships through his work is one of the most valued rewards of the garden designer. I mention this fact because through my published works I not only gained new clients, but found in these clients new friends, and so added momentum to my progress. So it always should be.

When I fall to " musing on man, on Nature, and on human life," as Wordsworth sings in the opening lines of " The Excursion," there comes to mind, among other things, the various motives which have actuated my clients in first consulting me. A very great percentage of my smaller professional friends have been real enthusiasts who have begun to lay out their own gardens, and have succeeded admirably up to a stage, when they felt the need of trained assistance in incorporating some feature which they have seen elsewhere and admired, or in effecting some improvement on their own scheme. Their unaided efforts may have shown that one small improvement has necessitated alterations to other parts

The Life and Work of An English Landscape Architect.

beyond the immediate precincts of the superadded features, such as walks already laid down, trees already planted, and borders already flourishing. These in turn have dislocated something else— so much so that, in the end, even the most enthusiastic sometimes get disheartened with their herculean labours. Like the attackers on the hydra-headed monsters of mythology, for every head they chop off, three others (difficulties) come in its place, and our amateur friends are distracted. When, however, they obtain a survey and a plan or policy on which to base all their work, they are surprised what little alteration is really needed. With a little pushing and squeezing, and a few minor camouflages which are never noticed in a garden, all comes right.

In the same connection one is reminded of that curious obsession which blinds its owner to any artistic possibilities in anything which bears evidence of design, especially in relation to gardens. Forgetting that there is a sweet, a noble, and a good side to human nature which should, and indeed must, express itself in all that its owners contrive and create, and especially in their dwelling-place and its surroundings, some demand that in everything intended to be pleasant to the eye " Nature " shall be slavishly copied. The logical result is a craze for the manufacture of sham wildernesses, the artificiality of which must be utterly repugnant to any person of discrimination and taste.

I have met with more than one very rich man seized with this passion for the manufacture of primitive wildness. I do not know whether it is a survival of those primeval instincts of mankind which Mr. E. T. Reed satirises so amazingly in his pen sketches, or whether it is a return to the dreams and imaginings of childhood. It is a strange obsession. I knew, or rather knew of, a well-known personality in Lakeland who used to paint fanciful landscapes depicting the country, as he said, " before the advent of man, when there were no ugly fences, walls, and barriers." He also painted portraits—and characteristic portraits they were,—refusing to use artists' brushes and laying on his colours (artists' prepared colours, by-the-by !) with a chewed hazel-stick. In keeping with these little inconsistencies, he lived a life on a par with his land-scapes, his dwelling being a cave on Mount Skiddaw. There, clad in only two garments, a wincey shirt and a pair of trousers torn off at the knees, he slept on a bed of spruce-fir boughs throughout winter's cold and summer's heat, without coverlet of any kind, the rugged rock being his only shelter from the elements.

ROCK GARDEN IN LAKELAND NURSERIES, WINDERMERE.

Hard Work and Experiences.

I can only explain this ruling passion in a rich man by saying once more that " extremes meet "—the extreme of luxury meeting with the other extreme of those who have no visible means of sustenance !

What I have said about the craze for the creation of wildernesses is not by any means in disparagement of rationally designed and placed informal or wild gardening, such as that which is directly associated with rock-work, nor as discrediting rock building even on a large scale. Nor have I any aversion to natural picturesque wildness when it is there on the site originally, or whenever the nature of the site or the materials to hand warrant it. In one instance I advocated the changing of the entire location of a proposed house on the Westmorland moors, in order that it might have as site a natural terrace of rock. The steps down to the lower garden were partly hewn in the solid rock, and partly built of a rugged character that accorded perfectly with the natural outcrop, and the whole garden on this, the principal front, was designed in keeping. With the exception of a border next to the house, mainly for climbers, all the flowers and shrubs were heather and heath arranged in affinity with the wildness around. What I do dissociate myself from is the importation of tons of stone from Yorkshire and Derbyshire in order to build rock gardens in districts absolutely devoid of the natural product, and where the surroundings indicate other methods altogether, and a *motif* in keeping with them.

Every art has its legitimate bounds, and when forced beyond those bounds its artificialities become repugnant. This truism, of course, works both ways, but in our present connection applies especially, say, to a rock garden composed of thousands of tons of Yorkshire grit and stone transferred to the lush lowlands of the Thames Valley, or to a site in a similar district where it stands uneasily perched on an obviously artificial mound.

My method of working in such cases is usually to draw up a plan showing the extent and general arrangement of the rock garden, often accompanied by sketches showing the treatment of the more important parts and the height to which they are to be carried. If the garden is built round a stream, I, of course, show whatever widenings, pools, and falls are to be constructed, and arrange the paths on my plan so as to open up consecutive vistas and tempt to further exploration. This being all that can be done on paper until we are ready for the planting plan, it will easily

The Life and Work of An English Landscape Architect.

be seen that rock gardening demands even closer and more detailed attention during the process of formation than any other.

The most successful rock gardens are, of course, those formed by laying bare a natural rock escarpment, as was done extensively in the creation, about the time of which I am speaking, of new and extensive nursery gardens made necessary by the rapid and continuous expansion of the business the foundations of which I had laid so many years before, and now in the hands of my sole remaining brother, Robert. The laying out of these was a real labour of love, and included the design and placing of a block of buildings containing a house for my brother, and, in a separate wing, offices and seed store, the whole being contrived so as to create a harmonious and attractive semi-public garden to which everyone interested might have free access without in the slightest impairing its usefulness for the nursery-garden business.

A prophet is not without honour save in his own country, and immediately it was seen that we were clearing the scrubby coppice with which the site was covered, much needless anxiety was expressed as to whether a vandalism was about to be committed by the commercialisation of a prominently placed piece of ground on the main highway between the villages of Windermere and Bowness. In particular, many anxious inquiries were made as to what we intended to do with a tall and extremely graceful silver birch which had long been a landmark and an object of admiration by all who used the neighbouring road. Needless to say, any fears that we should interfere with it were perfectly groundless. It was retained as an artistic asset of the utmost importance, and, in one sense, as a central feature of the design.

In the end, anxiety gave place to surprise and pleasure when it was seen what hitherto unsuspected views were opened up of the northerly reach of Windermere and of the mountains grouped round its head, and how these wonderful views were made the most of in our lay-out without the sacrifice of practical utility.

Among the new clients who came to me at this time I remember with special pleasure Mr. Richardson, of Lincoln, who, in addition to his business as senior partner in an old-established firm of oil-crushers, found time for the cultivation of many outside interests, of which the two principal ones were music and gardening, in both of which he excelled. With such a client, and with a site which had the great artistic advantage of including an old worked-out quarry, and from which magnificent views of the cathedral could be obtained, the garden designer was indeed happy.

Another commission which, though small, gave me great pleasure, and which is known to a great many people, was for the design, on lines equally practical and artistic, of a new recreation ground at Cleethorpes. This provided a good example of the manner in which, in cases where almost every inch of the site must be used for some utilitarian purpose connected with sport, effect can be obtained almost solely by the careful balance and disposition of parts. Not all my recommendations matured, however. I had a good plan, which, if carried out in its entirety, would have given a distinctive note to this enterprising seaside resort, but it was completely spoiled in execution, largely owing to its interpretation by local " geniuses " who had no appreciation of design or the value of carefully thought-out details. This was distinctly a case where unwise economy led to uneconomic results.

I also worked at Portmadoc for Mr. W. G. Greaves, on a garden of a very interesting character. The climate in this part of North Wales is most genial, and here my client had erected a very beautiful country house, occupying an elevated position on the site of an earlier homestead. From the house the ground fell rapidly to lower lawns and wooded stretches, through which meandered a beautiful brook, the margins of which had been successfully planted with aquatic and sub-aquatic plants, and here I saw growing for the first time in the open large masses of white arum lilies, which flowered most profusely after surviving the winter.

To connect the house with the lawns I planned a complete scheme of balustraded walls, with long, broad flights of steps connecting the house to the informal lower gardens, previously planted and laid out with great skill by the owner. Though not extensive, this work gave me great satisfaction, largely because my clients were so very appreciative, but more particularly because I felt I had succeeded in a task rendered difficult by the nature of the site and the necessity for conserving the work already done, by simple and straightforward planning.

Another client I remember with exceptional pleasure is Doctor Augustus Harboard, a Harley Street specialist, who owned a property of considerable extent on Detling Hill, near Maidstone,

The Life and Work of An English Landscape Architect.

and here from Friday to Monday he led the simple life, emulating Thoreau in his Walden shanty in the severe austerity of his tastes. His principal object, however, was to live on his property sufficiently long to be able to locate with absolute certainty the right position for the country house which he proposed to build. When he had arrived at a decision, he sent for me to advise him upon the type of house suited to his needs and its setting, and to plan the new drives, terraces, and gardens.

The site chosen was admirable, and opened up interesting discussions upon all aspects of the subject of the house in its relation to its surroundings and the needs of the proprietor. The first thing we agreed to do was to determine the accommodation required and to limit it to that and no more, and then to plan so that the house should not sprawl beyond the comfortable limits of the plateau on which it was to sit, giving due attention to the aspect of each part of the dwelling. All this is, of course, by no means omitted in such cases, but on this occasion it was entered into with a thoroughness, a depth, and zeal which could not but delight the professional designer. It was followed by discussions on the style best suited to the house, avoiding insipidities on the one hand and flamboyancy on the other. We were both in love with the homely Tudor style, which admirably suited the needs of the case, and which was adopted.

Next we turned our thoughts to the views, both outwards and towards the house, especially in relation to the placing of the purely utilitarian and domestic parts of the garden. In all these discussions with a client so deliberate and painstaking there were many searchings of heart! Many a time we came to a place where, as ever in architecture and garden design, it has to be " this *or* that," whereas the inclination is to struggle to retain " this *and* that "—very desirable, but, alas! impossible.

I had many delightful interviews and discussions of ways, means, and methods with my client, the more gratifying to my professional susceptibilities from their earnestness and thoroughness, and we felt we had worked out the main lines of an ideal scheme when, in the end, whether in despair of ever completely satisfying himself or not I cannot say, he decided to content himself by adding to one of the farmhouses on the estate. To meet a man so thoroughly in love with every phase of country life was delightful, and I shall always remember with pleasure the week-ends at Detling.

Hard Work and Experiences.

A very different man, but an equally delightful client, is Mr. William Galloway, for whom, as the reader will remember, I had already done considerable work. He is a bachelor, art connoisseur, a musician, and a lover of gardens. He inherited from his father " The Willows," overlooking the River Ribble and the Preston Docks. From my first introduction to it the house has suffered increasingly from the growing industrialisation of its surroundings, and I have always felt that it must have been my client's affection for his family that induced him to spend so much money on his house, its decoration and appointments, and the gardens. No other consideration could have justified so large an expenditure when a lesser outlay on a befitting site would have built a house complete with every amenity, and of a character more suited to his tastes and convenience.

Still, the house is a model of comfort, surrounded by gardens of exceptional interest, with a unique enclosed tennis court. This enclosed court is approached by a terrace connecting with the house, entered from one end by a fine piece of wrought-iron work designed by Dan Gibson, the central gate of which is hung with Spanish bells. This garden has been illustrated in both line and colour in the later editions of my work on " The Art and Craft of Garden Making."

In Mr. Galloway we have a typical example of the art-loving Lancashire manufacturer, a much larger class than many suppose, though of the existence of which contemporary artists have ample and material proof. What is more, these men really are genuine lovers of the beautiful, and not merely rich plutocrats with a pose, as some stupid writers of fiction have assumed.

These instances from a year's work might be very considerably extended, but they will be sufficient to show that variety has been one of the greatest charms of my work, and also the growth of interest in landscape architecture, and my contributions to its wider appreciation.

The years which followed were none the less interesting, nor did the momentum given to garden-making wane in any sense, but rather tended to gather strength.

Many new clients came to me in the year 1903, amongst whom were Lord and Lady Beauchamp, who were delightful clients. Madresfield Court was already well known for its extensive gardens, which for their variety and high keeping were famous. Lord Beauchamp, like many of my clients, was a scholarly

H

The Life and Work of An English Landscape Architect.

arboriculturist and gardener. I have always regarded it as a fortunate circumstance that I was thrown into association with so many famous amateurs, for they compelled me to keep up to date, and to follow the changing nomenclature as systematised by the Kew hand lists.

In 1904 I had fourteen important new commissions among many smaller ones. For Andrew Carnegie, Skibo Castle, extensive improvements to garden. For Walter Fenwick, Esq., Witham Hall, Bourne, Lincolnshire, remodelling of old gardens and considerable extensions to them. For Fred J. Monks, Esq., of Warrington, gardens to new residence on high ground overlooking the estuary of the Ship Canal.

Out of so many, space permits me to refer at length to only a few of the most interesting; and, first of all, I would like to retail a story about a family whose names I must not, for obvious reasons, disclose.

On the eve of my arrival I noticed evidences of child life, and heard the musical laughter of young voices in the distance. At dinner I was told that not only was I to meet the family at breakfast, but that I had been appointed judge of the children's gardens.

At breakfast I met a very friendly group, consisting of three girls and a boy—four cheery, healthy, romping children. The eldest was called Maude, who was probably a little over thirteen years of age ; then came Madge, say twelve ; then Betty, a little over ten ; and Bobby, about eight. After breakfast I was conducted across the lawns and beyond a group of beech trees towards the walled-in garden, on the south side of which the children, " all by themselves," as they carefully explained, had laid out and planted their gardens. I am glad they did them all by themselves, for otherwise I would have lost an insight into child character which was intensely interesting.

The first garden, which I saw from a distance, belonged to Maude, and was a perfect blaze of colour, the result of very little work and the expenditure of a few pence on packets of seed, mostly poppies.

The second belonged to Madge, who was evidently a keen gardener and had the instincts of a collector. In the small space of twelve feet by six she had got together a collection of old-fashioned hardy flowers, in which I discovered many of my own childhood's favourites.

When I had carefully examined Madge's garden, I asked Betty

Hard Work and Experiences.

to show me hers. "This is a potato patch, not a garden," I said. "It is my garden," she stoutly objected. "But why did you plant it with potatoes?" I asked. "Well, because cook said she would buy them from me. Then," said she, with an intense show of satisfaction, "I will get a larger patch and make more money."

At last I turned to Bobby, and asked where I could see his garden. "Well, sir, mine isn't exactly a garden. Come and look!" We came to a strip of mown grass, with an old pear tree at one end, to which was nailed a target, whilst at the other end was a small home-made shed, just the sort of shelter a boy would erect, with ample ventilation, to be sure. Between these two objects were two flower-pots let into the grass, evidently for the practice of putting. Thus, each child expressed herself or himself to the uttermost. Madge, of course, won the prize.

The Rev. D. Molesworth, who lived the life of a retired scholar at Pembury, was the son of Doctor Molesworth, of Rochdale, famous as the incumbent of the richest living in England, and the doughty antagonist of John Bright, yet who nevertheless in later life became the great tribune's staunch friend. From Mr. Molesworth I heard many interesting stories of the encounters between his father and the Quaker politician.

Lord Brassey I have always regarded as one of the most courtly gentlemen I have ever met, and a politician possessing a great fund of stories about well-known political characters. I was first asked to meet him at Normanhurst, an unwieldy house of little architectural merit, a fact no one appreciated more than my client, who would exclaim, "Look, look, Mawson, at the thing my father mistook for architecture!"

Lord Brassey had a charming way of telling a story against himself. On one occasion I had wandered to a distant part of the garden, and was struck with the curious and, I must add, rather stupid arrangement of walks. Here his lordship remarked : "You remind me of my old friend Edward Thomas, whom I once found standing just as you are standing now, on this very spot. By the way," he asked, "what do you think of it?" I replied : "I was just trying to make up my mind about it when you arrived!" "Shall I tell you what Edward Thomas said? He told me that no gentleman would do work like that—and he knew I did it."

Lord Brassey was building a delightful dower house for the

The Life and Work of An English Landscape Architect.

second Lady Brassey. It is a piece of exemplary English half-timber work, designed by Andrew Prentice. Here I planned the new drives and the whole of the gardens and terraces. The latter form a steadying line to the eye in viewing the house, which occupies a commanding site overlooking a panorama of rolling Sussex downs, extending in long undulations until lost in the blue haze of the horizon almost at the sea.

About this time Mr. Andrew Carnegie, who was a native of Dunfermline, founded the Carnegie Dunfermline Trust, to which he presented half a million pounds sterling for the purpose of bringing " sweetness and light " into the lives of the people of his native town. This was supplemented by the gift of Pittencrieff Park and Glen, the retention of which as a private domain had so far interposed a barrier to the extension of the city westward. Nowhere have I seen the dire results of private properties held against the advancing tide of population so curiously demonstrated, and I remember Mr. Carnegie telling me that as a boy of twelve he determined to buy Pittencrieff so that he might pull down the high wall which he was quite sure hid an earthly paradise from view.

Having got this large property to develop, and an ample sum to administer, the Trust requested Professor Patrick Geddes and myself to prepare separate schemes for the development of Pittencrieff as a public park, and to suggest any other improvements in the town which might appeal to us.

Our interpretation of these indefinite instructions was that in the field of imagination we were given free hands. This liberal interpretation proved, as will subsequently appear, our undoing.

To my scheme I brought every ounce of enthusiasm and hard study and imagination of which I was capable, spending, with an efficient staff, months of long hours and hard work in Dunfermline, investigating every practical avenue for the improvement of the city and its parks and surroundings. The result was the scheme which is now widely known to town planners not only in this country but on the Continent and in America. At the end of eight months I was able to present my proposals in a series of drawings, and a long preliminary report which pictorially, as in other ways, surpassed anything I had previously done. As an example of the landscape architect's art I have never been able in this country to surpass this effort, and if any work of mine is judged in future years to have advanced my art, such judgment

Hard Work and Experiences.

will largely be based upon my proposals for bringing " sweetness and light " into Dunfermline.

My scheme was first of all based on the following considerations :—

(1) Upon the financial possibilities derivable from the interest at five per centum on half a million sterling, and an approximate annual expenditure of this income over a period of fifty years.

(2) That Dunfermline had an opportunity of becoming a great centre for technical instruction on the lines of the Boston School of Technology.

(3) That, as the outcome of the work of its school, it would build up a number of artistic industries.

(4) That it would, through its schools, art industries, and the development of its parks and recreational facilities, attract a well-to-do resident population.

(5) That the natural expansion of the residential area was westward, and that the only logical approach to this area was by an extension of Bridge Street westward across Pittencrieff Park. Indeed this seemed to me to be the only logical way of expansion. This was the rock on which my ambitious scheme for Dunfermline broke down.

The Chairman of the Trust told me that if I would reconsider my scheme and remodel it so as to eliminate the extension of Bridge Street across Pittencrieff, he would propose my retention as landscape expert to the Trust. I explained that if I failed to emphasise a development so obvious, so practical, and so essentially logical, and agreed to delete it from my plans, it would be fatal. Reviewing all the circumstances, I think I proved myself a weak diplomat, and that it ought to have been possible to have made this concession, knowing that its adoption, sooner or later, was inevitable. As it was, my unaccommodating attitude lost me these clients. That my proposals were reasonable and inevitable is proved by the fact that the Trust have not only adopted this extension westward, but on my calling attention to this change of policy I was curtly told by the Secretary that they never contemplated anything else.

It was, however, heartbreaking to know that my efforts should not only fail to contribute to the evolution of Dunfermline, but that my action had given the Trust an opportunity of perpetrating an ungenerous act. I received not one penny for my many months of hard work. The sum paid to me barely covered my out-of-pocket

The Life and Work of An English Landscape Architect.

expenses. Dunfermline has, however, brought me a rich reward, for without my published report it is safe to say that I would never have been commissioned to replan so many Canadian towns, Athens, and Salonika. I suppose that even the Carnegie Dunfermline Trustees may have some doubts as to the wisdom of their judgment, and regret a certain Scotch keenness which might conceivably have ruined a career.

When I met the Trustees and submitted my estimate of the cost of the work involved, one of the members said, in a manner intended to crush, " To show how impossible your scheme is, you propose to spend one million pounds, whilst our total capital is only half this sum." To which I replied, " I don't propose to spend any of your capital, and only four-fifths of your income. By spending this for a period of fifty years you will have spent a million without dissipating one penny of your capital. In short, what I have done is merely to lay down a policy for your guidance."

My work in Dunfermline brought me in contact with Mr. Andrew Carnegie, who telegraphed to me one Wednesday afternoon to my London address, asking me to meet him at once at Skibo Castle, as he was leaving for America the following Monday. Eager to work for a man so famous, I left the same night *en route* for Dornoch, and reached it by Friday noon, where I was met by the agent, who conducted me to my hotel and arranged to call for me at nine the next morning.

On my arrival at Skibo, which had recently been rebuilt and enlarged on a colossal scale, and in a manner which incorporated every detail of Scottish Baronial architecture, ancient and modern, I was met by Mr. and Mrs. Carnegie. They were quite excited about the planning of the new gardens, proposing that we should at once begin our perambulations and take in the possibilities of the site. On the sloping ground to the south-east of the house there was an old-world garden surrounded and divided by a remarkable beech hedge. To the west of the Castle, and in a hollow, Mr. Carnegie had built a large bath-house, which must have cost a fortune. This building, with its fanlight roof, introduced a persistent jarring note; but this was not the only difficulty which Mr. Carnegie's energy had introduced, for everywhere there were the most feeble attempts at artificial rocky streams and rock gardens, and other mistaken attempts at garden-making scattered about in all directions. To my keen disappointment I found that Mr. Carnegie took a great pride in his amateur efforts, and it needed all my skill to outline a logical scheme of development which would not cause alarm. However, I think I must have succeeded fairly well, for at lunch Mrs. Carnegie said, " Well, Mr. Mawson, we like your ideas very much, so you had better get to work quickly, and let us have your plans on Monday morning." " So speaks the American," said Mr. Carnegie ; " quick's the word ! " Of course I had to explain that the work which I had outlined was very important, and that the most I could promise was to post to New York sketch plans in six weeks' time. From what I afterwards learnt, I am sure that a few effective lines drawn upon Ordnance maps would have satisfied Mrs. Carnegie, who would have left the rest to me.

I spent the rest of the day with Mr. Carnegie, walking over the property. It was a beautiful October day, with a clear sky, and the foliage was just taking on its most gorgeous autumn colours. There was a lilt in the air, and the first signs of that crispness which makes this period of the year so perfect for a walk in good company, and Mr. Carnegie was that : full of his schemes for the betterment of mankind, full also of his theories of paternal socialism, and at peace with the whole world, but all the time anxious to expedite the evolution of life. In particular, he was inordinately proud of being the possessor of Skibo. " The Duke," he remarked, " told me that his agent had charged such an extravagant sum for Skibo that he felt ashamed to look an honest man in the face." " What did you reply ? " I asked. " ' Duke,' said I, ' don't you worry about that, for if you had been Andrew Carnegie and I had been His Grace the Duke, you would have had to pay a lot more for it than your agent charged me.' "

Late in the afternoon we arrived at the view-point of the estate. There we stood overlooking the Firth of Dornoch towards the setting sun ; the scene was so sublime that we both instinctively took off our hats. Then Mr. Carnegie, turning sharp round to me, said, " Mr. Mawson, they say Heaven is a beautiful place, and I dare say it is true; but isn't this good enough to be going on with ? " " Perhaps," I replied, " this is a foretaste." " I hope you are right," said he, " for I have never seen in all my travels anything so beautiful."

Another interesting man I met for the first time at this period was Walter Fenwick, of Witham Hall, the son of the well-known Northumbrian banker. My client was a keen horticulturist, and a man of great taste, and with a wonderful sense of colour, a gift

The Life and Work of An English Landscape Architect.

possessed by many of my lady clients, but seldom by the men. My work was to lay out gardens to correspond with the house, which had been extended and remodelled to the designs of Andrew Prentice, and was a good example of his work. In addition to the gardens immediately surrounding the house, all of which were of a formal character, I planned a landscape garden on the margin of a lake on the north-west side of the house, and here we naturalised a large number of ornamental trees and shrubs, many of which were new introductions from China.

On one of my visits to Witham Hall I found my client in his billiard-room and in his shirt-sleeves, in the act, as I thought, of paper-hanging, the last occupation I would have expected him to take up. On looking round, however, I found him surrounded by about twenty saucers in which he had mixed his colours, which he was laying in large patches on the back of long rolls of cream-coloured wall-paper. These rolls represented his scheme for a great border of annuals, and was arranged to quarter the actual size. I was interested, and asked on what principle he worked. " Well, I lay down my ideal colour first, and then select annuals of the height, colour, and character required." To me the drawings were both interesting and instructive, and the result, which I had the pleasure of seeing the following summer, exceeded all my expectations.

Another client, Mr. Thomas O. Lloyd, whom I first met at Budbrooke House, Warwick, was also the owner of the well-known Elizabethan Priory near by, to which Wren added a new classical front, and which is known to connoisseurs as one of our most beautiful examples of domestic architecture. Mr. Lloyd possessed an interesting collection of early Quaker correspondence and literature, he being the direct descendant of the original Quaker Lloyd who for conscience' sake spent thirteen years of his life in prisons. Some of this correspondence has been published by the Society of Friends.

My work for Mr. Lloyd consisted of garden extensions at Budbrooke House, where we accidentally discovered an avenue-like arrangement of trees in the park to the west of the house, which needed only the removal of two trees to bring to light a long avenue in alignment with the house and gardens. For a hundred years these two trees had obstructed this opening, evidently without anyone being aware of it. Later I carried out work for Mr. Lloyd at The Priory, and also, at a still later date, planned a part of his property as a residential estate, which, when developed, should, I think, form an interesting addition to Warwick.

The following year allowed no alternative to hard work and economy, necessitated by my still expanding practice. The most notable commission during the year was a public park for the Corporation of Rochdale, which cost over £20,000. Falinge Park, as it was called, was originally the name of a large private residence which, together with its handsome stables, was built round a large courtyard. The mansion, and estate of about 30 acres, were presented to the town by Alderman John Turner, who added to his benefaction the cost of laying out the estate, including the formation of a wide balustraded terrace enclosing the carriage court on the south front. Other terraces, flower gardens, and conservatories were laid out on the east side of the house, whilst the rest of the ground was adapted in various ways to the needs of the townsfolk, who from the first took a special pride in their park, and have maintained it in a high state of upkeep.

Meanwhile, Henry A. Harben (afterwards Sir Henry) had bought an estate at Chalfont St. Giles, with its residence intact, to which his architect, Mr. Paul Waterhouse, had made additions. Mr. Harben's father was one of the founders of the Prudential Assurance Company, and as president had brought that company to the position of one of the most powerful financial corporations in the country. At the time I met Mr. Harben he had risen to his father's position as managing director. I found in him a sympathetic client, well instructed in horticulture, and one who discussed every detail and development of my designs with the keenest interest. The site did not offer any thrilling opportunities. The soil was not good for many varieties of shrub, though excellent for roses, nor were there any interesting vistas over distant landscapes. Nevertheless, we were able to introduce many features which added character to the estate. Among these was a garden court extending from the house and bounded on either side by pergolas, ending in garden houses, the whole designed in a classical style to accord with the heavy character of the façade on this side of the house.

My most notable client during this year was Mr. John Cory, the owner of an estate in Glamorganshire. Duffryn and its gardens are extensive in scale and well appointed. Here, as an extension of the existing gardens, I planned a scheme extending over many acres, into which every type of garden design has been happily

The Life and Work of An English Landscape Architect.

welded by my client's son, Mr. Reginald Cory, who is an amateur landscape gardener and horticulturist of insight and ability. The credit of the success achieved in these gardens largely belongs to him.

My connection with Duffryn and my friend Mr. Reginald Cory still continues, and associations have been formed which help to keep alive my interest in certain departments of horticulture and arboriculture which the claims of later years might have weakened.

Mr. Cory's interests were many, and extended to town planning and housing, and it was for him that I designed Glyn Cory, a projected model village some three miles north of Duffryn. The site was admirable for a beautiful model village, and possessed many attractive and unique amenities. Unfortunately, during my subsequent absence in America the work fell into other hands, and was shorn of most of those distinctive features which would have assured its success.

Although I possessed all the illustrated works on Italian gardens extant, both Mr. Cory and I felt that books were inadequate for our full education with regard to both the setting and the planting of the examples given, so we arranged a tour of inspection of many of the best known Italian examples, and of a few lesser famous but beautiful gardens, bringing away with us records of our investigations in the form of photographs and rough plans and sketches. At the same time, we visited the noted picture galleries and works of art in Florence, Milan, Naples, and Rome, for I realised that Italian gardens were but one phase of the expression of a great art movement which influenced all design.

At the end of one of our strenuous days we arrived on our patient and tired donkeys at the gates of a large palace which we had been advised to see, only to find them closed and no porter in attendance. At last, just as we were arranging to return, we espied a young woman peering at us from an upper barred window, and my friend addressed himself to her in the best French he could muster, but got no reply beyond quizzical smiles. Thus encouraged, my friend began again in French, asking if it were possible to get inside the grounds. At last she replied in excellent English : " Don't you think, gentlemen, we would understand each other better if you spoke in English ! " It was an amusing episode, which led to our addressing ourselves for the future in King's English, backed by a King's coin, and, strange to say, we were usually understood.

STAFF AT THE LANCASTER OFFICE BEFORE THE WAR.

CHAPTER X.

AN ESTIMATE OF PROGRESS AND HOME LIFE INTERESTS.

HERE I pause for a brief space, as at a half-way house, to review the pathway along which I had striven to secure at last a position of some stability, noting there, from the eminence gained, the turns in the road or the surgings of the tide which, as Shakespeare says, when taken at the full leads on to fortune.

From the first budding acquaintance with the writings of Repton, Sir Uvedale Price, and Kemp, I always felt that I was one of the party, although, when my father's disaster fell upon the family, to feel the assurance within me that here was the line whereby I would retrieve our name and public regard may be looked upon as mere boyish ambition. My pole star was brilliant ; nevertheless, it was approachable, and my ambition was healthy and reasonable. I hitched my wagon to a star, and, I am thankful to say, I had the courage, through failure and success, to hold on unswervingly.

Now I may say that the flickering early lights of mere personal ambition had given place to the dawn of desire to advance the profession of design as applied to gardens, and to parks and cities also. That which has hitherto befriended me has become, from a sense of gratitude, a passion of love and reciprocal desire. It is oftentimes so in human affection. From one act of kindness to another, gratitude is engendered, which in turn gives place to affection and irrefragable unity.

My ambitions ran beyond my educational advantages, and doubtless were not in keeping with my lack of scientific training. Thus all the more it becomes my wish to see some specialised curriculum for landscape architecture established in a separate college or in a school attached to one of our universities, as in America. But, given the necessary grit and ambition, youth will

The Life and Work of An English Landscape Architect.

get a fair substitute for an academic and technical training somehow ; what is more, it will not make technique or science an end in itself, as many erstwhile brilliant students do. Onward and upward is the young man's motto, and a good training in the school of hardship and adversity tends to fit him for the forward march. I early learnt to eliminate non-essentials and not to tarry gloating over successes, nor to waste energy lamenting failures, but to use them as stepping-stones to higher opportunity.

The initial training of an architect, a garden and park designer, or a town planner, I compare to the impetus which the yachtsman gives to his craft when he throws it upon the wind upon leaving the moorings. When a sufficient momentum has been gained, he rounds his craft up to the wind, and using the wind to defeat the wind, he now progresses full in its teeth, closehauled and tacking at some five or six points to it. A poor start is a disadvantage assuredly, when through obstacles or other causes the full momentum cannot be obtained; but it can be atoned for in the race by skilful manipulation. There is a kind of education to be gained from almost everything seen and met with. I have a warm place in my memory for Mr. William Leiper, one of the few architects honoured with the coveted R.S.A. He was one of those men who are always educating themselves by constant observation and subsequent application. The freshness of the fount within him was always springing forth in response to the beauty of the world around him, and bursting forth in spasmodic and stimulating remarks.

To take a casual instance. Travelling together on the road to remote Ballimore, he would suddenly remark in the midst of our professional conversation : " Eh, Mawson, look at that towering bank of cloud. Isn't it grand in its form, and noble in its poise ! " And then he would add, " There's your commanding effect, and there are your subsidiaries ranged in perfect ordering," pointing to the lesser drifts of clouds in shoals ranged round the upstanding pillar. That was only a sample of scores of such observations. I know nothing about Leiper's early or professional training. There was no trace of anything pedantic about him or his work, but I felt assured, by his general remarks, that he was the man to send for when it was a case of reducing chaos to order, and, further, to cast over it the glamour of imagination.

It is a pleasure to rub shoulders with and to meet such men. Many of us observe and are unable to put into words what we feel, much less comment upon the lessons we store as we go along. I have met many men who are very highly trained, who are without this spark of genius, this Midas-touch which transmutes all they handle into gold.

This by the way. Now to my narrative.

Owing to the expansion of my practice in the South and South-West of England I began to find more and more that Windermere and Lakeland (of which I was passionately fond) were too remote from most of my work. A number of my clients were City men who could only get away from business for the week-ends, and so desired interviews on either Friday evening or Saturday, which seldom left me time to reach home until Sunday, if then. This meant week-ends in town, followed by a week of visits to works in progress, and consequently longer absences from home and office than was convenient or desirable. To obviate this, my family stayed increasingly at Hest Bank, a seaside suburb of Lancaster, where, as already stated, my wife and I had built ourselves a bungalow, originally intended as a holiday home for the children. From Windermere and our many social ties there we gradually and regretfully withdrew. We had pictured ourselves as living our life in the home at Windermere I had specially designed and built, commanding a magnificent panorama of rolling woods, lake, and mountains; but fate willed otherwise. The Corbels, Windermere, is treasured in our memory as well as in the memory of our children, for there most of them were born. The house and its garden were just suited to our needs, and we had the advantage of the Windermere Grammar School for the boys. We had also taken our part in the religious and social life of the village, and made a host of loyal friends.

Although only thirty miles south of Windermere, Hest Bank, being midway between the important railway centres of Carnforth and Lancaster, and only thirty minutes from Preston, was infinitely superior as a railway centre, as may be understood when I mention that I could reach London by 1-30 p.m., whereas from Windermere it was 4-15 p.m. before I could arrive. The latter allowed me but half an hour with my staff in the London office before closing, whereas the former gave me a clear half-day, while on the return journey the advantages were even greater. The difference meant that, while I very often could not get home to Windermere for the week-end, I seldom failed to return to my family when at Hest Bank.

The Life and Work of An English Landscape Architect.

The place had special attractions for us all. We had conceived the idea of building a model village of our own on a site which was in many respects ideal, and, as a hobby when on our holidays, we planned out the village. Our plan extended over a wide area in order to ensure logical expansion towards Lancaster in one direction, to Morecambe in another, and to Carnforth in another. Now that the lapse of time has thrown our actions into proper perspective, it is easy to see, after the event, that at this time we ought to have removed our headquarters to London. Our not doing so was a tactical mistake. The London office had the practice in its grasp, and the provincial practice was subsidiary to that of London. Indeed, I had worked out a scheme which, had it been carried through, would have given a great impetus to my practice. This plan included a small colony built round a studio in a large garden, to accommodate at least twenty assistants. It was to be situated about half an hour's journey from London, and directly connected with my consulting room by telephone. The lure of the North of England frustrated this intention, and the alternative finally decided upon was to make Hest Bank a place of residence, and Lancaster the place of business.

Our bungalow of which I have spoken was on the shore, with two acres of lawn running down to the bay, and miles of yellow and light-brown sand alternating with the tidal waters, stretching away into blue and green distances, backed by the Lakeland mountains. Ulverston sands, as they are sometimes called, have been so well depicted by Turner, De Wint, and David Cox, that my readers have already some idea of the fascinations of our surroundings. To me these unbroken distances had a great charm and a distinct educational influence, and I am sure led to my work becoming broader in its conception and planning. I revelled in plain unbroken spaces, and planted still fewer shrubs. The contrast between the multitudinous detail of Lakeland landscapes and the quiet spaces of Morecambe Bay was fascinating.

The pleasure of having one's family around one must always be greater than that of living in a beautiful locality, and in the case of a large family such as ours there are many compensations. Sisters are splendid tutors for their brothers, and develop their sense of chivalry. Then both form a kind of club amongst themselves into which they intuitively admit others of similar age and diverse aims and tastes.

Progress and Home Life Interests.

Such was our home circle at the Bungalow, in which the young people found scope for outdoor athletic amusements in summer, while in winter, having a music-room and a pipe organ, we had many glee parties together, with part singing and instrumental orchestral music also.

These week-end parties were delightful; but, alas! very many of the bright young fellows who were so full of the joy of life, and so ambitious for the future, are no more. They played their part in the great struggle, and made the great sacrifice with brave hearts, anxious only for the triumph of right and the honour of their regiment.

On Sunday morning we all met at the little Free Church, one of the smallest in the country, holding, when packed, just one hundred worshippers, including the choir, which was largely confined to members of my own family and their friends. This church was presided over by the Rev. Herbert Gamble, M.A., who speedily endeared himself to us by remarkable gifts as a preacher, combined with a rare genius for understanding young people. He was the most lovable of pastors, wise in council beyond his years, and fully alive to the claims of beauty as an element in worship, he developing a form and order which were unique for a small village church.

From this service the children and their friends and the pastor would troop down to the Bungalow for lunch, where we usually sat down to the number of eighteen. The afternoon we spent at tennis or other forms of recreation. If the day was wet, then we would have a talk about our favourite authors, a subject on which Mr. Gamble was well informed. After tea there was the early evening service, and there was no difficulty in securing full attendance, for the sermons were always anticipated with the utmost interest; and no wonder, for they were perfect cameos, and always finishing to the second—twelve minutes in the morning and eight minutes in the evening. The entire service was full of beauty and helpfulness, though lasting less than an hour.

At Mr. Gamble's request I gave the children's address, limited to five minutes. This in a large number of Free Churches is a feature of morning worship, but I always think ours was somehow different. There was no attempt at theology, but a frank recognition of the mental capacity of young folk, whose powers of observation and love for all created things we endeavoured to cultivate, so that I made practically the whole of my children's

The Life and Work of An English Landscape Architect.

addresses short, simple studies of nature. I think the young folk took a lively interest in these little talks. At any rate, they used to set their parents an occasional poser, and one little chap asked his farmer father if he knew the names of every grass in his meadow. I always think that these talks to children were a fine preparation for the lectures by which in later years I endeavoured to popularise and encourage the study of Landscape Architecture in its application both to town planning and to the design of gardens. What I mean is, that the simplicity of style essential in the address to a child's understanding provides a quality of definite value and a direct style of diction equally invaluable when appealing to adults.

The work in the Windermere and London offices was now under good control owing to my policy of training my own men and retaining their services. The advantages of such a course could not be doubted, and the fact that every member of the staff regarded himself as the genius of the organisation without whose co-operation it would fall to the ground, in no sense diminished the advantages of this arrangement.

The knowledge that I was supported by a competent and loyal staff enabled me to cultivate a closer control of work in progress, make more frequent meetings with clients, and give, what is always so essential to success in a landscape architect, a closer study of the site and the proper adjustment of the design to it. In this way I was continually meeting new people, getting new angles of view in respect to many things, and solving new problems.

Every person who has carried his life forward with any measure of success proves what he is made of in the early stages by the force of his character. This is proved by the way he meets difficulties, obstacles, hindrances, and drawbacks, which, if he is a spirited competitor, he will, in spite of falls and mishaps, surmount with resolution and fortitude. Then follows a stage when he realises his place in the universal scheme of things, and he sees his life and his work in their true perspective. As I reflect, I am convinced that many failures to make good and reap the harvest of life are due to the fact that so many men and women never arrive at this restful stage. They never lend themselves to it, but go on fighting, and go under, submerged by trifling things which ought to have been side-tracked.

I must not omit to mention that it was at this transitional stage of my career that my first foreign commission occurred.

Progress and Home Life Interests.

It came to me in a letter received from Baron von Boeslager, of Schloss Hessen, near the town of Hamm in Westphalia, asking me to advise him upon the restoration of his garden, which had been much neglected during the years of exile from his native land that he and his father had suffered, on religious grounds. His father had been exiled by the Government of William I., the family being regarded as political Romanists and as wielding an influence antagonistic to the Lutheran dynasty. At this time they were living near Bournemouth. Here I first met my client and his wife, who were about to leave for Schloss Hessen, one of their nine ancestral homes. I made my arrangements to meet them, and a month later started with an assistant. Schloss Hessen is an old fortified domain situated in the centre of a very rich but otherwise uninteresting agricultural district on the banks of the sluggish river Lippo. The site of the residential part of the estate is triangular, being bounded on one side by the river and on the other two by a canal. The intake of the canal is some distance up the river, which provides power for a water-wheel where it reunites with it some distance below the Schloss. This island is approached by a bridge and quaint picturesque gate-houses, the drive passing through an enormous stable-yard arranged for five hundred horses, the maintenance of which was one of the conditions on which the barony was originally granted, along with accommodation for the stable-men and a military escort.

From the stable-court the house is approached through wrought-iron gates with handsome pillars, the spaciousness of the stabling giving a dwarfed appearance to the house, though the latter was not by any means small. With its mansard roof it was reminiscent of the French chateaux, and was, along with the stables, built of beautiful shallow hand-made bricks with stone dressings. The designer had evidently set his house in a garden in every way characteristic of the building, furnished with statuary, balustrades, triangular sundial, and a classical garden house, with a quaintly decorated dome ceiling. The whole of the garden was overgrown with weeds and rank growth. My work consisted of replanning it entirely and making a complete survey of the original work, my completed plans being more for a scheme for restoration than for a new design. These, along with suggestions for a few necessary additions to the house, such as those of a sanitary character, together with bathrooms, etc., we submitted in due course, and they were executed by the local builders and native

The Life and Work of An English Landscape Architect.

workmen. Before leaving Schloss Hessen my client asked me
to accompany him to one of his homes in his forests some sixty
miles distant. We left early in the morning and arrived after a
journey of about two and a half hours. Our purpose was to study
the approach and discuss possible additions to the house. What
attracted me most was the possibility of seeing a well-managed
German forest, and I was not disappointed—in fact, I had never
imagined that forestry lent itself to such scientific organisation.
Covering an extent of many thousands of acres, it was as accurately
laid out as the up-to-date modern city. Intersecting it was a
railway and a canal, and between the two was erected the extensive
estate saw mill, with light railways radiating from this centre in all
directions, thus providing cheap transit to the mill for each year's
cut. On a level site were laid out the forest nurseries, and
surrounding them was the foresters' village, with church and
school and every village amenity. I was shown the plans of the
entire forest, delineating each year's cut and each year's fresh
planting, and I was told that this plan had to be approved by the
Government Department of Forestry.

I left the Boeslager forest much impressed with the status
and importance of the forestry industry of Germany.

Thornton Manor, near Port Sunlight.—The Garden Forum.

CHAPTER XI.

I MEET MR. W. H. LEVER AND VISIT AMERICA.

THE years 1905 and 1906 were the most momentous in my career. In the first place, it was in the year 1905 that I first met my client and friend the late Lord Leverhulme. The manner of our meeting was both interesting and unique. It came about in this way:

I have already referred to the little church at Hest Bank, and it was my interest in this church and its adornment which brought about this life-long friendship.

I had designed for the church a carved folding screen to enclose a smaller space for the greater comfort of our sparse winter congregation. When thinking about ways and means for its execution, it occurred to me that I might induce members of Parliament, of both parties, whom I knew sufficiently well, to give their support. I succeeded admirably up to the last panel, and here the member on whom I relied to complete the scheme, a man of wealth and Free Church principles, failed me. He handed me ten shillings in such a manner that I prefer not to think about it.

As a last hope I wrote to Mr. Lever, whom I had never met, and upon whom I had not the slightest claim, excepting that we were both regarded as High Church Nonconformists. I pointed this out in writing, and enclosed a copy of my design for the screen, which evidently appealed to him. His reply was characteristic, and revealed that vein of humour for which he was so widely known, along with the kindly generosity which never lost a practical opportunity of helping forward worthy causes.

The Life and Work of An English Landscape Architect.

The letter was dated from Thornton Manor, Thornton Hough, Cheshire, and reads as follows :—

Dear Mr. Mawson,

I am very pleased to have the opportunity of sending you my cheque for the remaining carved panel in the screen of your beautiful village church, and wish you every success in your endeavours still further to improve its services.

Now that you have had the courage to ask me for a subscription, may I be so bold as to ask you to come and advise me upon the improvement of my garden at Thornton Manor? I have wanted to consult you for the last two years, but all my friends warned me that it would be useless, as you never worked for anyone holding less social rank than a Duke, whereas I am only a poor and indigent soap-maker. Let me know if you can come, and when, naming two or three alternative dates.   Yours faithfully,

WILLIAM HESKETH LEVER.

So began my association with Lord Leverhulme, of which I shall have much to say in this and following chapters. It was quite an unexpected reward for my interest in the work of our little church, and one which I certainly did not anticipate.

We fixed a mutually convenient date, and it was arranged that I should stay two days at Thornton Manor, a residence in the Elizabethan style, and even at that time of considerable extent, showing in its design perhaps a little too much emphasis on detail, a fault which has been eliminated by later extensions. My client had already initiated alterations reminiscent of the best work of the period. All this I took in at a sweep as I passed through the house to meet Mr. Lever, who was among his pictures in his palatial music-room. I was received with a smile and a hearty handshake, which put me at my ease at once.

William Hesketh Lever was, I quickly realised, a man of strong personality, who had absolute control of himself and all his interests, in which I include those interests which absorbed his few leisure hours. At this our first interview he struck me as a veritable Napoleon in his grasp of all the factors dominating any problem he tackled, in his walk and pose, and in his speech, which contained the concentrated essence of thought. There were all the characteristics which we associate with the " Little Corporal." After dinner we had a long walk backwards and forwards on the south front of the house, discussing industrial problems, politics, and certain aspects of sociology, in which I found he was deeply interested. Mrs. Lever was a perfect complement to her husband, quietly interested in all his wonderful projects, but not a little anxious to know when it would all come to an end, so that

Mr. W. H. Lever—and America.

they might be able to enjoy their home in peace. She was charmingly hospitable and careful for the comfort of her guests, and always shed the radiance of a truly gracious spirit over the household. Mr. and Mrs. Lever, though widely different in temperament, and probably because of this, were a most devoted couple. Seldom one left home without the other, even when the purpose was a purely business one.

On parting for the night, Mr. Lever said, with something of a twinkle in his eye, " I shall be out in the garden at a quarter-past six ; I hope this is not too early for you. I can give you an hour and a quarter, and we breakfast at half-past seven." I answered that this was quite convenient to me.

Prompt to the time he was there in riding attire, having just returned from the morning canter in which he always indulged after going through his private correspondence. I began to wonder how many hours' sleep he thought necessary. However, here he was with bundles of plans drawn out by himself, outlining great extensions to the gardens. He explained, however, that I must not allow myself to be too much influenced by these plans, as they were merely the work of an amateur. As the work of an amateur they were truly remarkable.

His scheme outlined a formal garden of heroic proportions, adapted to the changing levels of the site, and I have never met a man, layman or professional, who could reckon up so rapidly the amount of " cut and fill " required to form the levels he had planned. Mr. Lever also proved to have an intuitive faculty of visualising my emendations and alternative proposals to his scheme. I realised as never before how such men as Sir Peter Pindar, for instance, came to build such unique dwellings, characteristic of their personal selves, when they were no architects in the true sense of the word.

I found myself encouraged to give my views and criticisms quite freely, pointing out where the designs failed to take advantage of some notable feature in the landscape or in whatever way my experience suggested, with the result that by breakfast time we had arrived at the main outlines of a workable scheme. Thus began the professional connection with my best client, and a firm friendship which the passing years served only to cement more firmly. Some of the work resulting from this connection has been published in " The Art and Craft of Garden Making," and my other works on Landscape Architecture and Civic Art, as well as in my special

The Life and Work of An English Landscape Architect.

articles in "The Studio" and other publications. The plan, which will appear in my forthcoming book on Lord Leverhulme and his gardens, is interesting as the first which I prepared for Mr. Lever. The greater part of it was actually carried out.

About the time that this scheme for Mr. Lever was well launched, an American gentleman who was making a prolonged stay in the Lake District made a friendly call upon me. This was Mr. Theodore Marburg from Baltimore, later America's ambassador to Paris. With him I spent occasional evenings during a lovely summer memorable for its glowing sunsets, conversing upon scenes and topics dear to both. More than once, as we watched from the terrace of his hired mansion (the grounds to which, by the way, I had laid out several years before) the sun dip behind the majestic barrier of mountains at the head of Windermere, we were awed to silence. The spell which others than poets have felt in this district, was upon us. Personally, I admire those Americans who escape from the terrific rush which you feel immediately you land at New York, to make a prolonged stay in the Lake District, drinking deep of "its peace, its awe, its rapture." Instead of being a stretch of idleness, such an experience is a fount of inspiration to all who come under its spell. It imparts power and high tone to one's practical efforts.

My conversations with Mr. Marburg often took a practical shape. He was president of a civic league for beautifying and ennobling his native town of Baltimore, and I likewise had begun my studies in civic design, and had written essays upon it which I was later to incorporate in a book on the subject. We having so much in common, his departure for America left a distinct sense of loss, but shortly afterwards I received a letter from him telling me that a young friend of his, the direct heir to one of their colonial mansions and estates, situated at Green Spring Valley, Massachusetts, would make an appointment with me when over in England, to consult me about his gardens.

In due course I met and dined with Mr. and Mrs. Carroll Brown of Green Spring Valley, at Claridge's Hotel, London.

My new clients proved to be an interesting young couple, very much enamoured of the spirit of the English gardens, and anxious to reproduce some of the charms of these at their home. We arranged to spend the following day in touring part of Surrey and Kent, making Canterbury our objective, and inspecting private parks and gardens on the way. Such, however, was the speed at which we travelled in their 60-h.p. car that there was no opportunity of seeing anything except the road and the fleeting landscape on either side. Since then I have sat behind many reckless drivers in many countries, but this journey stands out in my memory as the champion hair-raising performance. The weather was fine and warm, and I enjoyed the run whenever I could manage to forget our danger. We got back to London, having done Surrey and Kent, in time for dinner, afterwards fixing up terms and time of sailing for America. Although I am a bad sailor, and always ill on the flimsiest pretext, the joys of the anticipation of this trip to the United States filled me with boundless pleasure. My eldest son, who had just completed his second year at the London School of Architecture, caught my enthusiasm, and finally persuaded me that he was essential to my success. Accordingly we took passage together.

We sailed by the Cedric on the 26th September, and after one of the stormiest voyages on record arrived at New York eight days later. We made many friends amongst the passengers, some of whom extended hospitality to us, and afterwards helped me in many ways in my later trips to Canada and the States. I had often heard of the liberal hospitality of the Americans, but my experience is that it surpasses anything one can imagine. Americans have indeed the will and genius for hospitality.

At this date the rising mass of "skyscrapers," now grown into a perfect mountain of masonry, gave a unique first impression of New York, especially by night, when outlined with myriads of electric lights. With insular British contempt I had regarded "skyscrapers" as monstrosities. I now began to see that they represented a new and necessary phase of construction, which possessed imaginative and scholarly potentialities. It is interesting to me to realise that so long ago I could cut adrift from English conceptions of art to the extent of studying new forms of architectural expression with an open mind.

After passing the customs officer I offered the man who had helped us a dollar, which he politely refused. "No, sir," said he; "you are now in the United States, where every man is paid for his job." So with a hearty good-day and a handshake he put us into a conveyance and directed the driver to an hotel.

The train journey to Baltimore, the divisional point at which we had to change and stay the night, was instructive. The note

The Life and Work of An English Landscape Architect.

of smartness and perfect organisation which had gripped me immediately we landed, and which had so impressed itself upon my mind, was again manifest in the planning and the outer architectural expression of the up-to-date hotel where we stayed. The decorations and furnishings sustained the note, as did the well-cooked and well-served dinner, and the absolute all-pervading cleanliness of everything. The details, such as pottery, glass, napery, and flowers, were in perfect accord.

After breakfast we caught an early train for Green Spring Valley, about twenty-five miles distant, a train journey of nearly two hours. Now we saw the picturesque New England aspect of America in contrast to its modern smartness. The train leisurely jogged along a sinuous course by the side of a river most of the way, the country being interspersed with abundant copses of trees and native shrubs. Here and there were little farmsteads and timber-built churches of the colonial neo-classic type. The native trees and shrubs were deeply interesting to us, seen as they were in the full splendour of their autumn glory. The American autumn has notes of harmony distinct from our English display, which struck home to me with pleasure, and made what would have otherwise been a tedious journey most instructive. It was one of those dreamy autumn days of the New England Indian summer such as we also enjoy on this side of the Atlantic during the later part of this season of mists and mellow fruitfulness. The American poets Longfellow and William Cullen Bryant have described this period of their year, and, in seeing it, I was able to enter into their sentiments and feelings as never before. Their seasons are more regular and follow one another with more precision than ours. Most of the meadows as we went along were bathed in a sea of silver mist, out of which rose the knolls and hillocks and lordly groups of gorgeous sumack, hickory, and red-leaved American oak, towering up magnificently, their tints fired with the glow of sunshine playing up against the dark-blue sky. They have an ample reserve of russet and sober grey-green in such trees as the sugar pine as a foil to the richer tints, and altogether I felt some compensation for missing in their autumn glory the Lakeland scenery, and that of the Trossachs, where my work had led me several autumns in succession.

At last we arrived at Brooklands station, where my client was waiting for us. Brooklandwood, his mansion in the Green Spring Valley, was about a mile and a half distant, and reached by

Mr. W. H. Lever—and America.

a deep-rutted, sandy road between a scrub of pine and hickory woods, all very picturesque, but not so well ordered as one would expect in the approach to a palatial residence built over two hundred years ago.

The site had been well chosen, and was situated on high, well-timbered ground overlooking the widest and richest part of the valley. The house itself was a fitting example of colonial Georgian architecture, built in a square block, with servants' quarters in a separate building. The orange and plum-coloured bricks, two inches thick, were, I was told, brought in olden times to the port of Baltimore as ballast, but how they were transported in those early days from Baltimore I never found out. The only explanation obtainable was that it had been a slave station, and therefore anything was possible.

There was the usual stoep, as the Dutch call it, or verandah, supported by long white columns. The roof of the verandah rose up two floors, finishing under the deep overhanging eaves, which latter were supported by beautifully carved acanthus consols or brackets, which gave a distinctly decorative note to the whole.

The views from the south front were varied and panoramic in breadth and extent. Looking at the house from the lawns, it had all the appearance of being embosomed in a richly timbered forest, the flanking trees behind being larger than any I have ever seen in America, except the sequoias of Vancouver. The distance from the house to the public road was about two hundred yards, and we decided to make a straight, dignified approach connecting them, with handsome wrought-iron gates, piers, and lodges, to mark the entrance. By the removal of a few trees it was possible to frame the view of the house and to obtain a ready-made avenue from the trees left standing on the lawns on either side of the drive. On the east side of this avenue the garage and stables were already built, forming a handsome block of buildings, and it was in the shelter of this block that I planned an enclosed garden in which the greenhouses and conservatories were to be erected. The extensive fruit and vegetable garden was on the west side of the house, and very irregular in shape. To give interest to this vegetable garden, as an alternative to the fruit trees, there were rows of specimen *Magnolia grandiflora* grown as standards, while hundreds of yards of rough espaliers were covered with American blackberry canes, which at the time were laden with luscious fruit.

The Life and Work of An English Landscape Architect.

The apples were not to be compared in flavour to our home-grown ones. I have since visited many American gardens, but I have yet to find one which can grow an apple equal to the Cox's orange pippin of my youth.

Between the house and the fruit and vegetable garden there was a deep gorge, with an abundant stream running through it, spreading out naturally at places into pools. On the south front the lawns lay in gentle undulations, but were otherwise barren and without interest, while the beautiful old house was devoid of any of the terracing for which it so insistently called.

We stayed three weeks with our clients, surveying, contouring, and planning out the whole garden scheme, which was completed in draft form and approved before we left. These plans we brought back with us, and prepared working drawings, details, and specifications for the whole.

My clients' home of Brooklandwood was the resort of the wealthier financiers and bankers, who together with their families and friends motored down from Baltimore on Sundays. In addition to their other hobbies the Browns were collectors of Chippendale and Sheraton furniture, and were proud of their collection.

Meeting Mr. and Mrs. Carroll Brown again in London the following Spring, I asked Mr. Lever's permission to show them his collection of pictures and furniture, which he readily granted. My clients were immediately and visibly impressed by the richness of the collection, and as we passed from room to room it could be seen that they had lost their pride in their own possessions. At last, when we had completed our round, Mr. Brown remarked with good humour: "There is just one note of completion which I could suggest. I think Mr. Lever should panel his doors with Romneys."

The intense interest of this trip to America was such that I felt determined to repeat it at no very distant date. It must be obvious that it is beneficial for a designer to get away from his drawing-board and desk for a time, and leave all the worry of his office for a spell. He comes back fresh, and tackles the problems from another angle, and I had felt this very much.

Shortly after my return from America I was introduced by Mrs. Chamberlain (sister-in-law of the famous Joseph) to another well-known American, Mr. J. J. Van Alen, who had purchased Rushton Hall in Northamptonshire, one of our best examples of

Mr. W. H. Lever—and America.

Jacobean architecture, where, in the triangular lodge adjoining it, the Gunpowder Plot was hatched. This lodge is in a good state of preservation. For many years previous to its purchase by Mr. Van Alen, the Hall had been allowed to fall into a deplorable state of disrepair; the gardens had fared worse, having practically disappeared. The terraces had all gone, probably during the " Capability Brown " period, and the lake which flooded the lower grounds was a mass of tangled alder and swamp vegetation.

." J. J.," as Mr. Van Alen was usually called by his friends, being one of those Americans who are obsessed with the beauty of mechanical perfection, was not the man to be the possessor of Rushton. Had I realised at the start that my client had really no feeling for Jacobean domestic architecture, or its equivalent in the garden, it would have saved me much loss and annoyance.

At my first interview with him I was asked to plan new gardens round the house, and to remodel the remainder in such a manner as I thought best. My first work was to reinstate the terraces which I was assured at one time ran along the two main fronts. The terraces were planned and approved, and instructions given to put the work in hand and to make as rapid progress as possible, so as to have them completed upon my client's return from America in six months' time. My experiences at Rushton were similar to those at Dalham. When we dug out the foundations for the terraces we came upon the footings of the original walls, and also found many pieces of balustrade, pier, and urn, which showed that our details followed the original somewhat closely.

Naturally I wished to build the new terraces in a manner to take on an appearance of age as quickly as possible. To secure this result I specified that the stonework should be left a little rougher on the face, and that occasional crevices be left, into which it was my intention to plant fumitory, chiranthus, rock roses, and campanulas, whilst the flags for the paths were self-faced and laid with occasional corners knocked off to allow of the introduction of thymes, toadflax, and lethospermum. The work was carried out very rapidly, and entirely to my satisfaction.

By the time my client returned the work was getting mellowed and weather-stained, promising in a year or two to be quite in keeping with the ancient Hall itself, which was what I desired. Mr. Van Alen, however, thought otherwise, and pointed to all the crevices and pockets as scamped work, for which he refused to pay, and a quantity surveyor was requisitioned from London,

The Life and Work of An English Landscape Architect.

the sort of man who spends his life calculating quantities for reinforced concrete, and of course he agreed that the stone ought to have been more neatly worked and all the joints should have been pointed in cement. In proof he pointed to the fact that the stone was rapidly becoming discoloured. As to the paths, I ought to have either had hard-sawn York flags laid on a bed of cement, or granolithic flags laid on sand with cement joints !

This unsympathetic disregard for the marks of time which the whole spirit of the place demanded caused me not only great disappointment, but a positive revulsion of feeling, so that my only wish was to run away and forget. This did not prove so easy as I imagined. " J. J." was determined to make me pay for what he regarded as bad workmanship. The matter was, by agreement, submitted to arbitration, and to my surprise the arbitrator was the surveyor, who thought in terms of cast-iron and granolithic ! Of course I lost, paid, and forgot as soon as I could. The experience was costly, but it was not without value. I have never since ventured to imitate old work without first being sure of my client. My garden scheme remains for the greater part intact as I left it, and I am not ashamed for the fact to be known.

One incident that occurred in connection with this work may be of interest to lovers of ghost stories.

When digging the foundations for the terraces on the south front, we came across what was probably a burial trench of the Battle of Naseby, which was fought close by, as we unearthed a number of skeletons. My brother, who was carrying out the work, saw the men throw out a skull. He took it home and had it on his office mantelpiece, set on a blue velvet cushion enclosed in a glass case. It had to be removed later and buried, because his imaginative office boy, with bated breath, declared that every morning when he opened the office, the skull took on flesh and grinned and danced in its frame.

My next client was Sir Walpole E. Greenwell, Bart., a typical city man, who, like many others, was also a keen sportsman and an enterprising and successful agriculturist. His country seat was at Marden Park, among the rolling pastoral scenes of Surrey so well described by Evelyn in his Diary. I have seldom seen more beautifully diversified park land, its hills and vales were so cleverly planted. This was, I understand, the work of Evelyn. The large house, however, was rather disappointing, not because of its position, size, and arrangement of block plan, which were

Mr. W. H. Lever—and America.

all good, but because of the introduction of aggressive red terracotta in the terrace balustrades on the south front.

However, the exercise of a little careful diplomacy resulted in my being allowed to introduce and include in my designs (this was a commission for plans only) stone instead of terracotta. The carriage turn was on the west front, and was approached by easy drives from north and south. Opposite the entrance the valley was rather narrow, the ground rising in one big fold with a grass glade on the central axis, with trees planted on either side of it. These trees rose far above the top of the folding ridge, giving a very picturesque effect from the entrance portico.

Owing to the direction of the valley, which runs north and south, the garden front to the south was necessarily very narrow, and there was no means of widening it. On the east side there were splendid opportunities for rising terraces, and of this I endeavoured to make the most, but it was a difficult proposition, taxing one's genius for design and practical planning to the utmost. There are many places where one doubts the wisdom of doing anything unless the house can be rebuilt, extended, or remodelled to fit the site. Far too many houses seem to bear but little relation to their sites. This criticism applies in a small degree to Marden Park.

My next client (to whom I was introduced by Mr. Lever) was Mr. Henry Gladstone, of Burton Manor, Neston, Cheshire. Henry was the second son of the great Liberal statesman, and was married to a daughter of Lord Rendell, who was a favourite with the G.O.M.

Burton Manor occupied a commanding site on the northern banks of the estuary of the River Dee, whence, looking across a wide stretch of sand, tidal river and saltings, one could just see Hawarden in the far distance. Henry was not directly concerned with politics, being more interested in his business as an East India merchant, and in his Cheshire property, particularly in his gardens, which the newly enlarged and entirely remodelled Manor House made essential. My commission was, like that for Mr. Walpole Greenwell, to prepare a design which could be carried out in annual instalments by the home staff. The scheme I subsequently prepared has been almost entirely realised.

Meanwhile my commissions for Mr. Lever were growing in number, interest, and importance, and now included gardens and terraces to Hall-i'-th'-Wood, Bolton, Lancashire, one of the most

The Life and Work of An English Landscape Architect.

famous examples of half-timbered mansions in the country. It had been thoroughly and reverently repaired and restored under the direction of Mr. Lever's architects, furnished in keeping with its period and traditions, and presented to his native town, where it is visited by large numbers of townsfolk and others interested in domestic architecture, furniture, and appointments. The garden space was small, but it demanded low balustraded walls and spreading steps, my designs for which were faithfully adhered to. There is no doubt that the restrained architectural treatment suggested by Mr. Lever was the right one to adopt, as it gave an immediate and harmonious setting to the whole.

Most people picture mid-Lancashire as a dreary congestion of mill towns overlapping one another with their multitudinous drab streets of houses built in unending sameness, wearying to a degree, as are most of the towns one could name in this portion of England. But few are aware that in the environment of several there are tracts of unspoiled moorland where the poorest citizens can repair with little or no expense, and enjoy to the full the invigorating sights and sounds of nature, and scan distances bathed in blue haze as clear almost as in Lakeland. As an added interest there is the glint and sparkle of tracts of water to enliven the views, for these moors provide catchment areas and storage reservoirs for the mill streams and indispensable dams of the cotton printers and bleachers. They are not by any means to be despised by the artist for their own sake. My friend the late Alfred East painted more than one Academy picture from the scenes I am about to describe. Not the least interesting are the characteristic old halls and manor houses which are to be found in these moorlands. There is sentiment to inspire poets, and romance for the novelist, to be gleaned in the history of some of these rambling many-gabled houses which intersperse this territory of rocks and heather, snugly roofed as they are with the characteristic old stone slates. The uplands are bleak enough, as may be judged by their bowed, bent, and broken trees, but on genial days they are delightful in their expansive breeziness, and they have a secret beauty of their own, just as Dartmoor and Exmoor have.

The sphere of my next and the most congenial commission entrusted to me by Mr. Lever was set in such scenes as these. On two sides of his native town of Bolton are vast stretches of moorland, from which it gains its old-fashioned name, Bolton-le-Moors.

Mr. W. H. Lever—and America.

A tract of land on the east side of this town, 400 acres of which were to be used as a park, and fifty acres for the garden of his private residence, known as Roynton Cottage, had been awarded to my client in an arbitration case with the Liverpool Corporation, and he proceeded to lay both out in the spacious manner that characterised all his undertakings.

The whole of the land in question lay on the western slopes of Rivington Pike, which rises to about 1,200 feet above sea level, reaching down to a chain of artificial lakes close upon three miles long, which supply Liverpool with water, his own private residence being on the higher slopes of the Pike, leaving the crest free to the public. The gardens to Roynton Cottage and Rivington Park were parts of one commission, and were to be laid out in perfect keeping with their natural environment. The park was to be made as free, as accessible, and as attractive to the townsmen of Bolton and to the public in general as possible, and the Roynton Gardens were for his private use.

In the first place, about twenty miles of good metalled roads were constructed to replace the former moorland tracks. Having arranged for these, we began our planning in earnest, there being a wonderful scope, such as is longed for by every client on the look-out for large ventures and big combinations. Both Mr. Lever and I felt that we had work that was congenial to us, and, unlike other clients I have mentioned, he never took alarm because my proposals appeared imaginative.

After providing access by suitable roads, most of which are now leafy avenues, the next question was shelter for the thousands of visitors. This problem solved itself, as there were two immense Saxon barns, picturesque externally, and with internal roof construction of the tithe-barn type, a pleasure to behold. These had previously been put into a thorough state of repair, and in part reconstructed in keeping with their original beam rafters and stonework, by Mr. Jonathan Simpson, my client's local architect, ample entrance porches and kitchens being added, where on fine days large numbers of the public are served with refreshments at moderate prices. If specially desired, visitors can be supplied with picnic meals, either under cover or in the open air, by their own caterers. Naturally this part forms the hub of the park, but a short distance away is the commodious, well-proportioned, and characteristic mansion of the former squires of the estate, known as Rivington Hall, which has been

The Life and Work of An English Landscape Architect.

converted into a Picture Gallery and Art Museum. Another interesting feature is provided by the paddocks, stocked with deer, buffaloes, emus, yak, and many other animals. But, after all, the chief interest was, and is, in the green fields and open spaces now intersected by wide tree-planted avenues, whilst large plantations of forest trees add interest to the landscape.

Roynton Cottage, the gem of the composition, was at first a wooden bungalow erection standing midway up the slope of the mountain, with fifty acres of barren and windswept land round it, without a tree or a shrub to give it homeliness. Thanks to the idiotic zeal of the suffragettes, the Cottage was burnt down, and while the loss of the treasures it contained was regrettable, good came out of evil in its replacement by a structure more worthy of and more in keeping with its unique surroundings. Among other things destroyed was a collection of samplers and needlework which South Kensington would have esteemed an acquisition, and the nucleus of a representative selection of pen-and-ink drawings by the foremost exponents of this art, such as Joseph Pennell, Hugh Thomson, Sydney Jones, and others. The building is now replaced by a stone structure sympathetically constructed with random coursed walling in conformity with the ancient Lancashire traditions, the flat roof of reinforced concrete giving little chance to the incendiary.

The new house bespoke a garden in keeping with it, and of all the gardens which have ministered to my professional enjoyment, none comes into competition with Roynton. The reason is a very human one. Everyone prophesied failure. All pointed to the tufts of bent and mountain fescue grass, the only growth to be found on the mountain side, and laughed at the notion of anything else growing. Some of them remembered that Scotch firs used to grow on the lower slopes, but that was when they were boys, and before there was so much smoke about. Undismayed by the pessimists, we laid out our nurseries and planted thousands of rhododendrons, including choice hybrids and many interesting species of Alpine varieties, along with Ghent Mollis and hybrid azaleas, kalmias, ledums, andromedas, ericas, dabacias, gaultherias, menziseas, vaccineums, and every other hardy peat-loving shrub, together with berberis, cotoneaster, hollies, and a host of other hardy trees and shrubs, many of which are rarely found in gardens. It was a bold enterprise, but we planted liberally, taking risks which in the event were abundantly justified—so much so that none of the

Mr. W. H. Lever—and America.

places I have planted for the same client in Cheshire, Hampstead, or the Isle of Lewis can bear comparison with this. Not only do Scotch and Austrian pines grow luxuriantly, but such difficult conifers as *Abies Kosterii* are growing better than in any garden or pinetum I know, and not only growing well, but colouring well, so that whilst the surrounding moors are as bare as ever, this enclosed fifty acres is the amazement of all who see it, and when they see it even the pessimists forget to croak.

The third extensive and interesting piece of work which I did for Sir William Lever (as he had now become) was the design and laying out of the gardens at " The Hill," Hampstead, to which I have already referred, which completed an ideally balanced trio of studies in landscape architecture. These were : (1) The gardens to a country house (Thornton Manor) ; (2) a mountain-side garden (Roynton Cottage) ; (3) a suburban garden (" The Hill," Hampstead).

In the last of these the difficulties were considerable, but the opportunities, as so often is the case, were correspondingly great. In view of his great love of panoramic views, it was not surprising that Sir William selected for his town house a part of Hampstead Heath overlooking the Common and leagues of open country centring upon Harrow-on-the-Hill, with the Welsh Harp gleaming in the middle distance, the whole framed in the foreground by enormous and exceptionally beautiful trees—beeches, horse-chestnuts, and elms. To look over this wonderful panorama from the terrace at " The Hill," one would never imagine there was a teeming population spread over the vast area visible, in part hidden away in slums, over which recurring groups of trees seemed to cast a foil. A difficulty presented itself in laying out the grounds from the manner in which part of Hampstead Common comes up to the boundaries of " The Hill " garden at a point somewhat popular with its habitués. The problem was how to hide this part of the Common so as to obtain a measure of privacy for the gardens, and at the same time to keep open the panorama without in any way introducing a jarring note to the view of " The Hill " from the Common. This we did by arranging a pergola the height of which was carefully fixed on the site. This entailed the raising of the ground at one place as much as twenty feet, necessitating thousands of loads of filling material. Ordinarily this would have been an almost impossible task in such a locality, but by the great good fortune which seems to follow some men's enterprises, the

The Life and Work of An English Landscape Architect.

Hampstead Tube Railway happened to be in course of construction at the time, and instead of Sir William having to pay for the filling required, he was actually paid a small fee per load for the tip. The accompanying Illus. Nos. 33 and 34 show the results attained.

Other work of considerable interest during this period was the remodelling of the Broomfield Park for the Southgate Urban District Council, which has remained our client ever since ; also Uplands, a very desirable property at Ben Rydding, for Alexander Walker ; The Shawms, Stafford, for H. J. Bostock ; Keffolds, Haslemere, for Commander Henderson ; Greenwoods Stock, for R. Adam Ellis ; and Ribby Hall, Kirkham, for W. Duckworth. These were all works of interest started during this period. Many of these clients still consult the firm, and most of them have, I am pleased to say, come to regard us as old friends.

Thus closed one of the most stirring periods of my practice. It was not an unqualified success. Work for two clients from which I expected much varied interest and profitable professional experience failed to mature. If the truth be told concerning the first of the two, it must be said that he considered that he had been neglected. When gardens are dismantled at the fall of the leaf in October, and for several weeks onward, it is scarcely possible to keep pace with the many calls from annual clients intent upon executing that piece of their whole scheme apportioned for the year, and with calls from new clients as well. All were anxious to get matters forward so that the planting might receive sufficient of the winter rain to tide it over the punishing spring droughts. In view of these calls I was compelled to try to pacify the first-named of the two, whose work would have been of a protracted nature, with a survey and preliminary sketch plan upon which to deliberate, since he had assured me he was not in a hurry. However, the elusive gentleman must have felt that he had been left in the lurch, and so he went off. Perhaps I would have fared better had I explained the whole situation to him—perhaps not ! It is useless to bother whether or no ! I have found in business that he who wastes time in vain regrets loses momentum.

The second of the two prospective clients had bought the bulk of the landed estates of a lord of the manor, minus the family mansion and gardens. This he wished to treat as a virgin site, according to his instructions to me, and I was asked to select the place for his residence, roughly plan its shape and limits for the architect, arrange the gardens for it, then fix sites for modern farmhouses (to replace the existent antiquated mudholes) equipped with up-to-date cow-houses and attendant buildings. After this I had to make provision for a farm bailiff's or steward's house (the tenant was to be estate agent for a few years), then gardeners' lodges, butlers' and artisans' houses, electric power-house and mill, together with the roads, fences, drainage, places for water reservoir and for sanitary disposal, and the other adjustments of a modern country squire's estate. I prepared this preliminary scheme and my report on it, dealing with both the ornamental and the utilitarian parts, showing the roads and drives required, the disposition of the buildings, and every other item, in a comprehensive way. Instead of calling in an architect and specialists to advise in each department, nothing was done beyond consultation and discussion. Had I been dealing with a client like the illustrious gentleman already mentioned in this chapter, the order would have been " full steam ahead," and I am afraid I was now spoiled for tardy ones.

About this time I received a communication from my manager to the effect that the fees on behalf of this new landed proprietor were mounting up inordinately, with a hint that it was time results began to mature. So I urged strenuously that the roads and the shelter plantations and other utilitarian plantations be proceeded with at once, requesting the gentleman's decision as to whether he wished certain of them to be for game and shooting. In any case, I urged him to order about a mile of rabbit-proof fencing, netting, posts, and wire, and begin operations. These plantations, together with the roads, would occupy him for a year, and give him time to grasp the responsibilities which his purchase entailed. First and foremost, I advised that he get hold of a capable specialist and make sure of an adequate water supply to tide him over all the seasons of drought. I am afraid that I appalled him with a sense of his new responsibilities.

To cut a long story short, we got so far as to send down one of my trained foremen, whom he purloined. The work was commenced in the ways I had indicated—but only commenced. Whether it was because of the spur of my manager, which led me to mention my fees, or whether my client resented my way of " educating father " up to the standard of responsibility laid upon him by the glory of his inheritance (or, rather, purchase, in his case), I know not : suffice it to say that the practical part of my

The Life and Work of An English Landscape Architect.

scheme came to an untimely end. I suspect it was the mention of my little bill, which after a little haggling we settled. I have never gleaned any definite information of this client since, nor have I had time to visit his estate, so I cannot say how his salvation (from himself) is being worked out.

So much for the newly fledged " squireen." On the other hand, if there is one person in this land of goodly homes that I have learned to admire, it is the country squire who has the heritage of several generations of paternal ancestors at his back, the man born of the family who have maintained the acme of perfection in house, grounds, and equipage, inside and out, for a hundred years or more. I know what this consistency of purpose means, and I have learned to distinguish those who can successfully attain it and maintain and live up to its traditions and the inculcation and preservation of the spirit of " each for all and all for each " throughout their little kingdom which is always so visibly marked, from those who have no such qualifications.

LOOK-OUT TOWER, ROYNTON COTTAGE.

CHAPTER XII.

A LEAN YEAR FOLLOWED BY PROSPERITY.

IN the year 1906 I was in some sense in good fortune similar to that of Lord Macaulay when rejected by the electors of Edinburgh. If I remember rightly, Macaulay, on his defeat, said it was his good fortune to be free to turn his mind to his long-cherished project of writing his history—as Rudyard Kipling would say, he had secured his independence. Now for my " history."

While this was the glad call of inner promptings, I am not so vain as to suggest that my contributions to literature are in any sense comparable to Macaulay's great classic, " that splendid fragment," as it has been called. Nevertheless, I was glad that a dearth of clients allowed me to make progress with my long-projected work on " Civic Art " as applied to the design and adornment of towns and cities.

My first intention had been to publish a companion volume to " The Art and Craft of Garden Making," dealing only with landscape architecture as applied to the development of park systems, the design of park and town gardens, children's playgrounds, and boulevards and avenues. Acting partly, however, on the advice of my publisher, Mr. Herbert Batsford, I decided to deal with other aspects of the æsthetics of town planning, the new social science which was just beginning to be recognised as the greatest factor in the development of our towns and cities.

It was a big project and a costly undertaking, for a book of this nature can seldom be made to pay its way, owing to the heavy cost of illustrating it, and its necessarily limited circulation. Town-planning books principally appeal to borough officials and a few architects interested in estate development, and landowners who have estates to develop. Town councillors seldom trouble with the literature of subjects relating to civic advancement. In America

The Life and Work of An English Landscape Architect.

and the Colonies there is a wider clientèle for books of this kind. In France the Government recognise the fact that expensive books of merit, technical or artistic, can be published only by granting subsidies, which usually take the form of the purchase of several hundred copies of the book for public libraries.

In a previous chapter I have spoken of the writing I did in the train. To this I now added drawing. The late Arthur Simpson, craftsman, of Kendal, made for me a handy and portable drawing-case with a fold-over lid, large enough to take half an Imperial sheet of drawing-paper. When closed, the case contained my mathematical instruments, scales, and small set-squares.

Thus provided, and generally alone in a first-class compartment, I would draw for hours, and was in this way able to relieve the tedium of travelling and prepare the rough drafts of plans and drawings which illustrate " Civic Art."

I have found this business of the writing of books invaluable in another way. It helps to clarify thought, and tends to give one breadth of view, and to restore that mental perspective which one is so apt to lose when daily and hourly distracted by the thousand and one puzzling technical details of practical work. The one task is preaching ; the other is living it out. Critical discernment, which is surely the most important factor required in the writing of a book, consists largely in bringing order out of chaos, and binding together the scattered elements by interesting links ; and so it is fortunate that, side by side with the theoretical work, came new openings for work for Sir William Lever during this year.

Constructional work at Thornton Manor was progressing, and opened up many new vistas for those improvements in progress which are so often suggested to the mind by the practical difficulties encountered, while the work at the Bungalow, Rivington, was much extended, many architectural features being erected, including an outlook tower and gatehouses (see Illus. No. 27). The glass-roofed pergola was also designed and carried out at this time.

Another outstanding figure amongst the more interesting clients of this year was Major Bolitho, of Hannaford, Ashburton, Devonshire. This gentleman is of a family which has done national service in many ways, and particularly in horticulture, having successfully formed several famous collections of shrubs and plants which others have found difficult to grow. My client's tastes

A Lean Year and After-prosperity.

were also architectural, but by no means was he pedantic in his preferences.

My commission at Hannaford was the designing of a formal lay-out for the terracing of the immediate surroundings of his new residence ; but while the scheme was formal in plan, the rough moss-grown granite of the walls, and the thousands of alpine plants inserted into them, gave to the whole an informal appearance as delightful as it was unique.

About the same time I also designed some interesting garden extensions at Maby Hall, Cheshire, for Mrs. Payne, and at Birch Grove House, East Grinstead, for Mrs. Macmillan.

If 1906 was a lean year, 1907 was a very full one, and one which not only brought many new clients, but also many new friends and much interesting work. Work now flowed into the office without any effort on my part. Clients first heard of me through friends for whom I had carried out work, or through my published works and contributions to the technical, horticultural, and architectural journals, and possibly in one or two instances through my lectures.

All this writing and lecturing was the outcome of my passion for creating an appreciation for landscape architecture, and I am afraid I often forgot the tax on my finances and physical and mental energy which this extra work entailed.

The first new client of the year was Mr. H. C. Moffatt, of Goodrich Court, Monmouth, a leading expert and writer of standard works on gold and silver plate. Mr. Moffatt was a nephew of Walter Morrison, of Malham Tarn, near Settle, Yorkshire, the millionaire philanthropist who so liberally assisted many worthy institutions. Having acquired on lease a very interesting old Tudor house, Codford Manor, Wiltshire, to which he was very much attached, my client, whose ambition was to restore the gardens to something of their original character and interest, called me in to assist him. Later I also helped him to plan out the site for a new house and gardens on his own estate. The house was built and the gardens were laid out, but I am afraid they only faintly resembled the plans and designs which I had prepared. Mr. Moffatt's charming after-dinner talks on organs, organ music, and organists so delighted me, however, that although I knew he would make mincemeat of my designs, I loved to meet him.

Following close upon Mr. Moffatt came Mr. George Douglas, the Chairman of the Bradford Dyers, who had acquired Farfield

The Life and Work of An English Landscape Architect.

House, near Bolton Abbey, a beautiful Georgian residence, probably the work of Carr of York. Unfortunately, whatever gardens had originally formed the setting of this noble house had almost entirely disappeared, except the massive gate piers illustrated in my book, " The Art and Craft of Garden Making."

The gardens as laid out to my designs are not extensive, but they are ample as an architectural framework for the house, and include a balustraded wall and many flagged paths, with garden courts on the north side of the house, along with rose gardens and extensive herbaceous borders. On the whole, and without any extravagant expenditure of money, a very charming garden was evolved, which rapidly improved as the stonework weathered and the formal hedges and herbaceous borders matured.

An important and somewhat unusual garden scheme was planned for Mr. R. S. Boden, of polo fame, who had just acquired Aston Lodge, near Derby. Aston Lodge is a very large house, simply designed in the later Georgian manner. This Mr. Boden put into a thorough state of repair, adding bathrooms and equipping the house with every modern convenience, and at the same time redecorating the entertaining rooms in accord with its period, the true character of which had been lost during previous ownerships. The new work was added with judgment and restraint.

Such a house demanded a garden scheme on a similar scale, but unfortunately the boundaries on the east side impinged irregularly on to the otherwise excellent and proportionate garden space on the south front, to a certain extent preventing this.

The gentle slope of this south front also demanded shallow, broad terraces, the upper one being balustraded in character with the style and period of the house. The second terrace was some sixty feet in width, and was laid out as a rose garden, with beds cut out of the grass. Below the terraces came a sloping lawn which led down to a large horsepond, which we converted into a water-lily pond with a fountain in the centre, contrived from a double tazza found on the estate. On the level land below this pond we laid out several tennis lawns, surrounded by yew hedges, which now give to this part of the garden a very quaint and ancient appearance. Between the lily pond and the eastern boundary there are a number of old elms, and near by, and extending above as far as the upper terraces, there was added an alpine rock garden. Aston Lodge emerged an ideal home for a busy manufacturer wishing to spend his leisure in garden pursuits.

A Lean Year and After-prosperity.

Early in the year I met, on one of my journeys to London, Colonel Leigh, of Leigh Hall, who told me he possessed one of the rare "Red Books" prepared by Humphrey Repton for one of the Colonel's ancestors about the year 1796. The book was illustrated by well-known sketches showing the landscape as it actually existed, and then the same pictures with movable slides showing the same views as it was proposed to alter them. Later in the year I was asked to advise in some improvements at Leigh Hall, where I was shown the "Red Book," and found it intensely interesting, especially when compared with the matured results. The preconceived accuracy of his forecasts heightened my respect for Repton, and confirmed my conviction that he was one of the truly great of my profession.

From Leigh Hall I travelled down to Cornwall on a visit to Place House, Fowey, the ancestral home of the Treffreys. This house had evidently been built in the period when Gothic was the prevalent style for both sacred and secular buildings, and occupied the site of a much older house. In the cellars there were the remains of very much older houses still, the doors therein being solid slabs of slate swung on huge wrought-iron hinges. The spirit of the place demanded that the gardens should be somewhat in accord with the character of the architecture, and that there should be a sense of seclusion and snugness within hedges. This was the more necessary from the fact that the site was a breezy hill perched more than a hundred feet above and overlooking the picturesque harbour of Fowey, with its ever-moving flotilla of fishing craft. Only a small part of my scheme was ever carried out, and from the first I realised that the trend of the gardening at Place House was altogether horticultural, a condition which, while I was in no way inclined to overlook or neglect it, should not, I felt, result in an entire neglect of the broader problems and possibilities of garden design and construction. A seaside garden on limestone is, of course, always a difficult problem, and demands a very careful selection of trees, shrubs, and plants, a department of my work in which I always took pleasure. The problems presented were unique.

About this time I had a letter from Mrs. Franklyn, of New Place, Botley, Hants, saying she wished me to advise her upon the lay-out of a garden there, where the house was being built for her son by Mr. Edwin Lutyens. "Surely, with Mr. Lutyens," I said, " you don't need anyone to design the gardens." "Well,

The Life and Work of An English Landscape Architect.

the fact is we wish you to do them, and Mr. Lutyens knows this and understands." Notwithstanding, I urged the claims of her architect, and his certain disappointment at having the work of the garden placed in other hands. Before accepting the commission I agreed with Mrs. Franklyn that I must see Mr. Lutyens and learn whether or not my collaboration would be agreeable to him. When I met him, in the kindest way possible he assured me that as he was not allowed to design the garden, there was no one he would rather co-operate with than me, and so I undertook the commission. But it was a mistake, for notwithstanding the encouragement of an appreciative client, I never felt happy in my work. Looking back, I am certain that Lutyens without me would have achieved a greater success; and, on the other hand, I am sure that I could have done a much finer garden had I been left entirely untrammelled. My partial failure resulted from my attempts to interpret Lutyens in the garden, he having one set of conventions and I another, a fact which is peculiar to us all.

My work at Hartpury House, beautifully situated on rising ground about three miles from Gloucester, for Mrs. Gordon Canning, differed in every respect from that at Botley. Here the house had been considerably enlarged and almost entirely remodelled to the designs of Mr. Guy Dawber, whose book on the architecture of the Cotswolds is so well known. The gardens, so far as they had been laid out, were designed by that well-known painter, Alfred Parsons, R.A. Although I had read about the work of the painter as landscape gardener, I had never seen the energies of a landscape artist directed to the construction of gardens. I had such a high regard for Alfred Parsons' work as a landscape painter and book illustrator, that perhaps I expected too much. However this may be, I have since come into contact with the work of artists and sculptors of unquestioned ability who have turned garden designers, but in almost every case I have been disappointed with the result. There are exceptions, as in the case of Nasmyth, who was a landscape painter before he became garden designer. I have a few of his original lithographs, and these of themselves show that his bent even as a painter and draughtsman was more in the direction of design and fancy than in copying Nature, as in most modern landscape painting. The inability of artists to realise the necessity, in gardens, for definite architectural motif and scholarly detail when working near the residence is most marked. Perhaps the reason is to be found in the lack of virility

GATES AT HARTPURY HOUSE, GLOUCESTER.

in English architecture, which has so profoundly failed to impress itself on the other arts.

The plantations by Mr. Alfred Parsons were well and artistically arranged. The rhododendron beds in particular were planted in large masses, rising out of a surrounding irregular carpet of choice ericas.

At Hartpury House the problem was to infuse a little form and order into the garden, and to bring it into character with the house, using in the walls, and as a base for the balustrades, the beautiful rag-stone which gives character to the architecture of Gloucester-shire. I also planned an extension to the gardens, in which we arranged for additional tennis lawns and herbaceous borders, while practically all the walls were utilised for alpine plants, which quickly gave to the terraces a wall-garden effect. The wrought-iron garden gate shown in the accompanying photograph (Illus. No. 28) was the work of Mrs. Ames Lyde, the lady blacksmith of Thornham, in Norfolk, from designs by my son.

I was first introduced to Mrs. Ames Lyde in Florence, where she had a palace with a beautiful garden, at which she spent half the year. The other half was spent on her Norfolk estate, mostly in her blacksmith's shop, where she trained village lads in the craft of the smith, which has become a thriving village industry.

When I first met her at her palace in Florence I commented upon the examples of Italian ironwork upon the garden walls, the garden gates and grilles of intricate design and workmanship, the wrought-iron fencing, and a host of other examples of ironwork, each a museum piece and a perfect specimen of its kind. " Don't you know I am the lady blacksmith ? " she remarked. Much abashed, I had to admit that I did not possess this knowledge, which was rather surprising. Later she carried out considerable work for me, of which the Hartpury gate is a fair specimen. It was a delight to see her in her workshop, or to spend an hour in her company discussing roses, which she grew to perfection.

Nearer home I was commissioned to extend the gardens at Bailrigg, Scotforth, near Lancaster, the principal home of Herbert Storey, J.P., D.L., one of the most generous of the sons of his generous father, Sir Thomas Storey, whose benefactions to his native town, especially in the gift of the Storey Institute, has made every Lancastrian his debtor. Originally the gardens at Bailrigg were laid out by my friend Mr. Ernest Milner in his well-known landscape manner. On the north, south, and east

The Life and Work of An English Landscape Architect.

fronts this treatment was excellent, but on the west or main front it appeared too weak for the æsthetic support of the elevation of the house, and as foreground for the panorama which included in its sweep Morecambe Bay and the distant Lakeland mountains. My work was almost entirely confined to this side of the garden. The Alpine plants inserted in the crevices of the walls have been most successful. The fact I remember with the greatest pleasure in relation to my friend and client, Mr. Storey, is his collaboration with me in good work for disabled Service men, of which I shall have occasion to speak in a later chapter.

About this time I was called to Lincoln to advise on a garden at Cross O'Cliff, on the south side of the city, for Arthur Newsum, Esq. I had already done work in Lincoln for Mr. Richardson, Mr. Newsum's brother-in-law. The site for the new residence was well chosen, occupying as it does an elevated plateau from whence at no great distance is seen the Cathedral projecting its towers into the sky in sunshine and shade. Surely this alone should be sufficient to give the tone or the keynote to any garden.

The new residence was practically completed when I first met my client, and its proportions and the contours of the surrounding ground were peculiarly good for a garden which should be both commensurate with the scale of the residence and yet so compact as to reduce the maintenance charges to a minimum. Although originally the site was practically without timber, the garden and small park are now furnished with vigorous young trees already sufficiently grown to impart to them a mature appearance. The garden is almost entirely formal, but nevertheless avoids that rigidly balanced lay-out which occasionally produces such distressing monotony, while the walls are in every instance either clothed with beautiful climbers or garnished with Alpines. A charming effect was obtained by planting avenues of John Downie crabs together with yew-bordered grass glades.

A very difficult but not entirely unsuccessful piece of work was the garden at Maesruddud, which stood in the centre of a rapidly developing colliery area not far from Newport, Monmouthshire. The very thought of collieries seems incompatible with gardens, but my client, Mr. T. Brewer-Williams, was himself a colliery proprietor, who considered it his duty to live in the neighbourhood and in the old family home with all its disadvantages, which were intensified by an elevated wind-swept site resting upon a poor clay soil. The original house, which possessed no architectural interest,

A Lean Year and After-prosperity.

was much enlarged and invested with a definite architectural character by my client's architect, Mr. Edward Warren. The plan of this garden, which is a fair criterion of my ideal of the nature and extent of a garden at this time, is illustrated in " The Art and Craft of Garden Making." The work was practically carried out as planned. As a garden it is successful, but having regard to its locality it is rather like a jewel stuck into a lump of lead.

Other clients sought my advice about this time, but the resulting work consisted largely of consultations on the arrangement of permanent shelter belts and planting for broad landscape effect, a department of my profession in which I took an intense interest. Unfortunately, few landed proprietors of to-day retain that passion for ornamental forest planting possessed by their ancestors of a hundred years ago.

This year my most important public work was for the Southport Corporation, for which I redesigned the Lord Street Gardens, the Marine Lake, Park, and Promenade. The Corporation was composed of a progressive body of men keenly interested in their town, and, what is somewhat rare in municipal authorities, they fully recognised the commercial value of beauty, and particularly the economic value of parks and gardens, and also the necessity for providing compensating attractions for the fast-receding sea. Such a feat required imagination and courage, both of which qualities they possessed to the full.

The pride of Southport is its fine boulevard known as Lord Street, which it was intended still further to improve by converting the deep garden courts to the houses on the east side into public gardens, and also by improving the gardens in front of the Town Hall and Cambridge Hall. My designs for these improvements are well known, and promise to be realised in full.

Lord Street is one of the most amazing studies I have ever undertaken. Its fame as a boulevard is universally admitted; but in what does its beauty consist? It is level from end to end, a fact which in other towns would be regarded as monotonous. There is not in its length any commanding building of real architectural merit. It is certain that the majority of them were not designed by an architect, many of them being distinctly commonplace. In what, then, does its beauty consist? I think the answer is in its length in proportion to its width, which is not interrupted by curves or breaks, but maintained in such a cohesive manner as to yield a decidedly impressive street perspective.

The Life and Work of An English Landscape Architect.

This perspective is maintained by the alignment and sky-line of the architecture, the asperities of which are softened by the avenues of trees. To this is added the life and movement of a constant stream of motor-cars and street trams, whilst a kaleidoscope of colour is given to the whole by the gaily attired crowds who frequent the street. It is an extraordinarily popular shopping centre for the many who visit the town.

Three notes are absent which just make Lord Street fall short of the perfect boulevard. It needs terminal architectural features to mark at both ends the focal point, and a perpendicular note in the centre. To supply this last feature, my collaborator, Mr. Mallows, and I designed a campanile clock tower, which we hope may one day be presented to the town by some patriotic citizen.

In September of this year my eldest son, who had already spent two years at the Architectural Association School in London, and two years in the office of a well-known London architect, took up his studies at the Ecole des Beaux Arts, Paris. Here it may possibly be interesting to know the reason of my preference for the French schools of architecture. It was based upon the conviction that in this country the training was grounded on wrong principles as a preparation for the practice of landscape architecture, by which I mean that young architects were taught everything except design, and were submerged in details long before they had learnt the elementary principles of composition. Imagination, instead of being encouraged, was suppressed. Instead of receiving instruction in axial planning, which was one of the fundamentals of the Georgian period, the aspiring architect was taught to regard the quaint eccentricities and irregularities of mediæval architecture as ideals to be followed, and instead of the relation of a residence to its site and environment being studied, the plan of the house was often evolved round certain predetermined details. In short, while in the French schools the student was taught to progress from small-scale compositions towards enlarged details, the English student was taught first to draw details which later were to be fitted into an expanded scheme. I am not criticising the English method of training; I merely say that landscape architects and town planners cannot be trained in that way. Since this time the English methods of teaching architecture have undergone great improvement, and now approximate to those in vogue in the ateliers of Paris.

PALACE OF PEACE.—VIEW FROM ENTRANCE.

CHAPTER XIII.

A YEAR OF EFFORT AND ACHIEVEMENT.

BY July of the year 1908 I had no fewer than twenty substantial new commissions.

By this time we were thoroughly well organised in our Lancaster office, ever since regarded as the head office and workshop of the firm. Here we had a staff at this time of about twenty-five senior and junior assistants, while the staff in London consisted of three only. This meant that the London office was used mainly as an address and call office, and as a convenient centre from which to control work in the southern and western counties.

An interesting addition to the staff, a man who has since made headway in Canada, was Mr. Howard Grubb, son of Edward Grubb, the Quaker editor. His manner of coming was unusual. Late in 1907 I had a letter from a Mr. Howard Grubb, a student of the School of Landscape Architecture at the Cornell University, U.S.A., saying he very much wished to come into my office. It was a very usual request, and I replied that while I congratulated the writer upon his evident enthusiasm for his profession, I advised him not to leave America, where I was sure the openings for advancement were better and more numerous than in this country. Notwithstanding this advice, three months later, when I had forgotten my correspondent's name, I had a wire from Liverpool notifying me of his arrival, and a few hours later he was announced at the office. When the visitor was shown into my private room I turned to look at him. He was an exceptionally tall, upstanding young fellow, and proportionate in build.

"My name is Grubb," he said.

"Well, what can I do for you?"

"I have come to work for you."

"I am sorry to disappoint you, but it is quite impossible. As you will see for yourself, every seat in the office is occupied."

The Life and Work of An English Landscape Architect.

" Well, sir, I have travelled all the way from America for the purpose of working for you ; so you must find me a seat somewhere."

" But, my dear fellow, I simply cannot do it."

" Listen to me, sir. I worked my way back from America on a cattle boat, so that I might have the honour of working for you, and so you simply must take me on."

What could I do in a case like this ? It would be wrong not to give such audacious youth its chance. Within two years Grubb was in charge of my London office.

Late one afternoon we were working overtime together, when I recollected that I was down to second Mr. Lutyens' vote of thanks to Miss Dunnington, a rising lady landscape gardener, who was lecturing to the members of the Architectural Association. " Close down quick, Grubb," I said, " and come along to hear Miss Dunnington lecture on garden design." Grubb was evidently interested, and made an excellent contribution to the discussion which followed the lecture. Afterwards I introduced Miss Dunnington to Grubb, and one morning three months later I received a letter from each of them, telling me of their engagement, and holding me responsible if the marriage did not turn out a success. The firm of Dunnington-Grubb is now the leading firm of landscape architects in Canada, and although we correspond fairly regularly, they have never asked me to meet any liability !

This may seem a digression, but reference to these two names raises a question often asked : " How can you possibly travel thirty thousand miles a year consulting with all sorts of people on a wide variety of problems, and yet do any actual designing ? " I have already in part anticipated this question by explaining how I built up my practice and trained my assistants, who gradually acquired the ways of their " chief," whose rapid sketches were often prepared on the site, in company with the assistant responsible for the working drawings. The " chief " attracts other men in sympathy with his ideals, who rapidly acquire the art of interpretation, so that eventually a score of assistants may be employed in working out important schemes from small-scale studies and suggestions. On the same principle that the patron of a French atelier directs by criticism the studies of his students, the expert directs to definite ends the development of his original sketches. This method gives wide discretion in detail to the

A Year of Effort.

imaginative assistant, and it has always been my policy to develop imagination and to direct it into practical channels.

Much the same may be said of the foremen who carry out the work on the ground. If they are men of insight, they acquire by experience various ideas for adapting the scheme to the levels of the site, and novel ways of effectively weaving in excrescences, rocks, groups of shrubs, and a hundred other things met with in the process of carrying out my schemes. These methods are not gained by memorising anything done here or done there previously. That is undesirable in landscape work, where there is all the variety which Nature is ever spreading before us, with which to deal. Every scheme or every difficulty differs from the last, and therefore those assistants and foremen who work by rote are of no use. Ideas and imagination are the desiderata, and these have to be brought forth quickly.

Looking back on this year and its work, I regard the period under review as one of the most interesting in my career. The work of 1908 is responsible for a greater number of illustrations in my published books than that of any other two years combined. First there was the work which I carried out for Her Majesty Queen Alexandra at Hvidöre, Copenhagen, work which came to me on the introduction of Mr. Samuel (now Lord) Waring. Shortly after this I was invited to accept an appointment as the British representative in the limited international competition for the gardens surrounding the Palace of Peace at The Hague. This was an exciting experience, and one which aroused my enthusiasm to the utmost. Naturally, I was soon on my way to The Hague, accompanied by my eldest son. Our first duty was to report ourselves to the British Ambassador, Sir Henry Howard, who received us with every kindness, spending nearly an hour in showing us his collection of pewter and explaining to us its history. Finally he gave us tea and wished us the best of luck, giving us the impression that the old sportsman was really anxious for his countrymen to win.

The next morning we made our way to the Buiterust Palace, the site of the Palace of Peace, and there met the resident architect, Mr. Van der Steur, and Mr. Cordonnier, the French architect whose designs were selected in the competition for the Palace buildings. We began at once to supplement the survey and contours supplied us, by a survey of all the old timber trees on the site. This took about a week. We then returned home, completing

L

The Life and Work of An English Landscape Architect.

our designs within the time allowed. This scheme included not only the lay-out of the gardens and terraces, but a little town planning in Scheveningen Avenue opposite the main entrance.

The scheme was duly despatched. I received the accompanying letter from Sir Henry Howard, notifying me of the result of the competition :—

BRITISH LEGATION,
THE HAGUE.

July 23/08

Dear Mr Mawson

Allow me to congratulate you on having won the competition for the plan of the gardens of the Peace Palace at the Hague. I am so delighted that you did so, and I hear that you won in a canter, as the designs of your competitors were immeasurably inferior, with which verdict I entirely agree, as I was shown the three designs the other day.

Yours very truly,
Henry Howard

This was my first intimation of our success. The next letter that I received was from Mr. De Wilde, the Belgian competitor. Mr. De Wilde congratulated me on the result, and asked me to give him a criticism of his designs. I found his plan so good that the assessor must have had some difficulty in making his award. I had no hesitation in giving him the criticism he asked for and congratulating him upon his scheme.

Very shortly after this I was requested to meet the Committee of the Peace Palace, over which Mr. Karnebeck, father of the Minister of Finance, and himself an ex-Minister, presided. The members of the Committee were a most capable body of men, conscientious in the exercise of their responsibilities, and before I was allowed to proceed with the work I was asked to present a carefully studied analysis of the cost. This was a task of some magnitude, and proved a most useful study, under conditions which were entirely new in almost every respect. In the first place, the soil was almost pure sand, into which had to be incorporated peat soil brought from a distance. The water level, which was publicly controlled, was only two feet below the surface over a large section of the ground; and, lastly, the varieties of trees and shrubs which could be relied on to flourish under these conditions were limited and different from those we usually planted in any of our home gardens.

Had I realised these difficulties in the first instance, I think my designs would have been different, and this fact I communicated to the Committee, who permitted me to present a revised set of plans along with my estimates. The result was that, as finally laid out, the garden, which I regard as one of our most successful efforts, bears but little correspondence to the designs which won the competition.

This work took two years to complete, entailing many pleasant visits to The Hague, where I made numerous friends. My son, who had just completed his studies in Paris, took active charge of the work on the ground in its early stages, but later it was in the hands of my Quaker pupil, Mr. Howard Grubb, and was finally completed under the direction of Mr. Norman Dixon.

The last time I saw Mr. and Mrs. Carnegie was at the opening of the Palace of Peace, which was a magnificent function, performed by the Queen of the Netherlands in the presence of a great concourse of foreign ambassadors and other distinguished personages. I received many congratulations upon our work, which I must admit

The Life and Work of An English Landscape Architect.

looked exceedingly well even at this early stage, and the effect has increased year by year as the trees and shrubs have assumed shape or been trimmed to the original designs. Incidentally, a study of the brickwork of the Palace during the period of construction was quite an education, for this work is probably the best example of the bricklayer's craft I have seen, and of a quality seldom equalled even by ancient examples. The revised scheme was one of the first works in which my son took an active interest with me, and much of its success has resulted from this collaboration.

Although our neighbours across the Channel are so clever and spacious in their designs (for French design is nothing if not heroic), there are certain Frenchmen who long for that homely charm which, wherever seen, we associate with our own native land. Some people contend that this elusive quality is more an instinct or passion of the soul than a phase of design. Whatever it is, when once experienced it will brook no substitute. Wherever seen, whether in the trim country cot in its garden (Wordsworth even goes so far as to give it its own sky) or in connection with our stately homes, it sheds its halo upon everything and lifts life's trivial round on to its own plane. It is my lode-star, and has been so ever since my youth, more or less ever since the essays of Price, Repton, Knight, and Shenstone inspired me. I am still pursuing the quest. I cannot say that I have attained the goal, but I am still following.

This much by way of introduction to my next client, M. Lazare Weiller, a Parisian banker and financier recommended to me by my friend Mr. Waring. This gentleman wished to find a house and garden in France with homely charms, and asked me to go with him and advise him in his inspection of several places mentioned to him by his friends and by the professional land agents. Together we visited remote parts of rural France and saw many delightful old places, but all were inconveniently situated for a man deeply immersed in business, so at last it was decided that his country home must be within an hour and a half's motor run from Paris, and Anglevillière, a small choice estate near Chatenay, was purchased.

There was no residence on the property of the dimensions my client desired, but there was a moderate sized villa, evidently intended as a dower house. There was evidence on the estate that a very important lay-out had been contemplated and actually started, and in searching the archives of the villa we unearthed some interesting plans by Le Notre, the French master of landscape architecture. In this plan there was a system of radiating avenues with a long central canal. This latter feature had been partly completed and flooded, and we adopted it as the main axis of our scheme. We had the privilege of co-operating with Mr. Weiller's Paris architect, and were able to draw a type of plan for the residence which took in every favourable vista which Le Notre's scheme sought to emphasise. The result is fairly indicated in the plan reprinted in my book, " The Art and Craft of Garden Making."

The soil with which we had to deal was quite different from that at The Hague. Not only the family of rhododendrons and other varieties of what are usually classed as American plants, but many choice flowering shrubs, and also the finest tea roses, succeeded admirably, so there was no lack of variety in this garden.

For Sir William Jaffray, son of the founder and proprietor of the " Birmingham Daily Post," I planned and laid out gardens at Skilts, near Redditch. Then there was dear old John Lancaster, a great coal magnate and the owner of considerable property at Dunchurch, near Rugby, on which he built a large residence designed by Mr. Gilbert Fraser, of Liverpool, and to which I added extensive terraces and gardens, these being realised almost in their entirety. Mr. Lancaster was a great invalid, who could move only a few steps with difficulty, but he was a courageous man, who, notwithstanding his disabilities, took the keenest interest in the development of his property. It was John Lancaster's father of whom it is said that he kept a pair of clogs in a glass case on his drawing-room mantelpiece to remind him of his early struggles as a collier, and to prove to all and sundry that he was the proud conqueror over early untoward circumstances.

Not far away, near Oxford, I met two other clients—Mr. Whitnell of Kidlington, and Mr. J. Heywood Lonsdale of Poundon. At Poundon Mr. Lonsdale had just built himself a house designed in the spacious Georgian manner and in the beautiful yellow sandstone of the district. Mrs. Heywood Lonsdale was a daughter of Lord Valencia, and had an innate love of pictorial gardening and garden design, whilst Mr. Heywood Londsale's preferences were for a garden furnished with vigorous masses of grand foliage summer and winter, with a leaning towards broad landscape effects. So between the two I had every

The Life and Work of An English Landscape Architect.

encouragement to realise one of those schemes composed of broadly outlined effects, yet inset with a series of beautiful incidents. This garden is, notwithstanding, very compact and easily worked.

Mr. Whitnell's home had been a farm-house, with picturesque gables and simple details. The garden was small—just the place for a young couple with refined tastes and fond of gardening. It was to satisfy these conditions that this garden was planned on quite formal lines, and on a very modest scale, so as to be within the capacity of a single-handed gardener with the energies of his employers thrown in. Such houses and gardens will be increasingly in demand, whilst the number of palatial houses and gardens will in all probability decrease. Moreover, the small garden becomes more personal, and consequently more lovable.

This year I met Mrs. Gerard Leigh, who had just leased Lees Court, Faversham, in Kent, from Lord Sondes. Lees Court is a stately old house, and one of the best known examples of the work of Inigo Jones. On my first visit I had a curious experience, for which I am entirely unable to account, because I knew nothing of the history of the place or its noble owners.

I arrived just in time for dinner, which was served in one of the smaller rooms, which, with the kitchen and a few bedrooms, was reserved for the use of my clients, the remainder of the house being in the hands of builders and decorators. Before retiring, my client informed me that my room was known as the Cedar Room, and was located in the oldest part of the house. This was reached by the original staircase, which had been retained when Inigo Jones added the main new block. The room was panelled from floor to ceiling, and had a fine old Tudor mantelpiece decorated with carriage and strap work. My four-poster bedstead and the furniture were in keeping, and suited my temperament and mood, being adapted to the repose of a tired artist. In bed I dozed uneasily instead of going to sleep. About midnight I had what I imagined must have been a rather horrid nightmare, for I saw in the corner of the room a desperate fight between two young men. The sight was so terrible that I still remember almost every feature of the struggle. The stronger and older of the young fellows, and the one who was gaining the mastery, was about twenty-five years of age, thick-set, rather under average height, with short, black curly hair, a broad square forehead, a face rather short for its width, and a pointed chin. His clothes were unusual in cut and material—a short blue jacket, dingy brown waistcoat, and green knickers. The other man, of whom I saw less, was much younger, and had light curly hair, and a round face which normally must have been pleasant to look upon, but was now marked by terror : he was getting the worst of the fight. At last the fighters were lost in a blue mist, and I went to sleep ; but on waking I still felt something of the horror of my dream.

In the morning I was met in the hall by my hostess, who asked if I had had a good night. I told her of my disturbed dream, when, to my amazement, she said, " You must have seen the historical murder which actually happened in this part of the house, the murderer being executed at Canterbury ! " If this was more than a dream, the explanation is possibly that the conditions in the room were precisely the same as on the night of the murder, the result being that I got " the positive " of the negative recorded. Yet I don't know, as our knowledge of these things is very elementary. It was an interesting experience.

The ground round the old house was very bald and uninteresting, there being no indication of the former gardens illustrated in old prints, except the orangery and the fruit and vegetable garden. The first improvement which I suggested was a big sunk garden on the south front to give elevation to this side of the house, and a substantial reason for a balustraded wall. This sunk garden extended for the full width of the house and for a corresponding length outwards, and was enclosed by double yew hedges with a wide glade between, divided by a wide central walk and long herbaceous borders on either side. The central sunk lawn was adorned by long criss-cross panels, each panel consisting of several beds, each bed planted with a separate variety of roses in harmonious shades and essential contrasts. The terminal point of the vista so created was marked by an arrangement of blocks of yew, supporting fountain basins and a central pedestal, raised by steps on a platform, an arrangement as effective as it was unusual.

At Lees Court I met many enthusiastic garden-lovers, including Lady Algernon Gordon Lennox, whose gardens in the Isle of Capri are among the best known of modern Italian examples.

The landscape architect is constantly engaged upon schemes leagues apart, and under totally different conditions of climate, soil, and local tradition, and one of his chief difficulties is to divest the mind of the influences of the last place visited, and to prepare

The Life and Work of An English Landscape Architect.

it for the reception of the problems of the next one to be dealt with. This is all the more so when the architect is given to enthusiasm and absorption in his work. This detachment of mind was largely induced by the literary work and drawing by which I relieved the tedium of long railway journeys. I also endeavoured, as far as was possible, to alternate my visits with those to other work of a very exceptional character. Thus, for instance, I would visit Grasmere, where I was developing a hillside garden for Mr. William Hoyle, a partner of Barlow, Jones and Hoyle, cotton manufacturers, of Bolton, which gave me all the change and contrast I needed. On another occasion I would take a trip to Perthshire, where I was designing gardens for three members of the Pullar family; or I might change my programme and visit the work I was carrying out for J. Pyman, Esq., at Penarth, or for his partner, Sir Thomas M. Watson, Bart., for whom I designed a garden at Newport, Mon., and a building estate at Maindee.

During the year I carried out many smaller garden schemes, some being extensions to and others remodelling existing gardens. These included plans for the garden at The Cliff, Warwick, for Sir Henry Lakin; terraces and other improvements at Rodborough Court, Stroud, for Sir Alfred Apperley; work at Gerrards Cross for Mrs. Moseley; at Edgemount, Stafford, for the Rev. A. Talbot; and at Sutton Coldfield for Mr. Tonks.

Not often does a new client introduce himself to you in your own office, but one morning at 28, Conduit Street a card was handed to me bearing the name of Mr. Humphrey Ward, who, on being shown to my room, told me that his wife was very fond of her garden, and wished to consult me at Stocks, their home near Tring. I had met Mrs. Ward's father, Matthew Arnold, at the residence of Mrs. Ward's sister at Ambleside. Mr. Ward proved a very pleasant caller, whom I now recognised as " The Times " art critic, and for this reason, coupled with my profound admiration for the writer of " Robert Elsmere," I was a little nervous; but I need have had no fear, for never have I had more appreciative clients. Mrs. Humphrey Ward in particular was most interested, and although many of the improvements which I desired could not be carried out, owing to prohibitive cost, within restricted limits most of my plans were realised. These included a new carriage court and a rose garden. Mrs. Humphrey Ward in many ways reminded me of her father. I found her a soulful person, who permeated her surroundings with her graciousness, a splendid conversationalist, demanding concentrated attention whether her talk was of politics, religion, or social reforms, and every utterance seemed to have serious purpose behind it.

The topic which always interested her most was her work at a London social centre to which she gave much time and interest. Having regard to her family traditions, I was rather surprised to find her attitude towards Liberalism to be one of profound distrust and dislike, leading her to write political pamphlets which must have given considerable disappointment to many of her admirers. Such, however, was her personal magnetism that it was almost impossible not to fall under her spell and agree with her conclusions, even though these were contrary to every political tenet one had ever held. To meet and talk with a celebrity of such outstanding serious mental power was in itself a liberalising experience. The facts that I had worked at Ambleside for Miss Arnold, her aunt, and that I was by adoption a Lakelander, proved very helpful, for Mrs. Humphrey Ward was deeply learned in the traditions, social life, and dialect of Westmorland, a circumstance amply demonstrated by " David Grieve," written, I believe, at Levens Hall, Kendal.

In the summer of 1910 my wife and I joined the organised tour arranged under the auspices of the National Housing and Town-Planning Association by its then secretary, Henry R. Aldridge. Our objective was Vienna, where the most notable town-planning conference in modern times had been convened. About sixty British delegates attended, but the full representation of all countries amounted to the total of some thirteen hundred. The trip was splendidly managed from start to finish, and the programme was carried out without a hitch.

Outward bound we spent a night at Salzburg, the town which has witnessed so many vicissitudes of war. The Miriabello Gardens, in their location, design, and maintenance, are perhaps the most perfect examples of town gardening I have ever seen.

Reaching Vienna, a city of great beauty and cleanliness, we proceeded to the Hotel Metropole, where quarters had been chartered for about half the British delegates. This was a most convenient centre for our rambles round the city. Arriving late in the afternoon, and although travel-tired, we went out to view the beautiful town gardens, including the famous Elizabeth Garden and the Prater, afterwards going to the opera, a large number of seats having been reserved for the delegates. Nothing could surpass the hospitality

The Life and Work of An English Landscape Architect.

of the Municipality and the Government, the sumptuous dinner given to us on the evening after our arrival at the Rathhaus being an example of perfect organisation for the comfort of their guests. I have attended many notable public dinners in London, New York, Ottawa, Athens, and other towns and cities, but none of these was so perfectly arranged as was this one at Vienna. Had the dinner been part of a great military pageant it could not have been more carefully organised or carried out with greater precision.

The banqueting hall is of immense size, lighted at both sides by deep Gothic traceried windows, filled with beautiful heraldic glass devices. At one end, on this occasion, there was a stage which at a height of about eight feet occupied the entire width of the hall. A military orchestral band took possession of this. At one side of the hall, and in about the centre, was a raised dais richly draped in coloured velvets and gold. To this dais marched, with stately step between uniformed supporters, to the strains of the Austrian National Anthem, a military looking gentleman. This richly apparelled officer mounted the dais and saluted the audience. Then followed grace by a church dignitary, after which the gaily attired personage took his seat, which was the signal for the guests to be seated.

The officer occupying the raised dais was the director of ceremonies, directing the band, the waiters, and the somewhat elaborate toast list. Nothing was done without his direction.

The spacious kitchens were placed behind the stage, and the huge space under the platform was used as a service room. At a given moment about twelve doors under the front of the stage flew open, and waiters about twenty deep emerged in such order as to give one the impression that the whole had been carefully rehearsed under the direction of the same master of ceremonies. Each man knew exactly where his place was and how many guests he was required to serve, and the entire movements of the waiters were so perfectly ordered that the return to the serving room was done without haste and without confusion. No doubt this perfect ordering expanded the generosity of the diners, when, after dessert, they were given an opportunity of remembering the waiters.

The work of the conference went without a hitch, and the greatest goodwill obtained on all sides. Herr Eberstadt, from Berlin, indulged in an eloquent speech, his subject being the good ship " Friendship," which had brought to Vienna a rich argosy of goodwill and contentment, destroying rivalry and encouraging competitive effort in seeking the greatest good for the greatest number. I often wondered during the war how far its spirit was genuine, or whether it was a clever piece of bluff.

It was curious to note the attitude of the English delegates during the conference. When big town-planning problems were mentioned they showed little interest, but when garden cities and housing were under discussion they were all alert and took the lead. That our delegates were obsessed with this aspect of their subject, to the neglect of others, was amusingly illustrated by one of our party who in an outburst of enthusiasm declared that he hoped to live to see London rebuilt on the basis of twelve houses to the acre! Fortunately, we have learned to take a wider conception of our responsibilities as town planners, and our study of Vienna, with its wonderful avenues and gardens and its splendid buildings, did much to enlarge our vision. What impressed us most, however, was the bold enterprise of the Municipality in securing wide belts of land for park reserves outside the city limits, and especially on the higher ground. That this was a popular move was amply proved by the crowds who during the hot season sought the open breeze-swept spaces and leafy shades.

On our return journey we spent a week-end in Dresden, and saw that city in holiday attire, and very gay and attractive it was. From a landscape architect's point of view I have never seen another city that impressed me so much. Perhaps this admiration was in part created by the railway station, a building in which expert engineering and fine architecture, set in a beautiful garden, gay with many-coloured, sweet-scented lilacs, conspires to give the right " first impression " to one entering the place for the first time. The avenues and boulevards of Dresden are also planted and maintained with greater skill than those in any other city I have ever seen. Dresden will ever remain in my memory as a lovable city of sweet-smelling lilacs.

The imperial capital Berlin was next exhibited to us from every effective point of view by its city planners and leading architects, and nothing was left undone that would impress us with its greatness. It certainly appealed to us as a city of wealth and efficiency, and in many ways as a beautiful city, but it is coldly grandiose and ornate. Its Siéges Allée, notwithstanding the mediocre nature of some of its statuary, and its Charlottenburg Strasse, are impressive and grand. The last is a rose walk of such interminable length that it palls long before it is traversed,

The Life and Work of An English Landscape Architect.

though as a great processional military road it is doubtless splendid. Probably the claims of imperial military display dictated its width and arrangement.

Somehow I am afraid that, notwithstanding every desire to appear grateful for all the efforts made to entertain us, I had failed to show the necessary number of thrills, because after dinner Dr. and Mrs. Haeggiman, both well-known exponents of civic art, called at our hotel and invited Mrs. Mawson and me to see Berlin by night. " We ought to explain," said Mrs. Haeggiman, " that we feel you are not properly impressed with our capital, but we are sure that if you see it by electric light you will say it is truly wonderful." We readily accepted the invitation, and for over two hours drove and walked from one interesting point to another, and I must admit that the enthusiasm of Dr. and Mrs. Haeggiman did much to modify our earlier conclusions, for Berlin by night is truly remarkable.

Hamburg I had previously visited, and as a town planner studied very carefully its more important improvements, and the excellent but autocratic method of acquiring areas for demolition and reorganisation and their reapportionment among the original property owners. We learned whilst in Hamburg that this drastic method of destroying and cutting up other people's property has proved profitable to all concerned. This was our own impression, for slum areas had given place to high-class business quarters. This was the special or legal aspect of town planning which we had put down for study, and a very helpful study it proved.

From Hamburg we returned home *via* the Hook of Holland and Harwich, the whole trip, with all its splendid opportunities for extensive study of the many-sided aspects of town planning, having been accomplished in a little over three weeks.

Reviewing the work of the year, which included many schemes in progress mentioned in previous chapters, I wonder how I managed to control so many varied interests to the satisfaction of my clients. The answer is that my clients were extremely considerate, and that I received far more assistance from my staff than I at the time imagined. One point, however, is quite clear : I was learning quickly to visualise landscape effects and to grasp the potentialities of the sites I visited.

HOME OF THE OLMSTEADS AT BROOKLINE, MASSACHUSETTS.

CHAPTER XIV.

HARD WORK RELIEVED BY A TRIP TO AMERICA.

ON my return from Vienna I found a letter from Mr. S. J. Waring saying that he had just returned from Hvidöre, Copenhagen, the Danish home of Queen Alexandra and of her sister the Dowager Czarina of Russia. Following upon Her Majesty's request he had recommended me to replan the Royal gardens. This necessitated a visit to the Danish capital, which, with its Amelienberg Platz, its beautiful squares and streets, and its many noble buildings, left a decided impression upon my mind. I consider Copenhagen one of the most interesting capitals that I have ever visited. Its people seemed to me to be vigorous mentally and physically, and to carry about with them an air of refinement and prosperity.

Hvidöre is a residence of moderate size, situated on an elevated terrace, rising some eleven feet above a public road, which divides the gardens into two separate parts, the upper part occupied by the residence and terraces, and the lower part running down to the sea-shore. The two sections are joined by a subway, necessitating a large number of steps. It was the lower half of the garden which we remodelled, a plot of some two acres in extent, and the task was as interesting as the opportunity was unusual.

The ground had an almost regular gradient seawards, and the soil was the deep sandy loam so favourable to flowers, but the stunted and leaning trees denoted that the wind must be combated. Accordingly we divided one garden into three simple straightforward lateral parts, each being a long herbaceous and panel rose garden, protecting all with trellis and hedges. The existing walls we hid with a plenteous profusion of interesting climbers and flowers. The whole when finished was just a snug floral paradise. A year later my son designed a two-storeyed tower to overlook this garden and command the views seaward. The

The Life and Work of An English Landscape Architect.

first part had evidently met with the approval of our Royal clients, for whom we felt it a great honour to work.

In the late summer of this year we planned a garden for Harold de Boyd of Kilfillan, Berkhamsted, a property situated on the high ground west of the town. It was desirable that there be one or two distinctive features to pronounce a base line along the side of this hill. This was secured by a pergola of unusual design, which is illustrated in " The Art and Craft of Garden Making." By this I do not mean that it was flambuoyant, to use a common expression. Matured designers turn from this order, or at the most use it very seldom. In truth, it was the climbers which gave the pergola its crowning glory. Architects have much to say, and rightly so, about smothering the beauties of their architecture with climbers, but these have a lawful province on houses and their accessory buildings, they filling up seeming voids and breaking up the persistency of lateral lines and angular asperities.

During this year, although a busy one, I did not carry out quite so much public work as usual. Notwithstanding, one or two small town-planning schemes were of sufficient interest to warrant notice. The first of these was a small improvement scheme planned for the Padiham Urban District Council,—a scheme, by the way, which was prepared in advance to provide work for the unemployed. in any possible period of great distress.

Padiham is a small and usually very prosperous cotton-manufacturing town of some 13,000 inhabitants, eight miles from Blackburn on the London Midland and Scottish Railway. It has a railway station which for meanness, inadequacy, and faulty location is hard to beat. It is one of the most depressing ports of arrival I know. The station looks directly on to the least desirable part of the town, although, on exploration, one finds that Padiham contains many quaint and picturesque features, including a fine modern town hall. The town is situated on a river which divides the site into an upper and a lower level. Flat cinder-strewn land prevails from the railway westwards to the river, and across the river steep grass-grown embankments (or brows, as they are locally called) lead up to the higher points of the town. It was this stretch of land extending from the railway to the top of the brow that I was asked to plan, partly as a recreational ground and a riverside park, and partly for building development. The opportunity was exceptional, permitting a treatment which, if the railway company saw its way to co-operate, would secure for Padiham a beautiful approach to the town·from the railway station, whilst travellers passing through would gain a fine impression of a town which in the meantime is æsthetically mean and uninteresting.

About a quarter of a mile down the river measured from the old bridge the water is spanned by the railway bridge, and from this point up to the old bridge the fall is so little that it would be possible, by erecting a dam between the piers of the railway bridge, to form a stretch for boating which would be almost unique in this part of Lancashire. Between the town and the railway bridge it was proposed to erect a footbridge giving access to the brow on the opposite side, which in turn was to be connected by graded paths up the brow, which we were prepared to afforest with suitable native trees and undergrowths. By this development residents on the tableland would gain a more pleasant and more direct connection with the railway station. As most of the land dealt with in my plans was already controlled or owned by the town, this scheme could be carried out very economically, and to the great benefit of the whole community. Indeed, I believe the results to be obtained, compared with the cost, would be so great that I gave several pictorial illustrations of my proposals in the fervent hope that some day a benefactor to the town might adopt the scheme and carry it through to a successful completion.

Another piece of promising town-planning work was at Nelson, a Lancashire cotton town which seems to have grown in the interests of the speculative builders of the more respectable sort. The property which I planned is known as Haw Lea, a private estate with a commodious mansion standing almost in the centre of the site, such as one usually associates with the Victorian cotton magnate—large, square, very comfortable, and eminently respectable.

This residence, with its gardens and sheltering trees, and a ravine, were retained as the central note, the remainder of the land being developed as a garden village, or, rather, garden suburb, with provision for houses of all degrees of size and importance. Nowhere were these to be more than eight to the acre, but ranging to sites of an acre or more. The character of the property, most of which was high land with rolling undulations, gave an interest to the scheme, and so suggested a delightful place of residence for those to whom amenity means so much. There is, however, from

The Life and Work of An English Landscape Architect.

the town planner's point of view, this drawback to nearly every town planning and development scheme : We have in such a scheme a plan and policy evolved in advance of actual needs, which for economic reasons can be realised only as and when the demand becomes insistent and need for action is imperative, and therefore the architect seldom lives to see the realisation of his dreams.

"The Art and Craft of Garden Making" met with a ready sale in America, where my publishers are the house of Charles Scribners Sons, who have been the American agents for all my later publications. This work led to an extensive and extremely interesting correspondence, securing me many friendships which personal acquaintance has ripened into permanence.

Some of my correspondents were professors of landscape architecture at those universities where the subject is an established department ; others were keen horticulturists ; others, architects interested in landscape design and the literature of the subject. This wide correspondence gradually crystallised into an invitation to take up a lecture tour in America. This idea was focussed by Mr. Robert Anderson Pope, a young and able landscape architect with offices in Fifth Avenue, New York, who had heard me lecture in England.

Mr. Pope undertook the duty of organising my tour, which commenced at the end of October and extended for six weeks.

For months every spare moment was devoted to the preparation of my lectures. The slides entailed much photographing, which was very ably undertaken for me by my secretary and manager, Mr. James Crossland. My subjects were divided into lectures on Landscape Architecture and Civic Art. The syllabus was as follows :—

LECTURES ON LANDSCAPE ARCHITECTURE.

(1) The Principles and Practice of Landscape Architecture.
(2) Gardens which were Builded and Gardens which were Planted. A description of ancient forms of gardenage, with modern examples wherein ancient principles have been adopted.
(3) Italian Gardens and the Gardens of the Renaissance.
(4) The Charm of the English Garden, with examples.
(5) The Charm of the English Village, with special reference to recent Model Garden Cities.
(6) A description of the Gardens of the Peace Palace (Carnegie Foundation) at The Hague.

Hard Work Relieved by a Trip to America.

LECTURES ON CIVIC ART.

(1) **City Planning.** Ideals and first principles in City Building.
(2) The Civic Survey and the collection of data upon which to base a City Plan.
(3) Street Planning, with special reference to traffic problems, incidental to manufacturing, commercial, and residential areas.
(4) Park Systems, including civic centres, town gardens, playgrounds, public parks, reservations, and boulevards.
(5) The Equipment of Streets, Parks and Gardens, and Promenades, for utility and adornment.
(6) Model Suburbs and Villages and Housing of the Industrial Classes.

The object of this arrangement was to induce important centres to arrange for a course of six lectures which were planned to cover in the round the whole field of the subject dealt with.

I left Liverpool on the 26th September, 1910, by White Star s.s. Celtic, the boat having a full complement of passengers, including many illustrious and well-known people. The voyage was ideal, the weather being perfect, and very soon friendships were formed and confidences exchanged.

At our table were four passengers, including a silent lady, and conversation covered many topics. At dinner on the second day the lady spoke, and in doing so startled us. In a beautiful voice she said, " Gentlemen, I have been listening to you for two days discussing things which don't matter anyway ; as we are to travel together for another five days, don't you think we might discuss matters of vital importance, as, for instance, the relations between capital and labour ? "

For the rest of the journey I sat and listened. The case for labour was championed by the lady, and the case for capital by the passenger opposite to me, who was an ironmaster with hundreds of employees. Never have I heard an argument so long, so tenaciously maintained, or one which was conducted in better academic form or with such understanding and forbearance. But the lady won. She was Mrs. Finch, one of America's best known educationists, a barrister-at-law, and at that time a recognised leader of intellectual socialism.

On this and succeeding visits to America I always lectured at the school organised and established by her, at which daughters of American millionaires sit at the feet of a militant but eminently sane socialist.

For a year past I had been working hard at " Civic Art," which was in the printer's hands, and I decided to devote the week on board to a final correction of the proofs. I was doubtful about

M

The Life and Work of An English Landscape Architect.

the wisdom of publishing this work, as friends who made great claims to literary criticism had advised me not to proceed, or, if I did, to eliminate the first five chapters, my critical friends asserting that they were too imaginative to be of any practical service. On board I realised Mrs. Finch's critical ability and her practical interest in the subject in hand. I therefore asked her to read through my proofs and to give me a frank and candid criticism. She devoted about three days' close reading to my proofs, at the end of which her verdict was : " I am not conversant with the strict technique of the last seven chapters, but I am confident that the first five will sell the book in America. They are the best exposition of practical idealism I have ever read." This declaration gave me heart, and I am assured the suggestive sales in America and in this country have proved the truth of it.

The idea underlying the book was to set forth the claims of landscape architecture applied to cities. Notwithstanding a somewhat cool reception by one or two of the professional journals, the reviews were on the whole very encouraging. The three following extracts may be taken as typical of the remainder :—

EXTRACTS FROM PRESS NOTICES.

" Nothing but praise . . . can be accorded to the boldness with which Mr. Thomas Mawson meets—and sometimes solves—the complicated problems of town planning."—*The Spectator.*

" Mr. Mawson possesses to a remarkable extent the power of visualising his ideas, and to do this is due to much of his success in garden architecture. When he applies himself to work on a larger scale, such as he deals with in the present volume, the advantage of the gift is inestimable."—*The Studio.*

" In a crown folio volume of some 350 pages, handsomely and strongly found in buckram, he has given us a book fully worthy to rank with his well-known and highly esteemed volume on ' The Art and Craft of Garden Making.' "— *The Liverpool Post.*

On arrival in New York I was met by Mr. Pope, who told me that my first lecture was to be given the following day, and that I had only a few hours in which to make all final arrangements for my tour. I was to begin at Harvard, where I was to give two lectures before the students in the School of Landscape Architecture. One of the lectures was to be given at 10-30 the next morning, and the second one at 8 in the evening.

I arrived at Boston late that evening and went straight to an hotel, where Mr. Fred Law Olmstead, the Eliot Professor of Landscape Architecture at Harvard, met me at ten next morning.

Hard Work Relieved by a Trip to America.

I had long corresponded with Mr. Olmstead and his brother John, for whose attainments and traditions I had a profound regard. It was therefore a delight to meet a man so eminent in the art, and to be introduced by him to Professors Pray and Hubbard, and the students of the School of Landscape Architecture at Harvard. That Professor Olmstead was popular with both students and tutors was very evident ; and I do not wonder, for his is one of those rare personalities which carry with them an atmosphere of enthusiasm for whatever they espouse. In addition to a vast fund of practical experience, he combines great power of clarified expression and the direct initiative qualities which are always dear to the student.

In my lecture I spoke of the art and craft of garden making as practised in England, illustrated by many slides showing how we collect our data, prepare our studies, and finally present our designs and working drawings, and then presented photographs of the results attained—principally, though not entirely, by examples of my own work. I do not know whether the lecture was a good one or not, but I do remember the eager faces of my youthful audience as I passed from point to point, and the shower of congratulations at the end of my lecture, when I was assured of a big crowd for the evening.

Never before did I experience the thrill of being able to influence a body of keen, intelligent, and enthusiastic young men and women who were to be the future leaders of a great and lovable art.

After the lecture Professor Olmstead motored me to his home at Brookline, where his famous father had established himself many years before. The group of picturesque buildings which comprised the house, offices, and laboratory suggested the history and growth of the firm. The house itself was very much in its original form, but the offices comprised many extensions to meet the ever-growing staff, imparting to the whole an aspect of straggling picturesqueness, the charm of which was heightened by its setting in a rural example of suburban gardening.

To an Englishman used to rapid transport facilities and nearness to a railway terminus, Brookline seemed rather remote ; but as a matter of fact the firm of Olmstead is so firmly established that the location of its working centre does not greatly matter. There must, however, be certain advantages attaching to Boston, of which Brookline is a suburb, seeing that it is rapidly becoming

The Life and Work of An English Landscape Architect.

the acknowledged centre for landscape architects, of whom there are a large number in practice in the town and neighbourhood.

On arrival at this notable home I was at once introduced to Mrs. Olmstead, the mother of Mr. Fred Law Olmstead, and also to the wife of the aforesaid gentleman. Mr. John Law Olmstead also gave me a warm welcome and made me feel quite at home. The American people overwhelm one with kindness. They possess the gift of entertaining to a remarkable degree. There is a charm of spontaneity and naturalness about their hospitality.

After my introduction to the several members of the family I was shown round the offices, which, notwithstanding their straggling arrangement, proved to be most orderly and convenient. Indeed I soon realised that in the matter of office organisation we in England have much to learn. Also their survey and contour work, which formed the basis of every plan, was done with a thoroughness seldom attempted at home. The method of preparing the plans by regular stages, ending with the work of the men who take out the quantities for the trees and shrubs required, all carefully noted on the plans, was a revelation to me.

The filing of records of executed works and "progress photographs." was reduced to an up-to-date card system. The records of expenditure upon all the work passing through the office were tabulated with a thoroughness which I was quick to praise. But I think that Mr. Olmstead's rejoinder was right when he explained that whilst they in America paid more attention to the business side of their practice than we did in England, we in this country paid greater heed to design and the originality of ideas. When I came to think the matter over I realised that we had in our landscape foremen men who were able to interpret our designs, and therefore we did not need to detail the work to the point of saying where, when, and how the last flowering shrub should be planted ; whereas in America, with work at such vast distances from headquarters, plans and drawings must be foolproof. Nevertheless, I learnt from the Olmsteads many valuable lessons for application on my return to England.

The luncheon party was a very happy one, set in a room of classic proportions, opening upon a gently undulating shrub-planted lawn. The furniture and the appointments of the room and table showed both quaintness and refinement, but I was soon too much absorbed in Mrs. Olmstead, senior, to pursue any other investigation.

Hard Work Relieved by a Trip to America.

A remarkable little figure, quaintly dressed, she seemed to have carried down the ages the quiet refinement of the Puritan maiden with the vivaciousness of the times. She was the widow of America's greatest exponent of landscape architecture, the true helpmeet, aider and abetter of her husband's enterprises ; having herself played an important rôle in political and artistic circles, she was evidently proud of her distinction. Very soon Mrs. Olmstead and I were engaged in animated discussions and descriptions and impressions of things English and American, and I soon discovered that her interests were world-wide, and that she had in particular a very intimate knowledge of England and France.

When I left England there was a sensation in the newspapers owing to the feared sequestration of the communion plate of the Church of the pilgrim fathers, who, if I remember rightly, originally came from Camberwell. The church had got into financial difficulties, and sought relief by converting its historic plate into cash at one of the London salerooms. A few wealthy men, English and American, had purchased and restored it to the church under a trust deed which would make it impossible for the same thing to happen again. This news I told Mrs. Olmstead, thinking it would interest her, but I found she was decidedly incredulous as to the accuracy of my story. " No, Mr. Mawson, your story is wrong somewhere," said the old lady, nodding her head, with its quaint head-dress. I protested that my story must be correct, because our home newspapers had been full of it. " Still," she protested, " I think you are wrong. Where did you say these pilgrim fathers came from ? " " Camberwell," I replied. " When did these pilgrim fathers come from Camberwell to America ? " " In 1632," I replied. " There ! " she exclaimed exultantly, raising her finger at me ; " I knew you were wrong. We came over in 1622 ; and remember, Mr. Mawson, there is a world of difference between us who arrived in 1622 and those who did not arrive until ten years later." It was quite evident that America's aristocracy was founded in 1622, and that Mrs. Olmstead was of the elect. I was quite delighted to find a dominant English line of ancestry in America, and my hostess appeals to me even now as one of its most delightful and distinguished members.

After tea—dispensed, I am sure, for my special benefit—we motored back to Harvard, my host pointing out to me on the way

The Life and Work of An English Landscape Architect.

certain features of Boston's famous park system. Arriving at the University, we found that a great reception was taking place in the hall in which I had lectured in the morning, and a crowd of students waiting to conduct me to a hall in Cambridge, where it had been decided that the evening lecture should be given. Very much to my astonishment, when the time arrived for the lecture to begin, the hall was nearly filled. How the students had managed to get me such an audience together in so short a time I didn't know ; but it was evident that they had mastered the art of rapid publicity. My subject was " The Charm of the English Garden." My depiction of the qualities of our home gardens, and my fine series of slides, were evidently greatly appreciated.

After another night spent in Boston I returned to New York to prepare for three lectures which had been arranged for me in an old American city a few days later. This was my best engagement. It represented a remuneration of 300 dollars, an aspect of my tour which, unfortunately, I could not afford to ignore. On arriving in New York, however, I found waiting for me a letter from the secretary of one of the societies before which I had arranged to lecture, informing me that his society had, for the purpose of my lectures, amalgamated with the other two societies, and therefore they would not require me to give the separate lecture as arranged. The next morning I received another letter from the secretary of one of the other societies informing me that the three secretaries had concluded that one lecture with an assured audience would be more agreeable to me than three smaller audiences, and therefore they would require me to give one lecture only. The secretaries had, however, arranged for my hotel, and proposed to invite me to dine with the committees and friends of the three clubs which I would address. The result was that I lectured to an audience of 700, each one of whom, I was informed, had paid a dollar for admission. Out of this I was paid my 100 dollars, which covered my expenses, but little more. A good bargain for the three societies, but not a very good one for me.

I would not have minded had they provided a good lecture hall. The one in which I spoke was the worst in which I have ever addressed an audience. The conditions taxed both the strength of the lecturer and the patience of the audience. At the close of the lecture questions were invited, and much criticism was indulged in.

In my lecture I had shown some beautiful slides of a number

Hard Work Relieved by a Trip to America.

of walls planted with Alpines and ferns. These took my audience by surprise, and they were quite certain that no such effect could be obtained over there, and that I was wrong in advising such treatment in America. Fortunately, one of their most famous architects, Mr. Frank Miles Day, was present, and in a short and pointed address supported my contention. He remarked that in laying out a garden some few years before he had followed the suggestions contained in " The Art and Craft of Garden Making," and reached results in every way equal to those shown on my slides, and said that whoever doubted his statement was at liberty to see the garden for himself. I was never so pleased to have a supporter, for my audience treated me rather severely. Some of the questioners reminded me of a dear old lady who attended a course of lectures I delivered a little later before the Royal Horticultural Society. At the close of the last lecture she said : " Mr. Mawson, may I ask you a question ? I am awfully worried about my gooseberries ; how would you advise me to plant and train them ? I have attended all your lectures, hoping you would tell us."

My next lectures were delivered before the School of Landscape Architecture at the Cornell University, at this time under the direction of Professor Bryant Fleming, a landscape architect of good repute.

The Cornell Campus is built amidst noble scenery, occupying a high tableland with steep bluffs, reminiscent to me of Martin's famous picture, " The Plains of Heaven." On this tableland, which runs into hundreds of acres, are grouped the University buildings, none of them particularly striking as architectural units, but together forming an impressive and extensive group to which new departments are being added from time to time. I was met on arrival by Professor Bailey, the Dean of the Faculty of Agriculture, and Professor Fleming ; and I was introduced by Professor Bailey to the largest class in landscape architecture I have ever met. This class was a fine body of students, male and female, who followed every word and every slide with the closest interest. Somehow I am always at my ease when addressing young folks, between whom and me there is immediate good-fellowship. After the first lecture I spent about two hours in the drafting-room criticising the work of the students.

Before undertaking the duty of inspection, and remembering my experiences in another city, I asked the students what they desired of me—whether they wanted me to say complimentary

The Life and Work of An English Landscape Architect.

things, or whether they really wanted me to help them. At once there was a chorus of voices calling, " Help, sir ; help ! " After this we had a very happy, and I hope a very helpful, time together.

Then I had an introduction which gave me very great pleasure, for no less a personage than Mr. Andrew D. White, the distinguished Ambassador to Germany and Russia, and the first President of Cornell University,* invited the Dean, the Professor, and me to tea at his house on the Campus. The interesting topic of conversation that evening centred round the work and influence of Goldwin Smith, for whom Mr. White had a great admiration, an admiration that seemed to be fed and fostered by a close personal friendship.

It was quite evident that Mr. White regarded England's loss of a first-class brain like that of Goldwin Smith as something approaching a calamity ; and yet he did not seem to think that America's gain (which he said was undoubted) was quite on a parallel with our loss, for, as he expressed it, " Goldwin Smith has come to America rather too late in life to be able to take advantage of the full flow of life and energy which surrounds him."

Since the above was written I have received the following interesting communication from my old friend, William Hill, who was editor of " The Tribune " during that Liberal organ's brief and chequered career.

Goldwin Smith was an eminent Oxford man who died in 1910. " He formed in his youth lasting liberal opinions on religious and political questions," and he attacked clerical ascendancy in the University. He was an effective writer at one time in the " Saturday Review," member of the Royal Commission on Education, 1858 ; Regius Professor of Modern History at Oxford, 1858-66 ; engaged on political agitation and pamphleteering, in which he defined his distrust of Imperialism and was denounced by Disraeli as a mischievous propagandist. In the late sixties he resolved upon prolonged residence in America, and became Professor of History at the newly founded Cornell University. He resented American hostility to England in 1869-70, and Disraeli's attack on him as "a social parasite" in " Lothair." He made a tour in Canada in 1870, settled in Toronto in 1871, and, marrying the widow of Henry Boulton of The Grange, took up his residence there for life. He then wrote on the daily, weekly, and monthly press of Canada, America, and England. He frequently intervened later on in the public life of England, and stoutly opposed Gladstone's Home Rule Bills, and opposed the South African War. Despite the unpopularity of his political and religious views in Canada, he won much

* Mr. White was the first President of Cornell University, 1866-1885, and after his retirement he continued to live in the President's house until his death in November, 1918, at the age of 86. He was the American Minister to Germany, 1879-81 ; Minister to Russia, 1892-94 ; and Ambassador to Germany, 1897-1902.

Dr. Andrew Dickson White, First President of Cornell University.

Hard Work Relieved by a Trip to America.

affectionate respect there for his enlightened activity on educational matters, by his advocacy of purity in public life, and by his philanthropy and public charity. He laid the foundation of the Goldwin Smith Hall at Cornell in 1904 (when he was President of the American Historical Association), and he bequeathed the residue of his large fortune to Cornell for the promotion of liberal studies.

I greatly enjoyed my visit to Cornell University, for Mr. White proved a brilliant talker and scholar, deeply interested in European politics and educational movements. He was locally known and revered as the father and patron of Cornell, and looked every inch a patron of the arts and sciences.

After tea our host took us to an organ recital in the college chapel, which was filled to overflowing. I do not recollect the name of the organist, but I remember his brilliant performance on an excellent instrument, and how impressed I was by Andrew White's interest in the music. From here we went to one of the University fraternity houses presided over by Professor Bailey, but run on democratic lines by an elected committee drawn from the thirty boarders. I was delighted with the atmosphere of good-fellowship which seemed to pervade the whole establishment, and the excellent way in which it was run.

My evening lecture on " The Italian Garden " was given in a large hall to a big audience, contingents coming from the other departments of the University.

From Cornell I returned to New York, where I gave three lectures before the School of Architecture at Columbia University. To these lectures the general public were admitted. The lectures attracted very good audiences, and were evidently appreciated, seeing that at each subsequent visit to America I was asked to lecture there again.

After the day in New York I had to give an evening lecture before an influential and flourishing society in Hartford, Conn., which city, my agent assured me, could be reached with half an hour to spare by taking the 5-26 train. I was informed that the train attendant would find me a compartment wherein to change for the evening lecture, and that I could dine on the train. Perhaps I got into the wrong train. Be this as it may, instead of the accommodation promised, the train in which I travelled was more like an English workman's train, but much less clean, and altogether unlike the Pullman-car express which I expected. The result was that I arrived dinnerless half an hour late, and, what was even more galling, tealess also.

The Life and Work of An English Landscape Architect.

The secretary was waiting at the station with a car, and in five minutes we were at the hall, where a great audience, many in evening dress, had been patiently waiting for me. Notwithstanding, they gave me a good reception. I took the opportunity of allaying their reasonable annoyance at my late arrival, and in such a plight. I prefaced my lecture by a short explanation, ending with : "Now I am sure you are generous enough to understand and forgive, but the dinner is a personal matter which I cannot forget." After that there was complete understanding, and the lecture was one of the most satisfactory that I have delivered in America. After the meeting the hospitality of the Hartford Club was extended to me, and I was given a dinner that fully atoned for my enforced fast. The news of my famished condition had evidently been broadcast.

As showing the difficulties with which lecturers in the States have to contend, I may state that my next engagement, at the historic old town of Richmond, in Virginia, meant three days' travelling, and this for one lecture only. The society engaging me, however, generously paid my expenses in addition to my fee. My Richmond audience reminded me of the audiences at home, excepting that most of the ladies were beautifully and simply attired, and were genuinely interested in garden design. My subject was again "The Charm of the English Garden."

On my return to New York I lectured to a large audience in one of the theatres at 11 o'clock in the morning, on "Garden Villages in England," quoting Port Sunlight as the most successful example so far realised in any part of the world, with Bournville as a good second. This statement was contested by the speakers who took part in the subsequent discussion, and I felt there was a suggestion of resentment that I had ignored certain experiments in industrial housing then being made in America. Perhaps it was only reasonable to expect this counterblast.

Whilst lecturing at Philadelphia I received a telegram from Graham Bell, of telephone fame, whom I had met on board the Celtic, asking me to visit him in Washington, and to be prepared to give a lecture on housing in England. Fortunately, I had left myself a few clear days, so that I might have the experience of a drawing-room lecture amongst the people who are ever intent upon education. Accordingly I accepted the invitation.

I reached Washington on the Wednesday morning, and was met at the railway station by my host, who motored me to his

Hard Work Relieved by a Trip to America.

home in the city, a commodious and eminently livable house, which I believe had been planned by Mr. Richardson, the American architect. Graham Bell was almost as well known for his lip reading and talking for the deaf and dumb as for his invention. The lip-reading was begun and prompted by his affection for his wife, who was thus afflicted. Notwithstanding this, she was a fine hostess, who had the power of communicating her buoyant spirit to her guests. I found that Mr. Bell had arranged for a lecture to be given in his great parlour each Wednesday evening, and I was asked to give my own lecture on the day of my arrival. As the company arrived I was introduced, but the galaxy of senators, ministers, and heads of Government departments made me quite nervous : seldom have I met so distinguished a company, or one so evidently interested in housing as an aspect of social amelioration. I was advised by Mr. Bell to discard my manuscript and give them a simple account of the housing movement in England. I followed his advice, and much to my surprise I had little difficulty in speaking extemporaneously. The discussion which followed was intensely interesting, and showed a real desire amongst the senators present to promote housing reform in America, a movement for which there was great need.

The next day I was shown round the capital, a tour which only tended to confirm my previous impressions that Washington is potentially the most imposingly beautiful capital in the world. After we had made a comprehensive tour of inspection—and, I may add, admiration on my part, particularly of the more important Government buildings—we inspected the new housing area for the negro population of the city, and most excellent I found it all to be. The cleanliness of the cottages and the robustness of the children equal anything I have seen in white industrial quarters. Perhaps the facts that the property was new and that the tenants were carefully selected accounted in part for the conditions. This visit to Washington was most enjoyable, and led to new friendships ; but apart from every other consideration it contributed very much to my grasp of town planning and architectural problems, for here, in this great capital, was to be found the work of many of the nation's most famous architects, who have contributed of their best.

From Washington I returned to New York, and then went on to Chicago, where I arrived in the early morning. At one o'clock I was entertained to lunch by the members of the Chicago Civic

The Life and Work of An English Landscape Architect.

Guild, a vigorous body of social reformers who had already accomplished much for their city. At the luncheon I gave an address on "The Town Planning Movement in Europe." I had frankly to acknowledge that our continent had nothing so ambitious as Daniel Burnham's scheme for the reorganisation of Chicago, and indeed I felt that in many ways Chicago was pointing the way to other cities and to other countries.

At four in the afternoon I lectured to a crowded audience in the Art Gallery at the end of Michigan Avenue, on "Ancient Gardenage," and was amazed at the keenness and interest of the audience in the subject of my lecture. At the conclusion groups of enthusiasts gathered round me, some to ask questions and some to congratulate me on the beauty of my slides.

The next morning I met Daniel Burnham, who introduced me to his colleagues. Burnham was a big man, with all the simplicity and modesty of those truly great. For two hours he talked to me about my work and about his own, and in particular about his great hopes for the improvement of Chicago. Looking back on his life's work, and looking forward to his end, of which he had already had warning, he said, "Whatever happens, I feel that I have done a day's work, and there is great satisfaction in that." Burnham's work on the Chicago Exhibition was in itself sufficient to make the fame of any one man, for it gave a new impetus and higher ideals to the profession of architecture in America. I think, however, that he valued still more his contribution to the replanning of Chicago, which was a revelation of what possibilities existed even in the most congested cities, where site values are at the highest.

This noble scheme had its inception in the City Club. In itself this fact was remarkable, for here you had men promoting a stupendous plan of reorganisation for the city, knowing that if the scheme were adopted they would be called upon to find most of the cost. What is more, these men formed themselves into a City Planning Commission, which met in Burnham's board-room for an hour each day for five days a week, for nearly three years, the Commission finding the money for the payment of the special staff, which, with incidental expenses, cost in all about £30,000. I believe Burnham's great services were positively given gratis to the work. This is one of the most remarkable examples in America of that spirit which is creating a new view of civic responsibility.

Hard Work Relieved by a Trip to America.

At the request of Earl Grey, then Governor-General of Canada, I visited Ottawa for the purpose of stirring up an interest in civic betterment. In this subject the Governor-General was intensely interested, and he desired its principles to be applied to the remarkable opportunities of the Dominion capital.

In Ottawa I was entertained by the Canadian Club, a spirited organisation run on lines similar to those governing the Rotary Clubs in England. It is a luncheon club, at which the guest gives an address extending to about half an hour. Many representative men, including Sir Wilfrid Laurier and other ministers, attended. I preferred, however, to await the larger opportunities which a second trip would give me, and so spent most of the time remaining at my disposal in interviewing representative men and in writing articles for the newspapers on " The Aims and Advantages of City Planning." My introducer for the propaganda was Noel Cauchon, a young engineer who had made a wide study of city planning from the engineer's standpoint, and who has since attained eminence as an authority on the larger aspects of the subject.

My lectures, articles, and interviews had received such wide publicity in Canada and the States that I was offered many lucrative engagements, but I decided to complete my programme and return home, because reports indicated that several of my best clients were becoming restive.

Financially the lectures barely covered expenses. I could not afford to lose much, but money-making was not my object. I wanted to gain new and wider experience in a different sphere in the master art in which my life and studies have been cast. Further, I wished to gratify a lifelong ambition—viz., to meet men of great grasp and compass, and discuss comprehensive problems with them; or, rather, to sit at their feet and listen. In all these respects the trip was a success, and I left America with a much wider appreciation of that great continent and the character of her people. In particular I was very much impressed by the young people I met at the universities.

Since this visit I have had a string of young scholarship students carrying letters of introduction to me from their professors, and it has been my joy to keep up the connection thus formed. This experience of American universities with their classes in landscape architecture filled me with a determination to do what I could to remove the embargo which lies upon this profession in England. Twice I have nearly succeeded, and it is the bitterest disappointment

The Life and Work of An English Landscape Architect.

of my closing years that I have hitherto failed. However, I still trust that a rich horticulturist with a leaning towards the arts will yet establish such a school—or, better still, a complete course in the constructive arts. Six years later, in a letter which I sent to a very dear friend who is now a peer, written on the eve of my departure for Greece to carry out the plan of Salonika, I said :—

My Dear W.,

Several years ago you and I had a talk about university training in the arts, and I then suggested that some day we might have a great academic course worthy of our traditions and ourselves. The idea I then ventured to suggest was three schools under one department :

(1) Landscape Architecture and City Planning, which would give students a wide grasp of topographical opportunities and the grouping of architectural units with natural features.

(2) A department of Architecture which would develop the study of architectural styles and motifs.

(3) The Decorative Arts, which should include a study of all forms of decorative treatment, and include also the design of furniture.

My object in writing you is to say that Mr. Fisher, the Minister of Education, some time ago asked me to draw up for his consideration a curriculum for No. I department, and I now hear that he is very favourably impressed and anxious to found the school at Oxford. I wish, however, that someone with a fervent desire to help in the work of reconstruction could induce Mr. Fisher to start the three departments, because if one could get a number of promising young men to go through the whole of the three courses, we would rear a race of constructive designers who would hold their own with the men of any country, and incidentally raise the status of British Art.

Now, please, don't think me too venturesome if I suggest the following as a great opportunity, and as the way to ensure the founding of this project :

(1) A Chair in Landscape Architecture,

(2) A Chair in Architecture,

(3) A Chair in the Decorative Arts,

each of which would be set up for twenty-five thousand pounds. This is probably not the time to introduce this subject, but as I am risking something in going to Salonika next week, I thought I would, as an old friend, venture to leave you this record of my suggestion, in case of accidents. What a splendid memorial this would make to your boy, whom I last remember as an Oxford undergraduate.

Yours sincerely,

THOMAS H. MAWSON.

Only so can we hope to maintain that pre-eminence in design and in the constructive arts which we have so long enjoyed.

The Hill, Hampstead, for Lord Leverhulme.

CHAPTER XV.

THEORY AND PRACTICE: MR. LEVER FOUNDS A SCHOOL OF CIVIC DESIGN.

NOW opens a period of enjoyable stress and activity. When in the strength and ripening fruition of his powers a man has an open field before him, and a clientèle appreciative and responsive, he in turn responds with the best that is in him. With his imagination freed from fetters he can express himself either by his art or in words which keep pace with his progress and freedom.

During the period covered by this chapter, in addition to calls in my practice, the opportunity dawned whereby I could give forth in connected form some of the lessons I had stored, not only in my practice, but also by the " harvest of a quiet eye " in my peregrinations up and down the country, on the Continent, and in America.

With the exception of three connected papers before the Royal Horticultural Society, the lectures I had hitherto delivered had been single ones concerning some branch of the art I practised, and consequently were limited in range and vision.

By the generosity of Mr. Lever the possibility arose whereby I could present co-ordinately the principles which underlie landscape design. When free and untrammelled, this art not only deals in beautiful bits of gardens, or even parks, public or private, but is able to grip the imagination in the largest sense, and impart an atmosphere. This is its ideal. Everyone in practice knows how his mounting Pegasus gets chained, and how her wings are clipped; but it is this very inner vision which sustains in the outer materialistic struggle. Finding himself hedged up— " cribbed, cabined, and confined,"—the man with the ideal soars above the commonplace and above disappointments— disappointments with his own productions very often.

I have always advocated that theory and practice should go

The Life and Work of An English Landscape Architect.

hand in hand in all thorough training, and it is a very shortsighted education which confines the student to practice alone. Theory is usually derided, and, like the word " sentiment," pushed into a meaning which is a falsity. " An ounce of practice is worth a ton of theory " is one of those fallacious axioms which pass from mouth to mouth without due consideration, but I maintain that practice which is not steeped in a sound theoretical education is a cul-de-sac. In training the youths in my own profession I have advised them to go further and deeper, and make a much wider survey, than the immediate problem set them involves, a method I usually adopt in my own practice in any scheme of magnitude and with possibilities. Oftentimes I draw up a comprehensive policy which may take ten, twenty, or more years to complete, and which, whilst it does not commit the proprietor to the whole or any part of it, stimulates his imagination and keeps it open to widening horizons into which each piece falls as a part of a whole. Such is the purpose of a school or academy, and such is the method pursued in the training of landscape architects in the American universities.

It was this very method of comprehensive design which led me to join issue with Town Planning and Civic Design. The latter differs somewhat from the former in that it gives freer play to the imagination and the æsthetic perception, but is not by any means divorced from its practical partner. Civic design would encourage the solution of idealism in the configuration and the planning of towns, much as the Paris Beaux Arts encourages ideal monumental architecture, yet by no means ignoring the practical part.

In meditating on these matters I was led, by my lectures and personal solicitation, to make an endeavour to secure in some one at least of our universities a branch of landscape architecture. A degree, I considered, might, as a token of proficiency, be used as an introduction to further studies in civic design, or as a commencement of practice. Those students who could afford to do so, might couple the diploma with an extended study of architecture and the decorative arts in general, as suggested in the verbatim letter at the end of the previous chapter. But whichever the system adopted, I am convinced that until we have a School of Landscape Architecture there is something lacking in our national university curriculum.

This project may seem ambitious, and some may read into it a suggestion of egotism, but I have always felt that as we plough

Mr. Lever Founds a School of Civic Design.

our way along, everything is lost to the toilers who follow, except the outward manifestation of our work, which is very often marred by others, possibly with the best intentions. Our inward thoughts, and the steps and stages by which we arrive at our conclusions, are usually more valuable than the finished product, and it is these that are of educational value. Although in England we have always had, in every emergency and in every profession, a few men who have been strong enough in their natural aptitude and acquired power to be independent of schools, the fact does not disparage academic training and study. Although without doubt the need to overcome great obstacles in their younger days accounted largely for the making of these stalwarts, they would have been thankful had their initial difficulties been simplified, and had the pace been set for them by a few like-minded in purpose and imagination.

The school I contemplated, which I maintain is sorely needed, would hold out good prospects for students possessing a fair share of imagination, and prepared to take the full course and make themselves proficient. It was not to be modelled altogether on the very strict technical lines of the American schools, for which I have nothing but the sincerest regard, but to be a school for the training of architectural minds on the widest possible basis. Not alone is it the purpose to plan, design, and allocate buildings, but in addition we must marshal the landscape, and, when called upon, be able to respond with a general indicative design for any part of the *tout ensemble*.

In quite a remarkable way, yet by no means the result of my advocacy, some approximation of my ideal was achieved by the founding of the School of Civic Design as a department of the already prosperous School of Architecture attached to the Liverpool University. The history leading up to the foundation of this school is interesting. It came about in this way.

In 1908 a group of newspapers attacked Mr. William Lever, the founder and chairman of Lever Brothers, for endeavouring to amalgamate a number of competing firms of soap manufacturers for the purpose, as was afterwards proved, of cheapening the cost of production to compensate for the soaring cost of raw materials. In this proposal the newspapers thought they saw the introduction of the American trust in its most pernicious form, and in supporting this contention went beyond the bounds of reasonable criticism. The result was an action in which Mr. Lever received very

N

The Life and Work of An English Landscape Architect.

substantial damages amounting to over £100,000. This large sum was presented to the Liverpool University for the purpose of increasing the usefulness of the School of Tropical Medicine, and to establish a new department of Town Planning, or, as it was designated, Civic Design. Early in January of 1909 I was staying with Mr. Lever at Roynton Cottage, when in a fit of enthusiasm I introduced my pet subject. My host allowed me to explain in considerable detail what I thought was needed, and at last quietly remarked, " So you have heard about it, have you ? " " Heard what ? " I replied. " About a School of Town Planning." I assured him this was my first intimation of it, and that I was delighted.

The gift was actually completed in March of that year, and Professor Reilly was despatched to America to collect all the available information and literature on the subject, and to investigate any school the curriculum of which included Civic Design or Town Planning. In October the school was formally inaugurated under the direction of Professor Adshead.

I had previously been consulted as to the curriculum and as to the part I would take in the work of the school. Reluctantly I had to state that my commitments were such that my share of the work would have to be confined to the lectures on landscape design applied to park systems, boulevards, town gardens, recreation grounds, and other phases of town development which depend for success upon the application of the principle of landscape architecture.

The acceptance of this lectureship added a new zest to life, and gave me the opportunity of trying to instil into the minds of the rising generation of town planners, some of my own passion for the art I have now practised so long.

It is not claimed that in a course of lectures one can make expert landscape architects, any more than a course in civic law can make expert town clerks, but it was possible to give the students a knowledge in the round of the necessity and opportunities for parks and gardens, and also a critical sense of what is good and bad. I felt that when these students assumed charge of comprehensive town-planning schemes they would be able to choose the right colleague and to give him his instructions for the preparation of working drawings. Many of the students have gone much further than this, especially those who started with a sound training in architecture and some general knowledge of

Mr. Lever Founds a School of Civic Design.

arboriculture and horticulture. In the future some of these men ought to contribute to the advancement of civic art.

The school has from the start done excellent work, and by its publication of the " Town Planning Review " has exercised a wide influence in many parts of the world, especially in promoting those aspects of town planning in which we in this country excel. To this review it has been my pleasure from time to time to contribute articles on the application of the principles of landscape architecture to town and city development.

Although the existing provision for teaching in this school falls far short of what I hope may dominate a University of the Constructive Arts, the instruction provided has already had one very important effect—it has given a status to the profession of town planning. By its research work and publications the school keeps every member in touch with the latest developments at home and abroad, inspiring the profession as a whole to higher effort in the development of town-planning problems. Moreover, any art or science which is supported by a university training wins a popular recognition not attainable by other means. Incidentally this university status made possible the founding of the Institute of Town Planning, which has become a strong and influential organisation.

My work for Mr. Lever, which was considerably restricted during the previous year, was now resumed with increased vigour, particularly at Roynton Cottage, Rivington, where considerable expansions to the grounds entailed the planting of many thousands of trees and shrubs. In this department of our work we now felt safe in forging ahead, because our experiments in the acclimatisation of hundreds of varieties had given us a full idea of what would and what would not grow.

At Mr. Lever's London house, The Hill, Hampstead, considerable improvements and extensions were planned. The extensions were possible owing to the purchase of the adjoining south-western property known as Heath Lodge, which forms a peninsular-like extension surrounded on three sides by Hampstead Heath and on the remaining side divided from The Hill gardens by the public lane.

The purpose of this extension was to provide a pleasant setting for the garden parties which are such a popular feature at The Hill, including each season the entertainment of the members of many artistic and learned societies. All the beautiful timber, including

The Life and Work of An English Landscape Architect.

several exceptionally fine beech trees, was retained and woven into the design, which included ample terracing with spacious pergolas and garden pavilions. This work was still in progress when war was declared, and had for several years to be abandoned.

Still other work was designed and executed for Mr. Lever at Thornton Manor. This included a large ornamental lake of twenty acres, and here we had a somewhat curious experience. The site chosen for the lake was on the lowest level of the park, and south-west of the Hall. The site was fairly dry, with no signs of springs or streams, and we had therefore, as we thought, to consider the filling and maintaining of the water supply. On this point we obtained the best expert advice available, with plans and a report, along with estimates for the water supply by means of borings and pumps. The cost, however, threatened to be so excessive that my client decided to delay the laying down of the new plant; but when the lake was completed and the margins and island were strengthened and planted, water began to appear, and finally filled the lake, and from that day to this there has never been any lack of water. The ground proved to be the natural draining point for a wide surrounding region, and there must have been some undiscovered springs. This lake is broken up by several wooded islands, which impart to it a picturesque interest.

Other old clients for whom new work was undertaken were Lord and Lady Erroll, for whom I had already laid out the gardens at Slains Castle in Aberdeenshire. This time the plan was for Barwell Court, a comparatively small but interesting place near Surbiton, and here I planned, to Lady Erroll's instructions, a simple arrangement of terraces, along with a panelled rose garden and flower-bordered lawns. This when completed had all the appearance of a garden laid out in the same period as the house.

Many new clients sought my advice during the year, a goodly number of them being introduced by old clients. Of this number was Mr. Joseph Bibby, of Bidston Priory, who was introduced to me by Mr. Lever. Bidston Priory occupies a site on the most elevated part of Bidston Hill, overlooking the Weald of Wirral. A large part of the hill, now divided into several properties, had been thickly planted with Scotch firs about fifty years before by a former owner, an inexpensive yet effective way of enhancing prospective building sites. My work consisted of new drives, terraces, forecourt, grass glades and retreats, all arranged with

GARDEN HOUSE AT THE PRIORY, BIDSTON, FOR JOSEPH BIBBY, ESQ.

Mr. Lever Founds a School of Civic Design.

the object of retaining the forests of Scotch firs, which had reached their picturesque stage ; also the garden house shown in Illus. No. 35. These delightful pinewoods lost none of their massed character by the introduction of the garden scheme. Notwithstanding, it was possible to add a note of delightful variety by the introduction of large masses of rhododendrons, azaleas, and other plants which thrive on a peaty soil, and always group well with Scotch firs. My client is well known as the editor and proprietor of that artistic publication, " Bibby's Annual." It pleases me to think that the garden which I had the pleasure of designing for my client produced in some slight measure the atmosphere essential to the responsibilities of high editorial ideals.

Other work in the year included garden extension at Isleworth, Hordean, Hants, for Sir E. Clarke Jervoise ; rose gardens at Breadsall Priory, Derby, for Sir Alfred Haslam ; and Bowden Hill, Laycock, Wilts., for Mr. Herbert Harris.

The last of these was a responsible piece of work, but the risks attendant upon the execution of part of the scheme were so great that the plans were modified and in part abandoned. We discovered that the house had been built on a mound of shifting clay, which was already bulging out in places, as is often seen along railway embankments, and the digging of the foundations for the proposed terraces threatened a landslide. We succeeded by other means in effecting some considerable improvements—by planting and rearranging the carriage court. A very successful rose garden was also laid out on the north side of the drive and carriage court.

Maer Hall, in Shropshire, is a characteristic old house owned by Mr. F. G. Harrison, a Liverpool ship-owner, and a generous supporter of good causes in that city and elsewhere.

As I first saw it after certain additions had been made in the Elizabethan manner by Mr. Doyle, a Liverpool architect, after the style of his famous collaborator, Mr. Norman Shaw, R.A., it called aloud for some features to accord with the spacious style which the architecture favoured. What is more, the levels of the ground were not unfavourable, although there were certain palpable difficulties. The Hall stood in front of a steep slope which had been cut about and adapted to fit the roads of the original mansion and its requirements, and Mr. Doyle's additions had also slashed into the same rather awkwardly. This was not apparent when viewed from the grounds ; on the contrary, the Hall nestled snugly into the background of terraced and wooded

The Life and Work of An English Landscape Architect.

slopes. But a mansion cannot live on its background, however impressively it may strike the visitor at first sight.

But it was on the opposite side, looking outwards, usually called the front view, with its intervening space of garden, and the park beyond, where the lack was most felt. All on this front was feeble and purposeless. A lake had been attempted, but it was not bold enough, and the lawns rolled in billowy swells, without anything to relieve them except indeterminate shrubberies and flower beds of the invertebrate tadpole shape. There were no upstanding groupings of paternal trees, which was all the more regrettable because the surrounding pastoral land was picturesquely interspersed with such groups. On this side the mansion simply sprawled, calling for a wide spacious architectural terrace of open design, and for a flower-bed design in a continuous strap-work in balanced harmonies quaintly framed with box. Thus a decided note would be struck. This done, I advocated a few small yet select groupings of beeches to frame the views beyond, and a few in the immediate precincts of the park, which would have supplied the motif lines of design. These would also have had the effect of aiding spaciousness by drawing out the eye in infinites and extended perspective. A vacuity of lawns and pastures, no matter how pleasing the curves of their crests may be, or, what is worse, the same lawns dotted over with specimen hybrid shrubs, planted solely for their rarity and individual interest, has the tendency to destroy breadth, no matter how contrary to reason this may seem. As it was, there were no subtleties. The long-drawn-out horizontals called out for vertical masses, as in a picture. This improvement effected, there were ample spaces to indulge in the smaller intimates of the garden—namely, beautiful shrub and flower effects, provided the work was done boldly. When good taste prescribes that a bed of shrubs should exhibit a few shades of one colour, the tendency is to worry it up with miscellaneous plantings of mixed and independent gems.

My client, who was a keen gardener, unfortunately preferred green slopes to a terrace and balustrade, and also irregular and sinuous lines to clear-cut lines near the house, which, however suitable in free and irregularly balanced mansions, were not in character with the immediate precincts of Maer Hall. I have often been met with such preferences, which is not surprising when it is remembered that the working life of such gentlemen as my client is spent in offices and in the business warehouses and unlovely streets of our seaport towns and distributing centres, where everything is hard and angular. A wise designer will always endeavour to meet such requirements wherever the existing conditions are favourable. Personally I dearly love the wild, but if we carefully observe the wild expanses of nature, we find there is design in them. There are usually one or two dominating kinds of plants or flowers, and all the others play up to them as the lesser instruments of an orchestra do to the pronounced leading strains.

The next call, the subject of which formed a great contrast to the conditions existing at Maer Hall, was to a suburban park and garden of considerable acreage—a green oasis staked out and held against the encroachment of the town of Leeds. The owner, Sir Wilfred Hepton, a manufacturer, and Lord Mayor of the town, had spent a considerable sum in altering the interior and the furnishings of his massive Georgian mansion to harmonise with the exterior, and now he desired a garden with similar distinctive characteristics. For a residence so near a large centre of population the site was excellent. A small park stretching away to the south, a fringe of umbrageous trees screening adjoining properties without hiding the spires and cupolas of the more important churches and other buildings in the line of sight, were the characteristics. On the west side of the house we converted the old vegetable garden into a rose garden, which, partly owing to the nature of the soil—a retentive loam—and the great cultural skill of my client, turned out to be one of the most successful rose gardens I have had the pleasure of designing. The effect was heightened by its circular form, and the pergola and garden house which enclosed it on its northern side. These are fully illustrated in "The Art and Craft of Garden Making."

At the same time I planned additions and alterations to the gardens at Holker Hall for Lord Richard and Lady Moira Cavendish, both keen gardeners. These gardens were somewhat famous on account of the fact that they were remodelled by Sir Joseph Paxton, the designer of the Great Exhibition grounds of 1852, and of the Crystal Palace. The large orangery at Holker (since removed) was also designed by Paxton, as were also many of the pleasing surroundings of the railway stations on the adjoining Furness Railway.

The gardens at Holker were intensely interesting. They contained many rare conifers, rhododendrons, and other peat

The Life and Work of An English Landscape Architect.

loving plants, some of which are probably now no longer in commerce. Thus we had the house and gardens laid out in a free landscape manner, the ideal setting for a low terrace and rose garden, and balustraded boundary wall. The result, which was largely influenced by existing conditions, was successful.

One day, during the progress of the work, Lady Moira and my client, Mrs. Gerard Leigh, who was a guest at Holker, offered to take me with them to Underley to see the wild gardens laid out by Lord Henry Bentinck. I had often seen the gardens at Underley when a boy, when Lord and Lady Bective owned the estate. I had no idea, however, that Lord Henry had developed such skill as a planter as was shown by the wild garden arranged on a most difficult site on a steep wooded slope on the opposite side of the river Lune, which forms the northern boundary of the gardens. In America I have often shown slides of this wild garden, which always brought shouts of applause. The way in which various kinds of foliage are contrasted, such as *Saxifraga peltata* with *Iris Kæmpferi*, is quite wonderful. When I told my American audiences that an English lord had planned this garden and also done a large part of the actual planting, they were amazed. It gave them a new point of view of our aristocracy. Perhaps I ought to have explained that although Lord Henry was an aristocrat, he was also a democrat.

It has always been my greatest pleasure to work for those who put their personality into everything that has to do with their homes. I am assured that the secret of the fame of our stately mansions, and even of our cottage gardens, is here to be found. These people seem to be able to hit the true pathos and sublimity of a garden, and to grip the objective of its design, which, as Wordsworth says, ought to move the affections under the control of good sense. These are the clients who continue the traditions of the early herbalists, who wrote with such simplicity, and yet with such intimacy with their subject and their pursuits, as to convey to us their own delight. This is just where horticulture, for its own sake, fails, with its false standards of showiness, size, and rarities. We are drawn away from the typical, with all its grace and charm, and made to occupy ourselves with the abnormal. It is a pleasure to return to one's own work and find that someone has understood and has placed the decorative notes just where they are needed—the masses and the lighter touches likewise.

Gardens of moderate extent were laid out this year for

Mr. Lever Founds a School of Civic Design.

Mr. F. W. Monks, an ironmaster of Warrington, whose residence occupied an elevated site on the south of the town, where a deep bluff on the west side commanded extensive views from east to west. Owing to its elevation the lay-out of the garden presented many difficulties, some of which were overcome only after many experiments. It is these difficulties, peculiar to every site, which give a zest to the art of landscape architecture.

The next call was from Somersetshire to the former residence of Hannah More the poetess, at Barley Wood, Wrington, now the property of Mr. Herbert Wills of tobacco fame. I found this lovely retreat all that I imagined the house of a poetess to be, and, as far as I could judge, very much as she left it in 1828, when she was driven out by the impositions of her staff of servants, whom she had treated too benevolently. As she left, at eighty-three years of age, amid the scowls and hostile demonstrations of these servants, on being helped into her carriage, she remarked : " I am driven like Eve out of Paradise, but not, like Eve, by angels." A little paradise I found the house and grounds to be, both within and without. As on other occasions in my practice on which I have been called in, I found all so happy and appropriate that I advised that no alterations be attempted beyond a little touching up here and there where the original intentions had been lost. I also designed a quiet panel rose garden at a part of the site, and in such an unobtrusive way that I felt the illustrious authoress would have approved, then left all to the pervading peace which breathes into the soul.

For Mrs. Aitken of Bodelywddan Castle, North Wales, I replanned the upper part of the gardens behind the Castle, and carried out some necessary improvements on a very difficult site. The soil was sparse, resting upon limestone, demanding great care and knowledge in the choice of shrubs and plants ; but here again a fair measure of success rewarded our efforts.

At the same time a garden near Wigan for Harold Sumner, Esq., of Ashfield House, Standish, was laid out. Mr. Sumner's large business and manufacturing interests in Standish fixed for him his place of residence, so he chose the best part of the district and purchased an old house with well-timbered grounds ; but the land was very retentive clay, which is always difficult to manipulate. Without dry lawns and walks a garden is not worthy the name. Fortunately, there was a fairly steep slope to the land, so that the outfall to the south was a comparatively easy matter ; but Wigan

The Life and Work of An English Landscape Architect.

clay is the most tenacious I have ever had to tackle. We laid out a complete system of herring-bone drains, a few feet apart, filling in a foot of dry clinker on the top of the drainpipe. By this means we converted a water-logged garden into thoroughly dry lawns, walks, and borders.

In the early part of November, 1911, I received a letter from the Town Clerk of Preston, desiring me to meet the Parks Committee at an early date to advise them on the completion of the Haslam Park, a tract of land admirably situated at Ashton-on-Ribble, presented by Miss Haslam, a representative of a highly esteemed Preston family. The site, which extends to over sixty-six acres, was originally pasture land, with a stream flowing through it. A start had already been made upon the work, to plans prepared in the Borough Surveyor's office, but Miss Haslam at this stage wisely decided that she would pay for the construction and all professional fees incurred, so that she might be assured that her gift would be dealt with in a worthy manner. The only way to secure this was to start afresh with a new plan, weaving in as far as possible what had already been done in the way of planting, together with the superintendent's house and the main entrance. This scheme was embodied in an illustrated report submitted and approved in the early part of 1912, and was successfully carried out on broad lines under the superintendence of two of my landscape foremen. Miss Haslam was keenly interested in the work as it proceeded, and was desirous that ample space and provision should be made for the children, which was accordingly done, since any concessions or advantages to be gained for the children in a park always have my hearty support.

BANFF, ALBERTA, CANADA : VIEWS SHOWING ITS LOCATION.

CHAPTER XVI.

THE YEAR 1912, THE ADVENT OF NEW RESPONSIBILITIES.

I HAD now, metaphorically speaking, annexed America, and made this vast continent a part of my sphere of influence. Already I had visited it in the autumn of 1910.

In the early part of the year Mr. James Langmuir, of Toronto, who was chairman of the Niagara Falls Victoria Park Commissioners, was in London, and interviewed me. He suggested that when I could make another visit to Canada his commissioners would probably wish to consult me about the development of their National Park at Niagara Falls. About the same time I met Earl Grey, then Governor-General of Canada, who urged me to give a series of lectures on the necessity for town-planning legislation in Canada. Also, in particular, Lord Grey pressed me to do what I could to promote a demand for the replanning of Ottawa, a city which he described as possessing the finest site of any capital in the world, with every facility for expansion, a fact he believed but few Canadians realised. A third attraction was the Town Planning Conference to be held at Philadelphia, which promised to be an historic gathering, as it indeed proved to be. It is not surprising that I found the call of the West irresistible, and that I proceeded to make my arrangements accordingly.

Two of my objectives failed to materialise. The Niagara Falls Park Commission decided that their funds could not afford professional advice; and the replanning of Ottawa, which came into the sphere of practical politics only through the success of my propaganda work, was assigned to Mr. Bennett, of Chicago, in spite of Sir Robert Borden's advocacy on my behalf. I was also strongly recommended to the Canadian Government by the Rt. Hon. John Burns, then at the Local Government Board, and by the Canadian Society of Architects; but unwisely I recommended Sir Robert to seek further credentials from the

The Life and Work of An English Landscape Architect.

Royal Institute of British Architects, of which I was an honorary associate.

For reasons doubtless known to themselves, the R.I.B.A. made a counter-proposal which proved unacceptable, and which ruined the chance of any of their own countrymen securing this important work. Inimical to my chances of securing the work was, again, the supposition that I had advised certain developments which the directors of the Canadian Pacific Railway regarded as being opposed to their interests. This certainly was not the case, but whoever spread the falsification, it served its purpose and brought me up against powerful railway interests, which eventually secured the appointment of Mr. Bennett—who, by the way, produced a very fine scheme, some part of which may in the far distant future be realised.

Although my immediate quest was a failure, the trip was very successful in other respects. Indeed, so many requests were made for lectures, and I received so many promises of work, that I arranged for another visit in the autumn, to be devoted to the propagation of city-planning principles and ideals.

Sir Robert did what he could to atone for my disappointment by recommending that I be selected to replan Banff in the Rockies, including a large section of the great national park there. The goodwill shown to me by the Premier (a fact which seemed to have become public property) was of the greatest assistance to me in securing introductions and requests for lectures on city planning from a dozen important centres, beginning with Ottawa, and including Montreal, Halifax (Nova Scotia), St. John (New Brunswick), St. Marie, Port Arthur, Winnipeg, Regina, Saskatoon, Medicine Hat, Calgary, Vancouver, and Victoria (B.C.).

These openings were very encouraging, showing on the one hand a vital interest in city planning, and on the other a leaning towards the Old Country for guidance and help. Having regard to the fact that every Canadian town site had been developed on the monotonous gridiron plan, which ignores topographical conditions and internal circulation of traffic, along with an utter neglect of zoning for specific needs of a modern, well-equipped city, the need and the opportunity were great. The acceptance of what I regarded in the light of an obligation was fraught with some difficulty, for, as some of my clients at home reminded me, my practice carried with it certain duties which I could not entirely ignore. I had, however, felt for a long time that my practice was very much a personal affair, and that my partners and staff would never reach their highest artistic or practical achievement without increased responsibility ; so I decided to launch forth.

Nevertheless, it was necessary that I should return to New York *en route* for England as soon as possible after fixing up my programme for the subsequent autumn. In New York I had lecture engagements, and also several new and prospective clients to interview, for some of whom I designed gardens. Work designed in this country and executed across the Atlantic by a foreign mind, from a garden standpoint never struck me as satisfactory—a foreman trained in the English school was essential.

The five months which intervened between my return home and my autumn trip formed a busy time. First the Peace Palace was satisfactorily completed, the final stages necessitating several visits to The Hague. My son and staff were responsible almost entirely for the executing of this work. Important extensions were planned to the gardens at The Hill, Hampstead. My client, now Sir William Lever, had razed Heath Lodge mansion, thus providing an opportunity rarely open to the landscape architect, as it called for special ingenuity in the contrivance of a bridge across a sunk path which divided the two properties. This solution was suggested by my client, as was also the extension of the pergola which screened the new extension from the public common. This extension was continued up to the early stages of the war, when the Ministry of Munitions prohibited further work, notwithstanding the fact that the youngest man employed was fifty-three years of age.

At the same time considerable alterations and additions were in progress at Thornton Manor, and also at Roynton Cottage, near Bolton. The additional work at Roynton included a new gatehouse and a Romanesque bridge over the new estate road. The bridged road is much used by visitors to the great park already referred to, and is a convenient route to the summit of Rivington Pike, the highest peak in this part of Lancashire.

I was again called in by my old client, Mr. H. C. Moffatt (for whom I had already worked at Codford Manor), to advise him on the lay-out of his gardens at Hampworth Lodge, near Salisbury. For the Union Bank of Manchester I laid out a building estate at Congleton on the lines of a garden village ; and the Southgate Urban District Council, for whom I had improved Broomfield Park some years before, had purchased a part of the Grovelands

Thr Life and Work of An English Landscape Architect.

Estate, and this they instructed me to lay out. This work was duly carried out, and it is interesting to note that at the time of writing my firm and colleagues are town-planning advisers to this Council.

For the well-known hunting man, Mr. W. Arkwright, of Hatton House, Warwick, we improved the gardens, adding several new features ; and for my old client, W. W. Galloway, of The Willows, Ashton-on-Ribble, near Preston, we completed the garden scheme which had been planned and partly carried out several years previously. It was his affection for the home of his youth, and a desire to preserve the old character of the home, that led to the postponement of a part of this scheme, and therefore it was with pleasure that I received my client's instructions to complete the work, and a still greater pleasure to hear him say on completion that we had done the right and only logical thing. This garden is illustrated in " The Art and Craft of Garden Making."

After months of hard work, in which my days were spent with clients and my nights in railway journeys, without a holiday for even a day, I sailed again for America for the fourth time, my wife accompanying me.

The day before we sailed, however, I had a great shock in the form of a letter of dismissal from Sir William Lever, my best client. The letter was couched in terms of personal regard and goodwill, but regretting that the time had arrived when he could no longer disguise the fact that his interests were not promoted with that assiduity which he had come to expect from me. The letter concluded : " I recognise that in many aspects I am losing a very able adviser, but you in turn are losing a client, whether a bad or good one is for you to judge." I saw the reasonable grounds for annoyance in a client who always adopted a generous attitude towards me, and who annually paid me more for my services than I could hope to earn by lecturing or working in America. I also recognised his reasonable disappointment in having his important work left in the hands of junior partners ; but I also saw that he rated my professional services far too high, whilst correspondingly under-estimating the value of the services which my partners and chief of staff were rendering. This did not alter the fact that I had received a stunning blow, and for a time I felt that the bottom had fallen out of my practice. I regarded the decision as final, and decided to accept the inevitable, but if possible to maintain the mutual regard which had grown up between us,

GARDEN AT ASHTON-ON-RIBBLE FOR W. W. GALLOWAY, ESQ.

which rested on several interests which we held in common. The first and chief work on board ship was the drafting and redrafting of a letter of reply. In this letter I decided to state frankly the reasons for my American trip—

(1) To give my sons wider opportunities and greater responsibilities by removing for a time my personal influence.

(2) That only in this way could my sons come into personal relationship with our clients and thus assure that continuity for the practice which it had been my life's work to promote.

(3) That I was very anxious that the English School of Town Planners should exercise a wide influence in Canada and the Colonies, and that for some unaccountable reason I seemed to be one of the chosen apostles whose appeal was exercising an influence.

This letter carried greater weight than I had hoped for, for within a fortnight I received a reply which, though it did not cancel my dismissal, asked me to let him know when I was returning, and wished me in the meantime a successful tour.

In New York I had several appointments with clients, and with others for the purpose of arranging lectures, including a very interesting drawing-room lecture to the members of the Garden Club, a vigorous and enterprising organisation. This lecture was given at the house of Mrs. Fred Hoffman, and was attended by over a hundred garden enthusiasts. My subject was " Rock Gardens," and many of my slides were colour photographs, which were greatly admired. I next gave three lectures at the Columbia University on " Historic Garden Design." These lectures were promoted by Professor Hamlin, himself an authority on Italian gardens, on which he had written several learned treatises.

From New York I went to Toronto, where I had arranged to give a week's lectures at the University on the " Principles of City Planning." On arrival at Toronto we were met by a number of enthusiasts, who entertained us to tea. They afterwards took us to the residence of the Principal, Dr. Falkener, with whom we dined before proceeding to the Auditorium, a striking building of majestic proportions, capable of seating over twelve hundred people. Great preparations were made for these lectures, and such prominent citizens as Sir Edmund Osler, Sir Edward Walker, and Sir William Meredith, acted as chairman on successive evenings. Entering the hall I found a company of about three hundred and fifty people awaiting me, composed mainly of those who had the weight of the financial burdens of the city upon their shoulders.

The Life and Work of An English Landscape Architect.

The audiences increased in number each successive evening, culminating in a full attendance of about twelve hundred on the Saturday, when my subject was " Garden Cities and Model Housing for the Working Classes." This subject was *apropos* and very urgent, because congestion was endangering the public health of the citizens.

Previous to my visit the churches had undertaken a survey of social conditions, which they threatened to publish unless the City Council adopted a more progressive policy. The Bishop of Toronto attended four of the lectures, and sent me a letter of apology explaining absence from the other two, but informing me that he was sending his representative, who would report to him.

The increasing popularity of these lectures was probably owing to the use which I made of local illustrations, many of which were supplied by the enthusiasts, who formed themselves into a civic survey intelligence department, the leading spirit being Mr. Hynes, a Toronto architect, who has since done notable service in the cause of city planning propaganda in the Dominion. In addition to citizens of Toronto, many representatives were present from other important adjoining cities, including Montreal and Ottawa.

On the night of the first lecture my reading desk was set far back on the stage, and when I began to speak I had the sensation of having my words hurled back at me ; then I noticed a look of bewilderment on the faces of my audience, which became so apparent that I stopped. Dr. Falkener came to the rescue. Ascending the platform, he explained that the acoustics of the hall were very faulty, and advised me to bring the reading desk to the edge of the platform and to speak much more slowly. I took his advice, and no further trouble ensued. The lectures, however, which were arranged to occupy an hour, took an hour and a quarter to deliver.

With that hospitality for which Canadians are famous, I was entertained to lunch each day, the most notable and interesting of these functions being arranged by the Imperial Club, to the members of which I spoke on the " Ethics of City Planning." Looking back, I am afraid that I allowed my subject to run away with me, and that I indulged in oratorical flourishes which sane propaganda does not call for. One of these flowery periods, I remember, was cheered by the Bishop. This followed a declaration that " city planners were out to save souls by communities, by providing conditions in which intellectual, moral, and physical well-being became a possibility."

The course of lectures served a timely purpose, and by the publicity given to them did much to stimulate the adoption of city planning legislation in the Dominion, and the establishment of a lectureship on city planning at the University.

Another interesting incident arose on the evening of the last day of my course of lectures, when a deputation, including Mr. Noel Cauchon, a very able and enterprising engineer, who had given great study to city planning problems, and Colonel Meredith (nephew of my first chairman, Sir William Meredith), an able architect from Ottawa, brought a message from the Premier, Sir R. W. Borden, asking me to make another visit to Ottawa, as he wished to consult me again about some prospective work for the Government. This was the replanning of Banff, to which I have already made reference. I here mention this work again, as it provided another example of the kindliness always shown to me by the Premier, who took occasion to introduce me to many of his responsible ministers. Incidentally, this encouragement was not monopolised by any party, for Sir Wilfrid Laurier saw me on many occasions, whilst several of the ex-Ministers invited my wife and me to lunch or dinner. Particularly I remember the charming hospitality of Mr. Fisher and Mr. Patrick Murphy, both Canadian gentlemen of stately courtliness combined with a great sense of humour.

Shortly after my arrival in Ottawa I was asked to attend a luncheon at the Rideau Club. I forget the special object of this notable lunch. It was some matter of general interest that called for concerted action on the part of all men of good intent and purpose, who were asked to rise superior to the expediencies of party. I believe the question at issue was the expansion of the militia.

At the luncheon I found myself occupying the place of honour between Sir Wilfrid Laurier and the Hon. Sam Hughes, and I enjoyed their conversation immensely. Sir Wilfrid, who had a pleasant voice, possessed great conversational powers, and a fund of wit and humour which bubbled over naturally and spontaneously. Sam Hughes' talk was that of a jolly good fellow impressed with the greatness of Canada and his own contribution to its assured safety by reason of his position as Minister of Militia. I could not have imagined, after all I had read in the press about the

The Life and Work of An English Landscape Architect.

preceding election, that politicians of opposing parties could meet together on terms of such evident social goodwill.

Naturally the Hon. Sam Hughes responded for the Militia, and then the fun began, for he evidently could not string two sentences together without some amusing *faux pas.* He commenced by congratulating Sir Wilfrid upon the evident physical benefits he had gained through being relieved of official responsibility. Then he referred to the generous treatment his Militia had received at the hands of Sir Wilfrid when the latter was Premier, to which Sir W. replied : " Of course, Sam, we always did the right thing." Mr. Hughes went on to urge the transcendent claims of the Militia as being the one Government department upon which Liberals and Conservatives ought to agree. " Gentlemen," said he, " divided we stand, united we fall ! "—to which Sir Wilfrid replied : " That's about right, Sam ; let it rest at that." When it came to Sir Wilfrid's turn to respond, the ex-Premier twitted the Hon. Sam unmercifully, but with such good humour that no vestige of resentment remained. This was the only occasion on which I heard Sir Wilfrid speak. I was much impressed by his oratorical powers, his grace and charm of manner, and withal his air of statemanship, which seemed to be a natural attribute rather than an acquired habit. He was a courtier to the manner born, and a statesman by nature. In this respect he differed widely from Sir Robert Borden, who in many respects reminded me of Sir Henry Campbell-Bannerman, minus much of the latter's idealism. As a speaker Sir Robert appealed to me as being the representative of solid, honest politics, hard working and most conscientious, a patriot perfectly loyal to the interests of the Empire. His oratory was clear-cut and terse, and was evidently studiously prepared, being delivered in a somewhat ponderous, earnest style, but lacking the light and shade which a sense of humour often imparts to the most serious subject. Still, that fine quality of conscientiousness which characterised both Sir H. C.-B. and Sir Robert Borden is often the strength of the politician.

On the third day of my stay in Ottawa I called on the Governor-General, His Royal Highness the Duke of Connaught. To my surprise, his secretary, Colonel Lowther, greeted me with the remark that he was glad I had called, because His Royal Highness had inquired for me. When, after a few minutes, I was shown into the Governor-General's room, His Royal Highness said : " So you have come at last ? My wife was asking at lunch only yesterday if I had seen you." After asking about my work and prospects in Canada, he continued : " Well, I promised the Duchess that if you called I would bring you along to lunch, so if you don't mind excusing me for ten minutes, we will go on to Government House together. There you will meet my wife and daughter, and we can all have a talk about gardens, and you can criticise my latest improvements."

The Duchess and Princess Patricia I soon discovered to be past-masters of that difficult art of graciousness which is so lovable and yet so rare a gift. I later saw much of the Duke and the Duchess and Princess Patricia, and I always found them the same considerate, kindly, helpful patrons. As some little proof of this, I was permitted to dedicate the fourth and enlarged edition of my work on " The Art and Craft of Garden Making " to Their Royal Highnesses the Duke and Duchess.

From Ottawa I went to Montreal, where a lecture had been arranged in the recently opened Art Gallery. Here I had a representative audience, including some of the leading architects of the city, and a goodly number of professors from McGill University. Before the lecture we were entertained to dinner by Lady Drummond, who is the possessor of a small but remarkably choice collection of pictures, including examples of Turner, Girtin, Copley Fielding, David Cox, and the best of the English and also of the French schools of painting.

I spent the next day with Sir William van Horne, whom I had met on previous visits to Canada. Sir William was one of the most remarkable men I have ever met. Himself a painter of some distinction, he was an authority on art, and in particular on Chinese and Japanese pottery, of which he possessed a superb collection. What was most remarkable was his catalogue containing an accurate scale drawing of every bit of pottery he possessed, with all the figure work carefully filled in and coloured like the original ; then in tabulated form there were notes of the history, period, and value of the subject of the drawing. These catalogues ran into many volumes. " When do you find time for this work ? " I asked. " Almost every night of my life between the hours of 12 p.m. and 3 a.m.," he replied. " But how do you manage to reduce with such accuracy the finer details of the originals ? " " I merely feel them in."

In addition to his pottery, Sir William possessed a unique collection of models of ships. In these he took great pride, especially in those of ancient barques. Amongst his pictures I counted no fewer than five Franz Hals. One room was filled with his own paintings, all examples more or less of the same impressionist work. Indeed I was told that three hours was his limit for any canvas. His interests were not all of an abstract character. He had practical interests as well, which he found just as absorbing : one was the division of Western prairie lands into triangular-shaped farms, with the farm homestead standing at the apex of each triangle. In this way he got his farms in community groups for economy and social intercourse, thus obviating the isolation and loneliness which go to the making of life on the prairies to many quite intolerable.

This plan, I hear, is now favoured by the Dominion and provincial Governments. But my host's interests did not end here, for at this time he was busily engaged planning model railway stations for Cuba, where he had large interests as a sugar-planter and farmer. Each station was set in a beautiful garden. Then he ran a model farm in Nova Scotia, stocked with valuable herds of pedigree cattle.

Yet this notable man started life as a ganger of navvies, and in his early years worked on some of the most difficult sections of the C.P.R., of which he later became the head. Sir William told me that for thirty years he spent only three hours each night in sleep, and that his average daily consumption of cigars amounted to thirty. " Now," he added regretfully, " the doctor has cut me down to fifteen." He was then over seventy.

From Montreal I travelled to Halifax, Nova Scotia, where I met the members of the City Town Planning Guild. After lunching with them, we made a tour of the city, which occupies a wonderful site and contains some excellent Georgian architecture, built under the direction of succeeding British Governors. In the evening I gave my lecture on " The Principles of City Planning " and their application to Halifax. There was a large audience, and a lively debate followed.

How I came to travel so far out of my specified route is to be explained as follows : Whilst visiting Toronto I met the late Frank Darling, the architect of some of the finest buildings to be found in the Dominion. Befitting the son of a rector, he had a great charm of manner in contrast with a robust vocabulary. He was a man whose face was always wreathed in smiles, and who was from force of habit constantly giving helpful assistance. One day

Taking on New Responsibilities.

he asked me to lunch with him at the York Club. After lunch he introduced business in the following amusing manner : " I hear you have been invited to give a lecture in Halifax ? "

" Yes," I replied, " and I have cabled my regrets that I cannot accept."

" Yes, so I hear ; but I want you to go."

" But I cannot spend five days on one lecture, for it practically means two days' travelling each way."

" Notwithstanding, I want you to accept, and you really must."

" Well, if you put it that way, I will go."

" That's fine. But now that you have decided to go, I would like to say that I don't care a button about your lecture, but I do particularly want you to plan for me the campus of the Dalhousie University."

This commission, added to the fee for the lecture, made the trip a financial possibility. Mr. Darling, of course, knew this.

The day following my lecture was accordingly spent with the Principal of Dalhousie University inspecting the site of the new campus. This was on a gentle southern slope, and forty-five acres in extent. Before leaving the site I had made all my rough notes and sketches and collected all necessary data for my lay-out scheme. This work proved absorbingly interesting, and prepared me for the larger university work to follow.

Returning to Montreal, I sought out the architects for the new Houses of Parliament at Regina, having been commissioned to lay out the surrounding public garden. I also called upon Messrs. Brown and Vallance, the architects for the University of Saskatchewan at Saskatoon, occupying the compass of three hundred and sixty acres, which my firm were asked to plan in conjunction with the architects. From both firms I received every help and encouragement, which led me to reflect upon the difference in attitude of architects towards landscape architects across the Atlantic and in England. In America the attitude is distinctly friendly and helpful ; in England, with rare exceptions, it is frankly resentful and unsympathetic.

From Montreal I proceeded to St. Marie, a small yet pleasing city, possessing an old-world character and an air of solid prosperity which rested on industry rather than on real-estate booming. At the time of my visit there were prosperity and an expectation of big developments, but on what grounds these hopes were based

The Life and Work of An English Landscape Architect.

I did not discover. The point of interest to me was that the leading
citizens had been smitten with the development idea, and desired
me to tell them how they should proceed. Fortunately, the town
had made a good start on a plan suited to its site, and had not spread
to that part of the town which presented topographical difficulties.
For this part I made certain suggestions in my lecture which seemed
to meet with immediate acceptance. Whether or not any progress
was ever made I cannot say.

My next lecture was given in Winnipeg before the Ladies'
Canadian Club, and the members and their male friends mustered
in good numbers. There was the usual luncheon address, and in
the evening I lectured to a very large audience under the auspices
of a City Planning Commission organised to study civic principles.
Already this Commission had engaged an Englishman and a staff
of assistants to make the preparatory civic survey and collect local
data. Although my lectures were appreciated and brought forth
very many compliments, I felt that in a large measure city planning
had, owing to towering real-estate value, become almost impossible
in Winnipeg. There was one very obvious traffic connection
needed between two very important centres, and to this I called
attention, but in the discussion that followed it transpired that the
property required for this obvious improvement was valued at
4,500 dollars per foot frontage at one end, and 2,500 dollars per
foot at the other. Assuming, therefore, a new 80-foot connection,
the property at either end alone would have cost over half a million
dollars, or, with the requisition of the intervening properties and the
cost of constructing a new road, well over a million dollars. This
was only one of many much-needed new arterial connections.
Farther away from the centre there were great opportunities, and
to some of these I was able to make reference. My arranged fee
for this lecture was 150 dollars plus out-of-pocket expenses, but
the Commission forgot to pay either. My terms for the future
in Winnipeg will be " cash in advance."

Winnipeg is a wonderful city, made great and prosperous by
its founders, who visioned the unique strategic position of the
site as the gateway of the Great North-West, and having at its
command the vast resources which the illimitable prairies so
bountifully provide.

On this visit I was shown the site for the new Parliament
Buildings, which was well chosen. The selected architectural
design in the subsequent empire competition (to which design

Taking on New Responsibilities.

the buildings have since been erected) revealed a worthy and scholarly building, which I am told embodies in effect all that the drawings promised. This building, along with the Canadian Northern Railway terminus, the Fort Garry Hotel, and other important buildings, gives a note of architectural distinction to the city, and atones for the monotony of its surroundings.

The next call was Regina, which had shortly before our visit suffered from a furious cyclone which had cut a gap through the city diagonally, razing everything in its onrush.

We were the guests of Governor Brown and his wife, whose carriage, with a splendid pair of horses and a cockaded coachman and footman, met us at the station. This is not a surprising sight at an English railway station, but an innovation in a Canadian provincial capital, where everyone almost runs a motor-car.

Government House is a comfortable residence on the west side of the city, surrounded by a well-planted garden with green lawns, probably the only garden of any importance in the city. Here was also a range of glasshouses, evidently managed by a gardener with English training, containing a collection of orchids.

In the evening I lectured to a very large audience. I again dealt with the principles of city planning and their application to Regina. Nearly all the questions put to me after the lecture had reference to the width of streets and side-walks, and the most desirable positions for avenue trees. I could not understand this concentration and the almost acrimonious discussion on side-track topics until I learnt there had been a heated discussion of the subject in the City Council, and that the opposing newspapers had made it a matter of local politics.

Nevertheless, the lecture seemed to have made an impression. Before I left I was commissioned by the Government to lay out the gardens and park surrounding the Parliament Buildings, also a building estate of about three hundred acres. The City Council also instructed me to prepare a complete plan for their city, reaching to the limits of the civic boundary. In the securing of these two important commissions I was deeply indebted to Governor Brown. The major part of the work for the Government has been carried out, but owing to the slump in real-estate values not much progress has been made with the city extension. In Regina I met many notable men and women. The then Premier, Mr. Scott, is a man of great ability and a progressive politician. Saskatchewan is probably the best governed province in Canada.

The Life and Work of An English Landscape Architect.

From Regina we went to Saskatoon, where I saw the amazing sight of a whole city under scaffolding poles. Although situated in the centre of a fertile wheat district, the strategic location could not justify such rapid extension. I am afraid that when the slump came many English investors lost heavily.

My business, however, was at the University, and not with the city. In collaboration with the architects to the University I had to lay out the entire campus. The scheme included the planning of the several departments in relation one to the other, and the site. The campus occupies a well-chosen site on an elevated plateau some three hundred and sixty acres in extent, bounded on the south by the Bow river. Several important buildings had been erected. University departments had been established, and already there were in residence many hundreds of undergraduates, who were working for degrees in theology, engineering, agriculture, and pedagogy. But the Governors were ambitious, and decided to plan in advance for the most complete campus in Canada, to accommodate 9,000 students. This was the basis on which our plans were prepared, and I trust that as the many departments are erected they will conform to the development plan. This is the only way to secure coherence and the economic arrangement of departments. I think it a mistake that the University was not erected at Regina, and thus contribute to the importance of that city.

In the early stages of my tour, before leaving Ottawa, I was requested to act as assessor upon the competitive drawings for the University buildings at Calgary. I was also asked to meet the Governors when I reached the town, to plan their campus. I preferred not to act as assessor excepting in collaboration with a Canadian architect, so Colonel Meredith, of Ottawa, agreed to act. Upon the decision of Colonel Meredith the whole collection of designs was rejected as totally unsuited for the purpose intended, and as being architecturally impossible. I therefore escaped from an embarrassing appointment.

On arrival at Calgary I had several conferences with the Governors, with whom I visited the site, which was about two and a half miles west of the city, on a bleak stretch of bare prairie land, without connecting roads or any public utilities, and I came to the conclusion that the scheme was being exploited in the interests of real estates. Nevertheless I supplied a plan of the lay-out, spending a great part of a week upon it, for which I never received a dollar, not even my expenses.

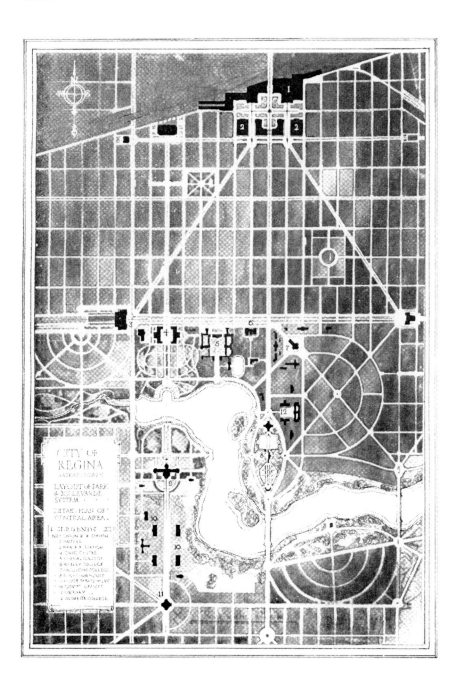

CIVIC CENTRE, REGINA, SASKATCHEWAN.

Taking on New Responsibilities.

The main object of my visit to Calgary, however, was to give a series of lectures as part of a propaganda campaign under the auspices of the Citizens' League, of which a Mr. Mark Lemon was the able and enthusiastic secretary and moving. spirit.

The publicity given to these meetings was effectively done, for the lectures were attended by large and enthusiastic audiences, who finally passed a resolution in favour of a city plan for Calgary. This resolution was sent to the City Council, who invited me to a conference, with the result that I left Calgary with a contract in my pocket for the preparation of a preliminary but comprehensive development plan. This commission was so well advertised through the City Publicity Bureau that I received inquiries for lectures from other Western cities competing for real-estate deals. As I had still other engagements on my programme, however, I had to refuse these invitations. One exception I made in favour of Medicine Hat, a nice little city on the main C.P.R. line, east of Calgary. Here I arranged to address the Canadian Club, the members of which turned up in record numbers. We foregathered in a large ante-room, where I was introduced to the members as they arrived, until an American, who tried to monopolise the whole of my time and attention, came in. He had been invited as a visitor, but I think his sponsors must have regretted his rashness.

"Well, Mr. Mawson," said this gentleman on shaking hands, "I never heard of you before, but my friend tells me you are a famous city planner. Well, sir, we have some famous city planners in the States—Mr. Olmstead, Mr. John Nolan, and many more who are carrying out big works and planning more! Yes, sir, things are very busy in your line in the States. Why, in the State I come from we are spending a million dollars on roads alone. That's some expenditure, sir, and we are considering some dandy motor roads for quick motor traffic."

This boosting he continued in loud tones throughout the luncheon, so when it came to my address I could not help trying to get even with him, and the fact that just then there was a panic on the New York Exchange added a note of piquancy to my sally.

"Gentlemen," I said, "I must apologise for being a mere Englishman, for according to some of our critics we are rapidly approaching the period of our decline ; but so ingrained are our historic associations and our love of industry that from mere force of habit we keep on doing things. In one important respect we are hopelessly behind the times—we do not advertise. For

The Life and Work of An English Landscape Architect.

instance, we have just spent fifty million dollars on one road, and are starting another one which will cost one hundred and fifty million dollars. We shall pay for both without turning a hair or causing panic on the Stock Exchange." (Laughter and loud applause.) I must say the American proved game.

"That was bully, sir," he said. "You did indeed get down to brass tacks, but I had no idea you were doing anything big in England. Why don't you have a publicity department ? "

Americans use the newspapers extensively for booming their interests, and know how to do it to advantage. Englishmen, on the contrary, shrink from publicity, often to their own hurt, and I was pleased when Sir George Paish reminded his audience in Ottawa that whilst we perhaps did not do as much for the development of the Dominion as we might, nevertheless we invested from sixty to seventy millions sterling a year in Canada.

From Medicine Hat I travelled to Banff, the St. Moritz of the Rockies, to make my first itinerary study of the town site and a wide section of the National Park which I was to develop, an area which included the three hot springs and the vermilion lakes.

We stay-at-home islanders have no idea of the glory of our Colonial possessions. I would suggest that those who go and return by the stock routes to the Alps, and who are registered amongst the Alpine climbing clubs, should make a change and go to Banff or to the neighbouring National Glacier Park, when I guarantee that their bosoms would swell with the pride of our own glorious heritage. If the distance be greater and the discomfort in reaching these parts of the Empire makes the pleasure prohibitive in winter, there are more thrills and greater diversion to be got from a summer holiday in these Western territories than there are to be found in Switzerland, particularly if the tourists are in the pursuit of the romantic and sublime, or if they combine the interests of the naturalist and the botanist. They will find in quite a brief period enough varied interest to keep the imagination keenly alive for months, and even years, to come, in the ever-changing panorama of scenic grandeur, which is simply indescribable. In both of these two national parks herds of wild game, such as the bison, elk, moose, antelope, wild sheep, wild goats, and yak, may be seen and photographed in the open, or they may be seen in the " visitors' park," near the superintendent's lodge.

In spring and early summer the region is a floral paradise, as are the Alps, with a distinct botanical classification of its own.

Taking on New Responsibilities.

When I visited the district the Dominion Parks Department were alive with enterprises, and had carried out a well-thought-out scheme of motor roads and pony tracks and hiking trails to open up this awe-inspiring region, leading up to the best views and the many lakes, and the châlets whence supplies are obtainable. The intention was to make Banff the combined antitype of the picturesque Swiss villages which we know so well at the foot of the Jaungfrau, disposing the town in such a way that it would group effectively at the foot of the amphitheatre of mountains behind it.

Already, when I visited it, the Canadian Pacific had, with their usual enterprise, erected a million-dollar hotel to accommodate the increasing crowds of visitors, and have since that date more than doubled the accommodation. The situation indicated a phenomenal increase of population, and my instructions were to study, report upon, and plan out the town as a tourist resort on a great scale, providing for its growth for the next fifty years. This had to be done in such a way as to co-ordinate the varied interests, amusements, clubs, museums, etc. The Government had already established zoological collections of the wild creatures which had inhabited the district, also a natural history museum which contained a representative collection of the fauna, botanical and geological treasures of the district. In the established hotels, the museum and the clubs, and a nucleus of shopping area, there are some indications of the prospective town to commence with.

Having allotted five days of my tour for my survey, I spent every available hour of daylight collecting data, making diagrams and sketches for my plan and report, motoring, and examining the whole site and its immediate environs.

I then took train for Vancouver, passing through the amazingly awe-inspiring Canadian Rockies. I had arranged to write my impressions of Banff and my preliminary report on the journey, but passing through such country—a country expressive of Nature at her grandest, aloof, austere, inexplicable, and incomparable—work seemed mean and useless by contrast. In the presence of such titanic forces and wondrous visions of God's handiwork, all human endeavour, life and death, and all man's conquests, are puny. In the presence of these majestic mountains, these sentinels of eternity, the ever-changing wonder of glaciers, white cloud-spitting peaks, roaring torrents, mighty pine forests interspersed with the expansive lakes, one is struck dumb with awe and reverence. O for a modicum of John Ruskin's powers of description !

The Life and Work of An English Landscape Architect.

I could write a thrilling book about the railway journey up the Rocky Mountains, and another about the journey down the Pacific side, but they would convey little or nothing of the realisation as you are pushed up in luxurious comfort by engines of three hundred horse-power. Albeit, when we were passing through one of the most glorious and inspiring parts I overheard two young ladies discussing the price of some lace they had bought !

On arrival at Vancouver a number of people who were interested in social problems called upon us. These callers were particularly interested in town-planning, which they were anxious to see adopted for their own city, but I had to explain that my business in Vancouver was limited to the improvement of Coal Harbour and the famous Stanley Park. It is interesting to note that this appointment came about through my introduction by Mr. Wall, at that time managing director of the " Sun " newspaper, an organ that wielded considerable civic influence. Mr. Wall was later Chief Commissioner for British Columbia in London.

No sooner did I get to work on a study of the problem relating to my commission, than I was literally bombarded by a troop of newspaper men. They were out for stunts, and I simply had to oblige, and thus day by day appeared columns of my opinion on almost every phase of city planning and the need for action in Vancouver. This brought requests for lectures and conferences with Ministers in Victoria. How I managed in such a maelstrom of conflicting ideals to maintain a clear, sane policy, I do not remember, but somehow I managed to apprise the citizens of several risks which ungoverned developments made obvious. I also worked up a good deal of enthusiasm for a co-ordinated park system, and upon the needs for a new civic centre. It was a rather audacious enterprise, but it caught on, and gave a new line of direction to local patriotism.

My tentative report to the Board of Parks Commissioners was approved, and I was definitely instructed to proceed with alternative schemes for the reclamation of Coal Harbour and the improvement of Stanley Park. The alternative schemes were a concession to two opposing ideas, both vigorously promoted. In the result I prepared three schemes, two of which followed the landscape style, incorporating the suggestions of the contending parties ; the other, a quite formal and much more logical lay-out (Illus. No. 41), was my own proposal, upon which all concentrated, the design being unanimously adopted.

Taking on New Responsibilities.

As I shall have more to say in another chapter upon the schemes which I was commissioned to prepare for so many new clients, I will merely add that this trip, extending over rather more than three months, constituted the biggest bustle of my life, but every day was inspiring, and the whole trip of great educational value—new problems to solve, new people to meet, new opportunities for achievement; furthermore, I felt I must justifiably give value for the confidence placed in me, and merit the unbounded kindness which the Canadians showed me.

There is one other decision which I had to face, which raised questions of business morality. Two firms of American real-estate agents sought my assistance in the subdivision of their estates for boosting purposes, offering me fees by which I could, with very little work, have earned three thousand pounds. I visited both properties, and found they were miles away from any centre of population, with no public utilities within reach. Concluding that my would-be clients wished to use my plans and my name for the promotion of sales of land in England, I refused the commission.

On my return to Ottawa I was consulted by a very responsible estate agent, with offices in Montreal, and commissioned to plan a model suburb of about 600 acres near to Ottawa. Here the site was splendid, quite convenient to the capital city, and reached by electric tram with a quick and frequent service. The estate was on the shores of Lake Deschenes, a beautiful sheet of water offering great attractions for aquatic sports and fishing. My terms for planning the estate were eighteen hundred pounds, and having some fear of the financial stability of the promotion, I insisted upon a payment of £500 before I started work, which proved very fortunate, as the balance of £1,300 was never paid, although I carried out my part of the contract. Notwithstanding this serious loss, I was very sorry for my clients, who were caught by the sudden collapse of the land boom and lost seriously. If they could have held on they might have weathered the depression.

It was on this journey that I first met Pauline Johnson, the Indian poetess (daughter of a chief of one of the Iriquois tribes), whose works called " Flints and Feathers " and " Legends of Vancouver " I had some acquaintance with. At this time she was a semi-invalid, but her conversation was in keeping with her poetry—full of nature, imagery, and imaginatively construed legends of local places.

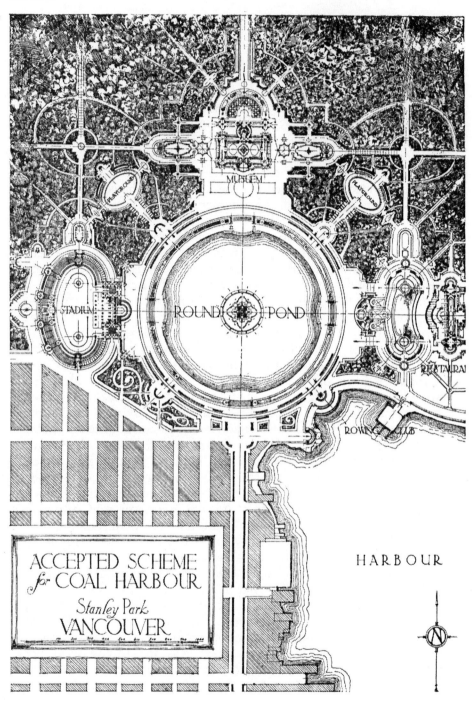

PLAN OF COAL HARBOUR, VANCOUVER.

HISTORICAL PAGEANT, ATHENS.

CHAPTER XVII.

A CALL TO ATHENS.

O N my return to England, my client who, as stated in the last chapter, had discharged me, asked me to meet him.

With some little anxiety I called at the time and place appointed. I was met in the most friendly spirit with the remark that I was to carry on, as he had realised that in my sons I was fortunate in having partners who would loyally uphold the standard hitherto aimed at in my work. Thus was attained, in part at least, one of the objects which justified my acceptance of commissions entailing long absences from home, and at last providing the requisite opportunity for those who would some day succeed me. As a result of this concession on the part of my clients, my work tended more and more to become advisory, with the preparation of preliminary plans. Thus the broad outlines of a scheme could be laid down, leaving to others the details and working drawings, but nearly always reserving to myself the arrangement of the plantations which finally give the dominant character to most garden designs.

In short, I was now applying to the work of my office the methods of budding French and American architects, who prepare the sketch designs to a small scale, after which these pass through the various stages and developments in the draughting office, under the direction of the chief, who supplies the criticism and suggestions during the stages of their progress.

This method of preparing preliminary plans led to many interesting developments. Increasingly it became apparent how intimately the house and garden are associated, and in town plans how every factor or feature has its bearing upon every other factor or feature. In the case of a new garden to an old house it was often impossible to obtain an ideal effect without serious alteration to the plan of the house—as, for instance, when the entrance hall and carriage court occupied the south frontage.

The Life and Work of An English Landscape Architect.

The consideration of the problems as a whole led unconsciously to the revival of the architectural side of our practice—or, rather, to a renewal of the position which obtained during my partnership with Dan Gibson, but now with my sons as architectural colleagues. Thus, when during these few months at home we extended the gardens at Brackley, Ballater, for Sir Victor Mackenzie, the work included a new billiard and smoking-room wing ; similarly, the extensive additions to the gardens at Thornton Manor called for as a part of our general development plan, extended plans for the mansion. Much of the latter has, in a modified form, been carried out. In some cases where this comprehensive planning was undertaken, we refused to act as architects, as our object was not to poach on architects' preserves, but merely to secure a general degree of harmony between the house and the grounds.

Before leaving New York on my last trip I was requested to meet Mr. E. P. Bonbright, a well-known New York banker, with offices in the City of London. Mr. and Mrs. Bonbright, like many other clients, had been content with a tolerably good luxuriant garden, but after studying the exemplary ancient and modern gardens in this country, had become dissatisfied with their American home.

The site I found was a good one, and large enough for ample gardens and a small park, but the soil was thin and poor, and lay on rock, which at places was very near the surface, and costly to excavate. I collected all the data and levels which were necessary for the preparation of a garden scheme, and during my stay in England developed my proposals for the improvement of these gardens and submitted them to my clients, who spent most of their time in London. Finally, I was instructed to complete my drawings, but whether or not my suggestions were ever carried out I cannot say. This is one of the disappointments inseparable from work at long distances from home.

For Mr. A. L. Langmuir of Cadbury Manor, Cadbury, Somerset, I replanned the gardens in such a way as to permit the scheme being realised by annual instalments. Mr. and Mrs. Langmuir spent much of their time in Canada, where they had property interests, and the intention was to have the alterations in the gardens carried out during their absence. Cadbury Manor is a very charming old-world house built in proximity to a peculiarly beautiful parish church of which the owner of Cadbury Manor is lay rector.

A Call to Athens.

At the same time extensive garden improvements were planned and carried out for John R. Barlow, Esq., of Greenthorne, Edgeworth, near Bolton. This gentleman is head of one of the most important cotton-manufacturing concerns in Lancashire, and for his partner, Mr. Wm. Hoyle, I had already done work at Grasmere.

One of the most successful bits of work in this garden was the conversion of a formal stream, hemmed in between irregularly built walls, into a series of rocky cascades.

An entirely new garden of considerable extent was planned and carried out for Herbert Noble, of Higher Trap, near Padiham ; whilst in association with my old friend and colleague, C. E. Mallows, I was continuing the work of laying out the gardens at Tirley Garth, Tarporley, Cheshire, for R. A. Prestwich.

Thus I was engaged at the one time by four gentlemen interested in cotton, in the planning of important gardens, and by three others in an advisory capacity. In my experience it has often happened that when a professional man has obtained an introduction into a particular circle it is soon found that he has been commissioned by many people having the same business interests, each anxious to outshine the others in friendly rivalry. Yet in the matter of garden-making there can be no real rivalry, for each garden problem calls for its own solution, and each stands alone and unique.

At Greenthorne the chief attractions of the garden are the cascaded stream and the stone-built bridge, whilst at Higher Trap the interest is found in the broad terraces. At Grasmere there are the extensive Alpine gardens and the terrace on the mountain side, while at Tirley Garth we are impressed with the variety and completeness of the several parts of the site, beginning with terrace and panel gardens, merging into the freer landscape treatment, where undulating lawns sweep in pleasing curves under the shrubberies and specimen trees.

One of the first matters with which I had to deal on my return home was the completion of arrangements for a course of lectures to be delivered at the Melbourne, Brisbane, Perth, Sydney, and Adelaide Universities. I had agreed to the terms offered by Dr. Barrett, who represented the Board of Governors of the Universities of Australia, and who was a keen propagandist of town planning. I was to give a course of six lectures at each University, for which I was to be paid six hundred pounds,

FOOTS CRAY PLACE.

inclusive of my expenses—not a very big fee, but a splendid introduction to the Government, which desired to consult me about town-planning legislation, a commission the completion of which would profitably employ my spare time. I was also asked to advise one or two city councils on the preparation of town-planning schemes, so that in one way or another the venture promised success.

At the same time I doubted the wisdom of giving my English and Canadian clients further openings for charging me with neglecting their interests ; this, notwithstanding the fact that I had learnt by hard work and quick intuition to work out my preliminary studies rapidly. The staff at home, fired with zeal by the widening horizon of interesting work ahead, gave me the assurance that the preliminary schemes for Regina, Calgary, Banff, and Vancouver would be ready to submit, as arranged, in the autumn.

Apart from financial considerations, I was genuinely anxious to contribute my quota to town-planning propaganda, and to give to Australian civic art something of the force and directness of English ideals. The factor, however, which finally decided me to accept the offer was the opportunity which it afforded for further travel, and the study of town planning and landscape architecture under new conditions. It is this ever-onward quest for new conditions that gives to town planning its unparalleled attractions.

The lectures were framed to admit of local references and slides showing Australian housing conditions.

I decided to leave England about the end of March, and to travel to Australia *via* Vancouver. My secretary, Mr. James Crossland, would arrive in Canada a month in advance of me, for the purpose of collecting data for the civic survey of Regina, Calgary, and Banff. This work, owing to the absence of up-to-date maps and the then almost daily changes of ownership, proved to be a more formidable task than we imagined.

During the intervening three months at home I met Sir Hubert Herkomer, R.A. I had stayed a week-end with Sir Joseph and Lady Swan at their home on the Surrey hills, and in discussing my prospects, and the need of a studio about half an hour from London, Miss Mary Swan, an old pupil of Sir Hubert's, told me that her old master had given up his school at Bushey, and that his studios were just what I wanted. I wrote at once to Sir Hubert,

The Life and Work of An English Landscape Architect.

asking if the property was to be sold, or if it could be rented. Sir Hubert replied that I was just too late, as he had demolished the studios and had decided to convert the site into a rose garden. To assist him in the preparation of his designs, he had instructed his bookseller to send him the most authoritative work on the subject, and as a result he had just received a copy of " The Art and Craft of Garden Making," of which he thought I must be the author. Now that we had come into touch with each other, he proceeded, he would like me to visit him the following week-end to advise him. This I arranged to do.

On arrival at Bushey station I found a luxurious car and a liveried chauffeur awaiting me. I thus proceeded in state to " Lululaund," Sir Hubert's Bohemian castle. Whatever may be the architectural merits or demerits of the home of the Herkomers, it was evident that the house had been built regardless of cost. What struck me about the place as I became further acquainted with it, was the original and unique craftsmanship which had been expended upon its decoration and appointments. Every hinge, every lock and key, had been specially designed, and each showed an amazing knowledge of the best traditions of the smith's craft. The wood carvings were largely the work of the artist's father, but the designs were, I imagine, the work of Sir Hubert. A striking feature was a frieze in modelled Whatman's paper, which looked as though it had been pressed in the pulp stage, but which had been worked similarly to leather-work and then tinted.

My famous client proposed at once that we should go into the garden and view the site of the proposed rose garden, which was covered from end to end with old building material. However, the character and extent of the site were easy to grasp, as were also the essential features which should dominate its design. So at once we plunged into details and agreed on the main outlines and proportions. The garden was to be separated from the kitchen garden by a brick-built pergola, with a handsome garden pavilion at one end. The centre of the panel rose garden was to be sunk two feet, with a fountain in the centre, and considerable spaces of ground were to be planted as foils against adjoining properties. Then we came to the discussion of probable costs, to my estimate of which Sir Hubert readily agreed. Finally, he remarked : "We have still to settle your fees, and I am going to make a suggestion which I hope you will accept. I think," he said, " you ought to have your portrait painted ; my price for this would be six hundred guineas. Let's swop. I'll do your portrait, whilst you design my rose garden, and we'll call it quits."

To this proposal I readily agreed, assured for once in my life that I had made a bargain. My friends regard the portrait, which is produced in tone as the frontispiece, as an exceptionally good rendering of the character of the sitter.

The last portrait painted by Herkomer was that of Governor Brown of Regina, to whom I showed a photograph of my portrait. Governor Brown wired Herkomer to ask if he could paint his portrait, and got in reply the following message : " If you can come immediately, think I can do it." Mr. Brown started for England the next day, and was just in time, for his last sitting concluded Herkomer's life-work. The distinguished artist died a few days later. As Mr. Brown remarked, it almost seemed as if he had had a premonition when he sent his cable. I felt Herkomer's loss keenly. During our short acquaintance we were drawn closely to one another. He was the most versatile man I have ever met ; his buoyancy was contagious, and he was a most delightful, companionable man, and a true artist—a Bohemian by natural birth and a Bohemian by temperament.

As already indicated, I proposed to travel to the Antipodes *via* Vancouver. I intended spending two months in Canada for the purpose of discussing preliminary plans with my several Governmental and municipal clients. Into the preparation of the Canadian town plans my two sons and my staff had put much interesting work, often interpreting my proposals from the roughest sketches, and with perfect success. They were certainly only preliminary studies, but in each case they were worked out in sufficient detail to focus discussion upon the essentials, yet were elastic enough to allow of adjustments where desirable. Other important events were now impending.

On arrival at St. John, New Brunswick, our port of debarkation, I found a cable from my son awaiting me, stating that His Majesty King Constantine wished to consult me about the royal gardens in Athens and a park system for his capital. This was great news, calling for immediate action. The possibility of working in this world-famous city under royal patronage was irresistible. Believing that my Australian clients would see in this call one of the greatest compliments which could be paid to British art, I cabled to them for permission to postpone my trip. At the same time I cabled to my son asking him to proceed to Greece at once with whatever

The Life and Work of An English Landscape Architect.

assistants he required for the preparation of surveys and the collection of data. In the meantime I would get through my work in Canada and join him in Athens as soon as possible.

My duties in Canada occupied about six weeks, and the amount of work undertaken during this period, the distances travelled, the number of governmental and municipal officials and committees interviewed, the voluminous notes which I made after my investigation of the town sites to be replanned, suggest that I had got into the stride of the American hustler. I had, however, got together the nucleus of a town-planning staff in Canada, with a well-equipped office in Vancouver under the direction of my second son, who was made junior partner in the firm, with my nephew, Robert Mattocks, as chief of staff. The help thus assured enabled us to work more expeditiously, and to check off our draft plans on the sites before submission to our clients, also to make such amendments as seemed desirable before returning these plans to our English office for final completion.

In some cases we found it possible to complete our drawings and reports in Canada. This applied particularly to the comprehensive lay-out of the Parliament Buildings, the gardens, and the real estate owned by the provincial government in Regina, and some interesting developments of schools and playgrounds in Calgary.

Returning home at the end of May, I found that my son had about completed the designs for the royal gardens at Athens, having obtained approval of his preliminary basic studies before leaving that city. Their Majesties proved most interested clients, giving my son interviews almost daily, and bringing ripe thought to the discussion of every feature as the work of planning proceeded. In addition, they motored him out to their villa at Tatoi and discussed the need of a new villa on a larger and better plan, to be built on a plateau somewhat elevated above the existing one. They also instructed him to prepare plans for their burial ground, which occupied the site of a beautiful knoll not far from Tatoi, though secluded from the villa. This knoll was surrounded by pine woods (since destroyed by fire), and on one side a vista had been cut which gave a wonderful view to the south-west, with Athens and the Acropolis in the distance. King George was buried on this lovely spot, and a small Byzantine chapel was perched on its highest part. King Constantine wished to enclose this ground

215

suitably, and to lay it out in the form of a simple terrace connected by a wide central path leading to the chapel.

Our Royal patrons were at the time preparing for their annual trip to Eastbourne, where we were asked to meet them at the Grand Hotel, where they stayed every summer with their family. These few intervening weeks gave time to detail our plans and to give them a businesslike appearance. At the time arranged (viz., at the end of June) I journeyed to Eastbourne, accompanied by my son, who introduced me to the Court Chamberlain, Count Mercati, in whom I found from this time onward a charming and helpful friend.

Next I was introduced to Miss Constavlos, lady-in-waiting to the Queen, who was keenly interested in all the improvements contemplated by their Majesties. In the afternoon I was introduced by Count Mercati to the King and Queen, who were delightful and entirely free from the formality which I had expected and feared. Like the members of our own Royal Family, they possessed the genius for putting people at their ease. "Your son tells me, Mr. Mawson," said His Majesty, "that you are a keen gardener. So am I; therefore we have interests in common." "And I," interposed the Queen, "am longing to see you at work on the re-housing of the working classes in Athens, where the conditions are deplorable. My royal mother-in-law erected many beautiful hospitals. I think better housing conditions might prevent the need for more."

For two hours we discussed alternately gardens and better housing, and finally the provision of planted public spaces, with coffee kiosks and restaurants where the working classes could rest in the shade during the heat of the day. In all respects the interview was very interesting, and gave me a new conception of the beneficent influence exercised by the members of royal families.

Before leaving Eastbourne I was introduced to the children, including Prince George, Prince Paul, and Prince Alexander (the last-named of whom in a few years succeeded his father on the throne), and also the Princess, who is now Crown Princess of Roumania, and was delighted to note the evident tokens of family affection.

The King finally approved of the plans for the royal gardens, and arranged that I should meet him in Athens in September. I was requested to call at Corfu *en route* to report on the possibilities

The Life and Work of An English Landscape Architect.

of improving the garden setting for the royal palace there, and also to offer suggestions for the improvement of the town of Corfu. "When you get to Athens," he remarked, " I will introduce you to M. Venizelos and the Mayor, and I hope you may be commissioned to prepare plans for the improvement of my capital. There," he said, " you will have the chance of your life, and ample scope for your genius. I ought to tell you, however, that we have already had one elaborate scheme presented by the Kaiser and prepared by Mr. Hoffman, his architect, who after a motor tour round Athens prepared a scheme which entirely ignored existing conditions and property values, overlooking those interests in the capital which have every claim for recognition. Therefore we had to reject his proposals, and we decided that next time the work should be entrusted to an Englishman."

In view of what has since transpired, this rejection of what was virtually the Kaiser's proposal is interesting. Later, when in Athens, I saw this scheme, which had been presented in elaborate report form, beautifully printed and illustrated. It certainly included many drastic proposals, but it also included a few suggestions that could have been incorporated in a revised plan. Its rejection must have been a keen disappointment, both to the Kaiser and to his architect.

In the interval between meeting King Constantine and the visit to Athens I made a brief return to my first love of private gardens, making a tour of the English and Scotch clients who had schemes in prospect or in hand. It was a delightful and restful interlude. Never before had I experienced the potency of that pregnant sentence of Lord Bacon's, that a garden ministers the greatest refreshment to the spirits of man. The change from the heavier toils of public work reminded me of what the late Sir Alfred East said about those occasions when he used to leave his ponderous easel work and betake himself off with pencil, notebook, and water colours, sketching from nature direct, returning with mind refreshed and ideas refurnished. It is one of the compensations of work that it compasses its rest in its own activities. The refined materials to hand wherewith to express one's ideals, and the freer rein given to the imagination, in private work, provide a pleasure after the restraints whereby civic work is usually hemmed in, and thus for ever running the gauntlet amidst vested interests. Speaking from observation and experience of clients, there must be a similar allurement in their case. There is apparently no end to garden

THE ROYAL PALACE, CORFU.

THE QUAY, CORFU.

A Call to Athens.

making, for when one part is improved it shows up disparagingly the other parts. If the owners of gardens only knew how far their initial experiments would lead them, their courage would fail at the outset.

At the end of August my son and I left for Athens, travelling *via* Paris, Rome, Brindisi, and Corfu, staying at the last-mentioned place for several days. The journey across the Continent was full of interest, and particularly the journey from Rome to Brindisi through prolific vineyards and olive groves, interspersed by white towns and villages, each one of which we would have loved to explore ; but the time at our disposal did not allow of digressions. Brindisi itself was disappointing. It had suffered greatly in an earthquake some years before, and many of the houses had lost their upper storey. The whole place had a lack of business prosperity, accounted for by the fact that the port was no longer a place of call for the P. and O. and other Indian liners.

We took one of the Italian boats calling at Corfu, arriving there the next morning ; but long before we reached the island we were on deck revelling in the beauty of the coast line, and noting the evidences of the Balkan war, which had just been settled in favour of Greece. The once prosperous little seaport of Santa Quaranta was in complete ruins, the result of a few hours' bombardment by the Greek fleet.

I had seen illustrations of the island of Corfu, the jewel of the Adriatic, which I had regarded as extravagances of the imagination in schemes of impossible colouring, but the reality far surpassed in beauty and depth of colour what I had regarded as merely imaginative. Every element of the picturesque was here embodied.

The town of Corfu, situated at the east side of the island, is a fascinating jumble of buildings devoted to every purpose, to which beautiful belfries and tall cupolas give a dominating note (see Illus. Nos. 45 and 46). The town occupies a cup-shaped slope with the higher promontory to the east and the rising ground to the west, crowned with fortifications and barracks. These fortifications are very massive in appearance, and reach down to the sea by a series of stone-built terraces, picturesque with masses of flowers and scrubwood breaking up the solidity of the heavy stonework. At places numerous cypress trees throw up their shafts of dark velvety green, their upright growth contrasting with the horizontal lines of the royal palace and the principal buildings.

The Life and Work of An English Landscape Architect.

On alighting to proceed to our hotel, built on the higher ground overlooking a pleasant bay to the south, we found the views entrancing: seawards to the south and westward over beautiful vineyards and olive groves, with the Kaiser's palace rising consequentially (of course) on its elevated site above the tops of surrounding woodland of cypress, pine, and olives.

The old part of the town, as we soon discovered, had been built in entire disregard of plan or arrangement, buildings of all sizes and shapes being placed at all angles, jostling one another and sprawling zigzag on to what should have been the streets of the town—roads which were actually narrower in many places than ten feet, whilst in some of the most important thoroughfares the width was no more than twelve feet. From the port to the royal palace there is a fairly good road skirting the shore, which must have required considerable engineering skill to construct. To the south-west there is a fine boulevard, promenade, and garden much like those at Torquay.

There were several well planned and constructed arterial roads extending from the town into the open country, and these, along with all the other modern improvements and the noble Georgian architecture, were a legacy of the British occupation. King Constantine, remarking on this fact, said that so far as the natives were concerned, they never promoted any improvement which added to the attraction or convenience of the island, having been spoiled by the English, who relieved them of every necessity to bestir themselves. His object was now to induce them to develop a little civic pride by introducing some of the improvements absolutely essential, and decencies worthy of the fame of the island, and thus attract an increasing number of tourists. Never, except perhaps in some of the remote Italian towns, have I seen such congestion as here, along with its accompanying unsavouriness; yet at the same time no town possesses such a beautiful environment or setting, or one which so readily lends itself to improvement without the loss of its picturesqueness or ancient character.

King Constantine had mentioned six main improvements to be incorporated in our town-planning scheme—

(1) An improved or alternative route between the port and the esplanade.
(2) A new hotel and casino.
(3) The improvement of the immediate surroundings of the royal palace.
(4) A new boulevard extending westward and past the Kaiser's villa.
(5) A model workman's suburb on garden-city lines.
(6) A park system for Corfu in which large planted spaces devoted to the growth of shade trees should predominate.

A Call to Athens.

Acting upon the King's suggestion, my son had called at Corfu on his return from Athens for the purpose of collecting the necessary data for the preparation of a town-planning scheme, and had reduced to a tentative plan his impression of what was possible and desirable. This plan met so fully with my ideas, that we presented a scheme, based on this study, to the King upon our arrival in Athens, elaborating and amending it after our discussions. It is interesting to note that in the early part of 1914 the Kaiser asked his sister, Queen Sophia, to convey to us his congratulations upon our scheme.

From Corfu we took boat to Patras, one of the busiest ports in Greece. After a ramble round the well-planned and well-managed town, we took train for Athens, travelling by the Patras-Athens express, which was supposed to do the journey in five hours, but generally, as on this occasion, took eight. The variety of scene, coupled with an excellent restaurant car, obviated all sense of tediousness, and at stopping places excellent coffee and delicious fruit could be procured at a price which in this country would spell bankruptcy to the caterer. *En route* we crossed over the Corinth canal, its stupendous engineering being very apparent, looking along it from the dizzy heights of the railway bridge.

My first sight of Athens (many miles away) from this railway was inspiring. The dim shadowy line of the Acropolis and its noble crown of ruined temples was softly silhouetted against a clear blue and purple sky, suffused by the dim evening light, the whole changing in mass and grouping as seen from various angles as the train passed round the frequent bends and curves. Whatever the point of view, the Acropolis is so imposing that scarcely for a moment could I take my eyes off it. This fascinating first impression of the world masterpiece I have never lost.

It was late when we arrived in Athens, but as we drove to our hotel we noticed that many of the thoroughfares were wide and well constructed, whilst in the Place de la Concorde and on the squares passed *en route* a distinctly decorative garden note was apparent. Many noble palms, mostly Latanias, Chamerops and Coryphas, interspersed with orange trees and beds of flowers, gave to the air a sweetness which reminded one of the favourite description of Athens—the city of sweet violets.

Further acquaintance with Athens, however, revealed a very low average of garden spaces, with practically no children's

The Life and Work of An English Landscape Architect.

playgrounds or other recreational facilities. True, there were the Royal Gardens, the Zappion, the Lycabettos, the Acropolis, the Mount of Phillapapos, and the open space on which stands the remains of the temple of Jupiter Olympus, but these were not readily accessible to the residents. They regarded the precincts of these ancient remains as tourist reserves.

Next morning we signed the visitors' book at the palace, and later received a note from Count Mercati, asking us to meet His Majesty at three o'clock the same afternoon. Punctually at the time appointed we were taken to the audience chamber, where the King and Queen extended to us a hearty welcome to Athens, hoping that great things might follow our visit. We were at once asked to sit down, a welcome request which surprised and pleased me. I had always understood that ordinary civilians were required to remain standing in the presence of Royalty.

The final plans for the royal gardens were approved, with slight modifications, and we were instructed to make arrangements for carrying out the work. This we did by co-operating with the court architect and the superintendent of the royal gardens, the latter a Greek who spoke excellent English.

Directly their Majesties had disposed of this work, the King told me that he had notified the Prime Minister (M. Venizelos) and the Mayor (M. Benachies), both of whom would have conferences with me in respect to the replanning and extension of Athens. The King then apprised me of some of the things which he wished to see included in the new plans. Among these were new parliament buildings on a different site, and a new dignified union railway station of ample proportions somewhere on the axis of Rue Constantine. Then we must consider the removal of all the shacks and hovels which had grown up around the base of the Acropolis, and also the removal of every obstruction within the precincts of all ancient remains. " It is very important," added the King, " that we should impress tourists by our care for that which they prize so highly." A new university campus to occupy a site then used as a military camp ; the improvement and connection of all important roads leading out of Athens, so as to encourage motoring ; finally, the scheduling of a wide belt of land for afforestation round the capital, were the other schemes propounded by His Majesty. This last-named scheme was his pet hobby, and one which he inherited from his father.

In giving his reasons for such amplitude of forest land he

explained that historical evidences proved that all the higher ground round ancient Athens was forest land, and it was also certain that in early times the river Illysus, with its roaring cataracts, was a river, and not a mere rivulet as now. He believed the drying up of the river was caused by deforestation, and that reafforestation would not only increase the rainfall, but by absorption equalise the river's flow.

"When do you propose to start work on your new forest?" I asked. "To-morrow morning," was the quick reply, "if you and the Queen agree to help me. I have thousands of young pines and cypresses growing in small pots, which may be planted out at once." This was quickly arranged, and we were to start work at the base of the Acropolis.

"And now," proceeded the King, "I wish to say that in any architecture which may be incorporated in your town-planning scheme I hope you will keep strictly to your Georgian tradition, for, in my opinion, no body of architects in any part of the world so truly caught the spirit of our classical Greek as did your English architects of the late seventeenth and eighteenth centuries." Passing for a few minutes into the adjoining room, he returned with a pile of books dealing with Georgian architecture, remarking, as he laid his load on the table, "I buy every book I can lay my hands on which illustrates good English architecture." My son had already told me of this preference, but I never guessed that his knowledge of the subject was so intimate.

When the King had taken in order all the points on which he was specially interested, the Queen, who had been listening, remarked that she hoped I would give early and serious attention to the rehousing of the working classes, whose existing housing conditions were intolerable and a menace to public health. When we had fully discussed our business, the King asked which way I was going, adding: "If you are returning to your hotel, I am walking that way, and we can go through the royal gardens."

Passing through Constitution Square and noticing the orange trees ladened with fruit, I remarked: "It seems to me that the boys of Athens must be peculiarly honest; in England we have yet to invent a fence which will protect our orchards." ·

"Boys," replied the King, "are the same the world over—these are bitter oranges."

At this time Constantine appealed to me as a very kingly personage who was interested in and adored by his people. One

The Life and Work of An English Landscape Architect.

story will explain this popularity. At the end of the second Balkan war, the King, in motoring back to Athens, saw a poor soldier who had evidently dropped out of the lines, lying exhausted by the road-side. At once the King stopped his car and asked the poor fellow to take a seat. " I can't," replied the soldier. " Why can't you ? " " Because I am worried with the lancers (?)," replied the soldier. " So am I," said the King ; " so jump in."

In the evening the King motored us out to see his villa at Tatoi, and I must say that I had only once previously travelled at such a pace. On this occasion, however, the road was a very bad one ; whereas on the other occasion the road was very good. When I alighted I breathed a prayer of thanksgiving.

I was delighted with Tatoi, which occupies a fine elevated site surrounded by thousands of acres of pine woods of thirty or forty years' growth. Before leaving we were instructed to proceed with the new villa, on a somewhat higher plateau. The special accommodation required had already been discussed with my son, and proved a delightful subject for study, as the accommodation of a royal palace is somewhat exceptional, provision having to be made for the sentinels on guard, and special exits provided for escape in case of an attack upon the life of the King. Then there are numerous secretaries to provide for, and private quarters for the lady-in-waiting on the Queen, and her clerical staff, consisting of secretary and typists. The lady-in-waiting at the Greek court is a very busy and important personage. We proposed to accommodate part of the staff in separate buildings.

After discussing the future gardens and terraces, we returned to Athens, covering the distance with almost lightning speed. Everyone seemed to know that the King was at the wheel, and scurried out of the way.

By arrangement we met at 2-30 the next day, at the palace, for our planting expedition, the Queen accompanying us to the Acropolis, where several waggon-loads of pines, cypresses, and shrubs had been deposited. A squad of men with picks and spades had been requisitioned, under the direction of an expert forester, to dig the holes and plant the trees as we set them out. Naturally a crowd soon collected to see the King and Queen setting out trees and shrubs, but my royal assistants stuck to their work, and the results which followed amply justified this much-needed piece of afforestation propaganda. Nearly every tree and shrub took root, and they are making splendid growth.

A Call to Athens.

At one point I paused to study the peculiarities of the site. "I know," said the King, "what you are thinking. You are wanting a little more variety, and so am I; but it can't be done." "But, surely," I replied, "we could import what we need." "Can't be done," again replied the King; "it's more than my job's worth. You see our phylloxera laws are very strictly enforced." "Then cannot anything be done in the matter?" "Well," replied the King, "the only suggestion I can make is that on your return home you buy a cheap piano, tear out the inside and stuff it full of shrubs and forward it to the Piræus by boat; but you must be careful to label it 'musical instrument.'" Just at that moment a smart wagonette with four young ladies and an older one, all demurely dressed in black, drove up and watched us at work. "These," said my royal client, "are the ladies of the last Turkish harem." This was the first of many delightful days spent with their Majesties.

Two days later I received a friendly letter from M. Venizelos, asking me to meet him the next day at the Mayor's villa at Kephesia in time for lunch, so that we could have a long afternoon together. He also said that this would give his friend the Mayor (M. Benachies) an opportunity of expressing his views on certain important aspects of town planning applicable to Athens.

Upon arrival, Mr. and Mrs. Benachies met me in the hall of their beautiful villa, and to my relief I found that both spoke excellent English, which they explained by saying they had spent the greater part of their lives in Manchester, and, they added, still loved England. I was then introduced to M. Venizelos in the library. He addressed me in French, though later he acquired the ability to sustain long conversations in English, in which he seemed to gain considerable mastery.

M. Venizelos accepted me at once as the chosen town planner for Athens, and was most friendly. Naturally I stood in some awe for a time of the man I had heard described by responsible politicians as the greatest statesman in Europe, but the kindly bearing and the merry twinkle in his eye immediately put me at my ease.

After an excellent lunch we three again adjourned to the library or salon, where the Prime Minister at once plunged into the subject we had met to discuss. The gist of what he said is as follows :—

"You have already had several conferences with the

The Life and Work of An English Landscape Architect.

King, who has doubtless given you his views upon the desirability of creating a noble park system for the capital, terminating in a fringe of forests. He also, I believe, emphasised the need for new parliament buildings and for Government offices ; also the desirability of improving the royal palace and its surrounding gardens. You have already spoken to the Mayor, who probably and properly desires a new town hall, and the re-housing of the working classes. All these are desirable, but need to be fitted into an organised town plan in which still broader factors shall receive recognition.

" Although approving of what has already been suggested, my view, as Premier, is somewhat different from that of His Majesty and the Mayor. I have to maintain a wider outlook, and the first thing I see is that the importation of tourists is our principal vein of wealth, and the one which has potentially the greatest powers of expansion. I notice, however, that visitors come and go in a few days, or a week, and therefore I maintain that your chief work as town planner to the Greek Government is to invent as many inducements as possible to prolong their stay. To this end the railway stations and approaches to the capital should be inviting, the city and its parks must be improved, all ancient monuments must be preserved and relieved of the accumulation of mean structures by which they are at present surrounded. New interests must be opened up, and additional ancient remains made accessible by fine boulevards and improved motor roads. But most important of all, material and physical comforts must be provided for our visitors, along with abundant recreational facilities for body and mind. The parks should also be as perfect as possible, whilst a chain of comfortable hotels should be arranged in convenient centres of historic interest. In short, modern Athens and the surrounding centres of interest must be beautiful, attractive, and recuperative to body and mind, as was ancient Athens."

Thus spake one of the wisest of European statesmen.

At lunch, M. Benachies, a generous patriot, had spoken as strongly and as feelingly of the deplorable Athenian housing conditions as had the Queen, and I told him of Her Majesty's keen interest in this problem, and also of her desire to see a great increase in the number of town gardens and shade trees. " Yes, yes," said the Mayor, " that, too, is very important, and you must show us what we should do, and how to do it." From this subject he went on to speak of the need of a new and more stately civic

Houses of Parliament, Athens.

A Call to Athens.

centre, which should include amongst its most important buildings a new town hall, post office, and opera house. After M. Venizelos had fully expressed his ideas, the Mayor returned to housing and the civic centre. The Premier spoke as a statesman, stating the first essentials of a metropolis of such historic sentiment as Athens—namely, proper accommodation for tourists, and residences for the well-to-do, who were increasingly making Athens their home. At this time its resident population was increasing at the rate of twenty-five thousand a year.

Taking M. Venizelos' ideas as my keynote, I wrote by way of propaganda a carefully-thought-out article on "Athens' Principal Vein of Wealth," which I handed to the press, urging the Council and Government immediately to schedule the few remaining suitable sites for hotels, or otherwise to acquire the sites and hold them in readiness for building operations, which could not long be delayed.

Next morning I had a visitor who said he had been impressed by my article, and wished to thank me for raising the question of hotel accommodation, which was so inadequate that hundreds were turned away every day during the tourist season, to the great financial loss and prestige of Athens. My visitor did not appear to me to be a man of substance, and as I was anxious to pursue my studies of the capital, I thought I would bring the interview to a close by asking to what extent he could support financially such an enterprise. Immediately he replied : " If you will get together a sound board of English directors to control the company, I will invest sixty thousand pounds sterling, and two of my friends will invest twenty thousand pounds each, and you may take it from me that at least two-thirds of the capital required can be found in Athens alone. The one guarantee needed is an English board of directors." This I regarded as the finest compliment to the probity and ability of English financiers I had ever heard. It shows that the financier, like prophets, has most honour abroad.

In anticipation of definite acceptance by the Town Council of our proposals as to procedure and fees, we spent long hours each day making a civic survey, especially noting vacant lands and low-grade buildings on the best plan of Athens which we could procure. Curiously, this was a survey prepared at the cost of one of the banks, which proved to be accurate in so far as it represented major factors, but was lacking in minor detail.

In addition to a survey of property values, we now inquired into the railway and traffic problems, and the opportunities which

The Life and Work of An English Landscape Architect.

existed for a co-ordinated park system, also inspecting alternative sites for the new parliament buildings and the proposed civic centre.

We left Athens with our contract with the Council duly signed and delivered, and a large amount of information dealing with every aspect of the problems to be solved.

Having received from His Majesty instructions to visit Corfu again, preparatory to the presentation of more detailed plans both for the royal gardens and for the town, we called at the island on our return journey. One day, whilst pursuing our studies, we saw a beautiful example of sacred art exposed for sale in a shop window immediately opposite the royal palace. This consisted of a frame divided into fourteen panels illustrating the life of Christ from the cradle to the cross. The work had evidently belonged to some church, and was the most exquisite example of miniature painting I had ever seen. After much bargaining I bought the work for six hundred and twenty-five drachmas, at that time twenty-five pounds sterling. We had the picture carefully packed and despatched by a boat sailing for the Port of London. Later it was delivered at our Lancaster office, and there unpacked and exhibited to the staff and many admiring friends. Before it had been in the office three days we received a letter from the Greek Ambassador in London stating that an important work of sacred art had been stolen from a Greek church. It had been traced to Corfu, where it had been exhibited in a shop window and purchased by two Englishmen. As we had recently been in the island, it was thought possible that we had acquired the picture, without, of course, knowing the origin or that it had been stolen. If so, the Ambassador would be greatly obliged if we would return it to him for transmission to Greece, and send at the same time an account of what we paid for it, and any other expenses incurred. We were much disappointed to lose our " find " ; but what could we do except willingly restore it, at our own charge, to its rightful place and use. Such a story as the picture portrayed, so reverently and beautifully told, must have solaced many a poor Greek, and may, I trust, continue to do so. The Ambassador refused to accept the return of the picture as a gift.

VILLA ACHILLEON, CORFU, THE KAISER'S RESIDENCE.

CHAPTER XVIII.

GREAT PROSPECTS END IN ANXIOUS DAYS.

FOR two weeks after my return I was engaged upon visits to my English and Scotch clients, followed by work on the preliminary plan for Athens ; but by the third week in November I was again on my way to Canada, *via* New York, with the main object of presenting our preliminary plan suggestion for the replanning of Banff, to the Parks Department of the Dominion Government, and the submission of our designs for Coal Harbour and Stanley Park to the Parks Commission of Vancouver, B.C. After much discussion the latter set of plans was finally and unanimously accepted and recommended for adoption. A plan of this somewhat bold scheme is inserted on page 206. Unfortunately, the City Council instructed their engineer to carry out the scheme, and as this gentleman was unsympathetic towards our proposals, and at the same time trained to a different conception of construction, the result, so far as realised, does not come up to our expectations or attain the high level aimed at in our designs. Here it may be urged that when the designer's intentions can be realised at a less expenditure than would be entailed in the carrying out of a mutilated scheme, it is seldom wise to depart from his proposals, nor is it fair to expect another man to interpret accurately another's intentions. Notwithstanding, my primary intention of converting Coal Harbour into a fresh-water lake has now been realised, and I hope that the three main structures which dominated our designs may be erected.

Vancouver settled, I arranged a visit to Victoria, B.C., to inspect and plan the new town sites for the B.C. Electric Company. The first of these two was known as the James Estate, of about one hundred and fifty acres. It is on the east coast of the island, and proved a most difficult site to plan, owing to the rough, rocky nature of the ground, which rose precipitously from the shore in a series of irregular stone cliffs. The cost of re-levelling any part

Thr Life and Work of An English Landscape Architect.

of this estate was so prohibitive that the line of roads and the subdivision of lots were in a large measure dictated by natural topographical conditions. Its proximity to Victoria, to which it is connected by electric tramway, and the picturesque character of the coastline, combine to make it a desirable residential estate.

The second was the Meadlands Estate, about five hundred acres in extent, situated on the west coast of the island about seven miles from Victoria. This was a much more ambitious

Illus. No. 49.

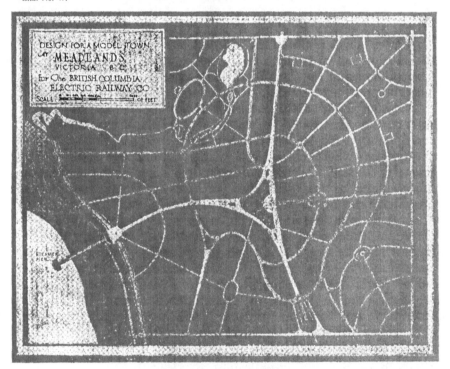

proposition. The site was a very favourable one for the purpose, lying in a hollow of a beautiful bay, with lovely white sands and ideal bathing conditions. Part of the estate had been cleared for agricultural purposes, and consisted of gently undulating pastures and arable land, with a background of noble forest trees and native shrubs. Beyond the estate the ground rose and fell in pine-clad mountains and valleys, giving the needed protection from the north and east. The levels favoured a perfect sanitation. The electric trams already reached to within a mile of the property, and it was intended to extend these through the centre of the estate, and finally to open up other estates for development.

On the whole, the property offered one of the finest opportunities in British Columbia for a summer and winter pleasure resort, and the plan was drawn with the object of realising this intention. A wide boulevard ran from north to south through its centre, winding through a gentle depression in the land, with a long curved junction extending from the central boulevard to the pier. The pier was to be treated as the tram terminus and as a feeder for the service of steamers, which would call at regular intervals. There was eventually to be a tram service running north from the pier, and the triangle formed by these converging roads was to be developed as a civic and shopping centre, with ample accommodation for stores, banks, post office, central hall, and estate offices. At the north-west corner of the estate was a wooded swamp to be converted into a public park, with a lake and a rocky stream, but all the level ground was to be utilised for tennis and other popular forms of recreation. At the promenade end of the piers we proposed to erect a commodious block of buildings, with waiting and refreshment rooms, parcels office, and all the conveniences of a well-equipped railway station. The triangular plots opposite this station were reserved for hotels. A large site was also reserved for a school, others for churches, and another site north-west of the civic centre was to be reserved for a large residential hotel. Altogether, as will be seen from Illus. No. 49, this was a very interesting project, and one which should eventually fully justify the enterprise of this progressive company.

During my stay on the island I had many opportunities of meeting the Premier, Sir Richard McBride, who was a picturesque character and yet withal a statesman. He was impressive in poise, courtly in manner, a fine conversationalist with an alertness and sense of humour which made him very popular. He made many promises, but I forget whether or not he ever fulfilled them. I rather fancy not. I also met most of his ministers, but Sir Richard seemed to stand alone and dominate a very difficult crowd. At this period the opposition consisted of one member, but it was the Government supporters which at times gave trouble.

Before leaving Victoria I was asked to address the City Council and the public on the need and advantages of city planning for

The Life and Work of An English Landscape Architect.

Victoria. I thought I had made out a good case, but in the discussion which followed I was thoroughly heckled by an irate Scotch member of the Council, who said they knew their own business so well that they had no need for an expert from England. Perhaps he was right, but Victoria did not bear very much evidence of the fact. The site of the town is a peculiarly beautiful one, but its lay-out is amateurish.

On my return to Vancouver I was engaged with Professor Laird of Philadelphia, and Professor Darley of McGill University, Montreal, upon the preparation of a comprehensive report and plan for the new British Columbia University at Point Grey. A public competition had already been instituted for the buildings, and a decision come to that Messrs. Sharp and Thompson, the winners of the first premium, should be retained as the architects. But it was felt by the Government and their advisers that the disposition of the various departments on the site needed the consideration of experts possessing practical skill and experience in the arrangement of a university campus. In this conclusion the appointed architects heartily agreed.

The site, consisting of three hundred acres, which was selected upon our recommendation, occupied a magnificent position at the western extremity of Point Grey. Being placed in full view of all the shipping passing north or south, or entering Vancouver, it was imperative that the grouping of the university buildings should be worthy and impress beholders. This impression would be in part maintained by night, as the central or culminating note of the composition was a tower brilliantly lighted and rising to a height of over three hundred feet. This dominating feature would be a landmark from all directions.

The work of estimating the respective characters and strengths of the departments and their inter-relation, and the special charac-ter of the site, was in itself a matter requiring the ripest judgment of all parties. Along with this we had to dispose of the whole of the buildings so that they could be heated from one central power-house, the same to serve for the lighting and the power distributed throughout. Each specialist was by this working arrangement able to contribute to the success of our report and recommendations. The Principal of the University was also able to add many useful suggestions, as, for instance, the need for the extension and correlation of the horticultural and the agricultural departments, for which an additional eighty acres were acquired.

Great Prospects.

This completed my studies of the fourth university campus upon which I had worked in Canada. They were all intensely interesting problems, to the solution of which the authorities lent their energies with a will, visioning the time when not just the few, but the majority, will need to take a course of specialised college study in any and every subject they have chosen for a livelihood.

Two things impressed me greatly — viz., the splendid organisation of these universities, and the elimination of waste and overlapping. As an example of what I mean, let us take the theological colleges for different orders. At Saskatoon and Point Grey twenty-five acres in five-acre plots are allocated to five of the principal religious bodies—Anglican, Presbyterian, Methodist, Congregationalist, and Baptist. As to nine-tenths of the subjects, these are taken in class together, only distinctive church dogma and assured essential differences being taught in the separate colleges.

Here in their formative years these future leaders of the faith are brought into close and friendly contact with each other, and in this way learn to eliminate differences which when seen in their proper perspective lose much of their importance. This grouping is bound in the future to lead to greater co-operation. Whatever differences still exist—as, for instance, between the Presbyterian and the Congregationalist orders—is rapidly disappearing, and this when complete will further simplify the work of the universities.

Arriving home in the middle of January, I immediately fell to work upon the town-planning projects entrusted to me, and upon which my son, E. Prentice Mawson, had during my absence put in much preparatory work, so that my task was materially lightened. Naturally, Athens came in for a good deal of attention, for I was inordinately proud of this commission. Indeed, it was the pinnacle of my ambitions, and I regarded it as the prize which would add most permanently to my reputation.

At home I was engaged upon several planting schemes, and in this department I was receiving help from my third son, who had developed a keen sense of the possibilities of the horticultural side of our work—a department, by the way, much neglected by the majority of pupils, for the reason that this branch of the work depends upon natural aptitude and a keen love of nature. Possessed as he was of this gift, and with the schooling in art at the Ecole

The Life and Work of An English Landscape Architect.

des Beaux Arts in Paris for which he was preparing, coupled with a genial manner and a lovable disposition, I had great hopes for this son and his future. Many proud fathers at the beginning of 1914 saw similar prospects in their sons. Having reached the zenith of their own limited achievements, these fathers rested content, assured that their ideals had been attained, and that these would be maintained and completed by their successors. If these happy parents could have scanned the international horizon and seen the ominous war clouds gathering over Europe, they might have had many disturbing moments. Perhaps it was as well that we did not see and did not fear.

On the 16th of March I lectured before the Civic League of Antwerp on " The Principles of Landscape Architecture Applied to the Development of the City Plan." The Belgian Government had just presented the site of the old fortifications to the city for its extension. A competition had been held, and premiums been awarded. The winner had grasped comprehensively this large addition, and had arranged a series of wide boulevards, suggestive of the Ringstrasse in Vienna. Evidently the Civic League wished to learn what they could about English methods, with a view to rendering their new parks and boulevards as attractive as possible. Upon my arrival I was met by the members, who took me round their newly acquired territory to show me the location of the different parks, gardens, and boulevards. From time to time they pointed in the direction of their new fortifications, always with the remark that they were impregnable—yes, absolutely impregnable,—comforted with the thought that whatever might happen, they were safe.

In the evening I lectured to an audience of about four hundred, explaining the principles of landscape architecture and their application to Antwerp. I lectured in English, and was closely followed. Whether they all understood or not, I am not so sure, but the slides shown from time to time elicited applause. I was warmly thanked for my lecture by the speakers who took part in the discussion, but the chairman remarked that whilst they had everything to learn from England in the designs of private gardens, we could not offer much assistance when it came to public gardens. In my reply I admitted that this was a just criticism, the explanation being that our private gardens were the work of experts, but our public gardens were mostly the work of amateurs. This fact I have always regretted, for I am democratic enough to wish that the public, and especially the workers, should have the best. Town councillors as a rule evidently think otherwise.

From Antwerp I proceeded to Paris *en route* for Athens. In Paris I met my friend and client, Mr. Samuel Waring, who, after spending a few days in Rome on business for his firm, had arranged to travel with me, as there were certain projects on foot in the ancient capital of Athens in which he had an interest. *En route* we were to call at Corfu, where, by arrangements made by Mr. Waring, I was to be introduced to the Kaiser at his villa on the 28th.

On the 26th we arrived at Brindisi, where keen disappointment awaited us, for we learnt that the Kaiser had received an urgent call to Berlin, and that he had left Corfu the previous day. We spent the afternoon in looking round Brindisi and its immediate surroundings, trying to work up enthusiasm for Italian art, and failing abjectly. The news we had just received filled us with dark forebodings which nothing could dispel, for we both knew sufficient of European politics to guess what the Kaiser's sudden departure meant. We both felt that it was closely related to some pending crisis—perhaps war. Oppressed with these forebodings, we were half-inclined to return home. We decided, however, to proceed, and next morning we were in beautiful Corfu, enjoying, after a bath and change, a hearty breakfast at our hotel.

After breakfast we were driven to the Kaiser's villa by a pair of the usual very lean Greek horses, which could be induced to quicken their pace only by the application of cruel strokes from a heavy whip. Evidently the S.P.C.A. does not function in the Near East.

Villa Achilleon is situated on high ground nearly three miles westward from Corfu, and is approached by meandering roads which pass through two exceedingly picturesque villages set in vineyards and olive groves, where the natives, in their old national costumes, are equally picturesque. Arriving at the porter's lodge, we had to wait some time until the ponderous Prussian attendant made his appearance. At first he refused to allow us to enter, but after an explanation and a suitable present we were allowed inside the grounds to see the uninteresting interior of the villa, which had been built by the late Empress of Austria (Illus. No. 48). The views in every direction were superb, and the gardens lavishly laid out in level terraces richly decorated with sculpture, not very well chosen or placed, excepting for a great figure of the wounded Achilles

The Life and Work of An English Landscape Architect.

gazing seaward. From the edges of the terrace there were steep embankments leading down to the shore, in which zig-zag paths had been cut in the solid rock, all the intervening spaces being planted with trees, shrubs, and conifers in endless variety. The whole garden seemed to be arranged and appointed for its royal owner's delight, regardless of expense, but neither the garden nor the villa reached any high artistic level, and at times harshly violated the canons of good taste. Later in the day we saw the royal palace in Corfu, and also together inspected the proposed site for an hotel de luxe, a project first suggested by King Constantine. My companion, still apprehensive of trouble, decided to return home that same evening *via* Brindisi, completing his business in Rome *en route.*

After a night's rest and several interviews with important people interested in the improvement of Corfu, including Prince Ipsolanti, the Governor of the island, I took the boat for Patras, where I was asked to meet the Mayor, a keen loyalist, at whose charming house I met a number of well-known Greeks who were supposed to be interested in town planning. On this occasion, however, they seemed much more anxious to gather information about the state of European politics, and particularly to hear about our own domestic troubles, such as politics in Ireland, the suffragettes, and our labour disturbances.

The next day, after a stroll round Patras, I went with the Mayor to see the new cathedral, then in course of erection, and part of which was ready for its roof. It did not impress me. The site was not the best available, neither was the structure a success as an architectural conception, although the interior promised to be much better than the exterior.

On the day following my arrival in Athens I met the Queen, and it was then that Her Majesty conveyed the Kaiser's congratulations upon our plans for the improvement of Corfu.

Since our last visit we had presented our preliminary report advising the municipality of Athens upon town-planning procedure. This report was accompanied by several plans and drawings illustrating the main features to be dealt with and the problems to be solved. The preliminary work had been so thoroughly done that the Town Council mistook it for the scheme proper, and would have paid our fees on this assumption. I explained that this preliminary report was intended to focus discussion on the major problems involved in order to start our more serious work in full agreement with the Council as to its scope. The Council, however, merely indicated that they were in the hands of experts, and would be advised by us. This was probably the wisest decision.

On my informing the Queen of the Council's decision, she asked where we proposed to begin, to which I replied, " By asking your Majesty for an introduction to the most influential archæologist now in Athens." " You evidently know where to expect trouble," replied the Queen. " I will arrange for you to meet Dr. Karo this evening." Dr. Karo, to whom I was introduced, proved to be a charming man, who spoke perfect English, having lived many years in London, which he said he still loved very much. What, however, was very important to me was the fact that he was able to inform me as to the excavation work already accomplished. Even more important, he pointed out the direction and extent of future explorations. Nothing could exceed the kindness and the help he gave me, the result of which was that I was able to avoid many pitfalls and much criticism.

Looking back on the pleasant time that I spent with Dr. Karo, it is difficult to believe that it was his clever brain that engineered the German propaganda in the Near East ; and yet this is what I have since been told was the case.*

My stay in Athens extended to about five weeks, during which time I saw much of the King and Queen. During one of my interviews at the palace (when I was accompanied by my son, who had been in Athens for some time) a messenger arrived to tell His Majesty that a duel between two of his officers was about to take place in a building near the Zappion Gardens, and our interview came to an abrupt close. Out of curiosity my son and I hurried to the spot indicated, and through the chinks of a wooden barricade saw the two men at their deadly game. Although considering this duelling as a brutal survival worthy of contempt, we could not help being fascinated by the quick movements and the dexterity of the combatants.

The two men seemed fairly evenly matched, but at last one of them got a prick in the arm, and the fight was called off, just as the King's messengers arrived to stop it. I have wondered if these messengers purposely arrived late to allow the combatants time to settle their difference about the lady. After

---

* Wace, the head of the English School, was away. This is why Karo was consulted. He was head of the German School of Archæology in Athens.

The Life and Work of An English Landscape Architect.

the surgeons had dressed the wound, the two officers seemed to be quite friendly.

On the Saturday following we received an invitation to join the Royal party at the historical pageant which was to be held in the great stadium (Illus. Nos. 42 and 43). The sight was a great one. It was estimated that sixty thousand people attended. The royal stand was in the centre of the south side, and thus in the shade, a fact which we greatly appreciated, because the sun was pitiless. The discomforts of those on the opposite side must have been almost intolerable.

Hundreds of characters were represented in each of the succeeding scenes, which were presented in perfectly arranged sequence, always with those depicting one period entering the arena as the characters in the preceding one left it. Thus perfect continuity of historic events was maintained. As a great spectacular display the pageant was the most educative I have ever witnessed. The crowd could not have been better behaved or more perfectly controlled, and I instinctively felt that if the pageant had been allowed in any of our cathedral closes it would not have violated the much-prized sanctity of the Sabbath. On this and every other occasion on which I accompanied the King, either in the capital or in the provinces, the greatest enthusiasm for the dynasty prevailed. At this time, also, there was perfect unanimity between the King and his Prime Minister. On every occasion when the King, discussing town planning for Athens, had to make reference to his Minister, he did so in terms of appreciation. " You will find," he said, " that M. Venizelos is a very clever man, and that he has many ideas about the improvement of Athens which are worthy of consideration."

Nearly all my interviews with the Queen had reference to the re-housing of the working classes under conditions of comfort and decency, and Her Majesty again asked me to include in our plan ample provision in working-class and industrial districts for tree-planted spaces with cafés, so that working men and women might rest under the shade of trees. These objects seemed, so far as the Queen was concerned, to constitute the beginning and the end of town planning, and it was agreed that on my return to England I should immediately prepare a number of housing proposals for submission and approval pending their arrival at East-bourne in June. It was also arranged that I should organise a tour of our best gardens in the south and west of England for the

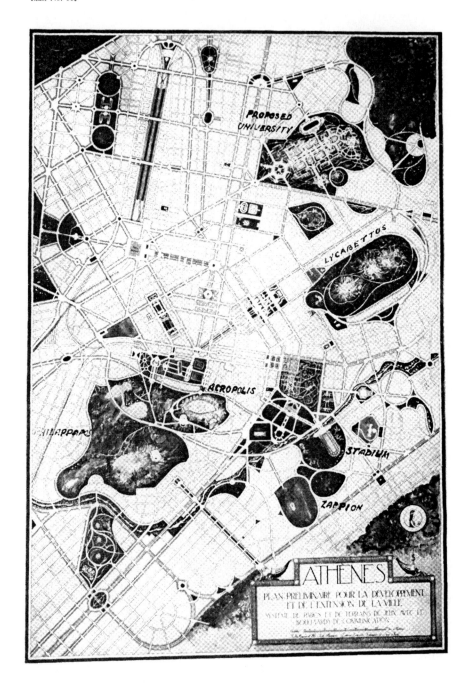

benefit of the Crown Prince, afterwards King George, who was as keenly interested in horticulture as his father.

Before returning home, my son and I again studied the railway problem for Athens, along with its traffic conditions. In particular we made an exhaustive study of the railway and tram systems in relation to each other, and made a rapid survey of all open spaces and dilapidated properties, as well as the location for the hotels which M. Venizelos so greatly desired, and toward which, it was understood, his Government was at this time prepared to make substantial subsidies.

Before leaving Athens I gave a lecture which was attended by the King, members of the Royal Family, and many of the Ministers and heads of Government departments. My principal object was to endeavour to incite the authorities to secure an ample water supply, without which, I argued, it was of little use considering park systems, or even housing extensions; in fact, I told them that the whole town-planning scheme for the city should be based upon the provision of utilities for cleanliness and decency. I found the topic was a live one, so I ventured to point out to the responsible members of my audience that they had been discussing the matter, with considerable heat at times, for forty years, that they had spent large sums of money on experts, but that they were no further forward, so far as I could see, than they were at the beginning; that every successive scheme had been turned down and another one called for.

My hearers thanked me heartily, and the newspapers likewise applauded me in their leading articles for the courageous step I had taken.

Except for a few artesian borings, the only results were the employment of more experts and the submission of new proposals. Athenians, now as ever, are in search of " some new thing." As I write, ten years have elapsed. Notwithstanding the increased burdens which the country has had to bear, an efficient water supply for the capital is now within the sphere of practical politics.

By the 16th of June we were ready to meet their Majesties at Eastbourne with working drawings for our housing schemes, which had already been approved in principle. All the types were to be built in tenement blocks suited to the climate, and with convenient and even ample accommodation, but lacking some of those modern utilities which an ample water supply alone could make possible.

The Life and Work of An English Landscape Architect.

As arranged, I proceeded to Eastbourne, staying at the Grand Hotel, where the Royal Family always stayed during their much anticipated annual English holidays. The King did not arrive for several days, but the Queen's sister, the Grand Duchess of Hesse, was there, and all the happy young princes and princesses, along with a number of court officials whom I had met in Athens. Our plans were approved and forwarded to Athens for presentation to the Town Council, who were urged to make an early start on the vacant ground we had allocated as a housing area.

On the following day I accompanied the Queen and her sister to the Agricultural Show, where we were shown round the exhibits by the President and the Committee, who afterwards entertained us to lunch. On returning to our hotel I was asked to map out a motor run for the following day, working in visits to country houses and gardens of interest. I decided to take my clients to see Lord Brassey's place, Chelwood Manor, and Mr. Douglas Freshfield's new home at Wych Cross, both places being about an hour and a half's motor run from Eastbourne. I wired my clients the same afternoon asking their permission, and both wired back a cordial invitation.

We had a luxurious Rolls Royce car, and the Queen and her sister were charmed with the open country through which we passed, frequently calling my attention to groups of cottages with their trim gardens. "I love England," said the Queen ; her sister did so too. "Do you know, Mr. Mawson," the Queen proceeded, "the happiest time of our lives was spent at Frogmore. Every visit revives those happy memories ; that is why I love my annual holiday so much."

On my part I felt depressed, for that morning the news was most disquieting : Europe was nearing its supreme crisis.

"Have you seen 'The Times' this morning?" I asked. "Yes, I have," replied the Queen, "and I know what you are thinking. You fear that England is going to be at war with Germany. You are quite wrong, Mr. Mawson. There is going to be a war, but it will be a war to end once and for ever the eternal conflict between the Teutons and the Slavs, and not a war between England and Germany."

Although subsequent history has proved this prophecy wrong, there is no doubt that the Queen expressed her honest convictions upon the situation.

We arrived at Chelwood Manor a little before three, and it

was immediately evident that Lord Brassey and the two Royal sisters were old friends, and that Lady Brassey also knew her visitors. The banter and laughter which followed certain references to my clients' visit as girls to the " Sunbeam " were quite delightful. After the merriment had abated somewhat, Lord and Lady Brassey conducted their visitors round the house, a beautiful example of half-timbered work reminiscent of the best old houses in Sussex. This work was designed by Andrew Prentice, a fact which Lord Brassey carefully explained, with many complimentary allusions to his architect.

Then we proceeded to the south terrace to admire the view over the Downs.

It was one of those dreamy summer days for which our island is famed. The atmosphere was clear and limpid, and the sound of the cattle and the sheep broke upon the ear with a sense of serenity and stillness in accord with the rapture that was all-pervading. The sunlit groups of dark foliage dappled the varying greens of the fields, with their shadows melting away into the blues and purples of the distance. After drinking deep of this feast of delight, we turned our attention towards the garden, passing each part in turn—a fragrant flowery way of early roses, long glades of herbaceous borders (then at their best), then along springy grass paths bordered with more and more roses, and still more roses clambering over the pergolas in endless profusion, the birds and the bees joining in the harmony of it all. Lord Brassey evidently knew how to set forth the charms of his garden—an enviable gift. At one place he jocularly made an impressive pause to explain that this was only a part of Mr. Mawson's dream, and in order that we might realise it in its entirety we were told that we must wait for the times to improve, our host finishing with one of his amusing smiles, which was received with a burst of banter and laughter at my expense. Admiring and chatting all the way, we returned to the house, where tea was laid.

Here Lord Brassey resumed his pleasantries, to the delight of his visitors. " What a dear old man Brassey is," remarked the Queen, as, after a last wave of the hand, we passed round a bend in the drive on our way to Wych Cross, where we arrived about half-past four, to be met by Mr. Douglas Freshfield and his daughter.

Here a considerable time was spent in the gardens, which are more extensive and more varied in treatment than those

The Life and Work of An English Landscape Architect.

at Chelwood Manor, and also a little more matured (Illus. Nos. 17 and 18).

After admiring the gardens we returned to the house, where tea was again served, conversational inquiries flowing freely meanwhile as to the history of many rare examples of embroidery and furniture, especially with regard to a small chest of drawers beautifully inlaid with ivory, a genuine old example of Sussex handicraft.

As we motored home, the Queen exclaimed : " Mr. Mawson, where do these old Englishmen get their manners—they are inimitable ? " A statement with which Her Majesty's sister enthusiastically agreed.

The Duchess then said she would be very pleased if I could arrange to visit her home in Prussia in August, when the German Crown Prince would be staying there. She expressed her desire to introduce me to the Prince with a view to my planning his gardens, as he was building a new house in the English style. This I regarded as an expression of keen appreciation of the two gardens we had just seen, and a compliment to myself. Six months later a sarcastic friend remarked : " What a pity Willie did not get his august father to postpone his little war until you had laid out his garden ! "

That same evening I returned to London to make final preparations for the five days' tour of the West of England on which the Greek Princes were to start the next Tuesday morning. To my intense disappointment I received a telegram from the Court Chamberlain on the Monday, informing me that urgent business of state compelled the immediate return of the Royal Family to Athens.

Again I had the feeling of impending disaster. This time, however, I felt the calamity was more immediate. I knew that only matters of the gravest concern could have led to the sudden change of programme.

KING CONSTANTINE OF GREECE.

CHAPTER XIX.

THE YEAR 1914 ENDS IN DISASTER, AND IN 1915 THE STRUGGLE CONTINUES.

BEFORE leaving London I had appointments with three of my oldest English clients, and, in each case received instructions to go ahead with further important work. I also met Gordon Selfridge, who told me he intended to purchase a property near Bournemouth, which he wished me to assist in developing. I soon realised, as I conversed with Mr. Selfridge, that this scheme meant one of the biggest private commissions I had ever been entrusted with. In spite of it all, however, I was so depressed that even the success of my new work on " Civic Art " could not arouse me ; and yet I had met four of our nation's leaders of commerce who were each evidently assured of security. Nevertheless, I still felt that disaster was in the air, and that we would be involved in the welter.

In this mood I returned home to work with my staff, which had now grown to thirty assistants, mostly young fellows loyal to their chief and keen in their ideals. The auditor paid his annual visit, and assured me that the firm was financially sound.

Newspapers and magazine writers were vieing with each other to prove the absurdity of suspicion. Had not Norman Angell proved conclusively that only nations that had lost the power of reasoning would be so mad as to go to war ? None of these things, not even absorbing myself in my work, gave me any rest. I felt that war was inevitable.

So the month of July, 1914, came to an end, my doubts as to the future ever increasing. Communications between embassies were constant, and their import became ever more and more disturbing. The air was electric and vibrating with plot and counter-plot. So the breathless suspense continued. Some sought peace diligently, others felt and said that a war would clear the atmosphere. Some said that the war, if it came, would be over in

The Life and Work of An English Landscape Architect.

three months, and end war for all time. A cabinet minister said that the burden of armaments in Europe was becoming so oppressive that a conflict would save Europe from ruin by ending for ever the competition in armaments.

Looking back, it seems to me that of our political leaders only two really grasped the situation, and both left the Cabinet at this crisis. They were John Morley and John Burns. " My dear Mawson," said the latter, one morning at the National Liberal Club, " I want you to write down my prophecy in case this unsettled state of affairs ends in war " ; and I wrote as follows :—

(1) A war with the Central Powers will last three years.
(2) It will cost us seven thousand million sterling.
(3) We shall lose one million men.
(4) It will end in world revolution.

At the time I regarded this prophecy as an exaggeration uttered under the pressure of nervous tension. I now regard it as the matured judgment of a remarkable mind. The three first were exceeded ; the last is being unfolded, page after page, with the Russian debâcle as a commencement, and the nations of Europe and Asia following in its train.

When, after several depressing days and sleepless nights, I awoke on the morning of August 4th, 1914, to find that war was actually declared, I almost felt a sense of relief. The suspense had become intolerable, and mentally and physically debilitating.

As I went to the office, the world seemed suddenly to have come to a standstill, with an entire absence of that purposeful business hurry to which we are daily accustomed. In its place there was an awed hush amongst the groups of whispering townsmen along the kerbstone, whilst knots of women stood at their doors talking in unusually quiet tones. Then would pass along companies of young fellows on their way to enlist. Their buoyancy was in strange contrast to the demeanour of their elders.

Arriving at the office, I found that every unmarried man, including my third son, James Radcliffe, had marched off to the Town Hall to enlist—a record in patriotism which I imagine few offices in the country could surpass. In one sense I was proud of the fact, yet in another way it was heart-breaking to see the growth of years and organisation breaking up, with no certainty of its ever being got together again. Two of my young men were Quakers, but they joined up, and later one of them won the Croix-de-Guerre, and the other gave his life.

QUEEN SOPHIA OF GREECE.

The Years 1914 *and* 1915.

Fortunately for the practice, my eldest son and partner was rejected on medical grounds ; but my second son, who was in charge of our Canadian work, joined up as soon as the local forces could arrange for his training.

It followed as a natural sequence that clients from every quarter immediately wrote stopping all work, or curtailing it to the smallest dimensions, and so we found there was scarcely sufficient work in the office for the remaining members of the staff. The men left to us were those who we knew would be indispensable whenever reconstruction became possible.

Knowing that I would not part with them so long as I was allowed to retain their services, they, of their own free will and accord, proposed that their salaries should be cut down by one-third. This was done in good faith, in the hope of helping the practice financially, but of course the arrangement soon proved unsound, for the staff found that with the soaring cost of living they needed not less, but larger, salaries, and these had to be found somehow. This expression of their goodwill was very cheering, and I made strenuous efforts in return to keep the practice going. There was still the completion of our plans for Athens, Regina, and Banff to work upon, whilst several of my clients, both public and private, with patriotic sentiments, decided to go ahead with certain works, and thus meet the demand for employment which was keenly felt during the early part of the war. Foremost amongst these was Lord Leverhulme.

Thus we could look ahead to a year's partial employment, with the compilation and illustration of another book if business became quiet. I had for some time been collecting material for two books, and Athens provided material for a third. I actually mapped out the syllabus for these, and as opportunity occurred and the staff became available, I made considerable progress with the illustrations. The titles may be of interest, and suggest enterprise in directions where I had previously feared to tread. They were as follows :—

(1) " Small Houses and Their Gardens."
(2) " The Art of Landscape Architecture Applied to the Extension and Improvement of Towns and Cities."
(3) "Athens Present and Future : An Account of the Replanning Proposals for the Capital."

My publishers urged that none of these works could be successfully launched until after the war, because it became

The Life and Work of An English Landscape Architect.

abundantly evident, as the war progressed, that the cost of printing would be absolutely prohibitive—a fact of which I was shortly to have an unfortunate reminder. Still, as I have remarked, a part of the MS. and some of the illustrations are ready, and I trust that my successors will complete that which I have begun.

The war, with all its horrors, defeats, and triumphs, has been so ably and graphically portrayed for us that we can, whenever we are in the mood, live those terrible days over again. My object here is to show how we, as an organisation whose work had largely consisted of the creation of luxuries for the rich and amenities for the poor, adapted ourselves to conditions in which life itself was cribbed, cabined, and confined. The nation as one man had one purpose—namely, to bend its whole mind and energies to the successful completion of the herculean task thrust upon it.

As the war proceeded and its proportions were more fully realised, more and more men were called for, and this call still further reduced our staff. A hard-working student from the University at Budapest, though an alien, was allowed to remain at his work under military oversight, but at the end of six months he was interned on a fruit farm in Gloucestershire, where he shortly afterwards died of pneumonia, greatly to the regret of all who knew him. Then some of the younger married men joined up, whilst the London and Vancouver offices, having lost their staff, became mere postal addresses. Soon all our work was concentrated in the Lancaster office, where the attenuated staff consisted of a lady secretary, a typist, a book-keeper, four men over military age, two pupils, my son, and myself—eleven all told : a fairly well-balanced group of workers, wishful to do our bit in whatever way was best for the nation.

Much in the same way as the American landscape architects afterwards offered their services to their Government to lay out the soldiers' training camps (or cantonments, as they called them), I felt that we could be of service to the Ministry of Munitions. The Ministry was at this time laying out a number of munition villages, such as that at Gretna Green. In a fit of patriotic fervour I obtained an introduction to the Secretary of the Department of Construction, who received me as if I were looking for a contractor's job. I explained the nature of our organisation, told him that we were ready and anxious for work, that my son and I were prepared to give our entire services gratis, and that the Ministry could take over the staff and offices on its own terms. I left my name and address for reference, after being told there was nothing doing.

After waiting a month I interviewed the Secretary again, having heard that considerable schemes were in prospect within an hour's run of our office, but was told that the work was already in hand.

At my club I met a young man who had made money out of the Ministry of Munitions, and who was later knighted for his " sacrifices." " Mawson," he said, " I heard of that offer of yours ; but why did you make it ? You surely knew it would be rejected ! They knew that you had an organisation which would be useful to them, but you made it impossible by offering your services gratis. If you had boldly said, ' Gentlemen, I am at your service, and my terms are two thousand pounds per year,' they would have accepted you on the spot." This was probably a gross exaggeration, but my friend's success gave reasonable colour to his statement.

Early in the year 1915 my son, James Radcliffe, who had joined the Pals Brigade of the 5th King's Own, having completed his training, was detailed for foreign service. He came home for a few days, bright, optimistic, and eager, assured we had got the Germans on the run, and that he would be home again by the end of June. He left us amid cheers and tears. Then came home breezy letters, but each succeeding letter a little more wistful than the last. " Tell father," he said, " that our camp is alongside a nursery half-full of young Scotch firs. If he wants a few thousand my mates and I can supply him cheap." In another letter he said : " The morning is fine and the country beautiful ; everywhere the hedgerows are draped in tenderest green. The birds are singing their sweetest, oblivious to the horrors of this terrible war." And in his last letter he told us : " The men are splendid, and beyond all praise. Whatever you and father can do for our wounded, I am sure you will do—nothing is too good for these brave fellows." I give these extracts on account of their sequel.

His end came soon after. He fell near Poperinghe on April 23rd, 1915. So ended one of my fondest hopes, for he had a wonderful grasp of the possibilities of his profession. He was just ready to complete his studies in architecture at the Ecole de Beaux Arts, after which I looked to his joining the firm and taking an active part in its development, especially on the horticultural side, for which he had a real genius. He also possessed irresistible

charm of manner, and was at the same time a diplomat who generally got his way. I might, for instance, send into his room a draft for the planting of a rose garden. In half an hour he would come into my room smiling, and exclaiming : " What a splendid idea that is for her ladyship's rose garden. She will be pleased ; but don't you think we ought to give them another three inches. You see, father, the soil is a strong loam." To which I would reply, " I think you are right." Then he would proceed : " Don't you think we ought to fill two of the beds with Madame Lavery, and these with Lady Ashtown ? And don't you think that Scarlet Rambler standards are rather coarse ? " And so when he returned to his own room he had got my permission to reconstruct the whole plan and arrangement.

And he was a humorist.

" What do you think of Herkomer's portrait of your father ? " asked a lady visitor.

" It is just splendid, and so life-like that I often talk to it."

" Talk to it, Cliffe ? Whatever do you say ? "

And, clasping his hands in the attitude of appeal, he replied : " I say, ' Please, father, give me a rise.' " And next week and onwards his allowance envelope contained an extra five shillings.

I might tell many many more such stories, but must keep them locked up as sacred memories.

His last letter home, from which I have quoted, now became a command. It called for action for the wounded, who were returning in vast numbers, and a large proportion of whom were rendered unfit to follow their former occupations. It seemed to my wife and I that herein lay our opportunity for the organisation of suitable employment under those ideal conditions which we felt a grateful country would seek to provide. Thus the death of my son was the starting point of an enterprise which for three years taxed my energies and resources to their utmost. To this self-imposed task I must devote a special chapter.

Early in the year I had been requested by Sir Vesey Strong, on the recommendation of Mr. John Burns, to submit a scheme for the King Edward Memorial Park on the site of the old Market, Shadwell, which had been acquired for the purpose. Sir Vesey, the Chairman of the Memorial Committee, said in his brisk, jolly way, " You ought to know, Mr. Mawson, that we have had several schemes presented to us, but as they are all inferior to

The Life and Work of An English Landscape Architect.

what I can do myself, I thought we would have another try. That's why we have asked you to help us."

In July, 1915, I presented our plans, along with a well-illustrated report. The solution pleased the Chairman and his Committee so much that, as he told me, they would like to carry it out at once, but the Government ban on employing workpeople for other than specified work made this impossible. Then Sir Vesey died, and the Committee finally passed over their responsibilities to the London County Council, to whom I offered my designs as a gift. I was, however, curtly informed by the Chairman of the Parks Committee that they had their own landscape gardeners. To this I replied that what I was offering was the work of a landscape architect, and not that of a landscape gardener. The poor man did not know the difference.

HOSTEL FOR DISABLED SOLDIERS' VILLAGE.

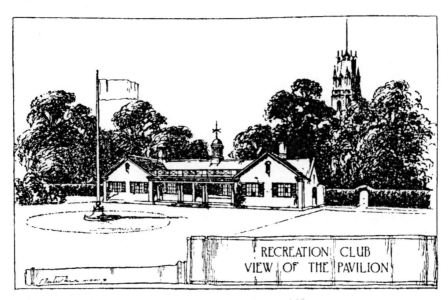

SPORTS PAVILION FOR DISABLED SOLDIERS' VILLAGE.

CHAPTER XX.

MY LAST VISIT TO AMERICA.

I HAVE already referred to my self-imposed task, in pursuance of my son's last letter, which was to take shape in a scheme of industrial villages for disabled service men. This scheme, when formulated, I presented to the secretaries of the Ministry of Pensions. Receiving no encouragement from that quarter, I determined to see what could be done privately, and so I had about thirty copies of the prospectus and report bound up and posted to influential men in England and in Canada, with the intention of inviting discussion upon the problems involved. After posting the Canadian copies, I notified each recipient that I would most likely follow up the report with a visit, as I had promised the King of Greece that I would make a tour of America to deliver a series of lectures on " Athens, Past, Present, and Future," although my lecturing tour would not be confined to this subject. King Constantine wished to popularise amongst American Greeks the remodelled capital, and I was to advertise these lectures as being delivered with the approval of their Majesties. The King regarded the solidarity of his subjects in all lands, and their love of their mother-country, as remarkable. He recounted many instances of this patriotic feeling shown during the Balkan war.

My wife and I left England for our last trip to America early in October, sailing by the St. Paul, thus minimising submarine risks, as America was still neutral. The voyage was a long one, the weather stormy, and the boat uncomfortably crowded.

My lecture agent had booked engagements at Columbia, Harvard, Michigan, Illinois, and Toronto Universities, and at several of the larger colleges for girls, including Mrs. Finch's school in New York, and those at Vassar and at Weston ; along with populous centres, such as Cleveland.

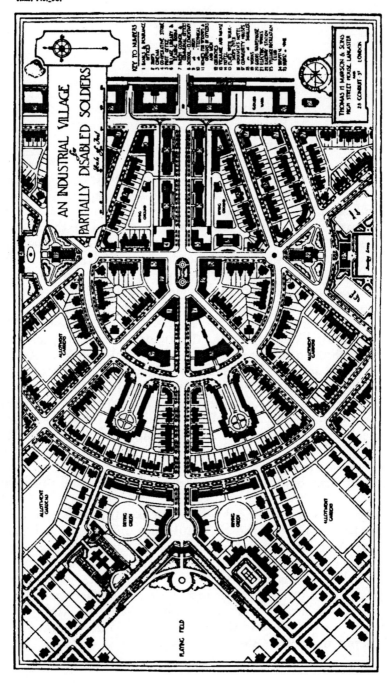

My Last Visit to America.

The university lectures were a great success. They served to seal the old friendships and opened many new ones. It was pleasant for us to see in the schools prints of my Herkomer portrait hanging in a central position, and my published works being used as text-books.

My wife and I were both delighted with Vassar, which is the most complete girls' educational colony I have ever seen. Readers of "Daddy Long Legs" will have an idea of its atmosphere, for it is at Vassar that the scenes in this charming story are set. You realise that the plot is laid in Vassar immediately you pass through the gatehouse into the College grounds.

The two lectures I was asked to deliver here were on "English Gardens." For these my slides and illustrations had been chosen with the greatest care, and with due regard to pictorial effect. There must have been over four hundred girls at each lecture. Their ages ranged from 16 to 20, and a brighter, happier, and more enthusiastic lot of young maidens I had never previously met. For the most part strong in mind and in body, they delighted me greatly with their sense of humour, every subtle joke and quaint allusion being appreciated.

At the Weston Ladies' College I had a very embarrassing experience, for which I must partly blame myself. I was told that I was expected to give one lecture on Greece, and given to understand that I should cover as much ground as possible in the time at my disposal. This school prides itself on its classical studies, and when, after tea, I discussed the lecture with the Principal, I found that the impression had been given that I was an archæologist. My knowledge of archæology is but an elementary one, and that mostly on those aspects which relate to ancient forms of city planning. In vain I explained that, whilst I thought I could lecture interestingly and helpfully on Athens, past, present, and future, as a city planner, I would fail if I spoke from any other point of view. The result was disappointing. I made every effort to be interesting, but I never got the grip of my audience, who wanted minute studies of ancient architecture, whereas my purpose was to state the why and the wherefore of Athens as a whole.

At the close of the lecture, questions were asked which by their import only tended to prove how far I was removed in spirit and outlook from these budding archæologists. This is the sort of question which was asked: "Was the lecturer correct in describing the Erecthion as being on the north side of the Acropolis?

The Life and Work of An English Landscape Architect.

And could he tell us what was the position of the camera and the time of day when the photographs were taken? Otherwise, we cannot understand the angle of the projected shadows."

Through no fault of my own, admittedly I failed. All the same, I was disappointed when the cashier handed me a cheque for half my arranged fee, telling me bluntly that was all I had earned.

Precisely the same lecture, illustrated by the same slides, was given before a select audience of one hundred and fifty at the residence of Walter Cottingham, of Cleveland, Ohio, and, judging from the appreciation shown by my audience, it proved the most interesting lecture of the whole trip. We have here the point of view of a company of school girls immersed in the meticulous details of classical Athens, as distinct from that of an audience of widely read and travelled people. There are lecturers who, with half a dozen hastily prepared notes, can entertain almost any audience, but I doubt whether such cleverness would gain half-fees with a specialised girls' school. For me the preparation of a lecture is a serious exercise, and one that cannot be adapted at a moment's notice.

At Harvard I lectured to the School of Business Administration, under the presidency of Professor Gay, on " The Commercial Value of Beauty," and the lecture was greatly appreciated. I gave the same lecture before the Cleveland Chamber of Commerce, with only partial success. Again the difference was in the audience, and not in the lecturer. I am convinced that for a lecturer to attain success it is essential that he possess the oratorical faculty and the mental agility wherewith to win the interest of his audience in the first ten minutes. This done, he may stick closely to his manuscript, provided he read clearly with due emphasis and expression. In my later lectures I studied this aspect of my work, and left myself free to feel the pulses of my audience before entering upon the more serious part of my subject.

Mr. Henry Vivian, for some time member of Parliament for Birkenhead, and a pioneer housing reformer, was one of those gifted lecturers who had to a remarkable degree the power of winning over an audience. Sometimes this was attained by an amusingly audacious trick. During a visit to Toronto he was asked to lecture on " Garden Cities." Before the lecture, he visited, photographed, and made slides of the worst social and housing conditions to be found in the city. He arranged matters so that his Toronto slides would follow a number of introductory pictures of English slum conditions. He began something like this :

" It is my painful duty to show by photographic slides some of the conditions which make the Old Country a by-word and reproach amongst social reformers. If I had depended on artistic drawings, you would have said they were treasonable exaggerations ; but the camera cannot lie. So terrible are the subjects chosen that it would be an unpardonable lack of patriotism to show them anywhere outside the Empire."

He then introduced, in a descending scale of squalid conditions, twenty slides, each of which he eloquently described in his inimitable manner. When he reached the twentieth slide he stopped as if he had exhausted his vocabulary. Then, as if embarrassed, he said, in a subdued voice : " Ladies and gentlemen, I owe you an apology. The last eight slides are Toronto slums, and not London slums." Consternation reigned for a time, until the audience saw through his subtlety ; then they broke out into loud and prolonged peals of laughter. He knew then that he had touched the moral sense of his large audience, and he used the opportunity to finish the lesson.

" In England," he added, " there are reasonable excuses. We are an old country ; we have come into a heritage of bad conditions. But this much I am proud to say—we are all the time trying to remedy these conditions, and the modern garden city is one of the proofs indicating that we realise our responsibilities. What can you say in excuse for the slum conditions in Toronto, which you have created in your own life-time, and for which you are therefore entirely responsible ? "

On my first visit to Toronto people were still talking about Vivian's lecture, and I am sure that it was he who first implanted the desire for better housing conditions and for town-planning legislation in that city. It was after his visit that the churches undertook a drastic survey of social conditions.

On this visit to America I had the great pleasure of meeting at the Illinois University Mr. and Mrs. Charles Mulford Robinson, of Rochester. Mr. Robinson is the author of the most delightful works on modern civic art in the English language. These were followed by other pleasing readable works on street planning and cognate subjects. Mrs. Robinson accompanied her husband on many of his tours, and was just as keen a student of city-planning

The Life and Work of An English Landscape Architect.

problems. It is generally understood that she assisted him in the compilation of data and the preparation of MS. for the press. The esteem in which I held Mr. Robinson had led to a regular correspondence between us some time before I first met the distinguished writer.

At the Illinois University the students of city planning are for the most part post-graduates in landscape architecture, and the professors in both departments (namely, the City Planning and the Landscape Architecture) joined forces to secure me as special lecturer. Robinson and his wife worked in the classroom, and naturally won, by their assiduity and encouragement, the affection of every student. They seemed to be the foster-parents of a peculiarly live set of students, all of whom, I am sure, look back with pleasure to the time they spent with their scholarly and genial professor, whose career was so soon to come to an end.

Having undertaken the trip partly to escape from the depressing war atmosphere, we accepted many social engagements, staying for a week at Springfield, Mass., as the guest of Dr. Sylvester Mawson, a philologist, best known as the editor of the greatly enlarged new edition of Roget's Thesaurus, the *vade mecum* of every writer. At this time he was one of the revising editors of Webster's International Dictionary.

We went to Springfield for a rest, but as the American newspaper man was on the scent for copy, I was soon found out in my retreat, and induced, without fee, to say what I thought about the beauties of Springfield and the possibilities which it offered for becoming America's most beautiful city. This interview occupied pages in the chief local newspaper, along with rough sketches for a new civic centre, parks, and boulevards. Since my visit a comprehensive city-planning scheme has been promoted.

From Springfield we returned to New York, where I lectured to encouraging audiences on Athens. I also gave many interviews to newspaper men, and in connection with one of these I had a very pleasant experience. My friend, John O'Hara Cosgrave, one of the editors of the " New York World," told me that his friend the managing editor of the Munsey papers wished to see me at his office. Accordingly I called upon Mr. Davis, the aforesaid gentleman—a jovial, great-hearted man, who seemed to radiate good-fellowship. He put me at my ease by saying he knew all about my work. " But why don't you allow us to fix you up in America ? " he said. " What I really want to say to you, Mr. Mawson, is that

My Last Visit to America.

I would like to print an interview with you on Athens in the ' New York Sun.' If you will allow me I will send round one of my young men to see you at nine in the morning." To this I readily agreed.

Prompt to time, a neat young man arrived, quiet in tone and manner, very unlike the type I expected ; but I soon discovered that he was an expert at his work. After an introduction, he said : " Now, Mr. Mawson, I suggest that we should first of all look through your photographs and drawings, make a selection, and then with these as our basic factor you can tell me your story."

For two hours we talked about Athens, past, present, and future, but concentrating largely on the latter. My interviewer made copious notes meanwhile, referring now and again to the illustrations to make quite sure that he thoroughly understood the position. " Now," said he, " I understand, and you can be assured of an attractive illustrated article and a readable interview. I thank you for your patience and courtesy, and will do my best to produce a bit of newspaper journalism of which you will approve."

The full-page article which appeared at the week-end was by far and away the best bit of newspaper journalism I had hitherto seen. The facts were mine, but the form, order, and phraseology were those of the interviewer.

On Monday morning I called on Mr. Davis to thank him for such a splendid piece of work. " Mr. Mawson," he said, " I wish you would tell my young friend what you have told me. I never lose an opportunity of giving praise where it is due, especially where a young man is concerned. It will mean so much to him to have your appreciation, and he will write all the better for it." No wonder the old chief was so popular with his staff !

Whilst in New York I undertook for the " New York World " a long article on the parks and gardens of that city, with suggestions for their extension and improvement. This was an important piece of work, which to my surprise won the enthusiastic approval of the Chief Commissioner of Parks, who placed his car at my service and accompanied me on my itinerary survey. These articles necessitated days of strenuous work and several long evenings' writing.

The following week-end we spent with Miss McCary Thomas, the famous President of Bryn Mawr, a splendidly designed ladies' college occupying an enviously elevated site. The school buildings were in good Tudor, or Collegiate Gothic, as they call it in America. The details, I understood, had been drawn by Miss Thomas

The Life and Work of An English Landscape Architect.

during her holidays in England and Wales. Seldom have I seen such faithful imitations, even the rough texture which results from age having been faithfully reproduced. It was at Bryn Mawr that President Woodrow Wilson started his career as a teacher, conducting the classes in literature and history for six years. At this time there was no indication of his future greatness. The pride of the College people in the fact that the President had started his career with them, was discounted by their deprecatory remarks regarding his tardiness in entering the war, since America stood aloof at this time.

On the Sunday we took a motor trip to the battlefield of Fort William, where so much American history had been made. On our way Miss Thomas told us an interesting story of the late Lord Bryce, an old friend who just before his return to England paid the College a farewell visit. As in our case, it had been arranged to take him over this same historical ground ; " but on this occasion," said Miss Thomas, " I thought I ought to have the best historical authority procurable. I thought indeed that as a student of history your Ambassador would appreciate this little consideration, and so he did. But not in the manner expected, for within half an hour of our arrival at the Fort the teacher had become the scholar, and the scholar the teacher. And what a remarkable tutor he was," continued Miss Thomas. " So graphic were his descriptions of the opposing forces that we were almost able to repeople the ground with moving armies and revisualise America's greatest drama. Yes, Mr. Mawson," concluded Miss Thomas, " Lord Bryce knew more about our history than we even knew ourselves."

Our week-end at Bryn Mawr was in every way a delightful and instructive visit. To see Sargent's portrait of Miss McCary Thomas was alone worth a visit.

Shortly after my return home I met Lord Bryce one night at the National Liberal Club, and told him the story of our visit to Bryn Mawr and its sequel. He was evidently pleased, but modestly remarked : " Mr. Mawson, I can only give the reply which Mr. Gladstone once gave on a similar occasion, ' Appreciation is apt to become exaggerated.' "

The last time I met Miss McCary Thomas was in July, 1920, in Athens, where she was investigating, amongst other things, the site which had been purchased for an American School of Archæology for lady students.

My Last Visit to America.

During our travels we had ample opportunities of estimating America's attitude towards the war, and particularly towards this country, and it was pleasant to realise that the educated classes were overwhelmingly in favour of intervention. Occasionally the opposition was manifest. Once at a cinema in New York, when a film was shown of the submarine which had arrived from Germany, landing at Boston, there was round after round of applause, in which there was quite sufficient evidence of opposition to make the occasion a very unpleasant experience. In Chicago, where the Germans tried a vigorous propaganda campaign, the resentment was rather acute. Most of the literature published by the German bureau was clumsily compiled, defeating its ends by its exaggerations, which could not deceive any educated person ; yet it had the desired effect upon the Teutonic element so strongly in evidence in Western cities.

Before completing our tour we made another visit to Ottawa, where we were entertained by many old friends, including Sir Robert and Lady Borden, with whom we had breakfast, afterwards discussing the war and my proposals for assisting disabled men. Sir Robert said he had been so impressed with the possibilities which I had outlined, that he had sent my proposals to the head of the department responsible for the care of the military, and had arranged an interview for that afternoon. This appointment I kept, and was gratified with the evident care given to the study of my report, and the possibility of applying its recommendations to Canada.

For our return journey we could only secure berths on an English ship, the Orduna, a well-appointed liner which had had a remarkable run of luck. Sailing from New York on the 16th of December, the ship carried comparatively few passengers, the first-class numbering only forty, there being a few more in the second-class. There was quite a heavy cargo of produce. We hoped to reach Liverpool in time for Christmas, but did not arrive until the day following.

The Germans had already made their crossing by commercial submarines, and there was grave suspicion that their naval submarines had approached very near to New York Harbour. In consequence, there was considerable nervousness amongst the passengers, which was intensified by the prophecies of a lady in the second-class. These prophecies seemed to affect the ship's officers even more than the passengers, and I well remember the

The Life and Work of An English Landscape Architect.

captain telling me one night at dinner that he had spent the most miserable day of his life. " You know, of course, about the lady who is prophesying disaster ? Well, her prophecies have got on the nerves of my officers and men. She says we are all to go to the bottom on Sunday, and she is the only one who will be saved."

" Could you not take drastic action under D.O.R.A., and drown the lady, thus reversing the order and so breaking the spell ? " I asked.

" Oh, I am not afraid," said the captain. But, all the same, he looked uncomfortable.

As Sunday drew on, the tension became almost intolerable, and in the evening we all foregathered in the lounge, keeping an eye on the clock, and not till the hour of midnight had struck did we retire to rest.

On arrival in Liverpool I saw the false prophetess leaning over the deck railings looking very uncomfortable, and evidently desirous to evade the passengers. She had been made to feel her unpopularity in the interim between the momentous Sunday and our arrival.

PRESTON HALL.—BIRD'S-EYE VIEW.

CHAPTER XXI.

INDUSTRIAL VILLAGE SETTLEMENTS FOR DISABLED SOLDIERS.

I REGARD the organisation of disabled service men into self-supporting communities as the best piece of constructive policy I have promoted. The inception of the idea has already been recorded ; its practical début was as follows :

One evening in December, 1915, I was dining with two officials from the Ministry of Pensions, to whom I outlined my ideas of creating villages replete with industries, handicrafts, and horticultural pursuits, for the shattered men thrown upon the nation as the aftermath of war. I made a strong plea for the old-fashioned handicrafts and trades wherein the work carries its own interest, as opposed to the modern factory system, where work is subdivided into infinitesimally small fractions, as dull and uninteresting as can be. These villages were not necessarily to be new, but I suggested that in the first instance one or two of our old-world villages should be devoted to the rearing of young trees to replete the areas deforested by the war. Another village, new or old, might be devoted to the growing of flowers, or, where suitable, to the creating of bulb farms, or to osier-growing and basket-making, such open-air occupations being provided for tubercular or shell-shock men. Another village could be devoted to the making of small proprietary articles of woodwork ; another, to the scientific manufacture of black-lead pencils, an industry suited to legless men ; another, to the printing of artistic books for children, with high-class illustrations. Here was scope for literary and artistic men. At another village could be made artistic dolls. I also described a set of town-planning models, or of toys made to scale, by which the young could be initiated in arranging model villages.

My enthusiasm must have been contagious, for my guests requested me to crystallise my remarks, and they would bring the

The Life and Work of An English Landscape Architect.

report before their chief. They pointed out that of course the Government were granting pensions, and had shops where the men were taught useful trades, but the authorities had no schemes for opening out vistas of future employment, or for the building of houses, which were scarce even then. During the night I arranged my ideas in logical sequence, and in the morning dictated them to my secretary, spontaneous and complete, whilst the iron was hot, and sent the first copies to my friends at the Ministry. The reply received in the early weeks of 1916 stated that the report had been submitted to the chief of the Department, who objected because the proposals were based upon segregation, to which the Government were strongly opposed.

Everyone who has had experience of Government methods knows that departmental chiefs keep a plentiful assortment of such labels, by which they stave off troublesome people with practical ideas who wish to enlighten their darkness. They adopt nothing until it has proved itself a success by private experience.

However, I felt that I knew my work better than these chiefs of Government departments selected for short terms as an award for their political astuteness, and determined that, having put my hand to the plough, I would drive the furrow through.

The word " segregation " had been plentifully besmirched : the Pensions officials had seen to that, and for a time it met me everywhere. I was assiduous in proclaiming my scheme in season and out of season, no matter what the reception, yet everywhere the inevitable retort was " segregation." In vain did I point out to one group that the whole of our communal life was based on the principle of segregation from the cradle to the grave—that we segregate ourselves into sects to worship one God ; in the National Liberal Club we were a segregation of Liberals, and across the Park was a segregation of Conservatives, both segregations having in view the advancement of one State ; that I had just travelled from Bolton, where the population was segregated to produce cotton yarn ; that every time I travelled to London I passed through Crewe, Rugby, and Northampton, the first-mentioned town having a population segregated for the production and repair of railway stock, the second a segregation of boys under educational discipline, the third a population segregated to make boots for the men at Crewe and for the boys at Rugby ! Finally, on my arrival in London, if I wished to consult a doctor, I found a segregation of medical men installed in Harley Street and Wimpole Street.

Industrial Village Settlements for Disabled Soldiers.

But fighting Government objections is like waging war with the hydra-headed monster of mythology—for every head you chop off, three come in its place.

Notwithstanding my protests, the word stuck, and I became known as the man who wanted to segregate our soldiers and sailors.

Another form of objection, evidently intended to deflect me from my purpose, was first intimated to me by the Chief of the Pensions Department.

" Mr. Mawson," he said, " there is no problem of unemployment amongst disabled service men. Every man who can work can find a dozen jobs."

" Yes, I admit," I replied, " at present any man with one finger capable of pressing an electric button can find work at a living wage. It is not for the present time, but for peace conditions that we propose to legislate."

Opposition only increased my determination. I saw that my case must be put in an attractive form before the public, so with set purpose I decided to write a book describing the proposal in its broader aspects, fully illustrated with plans, perspective drawings, and also thumb-nail sketches, to set forth the many-sidedness of my proposals. The cost, quite apart from printing and binding, and the time taken to prepare it for the press, was considerable.

The first edition of six hundred copies, published under the title, " An Imperial Obligation," with " Industrial Villages for Partially Disabled Service Men " as a sub-title, was circulated privately in February, 1917. These were sent to members of the Royal Family, Ministers, and important members of both Houses of Parliament, to church dignitaries, poets, writers, artists, leaders of industry and commerce, mayors of boroughs, and also to Colonial Premiers and foreign ambassadors in London, with requests for criticism and suggestions.

The response was amazing, and for the most part encouraging. Almost every Minister, with the exception of Mr. Lloyd George (who was otherwise engaged) and one or two previously noted, sent me their congratulations, as did also the bishops and leaders of the churches, university professors, great soldiers, writers, and men of affairs, all urging me to go ahead with my project, and some offering financial help. The only criticisms offered were of the " segregation " order—the dying echoes of the Ministry of Pensions.

The Life and Work of An English Landscape Architect.

It is possible to select only four short quotations from this correspondence, and these are typical of the remainder :—

LORD LANSDOWNE wrote :

We ought all of us to be grateful to those who make, as you have made, a determined effort to grapple with the difficulties of the problems which will have to be solved in dealing with our disabled soldiers. . . . I do not think we should get on at all unless we had dreamers amongst us, and your " dream " seems to me a very bright and attractive one.

GENERAL SIR WILLIAM ROBERTSON :

I can assure you that any practical solution for meeting the necessities and deserts of the men who have fought in the war has my utmost sympathy and best wishes for success.

JOHN OXENHAM :

I agree absolutely. . . . If your fine scheme can be carried out, it may save Britain from some of the evil times which I fear await her when the settlement comes, which may be more of an unsettlement than anything we have yet seen in this country. . . . Every good wish to your great work. Carry it through somehow and you will deserve well of the world.

HERBERT STOREY, D.C.L. :

Your scheme attracts me so much that, with the approval of other members of my family, I propose to make possible a practical beginning by offering as a gift the residence of my father, the late Sir Thomas Storey, along with fifteen acres of excellent building land on which to erect cottages and workshops. The only condition I make is that preference should be given to Lancaster men and any disabled member of the 5th King's Own Regiment.*

Such letters were sufficient spur for continued effort. Scores of others might be quoted, unanimous in urging me to go ahead. Here was evidence that the best-informed minds in the country were alive to the need for a great voluntary effort, which I still hoped might win the commendation of the Ministry of Pensions. The hope, as appears later, was doomed to be a false one. From the first the Minister of Pensions damned the scheme with faint praise, whilst the chief secretaries were hostile.

The book was revised, the new edition containing a new chapter compiled from the mass of criticism and appreciation, in order to stimulate further effort. Then we lost six precious months in the hope that Lloyd George would consent to write a foreword. Many influential friends, including men who were in close, almost daily, contact with the great man, used all their persuasive powers to obtain an invaluable service, but failed. Possibly he was obsessed with " segregation."

* The value of this gift, which is admirably situated opposite the well-known Giant Axe Field, and within three minutes' walk of the principal railway station, is at least £15,000.

Industrial Village Settlements for Disabled Soldiers.

At this juncture someone inquired if we had approached Field-Marshal Sir Douglas Haig. The suggestion was at once acted upon, and I received the following sympathetic response :

General Headquarters B.E.F.,
France.

Dear Mr. Mawson,

While I greatly appreciate your kindness in sending me advance proofs of your book, " An Imperial Obligation," I regret that, so far, my many engagements have prevented my giving them the attention I hope to at no very distant date, for I feel that the subject which you have tackled, the amelioration of the lot of those of our countrymen on whom this war has placed the dreadful burden of life-long disablement, is not only the most worthy to which it is possible to bend one's energies, but one which should receive immediate attention if we are to be ready for the emergency before it becomes overwhelming.

This much, however, I can say as a " Foreword " to your book : Any scheme honestly conceived and energetically and skilfully pursued for such a cause, is one which I feel confident will command the practical sympathy of our countrymen, and, as such, will have my hearty approval.—Yours faithfully,

21st June, 1917. (Sgd.) D. HAIG, F.M.

The second edition of "An Imperial Obligation" was a much more attractive book than the first, and to this improvement my secretary as literary editor, and my son as illustrator, contributed considerably. Mr. Louis Raemakers also contributed an appealing cartoon—"The Wounded Soldier Looking Into the Future."

Whilst awaiting the publication, I spent nearly the whole of my time in getting together an interim organisation, with an executive committee, primarily for the purpose of investigating any openings for promoting the interests of disabled men in need of homes and suitable employment, and the promotion of settlements or colonies, as recommended in my book. The success of my efforts to provide the nucleus of an organisation that would command respect is shown by the following print of our first note-heading :

INDUSTRIAL VILLAGES & SETTLEMENTS
FOR
PARTIALLY DISABLED SOLDIERS & SAILORS.

Interim Committee dealing with the Work of Preliminary Investigation.
WARWICK H. DRAPER ; THOMAS H. MAWSON; WALTER S. ROWNTREE; GORDON SELFRIDGE;
HERBERT L. STOREY; S. WARING; WILLIAM H. WHITING, C.B.

Treasurer:
LORD AVEBURY
Joint Secretaries:
WILLIAM HILL
JAMES CROSSLAND.

32, Orchard Street,
Oxford Street,

LONDON, W.1

The Life and Work of An English Landscape Architect.

A fund of about £1,500 was subscribed for working expenses. Excellent offices were provided by Mr. Gordon Selfridge in Orchard Street, rent free, and these were handsomely furnished and decorated by Mr. Samuel Waring at his own charge.

Then came the publication of " An Imperial Obligation," which was sent out to a large number of editors, who gave the work a splendid notice. These notices included leading articles in the great London dailies and the more important provincial newspapers, and special articles contributed by some of our best known journalists to the most influential magazines and reviews. The general tenor of these articles may be best shown by the following short extracts :—

> Mr. Mawson's scheme . . . is both ideal and practical.—*The Times.*
> Here is the book of a dream made practical.—*The Morning Post.*
> It is to be hoped that Mr. Mawson's book will achieve the success it richly deserves, both by reason of its inherent interest and the objects it has in view.—*The Daily Telegraph.*
> Here is no mere visionary : his eye knoweth what his hand can achieve.—*The Daily Chronicle.*
> The principles and proposals alike to be found in these pages are full of that new conception of what life means, which is one of the most lasting compensations the war has brought us.—*The Observer.*
> Such a scheme as Mr. Mawson's, if properly executed, would, by the creation of an exceptionally favourable environment, help to increase the fruits of the work of the recuperative and training organisations a hundredfold.—*The Manchester Guardian.*
> Mr. Mawson's project is a well-thought-out plan destined to meet the necessity for fulfilling in a spirit of the greatest generosity our duty to our mutilated countrymen.—*The Scotsman.*

Most of the approving reviewers dwelt too much upon " the dream "—the theme of the first chapter ; consequently the three succeeding chapters, which dealt respectively with " The Business," " The Finance," and " The Retrospect," were not accorded their full weight and importance. The purpose was not merely to erect a stage whereon to project the disabled soldier as an appeal to charity, but to set forth a complete circle of reciprocal life, with its flow and return augmenting the national river, since it was a scheme to supply nothing more than commonplace necessities. The pensions were part livelihood which, together with a modicum of generosity for a start, would have launched the enterprise.

As a town planner having to deal with sociological and collective schemes of habitation every day, and having made a

Industrial Village Settlements for Disabled Soldiers.

wide study of village life, both industrially and in the matter of habitations and gardens, I could give the assurance that once the initial support was forthcoming the professional guidance and the handicrafts would not be behindhand. Being an old member of the Art Workers' Guild, I knew that its members (who represent the best-informed minds of all the principal arts and crafts in the country) could be relied upon for advice, help, and support.

To show how this town-planning experience came into operation, I give the plans of a suggested model village from "An Imperial Obligation" (Illus. No. 56), and the two perspective views (Illus. Nos. 54 and 55) show parts of this latter village.

At this time the domestic policy of the country was concentrated on housing. Why not, therefore, I argued, begin by housing the wounded men and their families in these villages—say, twenty to fifty families in each, providing for their training and employment in those crafts dependent upon the building trade? Thus one village colony could be devoted to the making of lead lights and ornamental glazing; another colony to the making of fibrous plaster for plain and decorative work; another, to fitments for plumbers, and so on, the whole grouped together for publicity, collection of orders, and the distribution of finished products through some central place in the adjoining town.

This is regional planning for the purpose of production and distribution. This plan would have involved very limited segregation.

A study of this plan will show that no detail of the ideal model village was omitted. It is complete in every necessity of the ideal village community. The examples were not intended for exact reproduction, but to illustrate principles, and incidentally to prove the advantage of logical planning.

Our chief object, in which we failed, was to induce the Ministry of Pensions to see the possibilities of constructive effort on behalf of the wounded service men. What a splendid result might have been secured if Government villages like Gretna Green, now partially derelict, had been planned with a view to the reception of wounded men and their families at the end of the war, and the establishment of suitable industries.

The outcome of all these press notices, and the further publicity which was given to the subject by the clergy and public speakers (political and otherwise), was many requests for the plans of

The Life and Work of An English Landscape Architect.

operations. Several preliminary committees were set up in many parts of the country, who sought affiliation with the " London Interim Committee." This led to voluminous correspondence and daily interviews, the Committee having one or more sittings each week to deal with the more important matters arising therefrom.

In the meantime our deeds of association were formulated— a rather formidable task, involving prolonged interviews with our solicitors and counsel, who worked without fee or reward. Then came the consideration of rules of association for societies seeking affiliation, and rules for their constitution.

Meanwhile, Government Departments in allied countries and the Overseas Dominions sent for further copies of the book, and advice on the best manner of carrying out the recommendations contained therein.

At the same time, many people, including the late Princess Christian, who sent for an extra dozen copies, also began to interest themselves in our work. Property owners began to make inquiries, sometimes with a view to presenting a site for a village, more often with a desire to sell us one. Then came letters from owners of small industries and processes which they thought could be adapted to the capacities of wounded men. Many of these offers were exceedingly attractive, and were investigated and reported upon. The properties were generally inspected by Mr. Storey and myself, but we very soon found that the whole of this detail work could not be undertaken by the central office, but that, on the contrary, every scheme should be promoted and partly financed by a strong local committee like the one already founded for the promotion of the Westfield Village at Lancaster.

Nevertheless, the Central Committee hoped that by liberal public support and subsidies from the Government they would be able to help these local committees materially, and also to advise them upon the planning and industries suited to the colonies. We also decided to promote interest in our proposals in important county centres, and accordingly arranged lectures, to be illustrated by many interesting slides.

The first lecture was given by one of the secretaries, to an influential gathering called by the Town Clerk of a western town, under the chairmanship of a noble lord who was the largest land-owner in the county. It was illustrated by many plans of suggested

Industrial Village Settlements for Disabled Soldiers.

colonies, including the one at Lancaster. This was followed by a conference attended by the local representative of the Ministry of Pensions, who declared that he was instructed to say that his department was entirely opposed to the scheme outlined in " An Imperial Obligation."

It will be readily understood that the Committee were naturally much discouraged by this Ministerial attitude, carried to the point of protests at our meetings ; and to bring about a better understanding they sought interviews with the Ministry—first with the Rt. Hon. George Barnes, and later with the Rt. Hon. John Hodge. Appointments were made, but nothing resulted. The Secretaries always took up the same unvarying attitude of hostility to the project as before mentioned.

We had now arrived at a period in our development when, if we were to make a big forward movement, we needed the financial support of the public. In response to an appeal with this object, we had many replies from potential subscribers, unfortunately not containing cheques, but asking one of three questions—

(1) Does the Ministry of Pensions approve of your proposals ?
(2) Is your organisation propagandist or constructive ?
(3) Where are your soldiers' villages to which you ask us to subscribe, and can we see them ?

If to the first we replied " No," our correspondents politely said they could not go in opposition to the Minister of Pensions and his responsible advisers.

If to the second we replied that we were propagandists for the purpose of rousing interest and winning financial support, they replied that they objected to expenditure on propaganda.

If to the last inquiry we replied that we were actually engaged on the development of Westfield, Lancaster, they replied that Lancashire was quite rich enough to pay for its own schemes without seeking help from other parts of the country.

All this was both unexpected and discouraging. Hitherto, nearly the whole of our increasing weekly expenditure had, in a most generous spirit, been met by the members of the Committee. Our work was growing, and called for active financial support, and this notwithstanding the fact that all the members of the Committee were not only giving freely of their resources, but, what was more, of their time, energies, and business experience, with a liberality quite surprising for men so deeply immersed in the control and management of big enterprises.

The Life and Work of An English Landscape Architect.

In spite of the position thus created, the Committee decided to go ahead on still bolder lines, to study six projects, including the one in Lancaster, and to issue six illustrated pamphlets at regular intervals, dealing with proposed developments in various parts of the country. For this purpose I visited many districts and properties north, east, west, and south, selecting the sites which I thought possessed special advantages, making surveys, taking innumerable photographs, planning out the sites for the colonies and workshops—or, if the estate was intended for co-operative small holdings, planning homesteads and holdings. In this way I travelled long distances, accompanied by Mr. Crossland, one of the secretaries, who was as enthusiastic as myself. He took down my notes and comments, which were woven by him into pamphlets.

By far the most promising and fascinating of these estates was Meathop, Grange-over-Sands.

Next to housing, the important note of political propaganda was afforestation. Promises to re-afforest our denuded country-sides were always applauded. The Forestry Department of the Board of Agriculture was strengthened by the co-operation of many of our most scientific foresters, who made practical surveys of suitable areas. The newspapers rang out with the economic importance of afforestation and the splendid opportunity at hand for energetic development of this needed industry.

Here was our opening. Why not establish forest-tree nurseries for shell-shock cases and those of incipient tuberculosis, to supply the huge demands required by the Government's promised afforestation policy? Some idea of what this promised to be may be gathered from the following abbreviated synopsis from the Government report of a Royal Commission :—

ABBREVIATED SYNOPSIS OF PRINCIPAL CONCLUSIONS EXTRACTED FROM THE REPORT OF THE ROYAL COMMISSION ON COAST EROSION, 1909.

(1) Afforestation is practical and desirable.

(2) Approximate available area in the United Kingdom is 9,000,000 acres.

(3) Best rotation to sustained timber yield requires 150,000 acres to be afforested annually.

(4) Temporary employment can be found for 18,000 men during the winter months, and an equal number in subsidiary occupations connected with forestry.

Permanent employment can be afforded for one man for every hundred acres afforested, employing 90,000 men when the whole area has been dealt with.

Ultimate conversion and manipulation of crops would afford occupation for a still larger population.

(5) Any scheme of national afforestation should be on an economic basis.

(6) There are sufficient unemployed persons who could be advantageously employed without a period of special training.

(7) The annual sum required for the full scheme is £2,000,000.

(8) After 80 years the net revenue at present prices should be 17½ million sterling.

(9) The afforestation scheme should be entrusted to a special Board of Commissioners.

(10) The acquisition of grazing areas, private or common, should present no difficulty which cannot be satisfied by arbitration and reasonable compensation.

(11) Afforestation creates a new industry; it does not compete with private enterprise. The conversion of comparatively unprofitable lands into forests enhances the productiveness of the adjacent areas, and should promote the development of the small-holdings movement. More than any other apparent remedy, afforestation will stem the tide of rural depopulation.

For this programme the Government would require four hundred and fifty millions of young forest trees each year. Why not, I urged, secure this for those requiring light occupation in the open air?

Meathop Flats, near Grange-over-Sands, presented a perfectly ideal opportunity. Here were five hundred acres of flat rich land, with easily worked sandy soil, which was becoming derelict owing to the protecting sea-wall having been broken through by an abnormally high tide and left unrepaired. This property, including extensive farm buildings, was offered for £2,500, and formed an ideal site for an afforestation nursery and bulb farm. Naturally, this proved a very attractive subject for our first illustrated pamphlet, which was published under the title of " Afforestation and the Disabled."

This pamphlet made an immediate appeal to the press, and Lord Leverhulme wrote to say he would like to visit the property. My old friend and client was delighted, and immediately gave me a cheque for £250 to close with a six months' option.

After our experience with the Ministry of Pensions, this option gave us a basic factor whereby to win the sympathetic support of the Board of Agriculture. It opened up a conference with the Board, from whom we hoped to secure the rebuilding of the sea-wall under the reclamation orders of the Government.

The departmental heads of this Ministry cordially approved of our object, which they said it was in their interests to support if the scheme proved practicable. They sent down expert foresters

The Life and Work of An English Landscape Architect.

to report on the suitability of the soil and site for the purpose of growing young nursery stock, and engineers to prepare plans and an estimate of cost for the reclamation works. The foresters gave a very good report, approving of the scheme, with the reservation that half the land should be devoted to bulb growing, the soil and climate being in every way equal to that of the bulb-growing district in Holland. The engineers reported that the reclamation of the land was a practicable proposal, and that the cost would be fifteen thousand pounds, part of which expenditure might be charged against the property. Thus, supposing that ten thousand of this sum could be charged against the property, making, with the purchase price, twelve thousand five hundred pounds, we would have had a splendid nursery ready for immediate cultivation at twenty-five pounds per acre, including extensive buildings and farm-houses and cottages for the use of the estate manager, packing, etc., etc.

The Board of Agriculture sent up a recommendation to the Treasury to grant the money, but, by a stroke of bad luck, the application was presented on the day upon which Lloyd George introduced his economy campaign, and therefore was promptly turned down.

I have no hesitation in saying that if the Government had risked the comparatively small outlay, and if we had also got a good subsidy in aid of the homesteads, Lancashire and Yorkshire would, in their patriotic generosity, have met the bill, and this beneficent enterprise might now have been in working order.

A Mr Mawson
souvenir affectueux
E. K. Venizelo

CHAPTER XXII.

THE RE-PLANNING OF SALONIKA AFTER THE GREAT FIRE.

ONE evening late in 1917 I was quietly dining alone at my club when I was startled by a slap on the back, accompanied by cries of " Congratulations, Mawson, congratulations ! This is splendid ! "

Turning round, I saw my old friend William Hill standing behind me, evidently greatly excited.

" Whatever is the matter now ? Has someone sent us fifty thousand towards our industrial villages ? " I asked, because our finances and prospects were the disturbing factors at the time, and accounted for my dining alone.

" Haven't you seen the tape ? " he exclaimed. " If not, come along."

Arriving in the hall where the tape clicked out its messages, we found a crowd of members gathered round to read the news, which was evidently causing some excitement. On my appearance these members came forward to offer their congratulations.

" But first let me see the tape, for I have not the slightest notion of what has happened."

The message read as follows : " M. Venizelos stated in the Greek Parliament this afternoon that he had requested Mr. Mawson, the English town planner, to undertake the re-planning of Salonika."

The message was followed by a telegram from the Minister of Communications in Athens. This I showed to Mr. John Burns, and asked his advice as to what I ought to do, especially having regard to the obligations that I had undertaken in connection with the industrial villages.

" My dear Mawson, whatever your obligations may be, you cannot afford to ignore M. Venizelos' request, which confers a great honour upon you, and at the same time pays a great

271

The Life and Work of An English Landscape Architect.

compliment to the profession of town planning as practised in this country. Personally, I should regard the acceptance of this work as a matter of national importance."

" But," I replied, " it is quite impossible to undertake the work without an adequate staff, and particularly without the help of one or both of my sons."

" That I see, and therefore I advise you to call at the Foreign Office at 10-30 to-morrow morning, and inquire for the Secretary of the Middle East Section. Place the whole matter before him, and ask for special facilities to enable you to get the necessary staff together. I think you will find him sympathetic and helpful."

So on the following day at 10-30 a.m. prompt I presented myself and filled in the official request for an interview. After half an hour's wait in the corridor I was approached by a young man who informed me that the Secretary regretted that pressure of engagements prevented his seeing me. The young gentleman, however, had been instructed to hear what I had to say, and invited me into his room.

" Well," said he, brusquely, " what is the business you wish to discuss ? "

" I received this telegram from Athens yesterday, and Mr. John Burns told me you would probably help me to get a staff together so that I might be in a position to accept the offer contained in the message."

" I may as well tell you at once," said he, after listening to a long argument on the advantages that might accrue to our home industries if this work were secured by an Englishman, " that we are not prepared to help you or anyone to secure contracts in Greece."

With this parting shot my first interview with an official of the Foreign Office ended. I have since had many interviews with Government departments, but have consistently refused to discuss my business with raw undiplomatic juniors. I never again received other than the greatest kindness and help from this august Government department, but I always remember this first interview with a sense of irritation.

Having failed so abjectly at the Foreign Office, I called at the Greek Legation, where I had a long interview with the Ambassador, M. Gounaris, whom I had met on previous occasions, and found that he had received a copy of the telegram. Unfortunately, I did not stand very well with the old gentleman, who had claimed to be the real author of my proposals for the re-planning of Athens. I had indeed acknowledged—as I thought, rather handsomely— my obligations " for much interest and generous help " ; but this had not been enough, for which reason M. Gounaris had not read of my new appointment with any degree of pleasure. However, he promised to interview the Foreign Office, and in the course of a fortnight I was asked to call again, when the Secretary for the Middle East would see me. Mr. Tyrill, whom I saw, grasped the importance of my commission, and promised to help me to the utmost of his capacity; "but, of course," he added, "the question of permission to release men from war work for work in Salonika rests entirely with the War Office ; but we will do our best."

In the meantime I replied to M. Papanastassiou, gratefully accepting the call of M. Venizelos, and stating that I would at once endeavour to secure, by the help of the Foreign Office, the release of several members of my staff whose assistance was essential. Unfortunately, even the release of my son (who was engaged upon munitions) was very difficult to arrange, whilst the work of securing visas for our passports was a tedious, wearisome business.

The result was that twelve precious weeks sped by before we were actually on our way to Greece, and then only with my eldest son, none others of our staff being released. The Foreign Office, however, promised to acquaint Sir George Milne, the British Commander-in-Chief at Salonika, with our difficulties, and to request him to give us all the assistance in his power.

The delay, however, allowed me to complete the propaganda work for the industrial villages, consisting of the study of six concrete proposals as laid down in " An Imperial Obligation." For the publication of these booklets my friends subscribed nearly three hundred pounds. I was thus able to leave this work with the Secretary and the Committee, with a good conscience, and got their approval for three months' leave.

In Paris *en route* we met M. Venizelos, and had long interviews with him. He was enthusiastic about the new Salonika, almost to the point of regarding the fire as being providential, seeing that it had provided an opportunity for creating a city worthy of the splendid site—the prosperous port and the seat of local government for Macedonia. He brought out maps showing the fire zone, which stretched diagonally from the Port Vardar to the White Tower, a distance of nearly a mile, approximately.

The Life and Work of An English Landscape Architect.

M. Venizelos then explained that a large topographical survey staff had been at work for three months, principally for the purpose of deciding the boundaries of separate ownerships. The owners, of whom there are many hundreds, he explained, " are a source of some anxiety ; they insist upon permission to rebuild up to the limits of their properties at once, which of course makes the re-planning upon which I am determined impossible. What would you suggest, Mr. Mawson, under these conditions ? "

I immediately replied : " I would at once pass through your Parliament an Act of Expropriation for the entire town site," to which suggestion he assented, with the remark that this was the only way, and that it should be done. Henceforth we could regard the site of Salonika more or less as a sheet of clean paper, and our task was simplified.

M. Venizelos then told us that it had been arranged that we should travel *via* Gallipoli on the Italian Peninsula, where we would meet the British Naval Commission and sail by the Greek torpedo destroyer Panther, which would convey the party to the Piræus.

After several days, including a night in Rome, we arrived late one evening in Gallipoli, meeting Rear-Admiral Brown and members of his staff *en route*. The naval party was accommodated at the British Consulate, but my son and I had to find an hotel in the town—and a weird place it was. The hotel had at one time been the Bishop's palace, and such, undoubtedly, was the impression it gave us. It was in a narrow, tortuous street, so planned for purposes of defence. The enormous rooms were bare and gaunt, and practically devoid of furniture The place was without sanitary convenience of any kind, and the food was execrable.

After our waiting two days the Panther arrived, and we were requested to join her. Before leaving our hotel we asked for our bill. The big, burly landlord protested that, as we were Allies, he could not accept anything—adding, however, that Englishmen who were determined to discharge this obligation usually paid him 30s. per day each. We gave him half this amount, with which he seemed to be entirely satisfied.

Of all the uncomfortable sea voyages I have ever undertaken, that in the Panther stands alone in its nauseating and terrifying experiences. The very rough sea, and the fear of mines and submarines, were as nothing compared with the corkscrew movements of the boat and its stuffy cabin. Fortunately, the passage

The Re-planning of Salonika.

was a rapid one, and once we arrived at the Corinthian Canal our dangers and discomforts were at an end.

In the interval which had elapsed since my last visit to Athens many changes had taken place. King Constantine was no longer on the throne. In his stead reigned Alexander, whom I remembered as a bright youth of about seventeen years of age. M. Venizelos, after his successful revolution, was in control, and very popular both with the army and with the people; whilst the young King, although popular, was entirely under the direction of his Prime Minister. "I am merely a dummy figure-head, exercising only the will of others," he bitterly said to me later. Sir Francis and Lady Elliot were no longer at the British Embassy. In their places were installed Lord and Lady Granville. At the Greek Ministries were many new men, whilst a new Mayor presided at the Town Hall.

I was much impressed on this visit to Greece by the war-like aspect of the people and the vast armies which were under training for the front. The war-like attitude seemed to be more pronounced here than in any of the other countries I had visited. There was a great scarcity of food. At our hotel (the Angleterre) we were fed almost entirely on vegetables cooked in oil. Even milk puddings were served only twice a week.

Following the usual custom, we first signed the visitors' book at the Palace, then left our cards at the British Embassy. Following this, we called upon M. Papanastassiou, the Minister of Communications, and spent some two hours in discussion with him. This gentleman was a lawyer by profession and a socialist in politics, but withal a great admirer of his chief. He had spent two years in London studying English law, and spoke English fairly well. I found him a hard-working, well-meaning man—one who, however, had much more sympathy with French ideals than with English.

This preference had raised a difficult situation, which the Minister was eager to explain—and with his explanations he hoped I would agree. Owing to the delay in my arrival he had acceded to the request of the French military authorities to be allowed to submit plans for the rebuilding of Salonika. Indeed, M. Hebrard was already in charge of an expert staff. M. Papanastassiou proposed that the French and the English should submit each a separate competitive scheme, one of which he would select. I pointed out that this was contrary to the statement

The Life and Work of An English Landscape Architect.

of M. Venizelos in Parliament, and to his own telegram, and that consequently I must proceed according to the terms of my instructions. I stated, however, that I would be delighted to work as the director or senior member of a commission for the re-planning of Salonika, the commission to include all the experts essential to the production of a development scheme in which every important factor should be correlated. This was agreed to, and I was informed by the Minister that he proposed to accompany us to Salonika in from five to seven days' time. Everything, he explained, depended upon his being able to secure fuel for the railway engine. In the meantime I could see the Mayor of Athens regarding my scheme for the Capital. I was also informed that a society with which M. Papanastassiou was connected would be pleased if I would lecture on " English Industrial Villages for Disabled Soldiers," the Minister having seen notices in the English press on the subject. To this I readily agreed, for I had brought a double set of slides with me in anticipation of lecturing to our men in Salonika. The lecture suited the occasion and the audience, because the Greeks are wonderful craftsmen, especially in metals, leather, and pottery, and I felt that with proper organisation useful and successful soldiers' settlements might be established by them.

The lecture was given to a crowded house, under the presidency of the Minister, M. Papanastassiou, in the presence of the King and his retinue, and M. Venizelos (who had returned from Paris the previous day) and his Minister. M. Papanastassiou introduced me to the audience as the re-planner of Athens, and the director of the new town plan for Salonika. Others spoke quite warmly about my disinterested contribution to the welfare of wounded soldiers. I never lectured with greater freedom. From the first I caught the interest and sympathy of my audience. At the close I received the congratulations of the young King, the Premier, and his Ministers. Then a member of the audience said he would subscribe one hundred and twenty thousand drachmas (at that time approximately five thousand pounds) towards the first village.

The next morning I was informed that sufficient fuel had been obtained for our journey, and that we would leave Athens at six in the evening. The Minister's party, we were told, would be provided with a restaurant car and sleeping berths. On arrival at the station I was rather surprised at the size of the party, and the elaborate provision which had been made for our comfort ; but when I heard that the fuel for our journey had cost one hundred and forty-six pounds, I concluded that the expenditure of a little extra for our comfort did not matter. The railway between Athens and Salonika had not been long opened, and at various points *en route* the military—in some cases English—were developing side tracks and sidings. What struck me greatly, so long as light lasted, was the fertile beauty of certain parts of the route. The flourishing condition and variety of the crops, which included cereals of many kinds, tobacco, and cotton, impressed me very much. Where the ground was too rough for husbandry it was planted with olives and sugar pine, interspersed with vineyards where the soil was not so rugged.

We travelled very slowly, with many halts, and with a long stop at Larissa, which we reached early in the morning. Here the Minister was met by the Mayor and officials of Larissa and adjoining villages. From Larissa the country increases in beauty and picturesqueness, and by mid-day we were near the foot of Mount Olympus, which towers majestically from out of the level plain through which the railway passes. Soon we were travelling through the Vale of Tempe, with precipitous rocky crags rising on either side, awesome in their grandeur of height and in their descent to the river which courses along the foot of this famous romantic vale. For miles the village and surrounding hills are thickly clothed with beautiful forest trees and rich undergrowth of flowering shrubs. Altogether this bit of Greece is in strong contrast to the barrenness of most of the native landscapes through which we had passed. From this point to Katterina the railway has been partly cut out of the base of the cliffs, with numerous bridges spanning the gorges. It was very interesting, yet withal the most circuitous stretch of railway on which I had ever travelled. After this we crossed the Vardar river, and so on to Salonika, where we arrived about six o'clock in the evening. Here a great surprise awaited me.

As we alighted from the train we were met by the Prefect, the Mayor, and a number of officials, to whom my son and I were duly introduced. Then we were introduced to others who, we were told, were the experts who were to be members of the town-planning commission for Salonika. As we left the station together, the crowd of spectators began to cheer ; whereupon I complimented M. Papanastassiou on his popularity, to which that gentleman instantly replied : " It is not me, but the English town planner who is being welcomed." I could scarcely believe my ears, and

The Life and Work of An English Landscape Architect.

thought the Minister was perpetrating a joke. The next day I discovered that this was really the case. The whole matter was a well-staged piece of political bluff. Every day, for weeks previously, the newspaper department had been busy with daily reports about myself, and the good fortune of the Government in securing my services. One article described my departure from England by " the special permission of the British Foreign Office." Another told of our safe arrival in Rome, and then in Gallipoli, where we were detained pending the possibility of a safe passage ; then a great burst of satisfaction was expressed on our arrival in Athens, where we were in consultation with the Minister ; and, lastly, we were announced to be actually on our way to Salonika, where we were to arrive about six in the evening. It was all very amusing, but it was diplomacy, because the de-housed population were discontented with what they regarded as the dilatoriness of the Government in rebuilding their city. Truthfully, the Government had shown great energy in adopting temporary measures, and had even built a model area of new houses to accommodate some of the seventy thousand homeless. There is no doubt that the Greeks, like the Americans, believe in publicity.

On the evening of our arrival we were entertained by the Prefect at his official residence, a beautiful villa in Kalamaria, at the east end of Salonika, beyond the fire-devastated zone. Unlike the majority of Western towns and cities, the east end was the section reserved for the élite. After dinner, which consisted of four courses of well-cooked and well-served food, we retired to the salon, where the members of the commission who had met us at the railway station, and also M. Ernest Hebrard, the chief of the French assistants to the commission, paid us a visit. I had previously met M. Hebrard in London, where he gave an address on Spalatte before the Town Planning Conference, and knew of him as an archæologist of repute and as a " Prix de Rome " student.

M. Hebrard (who later became a good friend) regarded himself as the man in possession, and he was naturally anxious to hear how long I thought my work as consultant would take me. The delay and our absence from the minutes of the commission had allowed him to assume that he was in control. I learnt the same evening that the French Commander-in-Chief had first approached the Minister to secure the work for his countrymen, and that he had released no fewer than eighteen assistants for the work, and also for some archæological investigations. The Frenchmen at

STREET SCENES IN SALONIKA.

least were alive to the advantage of " securing contracts in Greece."
I also met Captain Pleybair, a French engineer who had
worked out a plan for the canalisation or drainage of Salonika,
from which it will be seen that matters were rather complicated—a
position which was by no means relieved when I saw M. Hebrard's
scheme. This was attractive, but was planned purely from an
architect's point of view, whilst Captain Pleybair's scheme proposed
to turn the whole of the crude drainage into Salonika bay. In
this matter of drainage I fancy M. Pleybair had yielded to local
pressure.

Now was the time to state clearly the terms on which I had
been brought to Salonika, and how on my advice it had been
arranged to constitute the whole of the experts into a commission.
I again stated that all I would claim would be that I should act as
senior member of this commission, with a casting vote, which I
trusted I would never have to use. We then arranged that our
first meeting should be held at the Prefecture the following
afternoon.

Next morning my son and I called upon Sir George Milne,
the British Commander-in-Chief, and were most cordially greeted.
He stated that he was delighted that his own countrymen had been
engaged to re-plan the town, which, apart from the fire, was badly
in need of improvement.

Acting upon the aforementioned communications from the
Foreign Office, and after inquiries, Sir George found he could
assign us four young architects, and, if needed, a good photographer.
" Furthermore," said he, " we can do all your blue prints and
reproduce in black line your plans of the town, as you proceed.
Finally, I can place at your disposal a car and a chauffeur ! " I
learnt that one of my old pupils was in Salonika, and I begged
his release to replace one of the architects. Sir George also
recommended us to the officers' rest-house, for which the old
Turkish palace had been commandeered, and this proved to be of
the greatest help. I have no hesitation in saying that in view of
the number of men released by the French Commander-in-Chief,
we would, apart from Sir George's help, have had to return to
England with our task unaccomplished.

With our impromptu staff we set to work at once upon a rapid
survey of the city, in order to be fortified for the preliminary meeting
of the commission. We first obtained a number of military plans
of the town, along with other plans showing the burnt-out areas.

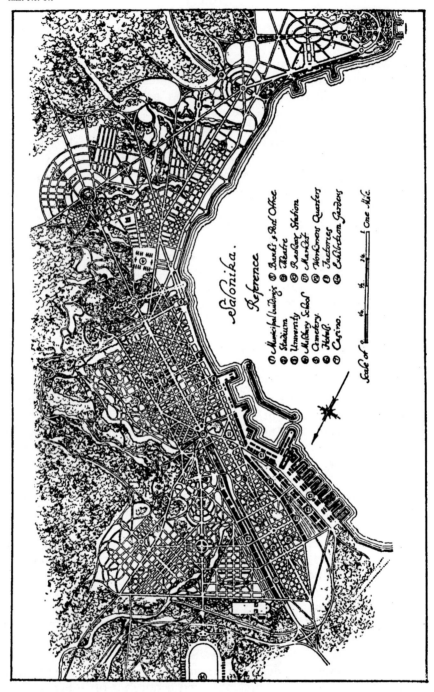

Salonika.

Reference

① Municipal buildings ⑧ Banks & Post Office
⑥ Stadium ⑨ Theatre
① University ⑩ Railway Station
② Military School ⑪ Market
③ Cemetery ⑫ Workmen's Quarters
④ Hotel ⑬ Factories
⑦ Casino. ⑭ Exhibition Gardens

Scale of 0   ¼   ½   ¾   1 One Mile

The Re-planning of Salonika.

Never shall I forget, in inspecting the town, the scene of desolation and the dejected knots of people camping on the ruins of their former homes or places of business.

The following account of the fire was sent me by my former pupil, Harry Pierce, then serving with the military at Salonika, who witnessed the scenes he describes :—

THE GREAT FIRE OF SALONIKA—AUGUST, 1917.

The afternoon of August 18th, 1917, was hot and sunny, with a strong " Vardar " wind blowing, and the cafés at the bottom of Venizelos Street by the harbour were curiously deserted. The usual crowds seemed to have forsaken their favourite haunts, and a curious uneasiness unsettled the city.

At the top of the town a thin spire of smoke rose into the clear air above the closely packed portion of the old city, where the native population crowded together in timber-framed houses whose upper storeys and projecting balconies nearly met across the narrow streets. This pillar of smoke grew thicker and denser, and the people, with an only too frequent experience of fires, became anxious.

The few loiterers in the cafés left their seats, and one of the waiters tersely remarked, " Big fire ; no water ! " The column of smoke grew darker, and people in every kind of dress began to hurry down the steep, narrow streets from the old town, across Via Egnatia, to the more open spaces of the modern town along the sea front. Slowly they came at first, but like a flood the volume increased rapidly, and soon the lower town was a seething mass of refugees.

Anxious tradesmen locked their shops and put up their shutters as the crowd swarmed past, all carrying some treasure which they valued most. One woman pulled along a small child and held up her apron filled with boots ; an old man clutched a leg of mutton ; another carried a live hen.

Carts soon added to the confusion—carts laden with weeping, excited people bringing with them what they could : a marble slab, a mirror, a sewing machine— the most curious collection imaginable. Strong porters staggered under huge loads of bedding or massive trunks, and still the crowds flocked from the stricken quarter. The flames, fanned by the strong wind, leapt from house to house across the narrow streets, and building after building crashed in ruins.

With nightfall the effect became vivid, and huge clouds of smoke hung over the burning town, streaked and licked with tongues of lurid flame.

By this time the troops of the various countries stationed in and around the town came to the rescue, and the battleships in the harbour sent help. Water was pumped on to the blazing buildings along the quay, and blocks of buildings were blown up to save the more distant parts of the city.

It is said that owing to the magnificent work of the soldiers and sailors not a life was lost out of the many thousands of people whose homes were burnt, and the refugees were lodged in temporary homes and camps without the city walls.

The fine old church of St. Demetrios, and the mosque of Hamza Bey, were destroyed, as well as the synagogues of the large Jewish population, and great damage was done to the modern buildings along the harbour front, but soon temporary shops were open amongst the ruins, trading as briskly as ever in the devastated city. Fortunately the Church of the Twelve Apostles (Illus. No. 2) was saved.

The Life and Work of An English Landscape Architect.

I soon realised the terrible extent of the havoc which the fire had wrought, and the heart-aching experiences of the poor. Later in the day I remarked to the Mayor that I had noticed that the British soldiers seemed to stand well with the native population. " I am pleased you notice this, for it is a fact, and for very good reason : they are the salt of the earth. I assure you, Mr. Mawson, that on the night of the fire the prestige of the British was raised higher than ever before. Indeed, they did more to strengthen the ties between England and ourselves than your Governments have done in twenty years." Then he told me of the splendid work continued throughout the night to save the population. Women and children followed our soldiers as if they were the natural protectors of these homeless sufferers, and these poor people were so grateful to our countrymen that they offered gifts and money. But this gratitude only made Tommy sad. He wasn't working for pay—he was simply doing " his bit," and enjoyed doing it. Nothing I heard in Macedonia pleased me so much as the Mayor's penegyric.

As arranged, we held our first meeting of the commission in the afternoon, one member only being unavoidably absent. The first business was to lay down rules for the smooth and effective working of the several experts. The French members of the commission objected to my being invested with the chairmanship, but all the Greek members, who were in a majority, and not very pleased with the attitude of their French confrères, supported my claim, which was duly approved. Thus my position was clearly defined. We next examined the work of the topographical survey department, which was entirely in the hands of Greek engineers, whose work was excellently done, and nearing completion. The whole of the burnt-out area had been surveyed and plotted to an excellent workable scale, suitable for our preliminary studies.

We decided to discard in large measure what had been put forward, and to re-study the whole of the town-planning problems from start to finish. We also agreed to meet twice a week to discuss the work in progress, so that each expert could offer suggestions for the proper correlation of his quota to the whole plan. In the first place, we divided the town into three distinct sections, each separated from the one next to it by a wide belt of park reservation. These reservations were to be plentifully planted in the form of irregular loops extending from sea to sea from a point near the White Tower inland north of the citadel, and *returning via* Porte Vardar to near the docks. The Eastern Section, which included the whole of Kalamaria, was the residential and social centre ; the Central Section, extending east to west from the White Tower to the docks, was the governmental, municipal, ecclesiastical, and business centre. The Western Section included the transport, warehousing, and industrial parts, with housing for the artisan classes. This was zoning for the purpose of fire prevention, and was probably the first occasion upon which fire prevention was the dominating factor in the planning of a great city in the Near East.

Transport facilities were the next factor which we sought to solve. This, however, was considerably influenced by several existing conditions beyond our control. In the first place, the military authorities had spent millions of pounds upon the construction of splendid roads radiating in all directions from Salonika. They formed the arterial systems which connected the hinterland with its port and business centre. The second controlling factor was the predominating importance of slow-moving traffic, which was gradually being modified by motor-driven transport, which the new arterial roads had encouraged. Our first problem was to connect our new street plan with these military-made roads, then to provide separate roads for quick and slow traffic within the town.

Our next care was to locate the main factors bearing upon a solution of the traffic system, and to define as carefully as possible the areas which would be subject to congestion. Thus we located the dock extensions, warehousing, and manufacturing area ; roughly laid out the goods yard and engine sheds ; located the position for the proposed new passenger station for Government offices, law courts and town hall, markets and theatre centres—in short, a fairly complete zoning plan ; after which we were able to predetermine the traffic system based upon ascertained and estimated needs. In this solution the planning of a complete tram system was a first essential, because most people travelled by car.

This method of solving our practical difficulties first by building up the plans upon the conditions of working efficiency before considering the æsthetic possibilities, was a great disappointment to our French colleagues. In the end they realised that there was something in this point of view ; but Frenchmen, with all their fine technical qualities, are not very friendly to compromise, and therefore, whilst recognising the great ability of French architects, I would not wish to repeat my Salonika experiences.

Thus, as the weeks sped by, we found that, whilst working in the closest co-operation with the Greek members of the commission, collaboration with the French members became less and less effective. However, by exercise of tact and patience we made headway, and arrived at agreements on all the controlling factors of the new plan, which quite naturally gave added opportunity for architectural expression where this was essential. In this department M. Hebrard and his assistants did excellent work.

I stayed in Salonika for about three months, and during this time was visited by the young King Alexander, who took a keen interest in our progress. M. Venizelos and his Ministers also paid us a visit, and the former was so pleased with our progress that he invited all the experts and their principal assistants to lunch at the White Tower Restaurant, and a very jolly affair it was. The Premier was in the best of spirits, and made a most complimentary speech when proposing the health of his guests. As senior member of the commission it was my duty to reply, and I remember I struck an interesting note by my free rendering of a passage from Ruskin : " The greatness of a country does not depend upon the extent of its territory, but upon the number of good men and women within its borders," from which I inferred that our work as town planners was to provide such conditions as would assure the upbringing and maintenance of good men and women. When I sat down, M. Venizelos gave me a hearty handshake, and asked where I got my quotation. Some time later, when standing with M. Papanastassiou, the latter pointed to the opposite side of the road. " See," he said, " there goes M. Venizelos with a volume of Ruskin under his arm."

By the end of three months I had, with the help of my son and staff, in full agreement with my colleagues, evolved a complete set of preliminary drawings, numbering thirteen in all. Herein every aspect, whether of traffic, fire control, civic centre, and manufacturing and residential areas, new training system, parks and boulevards, was shown, and also a proposed development of Mickra Point as a suburban seaside resort. I had also written a very full report, extending to eighty typewritten pages of foolscap. Although this report was entirely my own work, it was read over in French to the members of the commission, who severally signed it, so that it might go forward as our joint recommendations. Thus the preliminary scheme and our recommendations for its further elaboration for parliamentary approval were completed in three months, a record which I have never been able to repeat.

In addition to my work on the re-planning of Salonika I had many interesting experiences. In the first place, I undertook, at the request of General Ryecroft, to give a number of lectures on " Industrial Villages for Disabled Service Men," at the various depôts and halls provided for the men. My first lecture was given before a company of keenly interested men, with General Ryecroft in the chair ; but as my object in lecturing was to get at the men's point of view, and to have their frank criticism, I was disappointed that no one started a discussion. Then it occurred to me that the presence of the bluff old General overawed the men, so in future I decided to ask for a junior officer as my chairman. The plan worked admirably, and on every subsequent occasion we had a splendid discussion, which usually took up more time than the lecture. Usually there were some excellent speeches, generally tinged, to put it mildly, with socialism. One man, I remember, a graduate of Edinburgh, who had read theology for the Presbyterian ministry, asked a very pertinent question : " Can the lecturer assure us that their villages will not be under any sort of military patronage or dictatorship ? If they are, you will find the British Army to a man opposed to them. Military control is necessary in war, but we are determined not to tolerate it in peace time ! " The next questioner had been a leader-writer on one of the London dailies, and his questions were equally pertinent : " Will the Government officials exercise any control in their management, and will they be regarded as philanthropic institutions ? We object to the first ; and as for philanthropy, we have still a little self-respect, and cannot accept it." Then a third man, this time a citizen, got on to his legs slowly, and after carefully balancing himself, spoke as follows : " I would like the lecturer to know that we don't care a toss for the military government or philanthropy ; what we want to know is what wages you are going to pay, and who guarantees them. Also, my mate and me would both like one of those cottages the lecturer showed us. We suppose, of course, there would be no rent or rates to pay."

In some form or other these three questions were asked after nearly every lecture, from which it was evident that the men were anxious to return to the freedom of civil life again, and to be

The Life and Work of An English Landscape Architect.

for ever free from military control. On the latter point they often used the plainest language. After one of these explosions the speaker stopped suddenly and explained, " Of course, Captain [this to my chairman], we like you all right, for you are a white man," a statement which pleased both the Captain and the company present.

At the week-end my son and I were generally invited to one or other of the divisional headquarters, so sometimes we were on the Doiran front and sometimes on the Struma front. These frontal visits were at times exciting. Once when lecturing in a Y.M.C.A. tent at Langaza the Bulgars started a vigorous shelling of the road half a mile beyond us, along which they supposed a convoy was passing. The whizzing sound of the shells passing over us, and evidently not very high, followed by the explosion, was terrifying, but I continued my lecture. I am afraid, however, that a shorthand report would have read rather disjointedly. As the shelling continued, we dispersed at the close without waiting for the usual discussion or formalities, and walked back with our host, Captain Hamilton, through the dark and over a very rough path, along which we stumbled many times, the shells flying over our heads with sickening rapidity. At last we reached the Captain's dug-out, consisting of two compartments dug into the hillside, one being used as a living-room and the other as a sleeping-room. Here an excellent meal was provided, the table utensils being home-made productions, showing the ingenuity of our men under the most difficult and uncomfortable conditions. There was even a touch of artistry about the interior, the walls being hung with native rush-mats arranged in panels, which were decorated with suitable pictures cut from the magazines, mostly popular stage favourites.

Next morning we went to see the valley where we had suffered one of our worst reverses, in which our casualties amounted to over eight thousand—a battle, by the way, never mentioned in the published official reports. From this point we entered the trenches, which had been blasted out of solid rock, and finally to the outlook post, where, through a field glass, we saw one of our batteries shelling a party of Bulgars who were evidently intent upon throwing a bridge across the river. We had the satisfaction of seeing the Bulgars run.

On the Saturday night we were entertained by the Brigadier-General. After dinner we went with our host and staff to the pantomime, for which purpose a huge old bar had been fitted up with a stage, orchestra, and seating accommodation for about nine hundred. As we were so near the fighting front, the idea of running a successful pantomime seemed to me to be a very remote one, but it was the best show of its kind I have ever seen. The orchestra of forty instruments, and the stage scenery, were superb. The Colonel who was responsible for the orchestra told me it was amazing the many fine instruments the men possessed. Of course, he said, there were quite a number of expert instrumentalists in the army who had played in London orchestras. There were also many professional actors in the company. What struck me most was the way they had managed to collect their diversified and interesting costumes. I was told that these costumes (ladies' dresses included) had all been designed and made by the soldiers. Even the attendants were dressed in smart blue liveries, with long frock-coats and white trousers, all made by tailor-soldiers, and paid for out of the proceeds of the show.

During the performance I was delighted to find that I was the subject of the gags, some of which were very clever.

FUNNY MAN : Well, Bill, where'er you bin this last month ?
BILL : Bin in Salinka, of course, calling on the General !
FUNNY MAN : Now, that won't wash, Bill. Salonika is burnt hout.
BILL : Haven't you heard that Mr. Venizelos sent for Mr. Mawson, who has built it up again ?
FUNNY MAN : That ? All by the chap our Colonel sent for to build a garden city at Langaze ?
CHORUS (*pointing to me*) : Why, there he is—there he is—there he is !
Song : " When shall we live in the house that Jack built ? "

It was evident that Tommy had learnt the art of enjoying himself and of forgetting for a space the grim struggle upon which he was engaged ; for at this time the struggle in the Balkans was fraught with great anxiety.

On our next trip to the front our experiences were of a different character. *En route* we were struck by a Vardar wind, accompanied by a sand storm of great violence, we being without protection from any quarter. Our chauffeur, who simply wept, for about an hour lost all sense of locality as the wind swept over us with unabated force. With no signs of life visible, we feared we might be approaching the enemy country. It was an absurd fear, but when one is lost and in a conjectural state of mind, even imaginary fears assume reality. At last we saw signs of man's work in a camp road, and followed it to investigate. We came to a large shed,

The Life and Work of An English Landscape Architect.

when we heard singing in an unknown language. For a moment we thought of flight. But we summoned courage to knock at the door, which was immediately opened by the soldier on guard, who could not understand us. Then I saw that we were in an officers' mess—but of what nationality?

Although the soldiers were tall, robust, and manly fellows, I yet feared they were Bulgars. Several of them came up to speak to me, and fortunately the senior officer spoke good English. This officer, seeing my evident anxiety, explained that they were a contingent of Serbians. On hearing our business, and the name of the camp at which I was to lecture, the Serbians gave us very clear instructions, from which we found we had overshot our objective by only about six miles. Fortunately the wind had now somewhat abated, and we arrived at our destination only three-quarters of an hour late, with the audience still waiting patiently for the arrival of the lecturer.

I have experienced Chinook winds on the Canadian prairies, and other winds of bad report in other countries, but never have I experienced a wind which could cause such suffering and discomfort as the Vardar winds in Macedonia.

Having been requested by M. Venizelos to interest English financiers and contractors in supplying materials to rebuild Salonika, I decided to turn my steps homeward. We had now completed our preliminary scheme, and obtained the unanimous approval of the commission to its recommendations. With this in view I handed over to M. Hebrard the directorship, with my son in control.

On arrival in Athens I obtained permission to hold an exhibition of our drawings for the capital and Salonika, which was officially opened by M. Venizelos, and attended by Lord Granville, the British Ambassador, and a distinguished company. The plans for Athens occupied two walls of a large room, and the Salonika drawings a third. Again I took great care to share the credit of the latter scheme with my colleagues, by having a notice six feet long printed in big letters, stating that "These drawings are exhibited by the commission appointed for the re-planning of Salonika." The two schemes were highly praised by the Premier when declaring the exhibition open, and he asked me, before leaving, to proceed as rapidly as possible with the new diagonal road from the new station place to Monasterachi. When, however, I asked for an official instruction for this work, the Minister of

The Re-planning of Salonika.

Communication refused to ratify without a special vote of Parliament. Both M. Venizelos and the Minister commended my purpose in returning home, but the Minister in charge could not be induced to state specifically the conditions upon which they were prepared to accept this help. " See what you can do with the English contractors and report to me," said he.

By this time my second son, who had been an officer in a Canadian regiment, but who had been invalided home, had been granted permission to join us. He arrived in Athens, and proceeded at once to assist the Minister in formulating building laws and regulations for the rebuilding of Salonika. On the completion of the work he was appointed Director of Reconstruction of the sixty Macedonian villages, which involved the organisation of a very large staff.

Before I left Athens for home, the Embassy people arranged for me to cross from Patras to Taranto by a convoyed troopship. On arrival at Patras I was met by the British Consul, who informed me that the Italian Government had decided to prohibit the landing of all civilians at Taranto. He advised me to go on board the flagship and interview the captain, who might be induced to send a wireless asking for special consideration. The captain proved to be a Lancashire man, who at once instructed his operator to send a message ; but after waiting two hours and receiving no reply, I had to return to shore. That night this same vessel struck a mine and was cut in two, with a loss of a great part of the crew. Thus I had a providential escape.

After waiting three days in Patras I was allowed to join a vessel sailing for Gallipoli, which we reached in two days after a very anxious voyage. Probably the smallness of the vessel saved us from the attention of the submarines which at that time were the terror in these waters.

The only untoward event which occurred on this return trip was at Moderna, where we ran into a troop train in the dead of night, a collision that resulted in the death of some half-dozen men who with their regiments were proceeding to the Italian front. Fortunately I was unhurt, excepting for a fright and a shock.

On my arrival in England I was requested by the Board of Trade Department of the Foreign Office to write a report on the openings for British trade in Macedonia. I had the satisfaction of seeing this report published and freely circulated by the British Industries Association. The keynote of the report was that " trade

The Life and Work of An English Landscape Architect.

followed the town planner." This led to much interviewing and consultation, and also the formation of powerful groups of British financiers and contractors. One of these groups I introduced to M. Venizelos, who as a start gave out important contracts for railway and road construction. What the total value of these commissions amounted to I do not know, as I secured no financial recompense for myself.

THE SALONIKA TOWN PLANNING COMMISSION.

FRONT ROW.—Captain Jenkins (*Assistant Engineer*), M. E. Hebrard, T. H. Mawson (*Chairman*), The Mayor, Captain Pleybair, M. Kitsikis, M. Eleftheriotes.
BACK ROW.—J. W. Mawson, M. Zachos, E. Prentice Mawson.

CHAPTER XXIII.

STEPNEY GREETING AND RE-PLANNING OF LONDON'S DARKEST SPOT.

IN what proved to be the most anxious period of the war I received a pleasant surprise and an intensely interesting commission, and one that appealed strongly to my social and political instincts.

As a direct response to the issue of a limited number of roneographed copies of our report on the King Edward Memorial Park, I received a call from Mr. J. W. Kiley, then the Mayor of Stepney, and later member of Parliament for the five boroughs, who had been very much impressed by the town-planning and housing proposals. The possibilities of the immediate surroundings of the park led to a vision of the improvement of Stepney and Shadwell as a whole.

Mr. Kiley, who was a keen and sane social reformer, had also been impressed by a pungent magazine article by Mr. William Hill on " Better Housing Conditions for Returned Heroes," and was anxious that I should consider this aspect of Stepney's needs. The result was that I joined forces with Mr. Kiley and two of his friends, the late Sir Richard Stapley and Mr. John Nicholson, in the production of a town-development scheme for the whole of the district controlled by the Stepney Council and such parts of adjoining areas as impinged upon it, which it was necessary to include for the purpose of arterial road connections. None of the three gentlemen who acted as financial sponsors could in any way benefit by the regeneration of Stepney, as none of them was a property owner in the district. It was pure philanthropy taking its most practical form—viz., in the creation of conditions under which the denizens of the East End might attain a higher standard of well-being.

Never was there a built-up area which permitted of such economic development as Stepney, or one in which the need for

The Life and Work of An English Landscape Architect.

improvement was so sorely needed. Remembering that Stepney borough extends to within half a mile of the Mansion House, and that the southern boundary rests on the busiest and most prosperous reaches of the Thames, with its improved and expanding dock developments, one finds it difficult to realise why the rebuilding boom had not followed an eastern course and produced a great commercial locality in place of the squalid, unsavoury courts and alleys, whose phthisis charts are appalling documents. These conditions alone would justify any demolition, however drastic.

A civic survey of existing conditions soon revealed the reason for this depressing wilderness of human habitations, and for its low rateable value—also, shall we say, the reason for its failure to respond to that commercial pre-eminence which its position between the greatest financial centre in the world and the increasing shipping activities of the Port of London ought to have given it? I had no hesitation in deciding that the London and Southend Railway was the cause of this failure, and also for the creation of those conditions which were largely responsible for the high infant mortality and the high death rate, and, what was equally deplorable, the low physical and mental conditions of the slum dweller.

The great elevation of the railway, which ran east to west from end to end of the borough, starting at Fenchurch Street and rising like a solid rampart out of the level plain of Stepney, prevented the cross flow of sun, wind, and rain. It was a matter of much concern to me at the time, and still is, that in any part of England such conditions as I saw in Stepney should be allowed to continue, or that men and women should be content to live in such surroundings.

Feeling that no drastic improvement could be realised without removing the railway, and seeing that a great commercial boulevard could be created at a profit, I boldly proposed to place the London and Southend Railway underground from Fenchurch Street to a point near the Regent's Canal, or alternately to remove the terminus to a point near Albert Square. This would permit of a great boulevard one hundred and twenty feet wide on the ground now occupied by the railway. To do this it would be necessary to clear away the rampart-like railway to the level of the built-up areas on either side, and construct the new boulevard, which we called Stepney Greeting.* Thus would be removed the great

* This is a name given in America to promenades and park boulevards which are designed as social centres.

Re-planning of London's Darkest Spot.

blot on Stepney, and the primary cause of its unsavoury conditions, which also render any æsthetic improvement well-nigh impossible. The splendid opportunity which is here provided is shown by Illus. No. 53. The effect obtainable is by no means exaggerated.

As to the practical possibility of realising this improvement, I did not proceed without obtaining expert support for my proposals. I consulted expert railway engineers as to the feasibility of either placing the railway underground or of removal of the terminus, and was assured that both schemes were capable of realisation. On the financial side I worked in co-operation with the best known firm of estate agents in the city, who assured me that the construction of the boulevard would create land values of about three millions, whilst the value of property which would be erected on either side would create rateable values amounting to at least twelve millions sterling; so that, from a ratepayer's point of view, the inducements to promote this scheme were very great indeed.

With a boulevard one hundred and twenty feet wide it is possible to erect buildings of commanding height and importance. The best authorities on property in the city assured me there would be a strong demand for business premises, and particularly for importers' sample and sale rooms and offices for shipping and insurance companies. Looking at the strategic position between the world's greatest financial centre and its shipping centre, I was convinced that these splendid sites would be quickly occupied by commanding structures, all agreeing in general alignment and sky line, but relieved by the proposed war memorial, which it was suggested should take the form of a campanile two hundred and sixty feet high, so as to create a landmark for shipping entering the Port of London. We also proposed to create a stately civic centre in relation to the campanile, in which the two principal buildings should be the Town Hall and the Law Courts. For the Town Hall we adopted the first premiated design submitted in the Stepney Town Hall competition by Messrs. Briggs, Wolstenholme and Thornley, of Blackburn and Liverpool. This is the building shown in the perspective, and the Law Courts are a replica adapted to a court of justice.

Although the creation of the boulevard constituted Stepney's crowning opportunity, it was by no means our only concern. Our next care was to provide for the re-housing of the slum-dwellers. The problem presented was a very interesting one. Here was a

The Life and Work of An English Landscape Architect.

borough without vacant lands of any kind. Indeed, so intent had property owners in the past been to promote intensive development that the total area of public open spaces was approximately one acre to 4,500 population, as against the one acre to every 200 population which is now regarded by town planners as a minimum. In numberless instances even the restricted backyards had been used for the erection of workshops in which poor Russian Jews eked out a precarious existence.

In provincial towns expansion or provision for slum clearances can always be provided on the vacant lands by which they are intersected or surrounded, but Stepney is closely hemmed in on every side by other built-up areas.

Seeing that Stepney could not afford, on the one hand, to keep its slums, or, on the other, to lose any part of its population, how would it be possible to re-house these people under tolerable conditions, and at the same time provide increased playing spaces for the children? That was the problem. Instead of the mean two-storeyed houses, crowded so closely together as to keep sunlight from each other, we proposed to erect four-storeyed blocks of flats, far enough apart to permit the full rays of the sun to fall on each block, and at the same time provide considerable garden and playground amenities between them.

The housing proposals of our town-planning scheme for Stepney created some opposition from local and other housing reformers, who claimed that the only way was to clear out the whole of the slum areas and rebuild on the basis of twelve houses to the acre. In a borough like Stepney this is impossible of application, as it would be a needless hardship to the population, more than two-thirds of whom would be forced to seek housing accommodation outside the council area, and far removed from their work. By our proposals it would be possible to re-house the whole of the slum-dwellers under vastly improved health conditions, for it would be possible to secure for their tenements all the light and air possible in the case of cottages, which in any case would be out of harmony with the needs and appearance of the locality.

One of the next suggestions in our re-planning scheme was the restoration of the river front to the uses of the public. This we proposed to realise by setting the first floor of the warehouses back to allow of a promenade road on this level, thus permitting a direct connection between the wharf and the warehouses on the

Re-planning of London's Darkest Spot.

ground-floor level. This very practical and economical suggestion is by no means new, but has never yet been applied in any English seaport town. That the public would greatly appreciate this opening up of the river front is undoubted, for there is always a fascination about a river front, with its sea and river craft plying up and down the river in such varied and picturesque form and order. Thus to restore to the use of the public the very finest health promenades amid ever-changing but always picturesque surroundings would have been a great boon to the Londoner.

By the removal of the railway, the re-housing of the slum-dwellers on a different plan, and the restoration of the river front, we hoped in a measure to compensate for the lack of open spaces.

The study of the traffic circulation in relation to the docks and goods warehouses, and the principal points of collection and delivery, was most interesting, but the solution of these problems was much more easily attainable than might appear in the case of an area so densely built up. The reason was the new central boulevard as a traffic route practically solved the flow east and west, whilst the removal of the elevated railway would make it possible to arrange for the cross-traffic roads at points where property values were very low, or in positions where new traffic routes would become valuable business streets, in which case the enhanced land values would compensate both owner and local authorities for the cost of road-making.

It was never contemplated by the promoters that they should inaugurate any part of this work themselves. On the contrary, they regarded the scheme as a piece of necessary propaganda work which they hoped would promote interest in the town-planning possibilities of the East End of London, " so that heroes might have houses fit for heroes to live in." They also hoped that a scheme which showed both æsthetic qualities and financial possibilities, presented in an attractive form, would appeal to the Government, the London County Council, the Borough Council, the Port of London Authority, and the railway companies.

That the publication of this scheme, and the many reviews and articles which appeared in the press, created a widespread interest, is undoubted ; and I think I may safely add that Stepney Borough Council and the Port of London Authority would have favoured the adoption of the scheme. But the London County Council had already discussed the widening of Cable Street at a cost of a million sterling, an expenditure that would have been

The Life and Work of An English Landscape Architect.

unnecessary under our proposals. Probably one of the impediments to the interest of the L.C.C. in the scheme is their fear of any negotiations with a railway company. On the contrary, my idea was that, properly approached, the railway company would have favoured the scheme. We indeed hoped that the railway and municipal authorities would in this case come to recognise the fact that their interests were mutual. So far, however, the L.C.C. have made no effort to examine the proposals, although so influentially promoted and supported. It is true that the numerous plans and drawings were exhibited at Spring Gardens, and that some of the committees viewed them, but the only observation of these committees was that the plans were too idealistic to be realised. One must have proper sympathy with those councillors who without any expert knowledge are called upon to adjudicate upon the merits of a scheme of such vast importance to London's darkest spot. At a later period I renewed my efforts to influence the L.C.C. by approaching the chairman of their most important committee, to whom I was given a letter of introduction. In every case, however, I got the impression that the committees were very much overworked, and that they had no use for new ideas excepting when promoted by their own officials.

It is, however, a moot point whether such a vast scheme of public improvement would not be more successfully realised by a great financial combination working under a private Act of Parliament. Most of the notable achievements of the past have been promoted and carried out by financial enterprise; but after the financial success of Kingsway and other considerable enterprises which were undertaken by the old Board of Works, it was thought that the L.C.C. should consider the possibilities of the Stepney proposal before embarking upon the expenditure of large sums upon the widening of Cable Street and other existing streets.

After having given the whole matter my often renewed and earnest study, I am absolutely convinced that, given the will, the scheme is a profoundly practical one, that it would pay handsomely, and constitute the most far-reaching enterprise of its kind in the country. If in the future any work of mine is reckoned worthy of study by the town-planning student, Stepney will be the first which will be selected. I am even inclined to think that my solution of this problem will be recognised by some organising genius with sufficient moral power behind him to win for it the public support which I believe it deserves.

WESTFIELD SOLDIERS' VILLAGE, LANCASTER.—LORD HAIG SPEAKING DURING THE OPENING CEREMONY.

CHAPTER XXIV.

THE AFFAIRS OF THE INDUSTRIAL VILLAGES COMMITTEE.

WHILST in Macedonia I had devoted the whole of my leisure to interesting the British forces in the Near East in the work of the industrial villages, and in getting an inside knowledge of the soldiers' attitude towards the movement. I hoped that in my absence there would be a wide circulation of the pamphlets, for which I had prepared the necessary drawings and photographs, and I trusted that these would have produced a change for the better in the prospects of the committee. Instead, however, of the work being continued on the lines I had laid down, an almost opposite course had been pressed, which led to a searching inquiry, and finally, for financial reasons, to a curtailment of the work. Money had been spent and burdens incurred which were out of all proportion to our resources, and the sums which I had collected for the publication of the pamphlets on concrete openings for industrial villages had been spent upon exhibitions and expensive propaganda work.

It will be seen from what I have said that practically the whole expense of this propaganda work was borne by the members of the committee, the general public holding aloof because they would help established work only. The public heartily approved the scheme we had outlined, and would, so they said, support the villages once we could show results. My committee, being anxious to make good, prepared to make still further sacrifice to attain this end. I persuaded them to return to the policy I had evolved, and investigated two openings for industrial villages situated within easy reach of London. One site was very suitable for a co-operative fruit-growing colony, and on it had already been erected over forty excellent new cottages. The entire property was offered for seventeen thousand pounds. The other was a small factory, with manager's house and ample land for the

The Life and Work of An English Landscape Architect.

extension of workshops, whilst near by was available land for the erection of cottage homes. A successful industry in the manufacture of dolls' heads made from a peculiarly fine-grained hard clay dug in the neighbourhood, had already been established, and it was certain the same material could be adapted to the reproduction of small statuettes and other decorative modelled art productions. Reports were prepared for both colonies, along with a suggested form of business organisation to work them. Both schemes were carefully considered by the committee, and received their approval, subject to our ability to finance them.

For a time it seemed as if we were on the way to success, and we began to lay our plans for a big appeal based upon four definite proposals, one of which was, of course, the Lancaster village, which was beginning to take definite shape. The fourth scheme was the Meathop afforestation colony. A well-known firm of advertising agents whom we had consulted at this juncture wrote to say that in consequence of a great appeal to be launched by Mr. John Hodge, the Minister of Pensions, to aid disabled soldiers to start life again, he regarded the time for our appeal as inopportune. When we realised the tremendous scale of this rival appeal we sadly recognised the soundness of the advice given to us, and were reluctantly compelled to postpone further consideration of our new projects. Thus once more our efforts were frustrated by the Ministry of Pensions. The Hodge appeal is said to have realised a million and a quarter, which was dispersed in doles—in many cases, let us hope, with permanent results. How much better would the results have been had this large sum been devoted to co-operative efforts in industries specially suited to the needs of disabled men, along with the creation of housing facilities which might have been models and incentives to the country!

Meanwhile, disabled men were returning in ever-increasing numbers, so that even Government officials began to realise the enormous and pressing claims of the wounded men, who after having passed through the hospitals became clamorous for attention. The Government panacea was training centres and still more training centres, with craftsmen and professors to give instruction in every conceivable art, craft, or trade. For a time there was a demand for men whose six months' training was supposed to fit them for trades in which other men had served seven years' apprenticeship. Then trouble began, and the trade unions opposed dilution. What was needed at that precise moment was the conversion of the many munition villages into training and employment centres ; but, no, the men had been liberally dealt with, they had been given pensions and a trade, and some of these might be further helped by the John Hodge fund. A few might be placed on small holdings, but this was about the limit.

Then a change gradually came over the officials of the Government departments, and inquiries were made as to our activities. We were even told that if we could revive some of our schemes, especially Meathop, the Ministry would be prepared to give them very careful and sympathetic consideration ; but it was too late, for the cold reception of our efforts had weakened that driving force without which no great enterprise can succeed. Therefore, disheartened and sceptical of any adequate response commensurate with the energy and money expended, the committee decided to meet its liabilities and wind up its affairs. The offices were therefore given up, and the secretaries and the staff dismissed.

It seemed as if we were thoroughly beaten and " down and out "; but it is characteristic of our countrymen that they are blind to defeat, and can never grasp the most patent facts associated with failure. Chasing " the forlorn hope " is a positive recreation with some people, and incidentally such persons often prove there is method in their madness. In this category we may justly place Mr. G. Reeves Smith, who from the start had worked assiduously for the cause of the disabled, and it was largely by his efforts that Industrial Settlements Incorporated arose out of the ashes of the Industrial Villages Interim Committee.

The truly magnificent work accomplished by this organisation at Preston Hall, Maidstone, calls for a word of explanation as to its inception and achievements. Industrial Settlements Incorporated was fortunate in having Lord Queenborough as president, Lord Avebury as treasurer, and such active workers as Mr. G. Reeves Smith and Sir Edward Smith.

During the somewhat lengthy process of winding up the affairs of the old organisation, Preston Hall, an extensive, modern, and well-equipped mansion situated in the centre of a lovely Kentish landscape, with 100 acres of land in lawns, gardens, and park, came into the market. This property was, we thought, just what was needed, but the price was thirty thousand pounds, against which we had no credit whatever. What was to be done ? Some time previously Lord Queenborough had provisionally accepted the presidency of the revised organisation, and here

The Life and Work of An English Landscape Architect.

Mr. Reeves Smith again comes into action. If, said he, you can find anyone who will give the necessary guarantee at the bank so that we can conclude the purchase of the property, I think I can see my way within six months to raise the money required for purchase, furnishing, and whatever is necessary for organising the scheme. With this assurance I called upon Lord Queenborough and laid the facts and proposals before him, to which he replied : " I know the property, and the proposition is a splendid one, and of course I will be delighted to give the necessary guarantee." And he did. I did not know at the time how Mr. Reeves Smith intended to get the money, nor did I inquire ; but I saw that he, Waring, and Storey were putting their heads together, and at least I heard that a number of our friends were guaranteeing a clever scheme for raising a large sum of money, which had been devised by Mrs. Lyell. This proved to be the first Golden Ballot, which accounted for a balance of about £250,000.

Two-thirds of the new Council and Executive were old supporters, which showed that they had a deep interest in the work, even though, as we may now allow, some of them disagreed with the business methods of the Interim Committee. To these were added another third, all men and women interested in the disabled service man's welfare. Notable amongst these was Sir Edward Smith and Sir Nathan Raw, whose help was invaluable. To revive general interest in our work, Mr. Reeves Smith arranged for a conference at Claridge's Hotel, at which Lord Queenborough presided, and it was left to me to act as chief spokesman. The Ministry of Pensions and other Government departments were well represented.

The new organisation was given a room and an address, rent free, in the Savoy Hotel, and Miss Phillpots, the assistant secretary to the Interim Committee, whose keenness and ability had won the respect of all, was appointed secretary. The vast amount of work which was accomplished by Miss Phillpots did much to bring about the success of the new venture.

On the suggestion of Sir Nathan Raw, the first thing done after the acquisition of Preston Hall was to invite representatives of the Ministry to visit the property and report on its suitability as a colony for the training and support of men suffering from incipient tuberculosis. The report of these Government representatives was most encouraging, and they promised liberal grants for training and maintenance. It was therefore decided to proceed " full steam ahead." Architects were called in to report upon the necessary structural alterations and additions for the accommodation and training of at least two hundred and fifty men. Water engineers, heating and ventilating experts, were consulted ; a gardener was installed, with instructions to bring the beautiful gardens, which during the war had necessarily been neglected, up to their former condition. Negotiations were also set on foot to acquire an additional four hundred acres of land, and a deposit was paid : all proving that the new organisation had unbounded faith. Offices were taken opposite the Marble Arch, the meetings being held at the Savoy Hotel. In the meantime, the first Golden Ballot had been launched, and within a month it was evident there would be a substantial sum available for open-air treatment at Preston Hall. Later the Government offered a subsidy of £180 per bed. In 1920 Preston Hall was opened with a fully equipped staff under the direction of a medical expert, with about sixty patients, the number gradually increasing as accommodation could be provided, until the maximum of three hundred were at one time receiving training and maintenance. This of course meant a vast expenditure in workshops, machinery, and equipment, in extensive poultry farms and piggeries, and particularly in the development of the horticultural department, which was planned on the basis of an up-to-date commercial enterprise.

The men take a keen interest in their work, attend the lectures with regularity, and generally do their utmost to reach efficiency.

The preliminary scheme provided only for the curative and training period, but from the first it was recognised that if the men's future was not provided for, the enterprise could not be considered a permanent success. The scheme of village communities outlined in "An Imperial Obligation" was the only one which offered any solution and provided for the men's future, and so it was decided to test the men's wishes in regard to it. Segregation had, of course, been accepted as absolutely necessary for the curative and training period, but it was not known how the men would regard living and working permanently in a village erected entirely for their use. A ballot was therefore taken of the 214 men who were under training, with the result that 165 voted for the industrial village. In other words, practically every free man preferred segregation.

The next task undertaken, and that with great enthusiasm,

The Life and Work of An English Landscape Architect.

was to experiment in industries which would hold out the promise of a reasonable income which in conjunction with the men's pensions would provide a living wage. Out of a large number of industries which we tested, both as to suitability and as to profit-bearing, a number have given excellent results. Amongst the most successful has been the growing of tree carnations. Thus, again, when put to the test, the principles urged in " An Imperial Obligation " have proved trustworthy.

The result is that to-day there is a village growing up at Preston Hall which provides comfortable homes for the men, with their wives and families, whilst prosperous industries are being rapidly developed on sound business lines. Herein lies the future success of the venture, which, as the period of training comes to an end with the loss of Government subsidies, must rely more and more upon self-supporting industries. Thus by the tenacious faith and the organising ability of a few enthusiasts a fine local success has been built upon the ashes of the Interim Committee, and all connected with it have felt the joy of achievement.

Speaking for myself, I cannot claim any large share in this final success, but it is a matter of satisfaction that both Preston Hall and Westfield, Lancaster, are doing their beneficent work.

CHAPTER XXV.

THE END OF THE WAR OPENS UP NEW PROSPECTS.

DURING the late summer of 1918 it became increasingly evident that the resistance of the Central Powers was weakening, and that the end of the war was in sight. Many old clients then began to write about suspended works, and new projects began to spring forth, which sent me on my travels again.

Early in September of this year my wife and I paid a visit to Lews Castle, Stornoway, as the guests of Lord Leverhulme. I had not been on the island twenty-four hours before I saw I was booked for a busy fortnight. My client, who had recently purchased the island of Lewis, had begun to set his fertile brain and organising genius, not only towards the improvement of his own private domain, but also towards the industrial conditions of the island as a whole. The result was that I left Lewis with the data on which to base a report of the natural resources of the island, along with instructions to prepare designs for the Castle grounds, and also his lordship's tentative suggestions for the re-planning of the town of Stornoway. These commissions involved an amount of work which kept me busy for the next three months.

Thus I dealt with a wide range of possibilities requiring some knowledge in the round of architecture and town planning, tourist possibilities and sport, home industries and handicrafts, forestry and arboriculture, fruit-growing and horticulture, and finally the economic improvement of peat lands. All were subjects encountered in my varied life's work. Early in life, and all through my career, I had learnt to observe local conditions, including soil, climate, and tree growth. Working on this principle, it was comparatively easy, after observing the remarkable growth of *Abies Frazeri* on the estate, to estimate the value of similar land planted with the

The Life and Work of An English Landscape Architect.

same and kindred pines ; or, after seeing the remarkable crops of raspberries and bush fruit in the kitchen garden at the Castle, it was not difficult to estimate the value of a large acreage of bush fruits grown on similar land.

The report was presented later in the year. After reading it, Lord Leverhulme jocularly described me as the most imaginative man he had ever met; but whether intended as destructive or as constructive criticism I never knew, and did not inquire, for fear it might come under the first category. Be this as it may, I have seldom worked upon such a fascinating subject, nor upon one which seemed to be more my native element.

The chief subjects dealt with in this report were as follows :—

(1) The exploitation of Lewis as a tourist resort.

(2) The improvement of sporting facilities, especially of loch and river fishing.

(3) The utilisation of the vast quantities of peat for the creation of power, for fuel, for peat litter, and for horticultural purposes.

(4) The conversion of large selected areas of peat land into farm and forest lands.

(5) The creation of a nursery business for the raising and growing of young forest trees.

(6) The afforestation of large areas of the island for profit, shelter, and ornament.

(7) The development of osier beds, for which successful experiments had already been made on the island. These experiments and the increasing demand for osiers suggested the possibility of a large development of the basket-making industry.

(8) The development of small holdings for crofters.

(9) Co-operative fruit-growing on a large scale, including the cultivation of raspberries, blackberries, strawberries, gooseberries, currants, loganberries, and Siberian crabs.

(10) The development of herb-growing for drying and distilling.

(11) Bee-keeping.

(12) The creation of a well-appointed and scientifically controlled experimental garden for research work in the growth of New Zealand flax, etc.

Unfortunately, just as many of the proposals were entering upon the experimental stage, the now notorious raid began, ending with the eviction of the oldest and most enlightened farmers in the island, and the division of these cultivated tracts of land amongst the raiders. Obviously it was little use developing rural industries in places where there was no security for owner or tenant. But for these untoward incidents the Isle of Lewis might have proved an intensely interesting development which would have added enormously to the welfare of the inhabitants as a whole. These

End of War Opens Up New Prospects.

proposals were, of course, supplementary to the organisation of the fishing industry, upon which large sums of money were spent before the hostile attitude of a small but very insistent section of the islanders brought the whole of these experiments in industrial and social welfare to an end.

Following this failure, some years later Lord Leverhulme offered the island, upon which he had from first to last spent over a million sterling, as a gift to the islanders, but this offer was refused. One wonders what the disciples of Henry George would say to this rejection of ownership ; and yet the refusal is not difficult to understand. The tenant of a croft paid ten shillings a year rent, and his landlord paid the rates. This amounted to sixpence more than the rent, so why should the tenant (and a Scotsman at that) turn landlord and lose his " sixpence " a year ?

At this time, travelling beyond Inverness was as difficult as travelling abroad, and necessitated military barriers and passports, for which reason I did not visit the island again until after the Armistice.

The Armistice, which was signed in November, 1918, increased interest in national projects, particularly those which had to do with industrial reorganisation and the provision of better housing and amenities for the working classes. It also brought into practical operation much work for private individuals. Many old clients like Lord Leverhulme, Gordon Selfridge, Walter Cottingham, and Sir Samuel Waring, took in hand the completion of work which had remained in abeyance during the years of the war.

At this time the activities of the Ministry of Health, over which that practical idealist, Dr. Addison, presided, were directed primarily to the promotion of town planning with a view to fitting the proposed housing schemes logically into the expanding towns. These activities also aimed at improving transit facilities, the preservation of natural amenities, and the creation of those recreational facilities requisite for the higher standard of life which the returned war man demanded. Further legislation of an obligatory character was passed, calling upon all municipalities with a population of 20,000 and over to submit schemes before the close of 1923. This enactment brought considerable work to the firm.

One of the first calls in this direction came from the Wood Green Council, followed closely by our old clients of the adjoining

The Life and Work of An English Landscape Architect.

Council of New Southgate. For both areas we are still engaged in collaboration with the Council's engineers and surveyors. These two important North London districts are full of interest for the town planner, and both possess certain characteristics and features which ought to give a permanent value to the districts as a whole.

Wood Green, for instance, whilst in parts intensely developed, has the crowning advantage of Alexandra Park, a site of approximately one hundred and fifty acres, occupying the highest ground in the district. It also had the advantage of large undeveloped areas abutting the Tottenham, New Southgate, and Frein Barnet Council areas. The principal drawback had quite unnecessarily been created by the lack of co-operation between the railway companies and the local authorities. Here it may be remarked that without exception in my experience the railways have imposed the barrier to logical town planning. Further, I have yet to meet a case in which the railway lines, the stations, the goods yards, and the passenger department, might not have been better and more economically arranged had the railway companies and the local councils co-operated. Fortunately, owing to the discrimination of town-planning principles there is now growing up a more accommodating spirit which must inevitably lead to mutual advantage.

New Southgate's asset is its private domains, which are wonderfully interspersed with timber, set amidst expansive undulating park lands. These are some of the natural amenities which a town's development plan will seek to preserve. Two other advantages are its beautiful public parks and recreation grounds which a progressive Town Council has provided.

Another interesting commission was a development plan for the extension of the industrial and residential town of Grays in Kent. Here, again, we worked in collaboration with the district surveyor. The Council had acquired a tract of land for housing, thus giving us a starting point for the larger proposals. The result will be practically a new town, which, when fully built up, will contain its own shopping centre, churches, schools, and recreational facilities—in short, a model community centre.

By this time the housing of the working classes had become the slogan of every political party. The cries were for " houses fit for heroes to live in," and " conditions under which we could raise a race of A1 men." Every authority, whether county council, borough, or urban district, was invited to estimate its needs and

End of War Opens Up New Prospects.

to present schemes for the approval of the Ministry, which would then grant a liberal subsidy. So urgent was the supply of additional houses regarded, that their Majesties the King and Queen, accompanied by the Prince of Wales and Princess Mary, supplemented the efforts of their Ministers by giving a reception at Buckingham Palace on April 11, 1919. Representatives of the London and county councils associations, of borough and urban district councils, and rural district councils, were invited to send representatives. Additional to these public bodies, the National Housing and Town Planning Council was invited to send representatives, and I was one of the chosen delegates.

In all there were about five hundred present, each group being introduced by its chairman or secretary. Our group was introduced individually by Mr. Henry Aldridge. It was intensely interesting to watch these masters of royal courtesy making their guests at their ease, occasionally adding a word of compliment or making a short inquiry when any mayor of a town which had distinguished itself during the war, was presented. When it came to my turn, Mr. Aldridge presented me as the re-planner of Athens. The King gave me a cordial handshake. I then passed on like the others to shake hands with the Queen, and I confess I was more loyal still when the Queen told me she had been following my work with interest. It was so simply said, and with such apparent appreciation, that I felt at once under obligation.

After the reception the King read his address in a resonant voice, with excellent delivery, emphasising, with the accustomed skill of a finished orator, its salient points. The address created great enthusiasm, and undoubtedly did much to strengthen the housing cause.

Two paragraphs in His Majesty's address which were applauded are well worth quoting. They epitomise the high aspirations of the country for better housing conditions :—

" If this country is to be the country which we desire to see it become, a great offensive must be undertaken against disease and crime ; and the first point at which the attack must be delivered is the unhealthy, ugly, overcrowded house in the mean street, which we all of us know too well."

" It is not merely ' houses ' that are needed. The new houses must be also ' homes.' Can we not aim at securing to the working classes in their homes the comfort, leisure, brightness, and peace which we usually associate with the word ' home ' ? "

The housing boom was now in full swing, and we came in for our share, principally for the Wood Green Council, who had

The Life and Work of An English Landscape Architect.

acquired the Cline estate (fifty acres) and the White Hart estate of forty acres, both excellent for the purpose. For these two properties we prepared lay-out plans showing 450 houses for the first and 432 houses for the other. These schemes were duly approved by the Ministry of Health, and plans prepared for the whole of the cottages. Only fifty were built before Dr. Addison was replaced as Minister by Sir Alfred Mond, who reversed his predecessor's policy and practically brought housing to a climax. The results attained fell short by at least 80 per cent. of what politicians had advocated as a minimum necessity.

One of the reasons given for the abandonment of the housing policy was the combination amongst builders, merchants, and manufacturers to force up prices. In the early stages of the housing boom this was unfortunately only too true.

In the winter of this year I gave two lectures at King's College, London—the first on "The Re-planning of Salonika," and the second on "The Re-planning of Athens." The late Dr. Burrows, the Principal, a warm friend of Greece and its Prime Minister, was chairman. Mr. Venizelos attended, and proposed the vote of thanks in a notable address delivered in English. He spoke most kindly of my work, both as the director of the re-planning commission for Salonika and as the re-planner of Athens. Naturally, on such an occasion and with such a world-famous Premier in attendance, there was a large audience and great enthusiasm. At that time the Greeks were quite sure they were living in the early stages of a great renaissance.

Sir T. G. Jackson, Bart., R.A., our first authority on Byzantine architecture, was the chairman for the Athens lecture, and contributed many interesting facts relating to both classical remains and the Byzantine architecture of this ancient city. I was certainly most fortunate in both my chairmen, whose fame added numerically to the gatherings and infused the lectures with an amount of scholarly information on these great cities. My lectures were devoted for the most part to providing a picture of these two cities as they might be if Greeks the world over were minded to contribute the necessary financial assistance.

The lecture on Salonika was repeated all over the country. Everywhere it attracted crowded audiences, composed largely of men who had served with the forces in Macedonia, and who always applauded any picture representing such scenes as the congested traffic conditions at Porte Vardar, rechristened by them

End of War Opens Up New Prospects.

" Piccadilly Circus." They were also interested in my references to ancient forms of transport, which in the Near East still persist. For purposes of contrast I brought together in the same picture convoys of donkeys laden with scrub for firewood, as well as an ancient porter carrying the furniture of a household on his back, and the modern army motor-waggon. On the one hand was to be seen the smart modern Tommy with his alert, debonair carriage, and on the other the native muleteer, unchanged for centuries.

I also addressed companies of business men on the commercial and industrial opportunities of Macedonia, and always there was the same inquiry, evidently dictated by experience of business methods in the Near East : " How long credit do they require ? " This was a question I also was asking, for at this time I had not received from the Greek Government or the Municipality of Athens sufficient to pay out-of-pocket expenses.

The desire to obtain a settlement for our work in Athens largely led up to my next visit. I was also suspicious of certain political undercurrents which had for their object the promotion of French interests, notwithstanding the great popularity of the British throughout the Near East.

When I left Salonika after preparing our preliminary studies, which were approved as studies by M. Venizelos, it was clearly understood between the members of the commission that our report and diagrams were to constitute the basis of the final scheme. Further, I was to be regularly informed of the progress of this final scheme, and to be given an opportunity of criticising all deviations from the original proposals. Hearing nothing from my colleagues, I cabled my son to report to me, and found that the French members of the commission had rushed through the completion of the drawings and had held a public exhibition of them in Salonika and Athens, omitting my name entirely from the plans. Not until the Minister of Public Works protested was my name restored.

The compiler of the descriptive brochure of the exhibition thought to belittle our work by a contemptuous reference to it, which, translated, reads as follows : " Mr. Mawson, the English town planner, had visited Salonika and prepared several diagrams." I therefore, along with my son and our assistants, claim the authorship of these " diagrams," one of which is illustrated on page 280. This diagram is No. 13. I can now add that in so far as this " diagram " was departed from, the

The Life and Work of An English Landscape Architect.

" improvements " were of doubtful value, and often impossible of attainment.

Another thing demanding a further visit to Greece was the difficulty of settling anything by correspondence with the official departments. Before leaving Athens I had, as already stated, received explicit instructions from M. Venizelos to interest English contractors and financiers in the reconstruction of Salonika, and in this direction I had made some progress, but although I reported regularly to the Minister of Public Works, I seldom received any reply, so I felt that I could not go on spending my energies with so little result. I had learnt my lesson. The Greeks, notwithstanding many fine qualities, spend part of their lives in looking for some new thing, and the rest of it in procrastination.

In keeping with this resolution, we started (my wife and daughter-in-law accompanied me) for Athens, travelling *en route* Paris, Rome, and again by Gallipoli on the Italian peninsula. As Gallipoli was one of the few ports from which Italian and Greek boats were sailing, we were informed on the morning of our arrival in Rome that if we took the afternoon train for Gallipoli we would find a boat waiting. Following these instructions, we arrived at this port the next morning, only to find there had been no boat for a week, but that one was expected in two days. We had to stay for a whole week again at the hotel where we had previously experienced so much discomfort. Never have I met with a hostel in which ordinary comforts and decencies were so entirely neglected.

On arrival in Athens we again put up at the Hôtel Angleterre, which, after the discomforts of our journey, appealed to us as a palace of hospitality and cleanliness. There I met my two sons. They had been in Athens some time, compiling the conditions of sale and building ordnances for Salonika, and drafting out co-operatively worked homesteads for the settlement of returned soldiers on the land in Thessaly. In this policy M. Papanastassiou was following the lead of M. Venizelos, who on one occasion told me that he was not anxious to encourage new industries, even in Salonika, until the needs of additional cultivators of the land had been fully met.

My sons had prepared for me a résumé of the actual position of our work in Salonika and Athens, and the forces for and against its adoption, along with a lot of other projects in which our aid would be sought. They had also drawn up a programme for a

End of War Opens Up New Prospects.

month's hard work, which included a report on the principles to be observed in the re-planning of the sixty-four villages which had been destroyed in the Macedonian war zone, and the organisation of a town-planning department which was to be under the direction of my second son. At the same time, I was asked to select sites for four new hotels for the proprietors of the Hôtel Grande Bretagne. This particular company was promised special facilities by the Government, which at this time had adopted the recommendations of M. Venizelos for a chain of hotels as the first step in the development of the plan for Athens. The crowds of tourists who daily sought hotel accommodation in the Greek capital and failed to find it provided ample proof of the need.

The proprietors of the Hôtel Grande Bretagne had already prepared plans for extending its accommodation to the utmost limits of its site. They were now negotiating for the larger area of land between Rue de Stadt and Rue Université occupied by the Royal Mews, which was to be removed to a less valuable but more convenient site near the Crown Prince's palace.

Some idea of the land values in Athens may be gathered from the price (viz., £250,000) demanded by the Government for this site. The plan we proposed was to develop about half the plot for the new hotel, with the main entrance façade facing Rue Université, with an entrance from the Rue de Stadt flanked on either side by a long colonnade with lock-up shops between the hotel and garden court. Our most interesting proposal for a hôtel de luxe was the site on the rising ground south of the stadium, in a dominating position, which I still regard as the finest site for an hotel in the whole world. Its terrace would command such a panorama of natural features and historic remains as does not elsewhere exist.

Since my last return to England the Venizelos Government had endeavoured to prove their love of democracy by converting the larger half of the Royal Gardens into a public park. That this was greatly appreciated by the public was proved by the crowds of people who filled the walks and alleys of the park. A part of this ground abutting the east side of Constitution Square was greatly coveted by the group of hotel promoters, and it was hoped that I might report favourably upon it, and prove that it would add to the dignity of the square and the amenities of the Royal Park. I reported against the adoption of this site on both counts, and

The Life and Work of An English Landscape Architect.

recommended in its stead a much more spacious place along Rue Kaffissia.

Unfortunately, about this time the drachma began to fall in value, and has continued to fall ever since. This depreciation of the drachma was followed by lack of confidence and enterprise, so that little progress has been made in meeting one of Athens' most vital needs.

On the third morning after my arrival in Athens I was sent for by the young King Alexander, who had just returned from Salonika. As always, His Majesty received me with great friendliness, and asked about the progress of the various works on which we were engaged. I explained that we seemed to be like many other firms engaged upon construction schemes—every design seemed to meet with hearty approval, but made no further progress. "That," replied the King, " is the traditional attitude of Greeks, and you will find that they will keep you drawing out plans for ever if you allow them to use you so. Your only chance is to bring in foreign interests." The King then told me that he was chairman of a Trust Fund which amounted to over fifty thousand pounds left by an Anglo-Greek towards the foundation of a new collegiate school corresponding to Harrow or Rugby, for which several sites had been suggested, which he proposed I should visit the next day, in company with His Majesty.

As arranged, I presented myself at the palace at two o'clock the following afternoon, accompanied by the Mayor of the Piræus, who favoured a site to the south of the Piræus, or alternately a site on the other side of the town and harbour. Both of these sites were impossible, being barren rocks, which would have cost all the trust's money to level. I pointed this out to the King, who entirely agreed, but naturally the Mayor was very disappointed. The King said : " Seeing you cannot report favourably on either of these sites, can you make any other suggestion for a suitable site ? "

I replied without hesitation that there was an ideal site along the Singrosse Road, about half-way between Athens and Phalaron Bay—in fact, immediately behind the church built by King George as a thank-offering for a providential escape from death. I pointed out that this beautiful church, which was seldom used, would make an admirable school chapel, and that the ground to the east was practically level for sports fields and a group of collegiate buildings.

End of War Opens Up New Prospects.

King Alexander was so impressed with this site that he at once instructed me to prepare a scheme in which every building, whether of school-house, master's house, etc., was to be included. By the time these plans were submitted the whole position had been altered by the offer of a rich Greek to find the whole of the additional finances required to build and equip the school—a matter of two hundred thousand pounds,—subject to the school being built on the island of Spezia, of which he was the owner. When last I heard of this scheme the promoters were trying to find water on the island.

The reasons given in favour of the island site are very interesting, and worth repeating. The original sum of fifty thousand pounds was left for the purpose of introducing the English principle of public-school life into Greece, and one of the provisions was that the headmaster and the sports master must be Englishmen. It was pointed out, and I think with some truth, that under this system school control supplanted parental control, and that the only way to secure this in Greece was to take the boy away from the precincts of home, otherwise fond Greek mothers would be constantly showing their anxiety for their offspring by calling at the schools every other day, thus interfering with the discipline of the headmaster and his assistants.

We were inundated at this time with requests to take up work and establish an office in Athens. In addition to the projects already enumerated, we were commissioned to design an industrial village in Corfu for the well-known firm of Aspioti Brothers, with new works attached, whilst the Minister of Public Works promised us much Government work. This set me " furiously to think," for there was a great danger that our success in Greece might submerge our home practice. Already this Greek work was monopolising the entire energies of my two sons and nearly half of my own. I was approaching my fifty-eighth birthday, and, never being physically strong, I had to hesitate about accepting a suggestion that might have won me fame and fortune. With the favour of the Royal House, and the active support of the Government, anything seemed possible. The more I thought of it, the more I became convinced that either my home connection or the Greek one must go.

There was also the certainty that the dilatory financial methods of the Greeks would necessitate a much larger capital than I at the time possessed, and yet to give up a commanding position

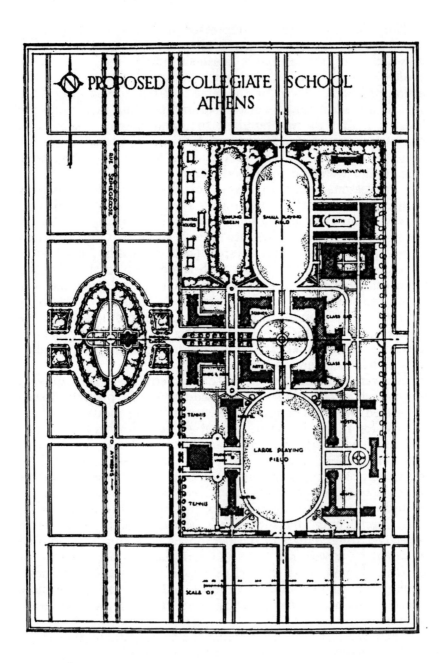

in Athens and allow the completion of the town plans to fall into other hands, was depressing.

I had been asked to lecture on " The Future of Athens " before the Society of the Men of Science, the most influential organisation in the capital, and I decided that I would then outline a policy for the completion of the city plans and the method by which the work could be spread over a period of twenty years. First I had a conference with M. Papanastassiou, and discussed with him the formation of a commission backed by its own executive staff as in Salonika. It was suggested that I should visit Athens for a period of six weeks twice each year, when the commission could meet in full representative force, and that, apart from my position on the Council, I should be entirely responsible for the park and boulevard system.

The lecture, which was delivered under the chairmanship of M. Zalacoste, and attended by the King and his suite, was evidently regarded as an important occasion, because the lecture hall was crowded to its utmost capacity, every profession and every important interest being represented. Greatly encouraged by my audience, I spoke for an hour and a half, laying particular stress again on the importance of an ample water supply as the necessary starting point in the improvement of Athens. Without it a beautiful park system would be impossible. A plentiful water supply would again make Athens worthy of its ancient title of " The City of Sweet Violets." I concluded by recommending the formation of a town-planning commission, outlining its compositions and functions. This was put in the form of a resolution and passed with acclamation ; but, to my great disappointment, I saw that the Minister of Public Works was not present, and I feared under-currents.

For the next fortnight I was daily interviewing Ministers and heads of Government departments, as well as the Mayor, trying to get support for my scheme for progressive development, both in Athens and in Salonika, but at every stage I found indecision and a refusal to accept responsibility. I was later to learn that all the Ministers were so entirely under the domination of M. Venizelos that politically they dared not call their souls their own. Greece, which had a very liberal democratic form of government, was really in the grip of the autocrat Venizelos, who ruled both King and Parliament. As a mere onlooker it seemed to me that this just suited the needs of the country under normal conditions,

The Life and Work of An English Landscape Architect.

because the Premier had the overwhelming support of the electorate and the fullest confidence of the Allies, and was recognised by friend and foe alike as a great personality. He was firm, yet courteous, wise, and far-seeing, and a thorough-going patriot, but in the completeness of his qualities he stood alone. Even Politis, with his great powers of oratory, did not approach the standard of Venizelos as a statesman. This autocracy worked perfectly so long as the Premier was on the spot to control the political machine, but for some time past he had been in attendance at the Peace Conference in Paris, and the work there absorbed all his energies, with the result that the political machine in Greece slowed down and gradually began to mark time, all hoping daily for the return of M. Venizelos. But the conference dragged on month after month, and the policy of marking time brought, as it was certain to do, unrest and dissatisfaction, for none of the promised plans for the rebuilding of Salonika or the devastated villages of Macedonia, or for the improvement of Athens, was begun.

The following incident will show how lax the Government had become :

At the exhibition which I gave of our plans for the capital, before leaving Athens on my previous visit, M. Venizelos greatly admired our proposals for a new diagonal road between the proposed new station place and Place Monastirachi, and said, in the presence of his Ministers, that he would like to see this improvement commenced at once. To him I replied : " It shall be done immediately if you can arrange for an Act of expropriation of the necessary lands, and also buildings (mostly slums) which stand in the way." " You shall have an Act passed through Parliament, Mr. Mawson," said Venizelos. Unfortunately, Venizelos left Athens a few days later, and this very promising and paying proposition was put on the waiting list, and there it is still. When on this visit I inquired what progress had been made, and was told that the Municipality refused to incur the expense. Of course M. Venizelos intended this to be a Government enterprise. Incidentally, I was informed that a French engineer had raised objections to the site I had chosen for the new Union Railway station, on account of its expense. This position had been mentioned to me by King Constantine as offering a convenient site on vacant land, and the finest view of Athens. Therefore the engineer's criticism was merely another effort at French penetration.

Realising the hopelessness of any progress, I returned to

End of War Opens Up New Prospects.

Paris to interview M. Venizelos, who was staying with his staff at the Hotel Mercedes. After waiting three days I had an interview with him, and arranged for a conference of representatives of the contracting groups in London. The upshot was that commissions were secured for several important schemes. To this extent my trip had produced good results, but I finally decided that in the then state of instability it would be unwise to risk my home practice for the allurements of Athens.

There is just one other matter of interest in connection with this trip which is worth noting. I have already referred to the work of afforestation which at the request of King Constantine I had included in my preliminary lay-out for Athens. This work had been continued with vigour each planting season over a very considerable area, with most promising results. In this way the slopes of the hills of Phillapapos and the Lycabettos are rapidly assuming a forest-like character, to the great æsthetic advantage of the capital. I was also delighted to find when I called at Corfu that the large spaces planted with cypress were flourishing.

On my return home I found much work awaiting me.

For a year before I left for Athens our surveyors had been busily engaged on the preparation of a contoured survey plan of Hengistbury Head, Christchurch, Bournemouth, which, with the adjoining meadow lands and tidal inlets, totalled over five hundred acres. This property had been acquired by Mr. Gordon Selfridge, one of those American business men who take to fine architecture applied to great projects as naturally as Englishmen take to old furniture, glass, or china.

At this time Mr. Selfridge was the tenant of Highcliffe Castle, a beautiful old house reminiscent of an old French chateau. Here I often stayed with Mr. and Mrs. Selfridge for long week-ends, and during these visits we evolved what was frankly intended to be a purely imaginative piece of work, and, being imaginative, we were not troubled by any of those material considerations, such as finance, which so often clip the wings of imagination. The only controlling factor was the topography of the five hundred acres, which include the well-known Hengistbury Head, to the west of the Isle of Wight, famous as the place of departure and arrival of migratory birds.

Mr. Selfridge explained the position, and his instructions were somewhat as follows : —

" For many years past I have spent my holidays visiting the

The Life and Work of An English Landscape Architect.

most remarkable castles and mansions in many parts of the world, many of them works of great antiquity, and all possessing architectural merit. Whenever I discuss these visits with my friends, I am told that the days of great architecture are past, and that we can never again hope to see such achievements. These are the pessimists, whilst I am an optimist. I believe it is just as possible nowadays to interpret human needs in grand architectural compositions as at any previous age. I am prepared to back my faith by co-operating with my architect and landscape architect in the creation of a castle crowning Hengistbury Head, with noble ramparts and terraces reaching down to the lower ground, these to be associated with gardens and a broad expanding park, with sheltered lowlands, extensive orchards and vegetable gardens and nursery, and every amenity and modern convenience, including a model village for the estate workmen."

It was to be a veritable castle in Spain, a dream domain. The designing of the castle was largely dictated by Mr. Selfridge himself; the garden part of the scheme and the park were entrusted to us. To gain an idea of the scale of this colossal proposal, imagine a castle occupying the entire bluff at the south-west end of the head, with its west elevation nearly nine hundred feet long, whilst the south elevation was six hundred feet in length, the rooms of this mountain of architecture being in proportion. The sculpture gallery was over two hundred feet in length.

I have tackled many big projects for daring clients, but here was an entirely novel experience. A castle in the air, conceived and carried through as such, to prove, if provable, that we to-day possess imaginative faculties equal to those of our forefathers ! In Mr. Selfridge we had a modern Piranisi, inspiring and directing the enterprise.

At first I thought it would be delightfully easy to work as an artist, untrammelled by conventions of style and practical considerations, but I soon found the difficulty of divesting oneself of the results of training and experience. When I submitted my drawings for the terraces, my client asked the reason why the lowest level had not been extended at least another hundred feet. " Because," I replied, " we settled the level at our last meeting, and the extent is decided by the number of cube yards of excavation available. In other words, the cut and fill are just about equal."

" I know you are a practical expert, but I hoped I should also find in you a great dreamer. That for the moment is the man I

End of War Opens Up New Prospects.

want. If to complete the dream castle we have to buy one of the South Sea islands or dredge the ocean, we may surely draw upon our imagination to this extent."

At every turn I found myself designing in accordance with the topography and practical possibilities of the site. In this respect I was more Greek than Roman, and more of a practical man than a great dreamer. I recognised my limitations. My plans were simply the interpretation of the possibilities of landscape art applied to Hengistbury Head and the adjoining lands, and I saw that my client was fettered by my practicability. My eldest son had by this time completed his work in Athens, so I suggested that as much of his training had been gained at the Ecole de Beaux Arts in Paris, where students are trained to develop their imagination, I would appreciate his collaboration. Some day I hope Mr. Selfridge will publish a portfolio of the drawings prepared by his architects and ourselves under his own generous leadership. The effect, I venture to suggest, would be to gain a wider toleration of and demand for the use of imagination in architecture and the allied arts.

Much other work came along, which included the preparation of a comprehensive town-planning scheme for Northampton.

The town planning of Northampton proved a difficult problem. As in most other towns, the principal difficulties arose through encroachments on the town by the railways, which paid so little regard to the rights of the public as to permit the main London road to cross the railway on the level. Meanwhile, valuable properties had grown up along the route, which would have to be demolished if a bridge were erected over the railway and on the line of the road. The hold-up traffic is a serious matter, and daily growing more intolerable, and one of our difficulties was to find a by-pass road to take this traffic. The solution for this important traffic road has been evolved, and we hope it may win the approval of the Ministry of Transport. If at one place the railway has created such a difficulty, the abandonment of the Midland Railway station, which occupies a central site, would provide opportunities for the development of the civic centre or other buildings of public or semi-public importance. The great opportunities for town planning in Northampton lie in the direction of the town's rapid growth, in the necessary zoning to secure increased open spaces and playing fields, and in the control of density of population and the location of industrial areas.

The Life and Work of An English Landscape Architect.

Soon after receiving the commission to re-plan Northampton, I was called in as consultant to advise the Windermere Urban District Council to work in collaboration with its very able surveyor, Mr. Charles Hines, to solve certain increasingly difficult traffic conditions, and to prepare a plan for the control of density of buildings and the preservation of the national amenities of the district.

It will interest motorists to know that in our report we recommend a road avoiding the two steep hills encountered upon entering Windermere from the south, by branching off in the direction of the lake after leaving the hamlet of Ings near the Hyning. Passing along in front of Blackmoss Farm it joins the high road to the lake at Queen's Drive, half-way between Windermere and Bowness. Another by-pass road to avoid the congestion in the lower part of Bowness branches off at the top of Cragg Brow, passing behind the Crown Hotel and joining up with the Kendal and Newby Bridge route at a convenient place clear of the village.

There are other new roads, all obviously needed to avoid several dangerous gradients, and generally so practical that some of them at least will surely be carried through as Government-aided relief works, being much more economical and more satisfactory than costly widenings, which are, after all, only poor palliatives for the relief of very serious conditions.

West Front of Dunira, Perthshire, for W. G. Macbeth, Esq.

Rocky Stream, Dunira, Perthshire, for W. G. Macbeth, Esq.

CHAPTER XXVI.

POST-WAR ACTIVITIES.

THE beginning of 1920 marked further progress in the post-war reorganisation of the practice. Old members of the staff resumed their accustomed work, and pupils whose studies had been interrupted returned to complete their course of tuition. Old clients looked out their progress schemes, and new clients for both public and private projects were filling the office with interesting work. The two most attractive schemes were Boveridge Park, Cranborne, Dorset, and Dunira near Comrie in Perthshire.

Both these extensive and notable estates had been recently purchased by well-known shipowners—Boveridge Park by Mr. Charles W. Gordon, and Dunira by Mr. W. Gilchrist Macbeth. In each place considerable work was being carried out in alterations and additions to the residence—at Boveridge by Mr. Guy Dawber, and at Dunira by Messrs. Clifford and Lunan, a well-known firm of Glasgow architects, through whom we were introduced to our new clients.

Boveridge Park is a large property, finely timbered, which imparts a dominating note to the beautiful but gently undulating landscape. The house is a large and somewhat austere Georgian example, occupying a commanding site almost in the centre of its own spacious park, all in such orderly stateliness as to suggest the work of Capability Brown or Repton. On my first visit to Boveridge the house was in the hands of the builders, but part had been partitioned off for the use of the family, and here I stayed with my clients, whom I soon discovered were keenly interested in their gardens. There was already an extensive garden in the formal manner, replete with a fountain, court, and grass glades bordered by cypress hedges. There was a terrace on the east side some distance from the house, but none of these features seemed to have any relation to the building, which called for a response in the

The Life and Work of An English Landscape Architect.

garden, and especially on the south side, where the park views are the most extensive. The mansion is approached by two long drives, the more important of which is from the south, Cranborne direction, and the other from the east. Both drives pass through mature and very picturesque beech and pine woods, and unite at the great carriage court which is on the west side of the house. As in many similar instances, the fruit and vegetable garden is some distance from the house, and in no way influenced the lay-out of the terraces and pleasure grounds. The new gardens, which for the most part are formal, are based on two main axes, which centre with the eastern and the southern elevations of the house. On the east side we confined our plans to the limits and levels of the original garden, but on the south the gardens were projected far into the park by way of a series of terraces of varying depth and width. First there is the stone terraces next to the house, then a grass terrace supported with a wall filled with Alpine flowers, followed by a terrace eight feet lower, laid out with panels of rose beds and a central canal for water lilies and other hardy aquatic plants. Below this, again, there is a green bowling alley, and finally an expanse of lawn large enough for several tennis courts.

As the somewhat thin crust of soil lies on chalk, the range of trees and shrubs planted with any hope of success was limited, and excluded choice rhododendrons, azaleas, kalmias, andromedas, and allied shrubs. On the other hand, all kinds of roses flourish, whilst nearly every known deciduous shrub grows vigorously, as do most of the conifers, evergreen oak, and holly. The chances of securing an interesting garden on chalk are equal to those on almost any other soil, but no other garden is so trying to the men who construct it, as a garden on a chalky base, especially if the chalk be wet. The adhesive nature of the chalk makes the work very laborious. Such was the case with the gardens at Boveridge. Nevertheless, the results attained were very satisfactory, and a credit to the firm responsible for its execution. My clients have continued to improve the quality of the soil and the lawns, which proves once more that gardens grow for those who love them.

Dunira is one of the most beautiful estates it has ever been my pleasure to study. The park, which extends to many hundreds of acres, is perfectly level, and the soil a rich alluvial deposit. Out of this plain rises somewhat precipitously a number of high mounds which suggest that these were at one time islands and promontories rising out of a lake, much in the same way as Windermere and its islands; in fact, when mist lies over the park it is easy to imagine a large lake studded with wooded islands. Beyond these islands are forest-clad mountains which completely encircle the estate, but at such a distance as to create an aspect of spaciousness. This encircling range of mountains reminded me of Grasmere as seen from Dunmail Raise, only they were even more picturesque in their rugged outlines and towering peaks, whilst everywhere the slopes and foothills were clothed with timber wherein groupings of Scotch firs gave a massive effect to the whole.

The large residence is in about the centre of the estate, and stands on a foothill seemingly slidden from the mountains which at this north side stand closely behind. The bluff extends to approximately fifteen acres, the level of the house being eighty feet above the lower park-lands.

Dunira is approached from the east or Comrie side by a drive of about a mile and a half in length, and from the west or St. Fillans side by a drive of approximately a mile in length. Both are well engineered, with pleasing curves adapted to the contours of the landscape, evidently the work of some person of taste.

The house was very large and well placed on the site, but although describable as Scotch Baronial, it was not built in a fortunate period of architectural taste. The architects, recognising its shortcomings, and backed by a generous client, prepared designs which brought the whole into harmony with Scottish traditions. These additions, mostly on the north side, comprise a spacious *porte cochère* on the centre line of the carriage court. This carriage court, which is now a feature, is framed in on the west side with the new billiard-room and on the east with the new kitchen wing.

Originally what passed for the gardens was a number of uninteresting grass slopes, unrelieved by flower bed or shrub, to all appearances arranged by a waterworks engineer with railway experience; all excepting the precipitous bank, which was the unfinished margin of the original lay-out, had been roughly planted with yew, hollies and timber trees, making a ragged outline across the southern view. On the northern side of the garden, and for a depth of about one hundred feet from the line of the drive, trees and shrubs, including many rhododendrons, had been planted and formed a pleasing foreground to the forest heights which rose on the opposite side of the drive. The walled-in kitchen garden was situated about half a mile west of the house, and near it were

The Life and Work of An English Landscape Architect.

the stables, garage, gardeners' and workmen's cottages and bothies, which are now transformed into a very picturesque, well-planned group.

My instructions were to design the gardens, in both their character and extent, as I would like to see them. In the main, these original plans have been followed, the only important omission being the panelled rose garden, by which we proposed to limit the west of the gardens where they join the park. We still hope that this feature, with slight modifications, may be carried through. In our designs we included the improvement of the fruit and vegetable garden and the erection of one of the most complete and extensive ranges of fruit and plant houses and accessory buildings I have ever planned.

Beginning near the house, we proposed first of all to improve the approaches and extend the carriage court on the north side ; then we endeavoured to secure an architectural base to the house on the west and south, by erecting a balustraded wall to take the place of the grass slope, providing ample width of steps to lower ground.

The remaining grass banks were replaced with retaining walls built of local black whinstone without mortar, the crevices being filled in with Alpine and rock plants. Flowering shrubs suitable for covering low walls were planted at intervals to break up the long lines of the masonry.

The long and very deep bank on the south front was entirely re-formed with diagonal walks rising from the upper bastion to the centre of the bank, then returning to the centre formed by the tea house, thus securing a convenient means of connection between the house and the six tennis courts (four green and two hard) on the lower level.

On the west side one of the most interesting features is the rose garden and lily pond, the pond fed from a wall fountain by way of a narrow canal which was constructed with a number of side recesses, planted with iris and reeds, as shown in Illus. No. 66.

The feature my client most appreciated is the rocky stream which enters the gardens to the north and passes southward beyond the line of the rose gardens until it loses itself in the artificial lake below. The rock-builders were fortunate in having to hand an abundance of picturesque moss-grown rocks, which they handled with great skill, to construct the cascades, pools, and the Alpine gardens (see Illus. No. 67). In this work we had the able assistance of Mr. Pulham, who continues the sterling reputation of his father and grandfather as rock-builders.

This part of Perthshire, like the English Lake District, favours the growth of hardy trees, shrubs, and plants of all descriptions, and fullest advantage has been taken of it. Very few gardens in Scotland are so richly furnished with plant life collected from all quarters of the globe, and everything planted is thriving. This work occupied a large staff for two years, working under the direction of skilled landscape foremen.

The above gardens were completed under the direction of my son during my last trip to the Near East. The why and wherefore of this visit were as follows :

(1) The commission formed to complete the Athens plans proposed commencing work under the chairmanship of Peter Calligas, a wealthy Greek who had formerly been in practice as a civil engineer. They were desirous to have my personal views upon the development of the park and boulevard system, which I had agreed to control.

(2) To report upon the site and erection of an hotel de luxe on the southern slopes of Mount Olympus.

(3) To avert, if possible, a threatened strike on the part of the English members of the Macedonian Reconstruction Commission.

On my way out I had to wait three days at Marseilles for the boat by which I had arranged to sail, staying at the Metropole Hotel, where were many English people, some outward bound for India, and others awaiting the arrival of friends who were expected therefrom. Amongst the latter was a lady of responsible years, stately, of dignified bearing, and who, I judged from her demeanour and evident organising abilities, held a high social position and was employed in some official capacity. Upon our venturing to make one another's acquaintance this lady told me that no mention of my identity was needed, since she recognised me from seeing a newspaper illustration of my Herkomer portrait; and, further, she had at the house of a friend seen a copy of my work on garden design. "So you see," she added, "you are something of a public character." She was awaiting the arrival of two Indian princesses, daughters of the Maharajah of Baroda, she being the director of their household. Having heard of the Maharajah as a progressive ruler with a bent for horticultural and arboricultural pursuits, and a patron of the arts, I was interested. "Would

The Life and Work of An English Landscape Architect.

you like to meet His Highness? "I was asked. I thanked her
warmly for the suggestion, and the next day I started for Athens,
and being immediately immersed in other matters, forgot all
about the lady and the promised introduction. The sequel to this
episode appears later.

On arrival in Athens I found an urgent telegram from my
second son, who was in charge of the Macedonian Reconstruction
Commission, which body included about forty English engineers,
architects, and town planners. The majority of these men had
been selected by myself, and were a fine body of men, and a
credit to their country and their profession. I was grieved to hear
there was trouble brewing.

A strike had taken place, and the reason given for the
dissatisfaction was the strangest I have ever heard. The
strikers wanted more work for the same money; they wanted the
Government to know that they were not earning their salaries,
and they held my son responsible for the appalling delays to
which the work was subjected. I called a conference of all
the staff and my son, and this was promptly arranged. The
men stated their case lucidly and with good reason. Their
discontent was so serious, they stated, that unless some real
improvement could be effected they intended to proceed in
a body to interview the Minister in Athens.

My son's reply took nearly an hour to deliver. It began by a
statement that, as he had been appointed by the Minister as
chief executive officer, he had always felt it incumbent upon him
to act loyally towards his chief, and within reasonable limits
accept full responsibility for the appalling delays and waste of
energy, which had become intolerable. He had even gone the
length of paying their salaries when cheques failed to arrive from
Athens. "Even now," he added, " I would have held my peace
but for the fact that I, too, have found the position impossible,
and have sent in my resignation. I am therefore free to tell you
exactly what I have endeavoured to do, and of the entire lack
of support which I have received."

He then read verbatim correspondence and cables to Athens,
to few of which had there been any reply. In many of these
letters he had urged the utter destitution and misery of the
inhabitants of the destroyed villages, and as a final appeal had
emphasised the fact that the destitution was creating grave political
unrest. But all to no avail.

Post-war Activities.

As these revelations were unfolded, a change gradually came over the temper of the staff, which later found expression in regrets for their action, although some of them thought they should not have been kept in the dark as to the true position. The sequel was that my son relinquished the post a month later, and the organisation, I believe, finally collapsed without accomplishing anything worthy of mention. With my own experience of the procrastinating Greek, I was very much in sympathy with the attitude adopted by my son. But, looking back, I think it possible that we both failed to interpret the Greek mind in this matter. What I mean is that it now seems possible that the Minister intended the commission to act on its own initiative and to take great responsibilities. That this was so was borne out by his own statements. He said : " I have appointed a commission of assured talent which has the entire confidence of the rural population of Macedonia, which knows better than I where the new villages should be planted, and how big they should be. As to building material, no one knows better than an Englishman where to get it, whilst as to cost, his honesty can be trusted. Why, therefore, should I bother ? "

This may be a possible explanation, but at the same time it could not be expected that Englishmen should take greater responsibilities for the Greek Government than they would take for their own.

On my return to Athens I immediately took up new work on the Athens Town Planning Commission, for the use of which ample conference rooms and a studio had been provided. Most of the members of the commission were known to me. The chairman proved himself a very able administrator; but here, again, I felt the influence of the French members, and did not fail to note that the work of the studio was not only under the direction of a Frenchman, but that the staff was mainly French, with a few Greeks in minor positions. This fact was perhaps fortunate from an English point of view, inasmuch as the completion of this scheme had a few months later to be postponed owing to the further rapid decline of the drachma and the Greek financial crisis. For the same reason I was never able to fulfil my engagement to design the complete park system, although the Minister had given me a Parliamentary order to pay on demand five hundred pounds sterling towards my out-of-pocket expenses. This payment order I still retain, but with the drachma standing at three hundred

The Life and Work of An English Landscape Architect.

to the pound instead of twenty-five, there is little hope of my
making use of it. What interest could there be in planning a noble
park system so long as the Government could ill afford to pay for
the plans, much less spend money in constructing and planting
the parks. Notwithstanding the somewhat disappointing composition of the commission, I attended its meetings, which were
bi-weekly, for a month—sufficient time to allow me to take part
in the consideration of the scheme affecting the work over which
I had retained control.

By this time the arrangements were completed for our journey
to Mount Olympus to select the site for the proposed hotel and
resort. The promoter of this project was M. Aspiotus, an
engineer of Athens and a man of assured status and influence in
business circles. There was, besides M. Aspiotus and myself,
a Mr. Cole, who had just relinquished a twelve years' engagement
as engineer to the Lake Copais Company, so that he was thoroughly
acclimatised and inured to the conditions we had to contend with;
but for me these conditions were very arduous, and even dangerous.
We started from the Hotel Grande Bretagne. The proprietor
arranged for the victualling of the party, and nothing was omitted
from either the baskets or the bill, which I had the privilege of
footing. Without mistake, the food and the delicacies were almost
endless in variety, the quantities ample, and the wines superb.
The gods of Olympus could have regaled themselves at our expense
if they would have allowed us the pleasure. Further, had I been
allowed to prefer a request in return for the favour, it would have
been for strength and endurance to climb the 3,000-ft. level of
the Mount sanctified by their sacred presence.

We left Athens by the evening train for Palmanova, which
lies a few miles south of Olympus, and near a ruined old castle
resembling one of our Border examples. Between seven and
eight on a lovely summer morn we arrived at Palmanova, where
mules and muleteers in native costumes, and looking very like a
company of cut-throat brigands, met us. The men soon spread
a roughly devised table with the contents of one of our baskets,
and never before or since have I so relished a breakfast, or felt the
tang of such winy air and the glamour of such wild scenery.

After breakfast, which we shared with the men, we slung
the baskets on one of the mules, then mounted our own raw-boned,
long-eared steeds and began the sharp ascent to the castle, which
occupied a most romantic site. The commanding panoramic

views over mountain plain and sea, for extent, colour, and variety, baffle adequate description. So entranced were we with the spot that we failed to notice the threatening clouds which were gathering to the south-west. Our guides pointed to these, and urged us to make haste to reach a village at the foot of the Mount, some five or six kilometres distant, before the storm broke. So we descended to the plain and followed a rough track through the scrub oak with which the place was covered for miles in every direction.

This road or track ran for about two kilometres parallel with the railway, which at this point was about a mile from the sea. Suddenly we heard a loud, terrifying noise, like the sound of a suction pump increased a thousand times. Looking in the direction from which the noise came, we saw the strange phenomenon of a cyclone travelling from the sea in the direction of Mount Olympus, the main or central column passing us within a quarter of a mile. We were within the limit of its action, so that we had to throw ourselves flat on the ground until it had passed us. When it passed we had a wonderful view of its form and appearance, and it was one of the sights of a lifetime, awesome and fascinating. In shape it was like a huge silver-lined gossamer curtain hanging from a heavy pack of clouds and reaching down to and trailing along the earth in a fanlike sweep. It seemed to us to travel slowly, but its motive was destruction, which it exercised in the way of suction. Directly this terror was over-past our chief guide spoke in grave and agitated tones to M. Aspiotus, who explained to us that the guide said that Jove was about to speak, and that we must avail ourselves of whatever shelter we could find. So we made tracks for a railway culvert spanning a ravine, the bed of which was dry when we entered it. No sooner had we entered than the storm burst in all its fury of thunder, lightning, and torrential rain, such as I had never imagined possible, so that within a quarter of an hour we were driven out by the oncoming flood, and by the time we reached the level plateau the dry river bed was converted into a fearful torrent. Our guide then informed us that there was a fisherman's hut about one kilometre distant, and so, drenched to the skin, we followed him. Without his help we could not have found the tracks which served as roads, for here and in the whole of this part of Greece there are no roads. The hut was a sort of fishing lodge, and not the regular abode of its fisherman-owner. It was quaintly and rudely constructed of

The Life and Work of An English Landscape Architect.

wood and cobble-stones, with a low roof and projecting eaves, suggestive of the home of a bold pirate of the sea. The interior consisted of one very large room and a small chamber, both open to the roof. There was a large open fireplace and chimney stack against the central wall. The floor was of earth, and in two corners were rough wooden benches covered with numerous skins. The occupant was a middle-aged man, unkempt like the rugged hut, and yet never did we receive more welcome or kindly hospitality. Immediately the fire was heaped up with drift-wood, the kettle boiled, and a delicious cup of coffee was prepared for us. At the same time, the fisherman's boy was busy collecting more rugs and skins for the benches, so we undressed and lay down whilst our dripping clothes dried before a furious fire. In an hour we were able to dress again and enjoy a rustic meal of fried fish, brown bread, and coffee. This repast finished, the sky cleared and the sun shone, so we decided to pursue our journey and climb the foot hill to the plateau on the three-thousand-feet contour upon which it was proposed to erect the hotel. Before leaving, we offered our host a suitable gift for all the trouble he had taken on our behalf. This was resolutely refused; but finally, seeing our disappointment, he said we might give his boy five drachmas. We gave him twenty-five, which the lad seemed to regard as a fortune.

It took us an hour and a half to cross the plateau to the village from which the ascent began, and the going between the masses of the thick scrub oak was very difficult. This first part was in no sense comparable with the difficulties of the climb up the mountain mule track, which in parts showed traces of ancient paving, a surprise to me, as it suggested that a village at one time crowned one or more of the plateaux on the foothills, and possibly the one we were prospecting. The villages, however, must have been very difficult to reach or to attack, and possibly this was the reason why they were built there.

The track, which followed the undulations and indentations of the mountain, rose on a regular gradient of about one in three, with occasional levels where the nature of the ground permitted them. At these we halted, and looked down the precipitous tracks we had ascended. All the way up the mountain side was thickly studded with forest trees, with thick masses of the Greek pine from which resin is extracted. Above the two-thousand-feet zone considerable areas were clothed with a spruce fir closely resembling the black American spruce, *Abies nigra*.

Post-war Activities.

At length our mules brought us to the hotel site, completely exhausted with the heat.

The prospect was entrancing, the position being admirably located as a centre for mountaineering, whilst in the neighbourhood were other plateaux well suited to winter sports. The drawbacks were the difficulty of reaching the site from the railway station, but M. Aspiotus had already planned a narrow-gauge mountain railway and a motor road, and these the Government promised to construct. Everything considered, and subject to the Government meeting their obligations previous to starting the hotel, so as to facilitate transport of building materials, I reported in favour of the site. Like many other Greek projects promoted about this time, this hotel scheme will have to wait until financial stability is restored. The proposal is an attractive one, and the position on the Athens-Salonika line advantageous. The coast is also convenient for travellers by sea. Being located on historic and classical ground, and the picturesqueness of the locality being so famous, the realisation of this project is certain once normal world conditions are restored.

As I had a few days unappropriated, we determined to explore the Vale of Tempe and the town of Katterina at the northern side of the Olympus range. So we proceeded to the nearest station, and found we had an hour and a half to wait; but there was an inviting inn quite near by—a long, one-storey building, reminiscent of an English village smithy, and about as black. Although there was no sign of other habitation for miles round, this inn was apparently a popular meeting-place. Its patrons seemed a very sober lot, and were keenly interested in us. The burly landlord at once set to work, placing a table and chairs for our use in the open air, where our Greek attendants spread for us a sumptuous meal from our two large baskets, which had taken very little harm from the day's storm, wind, and sun. The natives looked on in wonder at a spread which was sufficient for a dozen people. We soon found we were unequal to the task of clearing the table, so we handed the surplus round, making a special contribution of a chicken and a bottle of wine to a dear old priest and his wife, who seemed very grateful for our gift.

On leaving for our train we heard many expressions of good-will and *bon voyage*, whilst the priest gave us his blessing.

On arriving at Katterina station we found the town was about two kilometres distant, so we hired a ramshackle conveyance,

The Life and Work of An English Landscape Architect.

drawn by the scraggiest pair of horses I have ever seen, and thuswise we reached the only hotel of which the town could boast. It was a quaint colour-washed building of two floors. The lower one was a well-patronised public restaurant, the upper rooms being devoted to tourists. The accommodation provided was meagre, but everything was scrupulously clean, and the food good and appetising. Katterina should be a perfect goldmine for artists in search of strong contrasts in form and colour set in a framework of mediæval simplicity.

The busy little market town of Katterina was a revelation of logical and yet picturesque town planning. Its spacious open market place was an ideal model for the larger villages of Macedonia entrusted to us to plan. The central market was planted with shade trees and surrounded on all four sides with roads extending directly through the town and into the open country beyond. Those roads round the central market had the principal hotel at one end and the church at the other, and along the length at one side was the courthouse, flanked with the post office, and shops facing the schoolhouse and handicrafts on the other side of the street. The picturesqueness of the town was greatly enhanced by the colour of the various native products and by the number of handicrafts in metals, wood, leather, and pottery carried on under conditions which would have delighted the heart of William Morris or Walter Crane.

The principal industries were leather production in harness, boots, shoes, sandals, slippers, and sabots with wooden soles and leather uppers, finished to quaint shapes and decorated with red and blue tassels. Then came the wood-worker's craft, which included almost every utensil required for the farm or home, such as milking pails, water buckets, milk bowls, with lesser bowls and platters for table use, and many other wood articles the use of which I did not understand. The pottery was equally quaint, for the most part oil jars, wine bottles, and water jugs. Numbers of men were squatting on the floor making nails and chains. With a charcoal brazier on one side of them and a small anvil on the other, these men made shoeing-nails with a rapidity that was surprising. In addition to the handicrafts there were occupations followed by women, mostly in the production of hand-woven fabrics in many beautiful simple patterns. All that I saw in this lovely old-world town appealed to me : the customs and occupations were such as had been little changed through the passing centuries.

We were particularly struck with the number of healthy boys and girls, who were respectful and friendly. As it was the cherry season, the expenditure of about two drachmas secured an amazing supply of this fruit for equal distribution, which cemented our bonds of friendship. Thus we forgot modern civilisation for a few days, and thoroughly enjoyed the rest thus afforded ; and so we returned to Athens.

I had now completed the greater part of my programme, and only awaited an interview with M. Venizelos as to the settlement of my account, he being the only Minister in Athens prepared to take a decision, and this he usually arrived at very quickly, but with strict adherence to business principles, as in my case.

When I first quoted, drachmas were about 24-50 to the pound sterling ; when I met M. Venizelos they had depreciated to 31·58, making a difference on exchange of about £700 in my account, and most of this depreciation had taken place since the date when the account was rendered. This fact I explained to the Premier, who merely remarked that the depreciation was one of the fortunes of the war, and that as it had happened I stood to lose, for which he was sorry. So I was paid the exact amount in drachmas.

After this I began to pack for my return, and whilst thus engaged I received a letter from the Minister of Communication asking me to attend at the Ministry the next morning at 10-30. This I did, and was surprised to find an unusual air of bustle, and to receive the friendly greetings of quite a number of officials. On being shown into the Minister's reception rooms, I was quaintly informed that I was to receive a mark of the King's favour. I then stood up whilst M. Papanastassiou made a warm congratulatory address, thanking me for my work in Salonika and my preliminary scheme for the re-planning and extension of Athens. He then presented me with the Order of the Saviour (gold clasp), and the onlookers applauded. M. Papanastassiou then added : "And now I am going to ask you to convey the Order of King George to your eldest son, as an appreciation of the splendid help he has given to us and to yourself in the working out of the Salonika plans, and other special work with which we have entrusted him. As his father, to you we know this presentation will be a further gratification."

With a promise to return to Athens as soon as the work of the commission had made sufficient progress to justify it, I said

The Life and Work of An English Landscape Architect.

good-bye to the young King, whom I was never to see again, and to Lord Granville and the Ministers and all my friends. Before leaving, M. Papanastassiou gave me an order for £500 sterling towards the expenses of my next trip, and I was to devote the whole of my energies to the final planning of the park systems for Athens. Unfortunately the drachmas depreciated to such an extent that practically all public works were stopped, and the park-system scheme was the first to feel the financial pressure. I hope that the more stabilised currency which is now within sight, and the increasing prosperity of the country, will justify the Government going ahead with this part of their civic scheme. Already I hear they have secured a good water supply, which, as previously stated, is preliminary and essential to all other schemes of betterment.

THE AUTHOR IN HIS CONSERVATORY, CATON HALL.

CHAPTER XXVII.

1920 ONWARDS.

UPON arriving home ready for a quiet rest, I found that my house on the shores of Morecambe Bay, where I had spent many happy years, had been sold, and Caton Hall purchased. The Bungalow, which was really my wife's property, and had grown with the needs of the family, is a long, low block of buildings of many rooms, suggestive of comfort, and, internally, of restrained elegance. Its acre or so of forefront to the sea, though public property, is a great addition to its peacefulness and serenity. It is, however, somewhat remote and difficult to reach by car or conveyance.

Caton Hall, which had been purchased by my wife as a surprise for me on my return from Athens, is much more expansive, and pleasantly situated in the valley of the Lune. The hall is at the Lancaster end of the village of the same name, and stands in its own finely timbered grounds of eleven acres, three of which are an old-world garden, and eight a small park. Whilst retaining fine views to the north, west, and south, the property is perfectly screened from the east, on which side lies the village, containing many old quaint groups of cottages. Close by the entrance is an oak tree with fish steps bordering a stream at its base, and from these steps John Wesley preached on one of his itinerant tours. It is not difficult to portray the slight reverent figure of this evangelist, in his customary black gown and white Geneva bib, surrounded by an awed crowd of villagers at this picturesque corner. The tree and the steps are part of the property.

At Caton Hall, which now became my home, I conceived the idea of organising a school of landscape architecture, hoping thereby to solve in some little measure the question of academic training, accompanied by a certain amount of practical training in horticulture. I went so far as to publish a prospectus

The Life and Work of An English Landscape Architect.

and a preliminary curriculum, which received a very encouraging response, especially from America, the Colonies, India, and Continental countries. To this I will refer again.

In the stress of my work in Athens I had quite forgotten the lady I met at Marseilles, and her promise. The first letter I opened on my return from Athens recalled this incident. It was from H.H. the Maharajah of Baroda, asking me to arrange an appointment at his temporary home near Watford, naming an early convenient date, when he would be pleased if I could arrange to lunch with the Maharani and himself. I gladly availed myself of meeting such interesting prospective clients.

On arrival at the house I was shown into the library, where the Maharajah was seated. At once he explained why he had sent for me, and how my name had been brought to his notice by the lady before mentioned; also that on learning that I had written a book on landscape architecture, he had ordered five copies of " The Art and Craft of Garden Making," which he was sending to India. Then he explained that he had recently purchased Russell Park, near Watford, and the gardens required extension and improvement, and he would be pleased if I could undertake this work. He also said that as Russell Park was regarded as only a minor residence, and his occupancy might possibly last for only a few years, he wished me to advise him on the purchase of some other estate more suited in its scale and appointments for the recognised English home of his family. The Maharajah, who was of middle age and height, spoke with a very pleasing voice, and in excellent English and with easy fluency. I remark on this fact because in the following autumn he attended a lecture which I gave before the Town Planning Institute, when my subject was a plea for the exercise of imagination. At the close of the lecture the President asked the Maharajah if he would kindly contribute to the discussion. To this request he readily acceded, and his speech, occupying about ten minutes, was evidently the inspiration of the moment, his remarks following a logical sequence of argument, and, being poetically expressed, they gave great pleasure to all who heard them. There is no doubt that he appreciated the very hearty reception which was accorded him. But this is a digression.

At lunch I was introduced to the Maharani and the two princesses; also I met again the lady whom I had met in Marseilles, and also the Maharajah's secretary. The lunch was a very pleasant one (Indian curries notwithstanding), and I greatly enjoyed the table conversation, particularly that of Her Highness the Maharani, who I soon learnt was a progressive lady of considerable force and character.

After this I met my Indian clients at frequent intervals, both at Russell Park and at their London house, whilst the Maharajah made frequent morning calls at our London office to see how his plans were progressing. Occasionally he would call for me in the afternoon to accompany him into the country to inspect some reputed desirable property, but these visits resulted in disappointment, for His Highness had set a high standard for the permanent residence of the Barodas. If our return from these visits was in the evening, he would propose that we drop in at a restaurant and have a quiet dinner, and well he knew where to find the best.

The plans for the gardens at Russell Park soon took shape, and were accepted with but few alterations. The only exceptions were the new drive planned as a safer route to Watford station, as well as a new range of glasshouses. Both these desirable improvements will probably be carried out in the near future if this property is retained. As altered and extended, these gardens are very compact, and capable of being maintained in perfect condition by a modest staff.

About this time, Aldworth, the home of Lord Tennyson at Haslemere, was advertised for sale by auction. To me it was a matter of surprise that the Tennyson family should agree to sell, more especially as Lady Tennyson had looked forward to its being the permanent seat of the family. Even supposing it were sold with their full consent, I had hoped that the National Trust would acquire it, because of its public interest, and present it to the nation. The Maharajah requested me to go down and report upon the suitability of this house and estate. This report was duly presented, after which His Highness and I motored down to examine the property.

The day was fine, with a clear sky, and as we rose to the high moorlands above Haslemere, covered with heather, the prospect in every direction was enchanting. The climax came as we were about to enter the grounds, whence a panorama of great extent and exquisite beauty unfolded itself. Entering the grounds, we followed a steep descent to the eastern *porte-cochère* at the east end of the residence, a passable Gothic structure which it is

The Life and Work of An English Landscape Architect.

said was designed by an editor of the "Nineteenth Century," who was an architect by profession. There was little or no evidence of design in the interior or the decorations, they having no intrinsic value excepting the fact that they had been the possession of the poet.

Aldworth stands on a plateau carved out of the hillside on the eight-hundred-feet contour, the main elevation facing due south. It is a small house—too small in scale for a site possessing such a spacious character; but the stone terrace, with its Gothic balustrade, goes far to atone for this defect, whilst either by intent or accident a number of tall cypresses bravely break up the overpowering panoramic expanse. In this direction I was strongly reminded of the view from the terrace of the Villa d'Este, Rome. Whether this idyllic poet's retreat, remote and secluded, would suit the needs of an Indian prince equally well, was a problem.

The first comment made by His Highness as he gazed over the landscape was, "Yes, I think I can sleep here, and that is the great desideratum; but the house is much too small for my requirements."

We were, however, able to show him that the site called for a larger residence, and that it would be possible to incorporate all the additional accommodation in an extension which would double the length of the south elevation.

This was the day before the sale, and the next morning I was instructed to attend and bid for the property, and I purchased the entire estate, which was first offered in lots, for £30,000. We were then instructed to prepare plans for the extension of the house and the improvement of the grounds, with a new drive, the existing one being both inconvenient and dangerous. We were also to place an Alpine and water garden on the steep declivity below the second terrace. Farther afield we were to improve the fruit and vegetable garden and prospect for a cricket pitch, and to report on the restoration of the interesting old Georgian villa situated on the lower part of the property.

Altogether this was an important commission of surpassing interest, though one or two of our friends suggested that it would be sacrilege to alter the house of the famous poet in any way. We were able to assure these objectors that the Maharajah had given strict instructions that the rooms, including the library and bedroom used by the poet, were not to be touched in any way.

Moreover, the exterior of the existing house was to remain in its original state, whilst in any extension the construction and detail were to be copied. In the gardens every feature was to be preserved as Tennyson left it, and in particular the terraces and low grass lawns were to be maintained and relieved of many cumbering shrubs which were of recent introduction. Only when approaching the lower ground, or other points not observable from the house, were we allowed to suggest any considerable improvement to the gardens.

As the Maharajah was shortly to leave for India, we were instructed to proceed with complete plans on which to base a reliable estimate of cost. Although very wealthy and generous, the Maharajah is most businesslike in all his dealings, and careful to assure himself that all the expenditure he incurs will be of permanent value to his estate.

The matured plans were completed and forwarded to His Highness, who approved them as a whole. He decided to carry out the work in three stages, beginning with the necessary alterations to the existing block, and its decoration and furnishing, so that he might reside for a season at Aldworth to test its suitability and convenience before launching out into the larger scheme.

During this period we were engaged upon further extensions of schemes previously designed for Lord Leverhulme at Roynton, Sir Samuel Waring, and Walter Cottingham. Once a client who is fond of a garden launches upon construction work, such work develops into a hobby—and what a delightful hobby it is, lack of finality notwithstanding! If the whole scheme is first thought out to the point of settling its main provisions, this is the best way for a garden to grow. If, on the other hand, this annual upheaval is merely dictated by a love of change, the result is disastrous and extravagant.

At Roynton great developments were taking place. The most notable of these was the work entailed through a small stream which meandered almost out of sight in a deep leafy dell, which cut the lower garden almost into equal parts, imposing a difficult barrier to its unity.

We began by throwing two single arched stone bridges across the chasm and clearing the timber which intercepted the view. We then proceeded to divert the stream temporarily, laying bare the natural sandstone rock, which we quarried into rough receding ledges, using all the stone thus excavated for the

The Life and Work of An English Landscape Architect.

construction of a series of cascades, with a total fall from the intake to the outlet of over two hundred feet.

The tiny stream is not sufficient to justify the construction of such massive cascades, but we were able to divert several smaller runners, and these are augmented by the construction of a pond as a compensation reservoir capable of supplying an additional half-million gallons against dry weather. This is repeating under simpler conditions the hydraulic engineering feats associated with many of the Italian formal cascades.

It was about this time that my breakdown in health (to which reference is made in the Preface) took place. Whether this was the result of a mild sunstroke in Greece, or of a slight seizure, the doctors could not determine. In any case, I was advised to take six months' complete rest, a stipulation which I endeavoured to obey. But as complete isolation is foreign to my temperament, within a month I was in daily communication with the office, and gradually resumed my wonted interest in the work. My doctors and friends were disappointed at my rebellion ; but when a man is immersed in the most interesting forms of art expression, it is difficult for him to let his mind slip into vacuity.

For years I have been distressed in contemplating the baneful results of the lack of logical planning manifested in our seaside resorts, which suffer by comparison with those on the Continent and in America. Here at least the æsthetic possibilities should be made to influence the visitors educationally.

It may appear strange that in all the town-planning work of which I have dreamed, Blackpool appealed to me the most. The fact that I am a Lancashire man may account for this preference. Blackpool's unbroken stretch of golden sand, its bracing air, and the kaleidoscopic gaiety of its miles of promenade, combine to weave a spell of attraction. Already, according to the town's present configuration, the streets and railway terminals of the popular resort are taxed to their fullest capacity, with a resident and visitor population of 300,000. If the borough is to expand, as the Council anticipate, to accommodate over a million people, drastic alterations will be necessary. At present the expansion of the town is more rapid than that of any other town in the kingdom. Blackpool's phenomenal growth necessitates the provision of at least a thousand new houses a year, a fact which proves that a vast residential population is settling within the boundaries of the town. This, be it remembered, in addition to the increasing influx of visitors.

THORNTON HALL, LINCOLNSHIRE.—SOUTH FRONT.

THORNTON HALL, LINCOLNSHIRE.—NORTH FRONT.

1920 *Onwards.*

When these facts are taken into consideration, it will be inferred that a thorough overhauling of the design of this great Lancashire holiday resort is demanded.

It was with considerable satisfaction that I noticed about this time an able article by Mr. Ernest Lawson on " Town Planning for Blackpool," which appeared in the " Blackpool Herald," and in which the writer advised that our firm should be consulted.

As I had never even met Mr. Lawson, or communicated with him in any way, this article came as a surprise ; but having thus unexpectedly found a friend at court, I awaited developments, which were a long time in maturing. In July, 1922, I received a letter from the Town Clerk informing me that his Council had purchased two hundred and eighty acres of land for a park and recreation ground, and that they wished to consult our firm upon its development. I now knew that my ambition to re-plan Blackpool was possible of realisation, because it was inevitable that the periphery of the park and the sub-division of the residential areas would call for the application of town-planning principles, and this proved to be the case.

As to the park itself, the planning of nearly three hundred acres, two-thirds of which had to be devoted to recreation, was of itself a great project, calling for the application of imagination, backed by practical experience. Apart from this, the work appealed to me, and to those working with me, so much that it fired my old enthusiasm.

The practical part of the work was divided into five sections, each one of which would take a year to carry out at an annual expenditure of twenty thousand pounds, exclusive of the more important architectural structures. But the income from the many recreational features will, it is anticipated, fully cover maintenance charges and leave a surplus towards meeting interest on the loan.*

The commission quickly led to our being asked to plan the new South Shore extension, in collaboration with the borough engineer, Mr. Francis Wood. The South Shore includes a new promenade about a mile in length, reclaimed from the sea and protected by a stout sea-wall which forms the seaward boundary along the promenade. The extent is from the famous open-air baths southwards to the town's junction with the borough of

* The annual income from the park has already exceeded our estimates.

The Life and Work of An English Landscape Architect.

St. Annes, and including all the sandhills between a shore line fixed by Act of Parliament, comprising a total of about 127 acres, 23 acres of which were allocated to the promenade, and the remainder to be developed as a building estate. The spacious promenade is extended along in a gentle curve, its sweeping lines being pleasingly broken in the middle with a semi-circular bastion garden projecting seawards. This bastion garden and all the gardens along the promenade are protected from the sea breezes by panelled walls, the lawns, shrubberies, and flower beds being sunk two feet below the surface to secure a pleasing effect from the main roadway, which is crowded day and night by pedestrians, and tramway and charabanc passengers. The brilliant lighting of the promenade by night is a special feature of the scheme.

The building estate portion of the South Shore thus reclaimed will assume the appearance of a garden city, and be protected from the strong winds by the hotel and terraces of houses which continue for some distance along the promenade. The estate is divided into two parts by a spacious central boulevard, which runs parallel to and half-way between the promenade and the railway.

In connection with the central boulevard, note the position of the shopping centre, bank, and post office, and possibly a picture house. Note also the position retained in the design for the churches, which ought to add a note of interest to the whole. The remaining point of interest is that instead of gazing upon ugly backyards, visitors travelling by rail to the Central Station will look upon the fronts of houses erected in a shrub-fringed row and each set in a neat garden.

When this scheme was submitted, the idea of re-planning the whole town took hold of the imagination of the ratepayers and the Town Council, with the result that we were invited to submit terms for the preparation of a development scheme for the whole borough, and a little later we were instructed to proceed with the work.

The Blackpool Town Council are to be commended for giving us two test commissions before entrusting us with the preparation of a scheme of such magnitude, extending, as it does, to every quarter of the borough, touching every interest in it. It has entailed a vast amount of work of urgent importance upon the Town Planning Committee, who have had frequent sittings, these sometimes occupying a whole day before a decision is arrived at.

This commission was to be carried out in three stages as follows :—

(1) The Civic Survey, including all maps showing the progress made, with latest ordnances brought up to date, the collection and tabulation of health statistics, school-attendance charts, traffic conditions for railway, and also a regional survey to enable us to make suggestions for improved traffic facilities by rail and road, especially better roads for the rapidly increasing motor charabanc traffic. Also statistics relating to child welfare and children's playgrounds. Then the town plan had to be brought up to date, which involved drawing on to the ordnance maps over five thousand houses which had been erected since the last survey of the town. With all this information properly tabulated, we could proceed to the making of efficiency charts upon which the town planner depends so largely for the scientific solution of needs.

(2) The second stage of our town-planning scheme consists of what is technically known as the plan for submission—*i.e.,* the plan which has to be submitted to the Ministry of Health, and to which any objections are heard from property owners and others. This scheme includes the lay-out of all undeveloped areas and such improvements to the built-up areas as are necessary for the elimination of slums ; new or widened roads necessary for the development of vacant areas and the zoning plan fixing density of buildings for residential purposes, shopping centre and new park, recreation grounds, and generally the preservation of amenities.

This is the stage which most town-planning schemes reach and beyond which they do not proceed, as it is as far as the Acts of Parliament can be utilised. It is not, however, as far as the town planner usually wishes to go, for it stops short of the ideally perfect plan which sharpens his imaginative faculties and dreams of a town emerging in the process of years from chaos to order, and ever growing more beautiful as it takes on the likeness of the town planner's dream.

It is only to be expected that an ambitious and progressive Council like that of Blackpool should wish to explore every opportunity, existing and prospective, which would keep them abreast of the times, and help them to maintain their supremacy as the premier Northern resort.

(3) As a result we were instructed to propose a development plan in which we were given free scope to study every opening for the realisation of every improvement of the town in any direction, and to present our proposals graphically and pictorially, and in such a manner as to be adaptable for publicity purposes.

The opportunities associated with the re-planning of Blackpool have proved unique. First and most important, the Town Council is a far-seeing body of men who, notwithstanding the millions already spent on the promenade and other public improvements,

The Life and Work of An English Landscape Architect.

have managed to keep their borough one of the three lowest rated towns in the country. No wonder, therefore, that the Council has the intelligent moral support of the ratepayers behind any schemes of improvement which they promote.

In this connection the following story is appropriate. Shortly after receiving my first commission for Blackpool, I was staying at Roynton Cottage, where I met an old gentleman who was a typical Lancashire business man, a keen observer and a philosopher in his way. " I am glad you are going to make Blackpool beautiful, Mr. Mawson, for it really deserves it. Do you know," he continued, " if it wasn't for Blackpool there'd be revolution in Lancashire ? "

" Whatever do you mean ? " I asked in some alarm.

" I mean what I say, for down there," pointing towards the industrial towns, half-enveloped in smoke, which lay within the panoramic view, " men stick it as long as they can, and once a year they must either burst out or go to Blackpool ; and there they go, and after a fortnight they come back quietened down and ready for work again. Blackpool stands between us and revolution. May it long continue as the protector of social order ! "

At the end of my days it will be pleasantly restful to feel that I have added to Blackpool's attractions.

Whether or not the activity of Blackpool fired the competitive spirit of other resorts I am unable to say, but there has followed close on the heels of the Blackpool scheme many notable proposals for the improvement of seaside resorts, and we and our London colleagues were invited to accept commissions for the re-planning of Hastings and St. Leonards. The commission for Hastings and its suburb is on a scale almost equalling that of Blackpool, but the problems involved in the former are altogether different, as is also the clientèle for which Hastings caters. Everything in Blackpool is quite modern, its oldest parts—excepting for one or two groups of whitewashed cottages which are all that remains of the ancient fishing village of Poulton-le-Fylde—dating back only to the mid-Victorian era, of which the architecture is reminiscent.

Hastings and St. Leonards, on the other hand, have all the charm of historic association and architectural tradition, especially of the Georgian period—in the hotels, places of business, and terraces, suggestive of the Regency. In this respect these popular

II · CIVIC · CENTRE AND CENTRAL · STATION · BLACKPOOL ·

Town · Planning · Scheme · For the · County · Borough · of · Blackpool ·

resorts are almost as interesting as Brighton, to which they must at one time have been competitors. Even in their later develop- ments, whether of promenade, pier, or shelter, Hastings and St. Leonards retain their respect for good architectural detail, which helps to maintain that air of stateliness which is generally so lacking in our seaside resorts. Warrior Square, St. Leonards, may be quoted as typical.

Considered as a town site, Hastings and St. Leonards are very different from Blackpool. The latter suggests a lay-out which can go on expanding logically until it finally swallows Lytham and St. Annes to the south and Fleetwood to the north along the sea front, whilst to the east or landwards it has already included Poulton, and the inclusion of Thornton would seem to be a probability, as there are no natural topographical boundaries. Hastings and St. Leonards, on the other hand, scarcely permit further expansion except in the direction of Bexhill-on-Sea, which, for purposes of economic local control, ought to become part of the Hastings municipal area. In other directions the high ridges which practically enclose the town site, and the three valleys that run out tentacle-like from it, give a wonderfully varied and fine natural boundary, sufficiently far back to admit of considerable expansion of a character which promises to make this resort unique.

It is too early to specify all the improvements contemplated ; indeed, these cannot be published until the whole scheme has been approved by the Town Council and the Ministry of Health ; but I may state the nature of several of the most difficult problems which the town planner has to solve. They are :—

(1) To promote co-operation with the railway company for the reorganisation of the two railway stations, preferably on one site ; to improve the station approach roads to secure better means of collection and distribution of arriving and departing visitors, and to improve facilities for motor and charabanc traffic.

(2) Greatly to extend the parks and to give them a distinct connection with the promenade, and to clear and re-plan several congested areas.

(3) To zone the whole of the undeveloped lands with a view to restricting the number of houses to the acre ; to promote better housing facilities both as single self-contained cottages and as flats.

(4) To extend the promenade eastward.

(5) To plan a civic centre.

These were the factors most pressing for solution, and so far as the scheme has developed it seems probable that each of these needs will be solved.

The Life and Work of An English Landscape Architect.

A little later, in the spring of 1923, we were requested by the Urban District Council of Weston-super-Mare to design for them a marine garden, colonnade, and rotunda on the site known as Rogers Field, which extends to about fourteen acres. This work again proved a great incentive to creative effort, and the results prove what can be done with a progressive Council.

Many more interesting examples of town planning, landscape architecture, and domestic architecture are on the boards, but for the reasons given in the Preface my work tends to become more and more advisory, consultative, and critical. In other words, my mantle as designer has fallen on the shoulders of my sons and the other responsible members of the staff, who have grown up with the practice and imbibed its traditions. My personal work, on the other hand, has become more and more literary, including the revision of new editions of my published works, the compilation of illustrated reports, some of which, notably the Blackpool Park Report, have been published in book form, whilst others which are of even greater importance still await publication. In addition to these reports I have written many newspaper articles, especially three on " The Attitude of Railway Authorities to Town Planning," published in the " Manchester Guardian."

There was also the annual revision of my course of lectures on Landscape Design for the students in Civic Design at the Liverpool University to see to, for I made a point of giving my class the best of which I was capable. Thus in one way or another I was mentally employed in useful service, but physically I suffered increasingly from limitations, so that I had to reduce my travelling to a minimum. Fortunately there was much work at Blackpool and Roynton and other places within reach of a day's motor run, and it was my delight to keep in touch with this work.

Notwithstanding my disabilities, I kept in touch with the work of the Town Planning Institute, which under the able guidance of its honorary secretary, Mr. Pepler, and the experts who had passed through the presidential chair, was rapidly growing numerically, in responsibility, and in service. Although for a long period I was unable to attend its meetings, I usually sent a written contribution to the discussion of the many able papers read before the Institute. These written contributions were, I was glad to note, very much appreciated, partly, I was told, because of the optimism in which they were couched. From this it was quite evident that I still retained the goodwill of my contemporaries, and so· I was not surprised, though very gratified, when in October, 1923, I was raised from the position of senior vice-president to the presidential chair.

The annual conference was this year held in the city of York. A more inspiring rendezvous could not have been chosen. There was also the additional attraction that the city engineer was at the time engaged upon the preparation of a town-planning scheme in which was incorporated the premiated design which had been won by Mr. Reginald Dann, a member of the Institute and for some time the London colleague of our firm.

The conference was the most representative of any so far held. Not only did the members assemble in force, but our numbers were augmented by the civic dignitaries and officials of York, and members of the architectural profession. The excellent papers included " The Planning of Mediæval Cities," " The Historic Growth of York," and " The Town Planning of York," and an address was given by Mr. Barry Parker on Messrs. Rowntree's model industrial village of Earswick.

My own contribution was mainly confined to welcoming the city representatives and delegates, the direction of the debates following the several papers, and the response to the toast of the President,

At this time (the autumn of 1923), when politics were supposed to be at a low ebb, and when the short-lived Government of the day was travelling towards its Nemesis, there was gradually emerging into active performance a new conception of the place of art in the life of the nation. I refer to Mr. Stanley Baldwin's Fine Arts Commission, which received the approval of the King on the eve of the defeat of his Government ; but so popular was the measure that it received the hearty endorsement, without revision, of Mr. Ramsay MacDonald on the following day.

The united forces of artistic life in this country had long advocated the creation of an authoritative responsible body of experts to which Government departments and public bodies might refer the many difficult problems relating to civic art, its design, location, and setting. Experience had shown that these problems were often settled by the least informed section of the community. At the Board of Works the Fine Arts Commission found a keen supporter and a wise promoter in Sir Lionel Earle, who placed his wide experience at the service of the Prime Minister. I had always urged the setting up of such a commission, yet I

The Life and Work of An English Landscape Architect.

never, in my most ambitious moments, dreamt that I would be included as one of its members. Although I was convinced that landscape architecture was the master art, it never occurred to me that others would concede to it this claim. It was therefore with considerable surprise and a little concern that I received my nomination to the commission.

The first question which I asked myself was whether this recognition had not come too late. Five years ago, when still in full possession of my physical energies and mental enthusiasm, I would have revelled in the immense potential possibilities which the call provided to forward the claims of landscape architecture, but now the magnitude of the opportunities made me conscious of the limitations imposed by my impaired health.

In this frame of mind I discussed the matter with my doctor and my two sons, and one or two intimate friends on whose judgment and advice I could rely. All urged acceptance, my sons at the same time offering to relieve me entirely of any contribution to the work of the office. Thus it was that, with many misgivings, I gratefully accepted the Premier's call.

On the 24th of January, 1924, " The Times " gave the personnel of the Commission as approved by the King, which reads as follows :—

> Lord Crawford and Balcarres (Chairman).
> Lord Curzon of Kedleston.
> Sir Aston Webb, P.R.A.
> Sir Reginald Blomfield, A.R.A.
> Sir Edwin Lutyens.
> Mr. Alfred J. Gotch.
> Mr. D. Y. Cameron.
> Sir George Frampton, R.A.
> Mr. Thomas H. Mawson.

It is interesting to note that the Presidents of the Royal Academy, of the Royal Institute of British Architects, and of the Town Planning Institute are included, but whether this will become an established precedent or not remains to be seen.

The first meeting of the Commission was held at the rooms of the Society of Antiquarians, Burlington House, on Friday afternoon, February 8, 1924, under the chairmanship of Lord Crawford and Balcarres.

Tennis Lawn, Caton Hall.

THE AUTHOR AND HIS SONS, E. PRENTICE AND JOHN W. MAWSON.

CHAPTER XXVIII.

RETROSPECT AND PROSPECT.

THOSE who have formed habits of abstraction and contemplation upon the moving drama of life in the midst of the world's stirring activities, these possibly including extensive travels, half-welcome the call to cease the strain and slacken the tension. It is a natural instinct in the healthy man to be for ever striving to reach higher and yet higher summits of achievement. In the stress of it all we are like the swimmer—after a momentary gasp for breath we are ploughing under again. Amidst life's bustle we may have cherished, but never found time to express, those sub-conscious thoughts which have in a way kept pace with our practical activities. If we have this fount within us, we have a magnificent store to fall back upon. These relaxations keep the heart young, even though physical disabilities increase. There is rich compensation for the loss of practical activity—for those who stand apart see most of the game. Occasionally, however, furtive yearnings burst out, when we feel a strong desire to renew our youth and put into practice the riper results of experience, a temptation to be suppressed the next moment by the saner intention of placing these fruits of experience at the disposal of those still in the field, full of youthful ardour and hope. When in the evening of life we turn our gaze upon the pathway, we find it transformed by the ruddy glow. The parts that stood out so prominently in the morning's beam now assume their relative importance and their true perspective as we mark off a clear space whence to view them.

Every man who reviews his life and compares its achievements with its rosy promises, realises how far he has fallen short of the goal. If this is so in ordinary callings, it is much more so in the case of the creative artist, because his ideals are for ever expanding and leading forth to unexpected vistas and in new paths. These

349

The Life and Work of An English Landscape Architect.

truths apply particularly to landscape architecture, an art which is proving its universality, and which in many of its ramifications, particularly in its relation to town planning, is a new art, thus suggesting unexpected happenings and undreamt-of possibilities.

Success or failure in this art depends upon whether it succeeds in creating an atmosphere or not. The tremendous range of material which comes within the scope of the practitioner may of itself divert him from weaving the desired spell, and may just succeed in occupying the beholder's attention with novelties and surprises and other misguided objectives. Be this as it may, I am now, as my career draws towards its close, more in love with my profession than I was when as a youth before entering my teens I made it my definite choice. No other art could, I am assured, have made the same appeal to me that landscape architecture has, now that I have, after fifty years' study and experience, in some measure compassed its scope.

With no misgivings as to my choice of profession, and feeling a sense of responsibility for the continued growth and development of the art, I ask myself how, were I to begin anew, I would reorganise my life's programme, and how I would wish to be guided in my training. In the first instance I would devote my energies to a comprehensive study of the art of domestic architecture and make a more extended study of natural landscape and the work of great landscape painters, and seek to gain an expert knowledge of arboriculture and horticulture, with a view to designing that I might practise my chosen art in its fullest application, but with a wide knowledge of other correlated arts and the mediums by which they are expressed. I would undertake much less work, and seek compensation by doing the restricted work all the better.

Incidentally, I am sure I could have advanced the art much more by this policy. Nor do I think it would have been difficult to find a sufficient number of clients prepared to pay the advanced fees which this would have entailed.

Many of the commissions which I have undertaken have been sufficiently important to justify my throwing up all other work, had I had the courage to do so. My work in Canada or in Athens, or in Salonika, was quite sufficient to absorb my entire energies profitably, and might in either case have led to great results ; but the work which I most regret having delegated was that which I undertook in the interests of our disabled service men.

Retrospect and Prospect.

As my particular interests are largely associated with parks, gardens, and recreational facilities, I wish to observe that I have been very much impressed with the splendid work accomplished by Parks Commissions in America. These Commissions are in part elected and in part co-opted by the elected members, and are entirely free from the control of the municipal council, excepting in respect to their annual budget, which is voted upon by the council. If the budget is rejected, the Commission has to seek re-election. The main advantage of this policy is that many men of education and standing specially interested in horticulture and arboriculture are willing to act on the Parks Commissions, though they are not prepared for the rough and tumble of municipal government. In practice the members of such Commissions exercise far more influence in the progressive development of a park system than would the municipal bodies. Somehow, if the municipality requires land for any purpose whatever, it is generally regarded as " fair game " for the land-holders, whereas the Commission is so popular and self-sacrificing that it is encouraged from every quarter. To show how this works in practice, I was told by the late chairman of the Ottawa Parks Commission that the entire park lands for that city, extending in a practically continuous chain of fourteen miles, had been presented. Apart from this fact, however, I everywhere found these Parks Commissions pursuing a vigorous and intelligent policy, which never allowed the interests of their city in the provision of ample park and playing spaces to be submerged by other municipal enterprises. Everyone seems to realise the need for parks and gardens, and all know that nothing brings such ample return in advanced property values. Looking forward, I am convinced that, provided we can establish efficient training centres, there is a great future for landscape architecture both at home and in the Overseas Dominions and Colonies ; but in harmony with the growth of the civic spirit and a more equal distribution of wealth, and particularly in response to the desire of rich men to share their wealth with their fellows, much more attention will be paid to the designing and equipment of public amenities, whilst there will be less opportunity for the creation of private gardens on a big scale. These larger opportunities for serving the public will, I am sure, be promoted by a clearer understanding of the possibilities which a study of landscape architecture inculcates, and largely by the examples set by Parks Commissions and private

The Life and Work of An English Landscape Architect.

donors of parks, whose intelligence on such matters is usually of a much higher order than that possessed by the average town councillor.

I urge this consideration because at present the claims of landscape architecture are rarely recognised—so rarely, indeed, that it is probably safe to say that not one of our ten largest public authorities, including London, Glasgow, Liverpool, Manchester, and Birmingham, have consulted a professor of the art during the last twenty years. In other words, the authorities of these cities have during this period collectively spent millions of pounds upon public parks and gardens under the direction of amateurs. I have referred in this manner to this legitimate department of the landscape architect for the purpose of indicating the vast field which is still open for exploration and enterprise.

Already a good beginning has been made, and it is becoming evident that expanding knowledge of the subject is creating new demands, whilst the increasing call for town-planning and development schemes is providing new opportunities under conditions peculiarly favourable to the art of landscape architecture, and for some years to come unemployment problems will give this demand added impetus.

Supposing, however, that landscape architects were asked to design even one-third of the new parks and gardens which will in all probability be laid out during the next twenty years, would there be a sufficient number of qualified men and women to carry out the work? I very much doubt it, unless we can establish an efficient training centre such as that already outlined; and I can conceive of no other object worthy of sound and generous enterprise which would bring such splendid national benefits in its train as the setting up of a well equipped and staffed school of landscape architecture, where men and women could be trained for this vastly important work. Such a school ought to be located at either Oxford or Cambridge, so that the students might have the advantages of the fine botanical gardens at these seats of learning.

To me this subject of training is of such paramount importance that if I were asked which of my dreams I would like to see realised, I would unhesitatingly place the school of landscape architecture first. This is the one great scheme which would yield a result commensurate with the thought, time, and money expended upon it.

I have said that in all probability there will in the future be fewer large gardens laid out. I believe, however, that there will be many more small gardens of, say, an acre, or even less, which will call for the skill of the landscape architect ; and in the creation of such gardens the designer may find great interest and moderate recompense. If, again, as I have suggested elsewhere, the training of the garden designer has included the study of domestic architecture, and if in consequence he is entrusted with the design of both house and garden, he may accomplish greater artistic results than he has ever dreamed of.

As my energies decrease, my sons are accepting their heavier duties with courage and ability, and with a freshness of outlook which augurs well for the future.

Three of my daughters, denied the necessary encouragement to undertake the long and arduous training required in the practice of landscape architecture (an error of judgment I shall always regret), have with industry developed their artistic genius in other directions. They established a few years ago, at Thornton Hall, in Lincolnshire, the Thornton Art Industries. Here, surrounded by a band of lady workers, they turn out a considerable quantity of useful and ornamental articles, to which they apply their talent for colour and form and applied ornament. From the start their business has met with encouragement, and now the industry is well established. Two views are given of Thornton Hall, the residence of my son-in-law, Colonel Smethurst, where the enthusiastic lady workers pursue their separate crafts under ideal conditions.

Now I must bring this narrative of my life's work to a close, though I would fain continue to review the past, meeting old friends and acquaintances as they flit across my mind. Living one's days over again is a pleasant task, tinged as it must be with many regrets that one has not more fully realised the reasonably possible, but with a thankfulness that so much has been accomplished, and gratitude above all things for the friendships formed and for the encouragement of helping hands stretched out when the road was most difficult. Experience has taught me that the world is much more kindly than some affirm, and that it admires above all things courage and tenacity. Men and women who love trees and flowers are ever pleasant and understanding company, and my deepest regret is that I no longer possess the energy to tramp the road with them. Yet in imagination I am still walking with my clients through the gardens I have helped to

The Life and Work of An English Landscape Architect.

create, picturing the development of succeeding years, but regretful that I cannot curb wayward growths or reorganise and amend those portions which have fallen short of expectation—for a garden, like a family, has to be " brought up," and needs constant care if its character is to be developed. To me the garden and its design are still my highest pleasure. The green shades are my keenest delight, and my estimate of the ethical value of a garden is well expressed by Wordsworth in the following lines :—

> " A garden . . . . . . the place
> Where good men disappointed in the quest
> Of wealth and power and honours, long for rest ;
> Or having known the splendours of success,
> Sigh for the obscurities of happiness."

Like my friend Daniel Burnham, " I feel I have done a day's work "—and there is great satisfaction in the thought !

INDEX.

Index.

Index.

Index.

Index.

Index.

Index.

Index.

Lightning Source UK Ltd.
Milton Keynes UK
UKOW02f0652021013

218264UK00002B/8/P